TERRORISM AND
THE ETHICS OF WAR

Most people strongly condemn terrorism; yet they often fail to say how terrorist acts differ from other acts of violence such as the killing of civilians in war. Stephen Nathanson argues that we cannot have morally credible views about terrorism if we focus on terrorism alone and neglect broader issues about the ethics of war. His book challenges influential views on the ethics of war, including the realist view that morality does not apply to war, and Michael Walzer's defense of attacks on civilians in "supreme emergency" circumstances. It provides a clear definition of terrorism, an analysis of what makes terrorism morally wrong, and a rule-utilitarian defense of noncombatant immunity, as well as discussions of the Allied bombings of cities in World War II, collateral damage, and the clash between rights theories and utilitarianism. It will interest a wide range of readers in philosophy, political theory, international relations, and law.

STEPHEN NATHANSON is Professor of Philosophy at Northeastern University, Boston, Massachusetts. He is the author of several books, including *Patriotism, Morality and Peace* (1993) and *Economic Justice* (1998), as well as numerous articles on issues in ethics and political philosophy.

TERRORISM AND THE ETHICS OF WAR

STEPHEN NATHANSON

Northeastern University

CAMBRIDGE
UNIVERSITY PRESS

CAMBRIDGE UNIVERSITY PRESS
Cambridge, New York, Melbourne, Madrid, Cape Town, Singapore,
São Paulo, Delhi, Dubai, Tokyo

Cambridge University Press
The Edinburgh Building, Cambridge CB2 8RU, UK

Published in the United States of America by Cambridge University Press, New York

www.cambridge.org
Information on this title: www.cambridge.org/9780521137164

© Stephen Nathanson 2010

First published 2010

Printed in the United Kingdom at the University Press, Cambridge

A catalogue record for this publication is available from the British Library

ISBN 978-0-521-19995-7 Hardback
ISBN 978-0-521-13716-4 Paperback

To my sister, Joan Spivak,
and to the memory of our grandmother,
Tillie Dender Levy

Contents

Acknowledgments

Some of the people who have influenced this book have done so by carrying out horrific attacks against other human beings. I acknowledge their influence but offer no thanks.

My thanks are due, however, to the many students in my courses on war-related issues, to my department colleagues, to conference organizers and others who have given me the chance to present my ideas in public. I also thank and apologize to the many people whose writings I have learned from. I have not been able to discuss most of them, and even when I discuss individuals, I have generally been unable to do full justice to their thinking in the text.

I thank everyone who has questioned, criticized, and encouraged me in this project. A few need special acknowledgment. Mike Meltsner sparked the idea of writing a book that focused on terrorism and provided moral support along the way. Igor Primoratz has been my long-distance colleague, supporter, and constructive critic since I started writing on these topics. I have benefited greatly from his writings and edited works on terrorism as well as his comments on a draft of this book. For comments on and encouragement of my work in this area, I am grateful to John Basl, David Benatar, Michael Burns, Bill Crotty, Bernard Gert, Bart Gruzalski, Ron Hirschbein, Marvin Kohl, Nelson Lande, Bruce Landesman, David Lyons, George Rainbolt, David Schmitt, James Sterba, Michael Tolley, and John Troyer.

I thank Northeastern University for a sabbatical during which I wrote drafts of large parts of the book, Susan Setta for a course reduction to help revisions along, the readers for Cambridge University Press for their extensive comments, and Hilary Gaskin for her interest in, and support of, the book.

I also thank my friends in Newton Dialogues on Peace and War for camaraderie in difficult times.

My wife Linda remains my best friend and best supporter. I continue to be deeply grateful for her and to her.

The book incorporates ideas published in "Is the War on Terrorism a Defense of Civilization?" *Concerned Philosophers for Peace Newsletter* vol. 22 (Spring/Fall 2002); "Prerequisites for Morally Credible Condemnations of Terrorism," in William Crotty, ed., *The Politics of Terror: The U.S. Response to 9/11* (Northeastern University Press, 2004); "Can Terrorism Be Morally Justified?," in James Sterba, ed., *Morality in Practice*, 7th edn (Wadsworth, 2004); "Is Terrorism Ever Morally Permissible? An Inquiry into the Right to Life," in M. Sellers and D. Reidy, eds., *Universal Human Rights: Moral Order in a Divided World* (Rowman and Littlefield, 2005); "Terrorism, Supreme Emergency, and Noncombatant Immunity: A Critique of Michael Walzer's Ethic of War," *Iyyun: The Jerusalem Philosophical Quarterly* 55 (January 2006); "Terrorism and the Ethics of War," in Steven Lee, ed., *Intervention, Terrorism, and Torture: Challenges to Just War Theory in the 21st Century* (Springer, 2006); and "War, Patriotism, and the Limits of Permissible Partiality," *Journal of Ethics* 13 (2009).

Introduction

> "America must maintain our moral clarity ... Murdering the innocent
> to advance an ideology is wrong every time, everywhere."
> *President George W. Bush, farewell address*

This book, like many others, owes its existence to the terrorist attacks of
September 11, 2001. Nonetheless, the problems that it deals with existed
long before these attacks. Many of these problems have been preoccupa-
tions of mine for a long time. Although I have never fought in a war or lived
in a war zone, war, violence, and threats of destruction have loomed large
throughout my life.

While many questions can and should be asked about war and political
violence, my main focus will be on moral questions. Because of the
September 11 attacks and the subsequent "war on terrorism," I begin with
moral questions about terrorism. Much of the book, however, deals with
more general moral questions about war and violence. The reason for this is
that we cannot have morally credible views about terrorism if we focus on
terrorism alone and neglect broader issues about the ethics of war.

My aim in this book is to answer five questions:

1. What is terrorism?
2. If terrorism is especially wrong, what features of terrorism make it
   especially wrong?
3. If terrorism is especially wrong, why do moral condemnations of terrorism often lack credibility? Why do they evoke cynical responses rather
   than affirmations of respect for human life?
4. What conditions must be met in order for condemnations of terrorism
   to be morally credible?
5. Is terrorism always wrong, or can it sometimes be morally justified?

The methods I use to answer these questions draw on traditions of philosophical analysis that go back to Socrates. Underlying these methods is the
belief that difficult questions require careful thinking and that we can best

understand issues by trying to state beliefs clearly and examine the reasons for and against them.

My perspective on these issues is also influenced by my being an American and by my long-standing skepticism about the use of war and violence. While I am not a pacifist, both temperament and experience have made me wary of war and wary of people who are too eager for violent responses to problems. Officially, of course, almost everyone is against war. In fact, war is often attractive to political leaders and to ordinary people. The deep appeal of war, its great legacy of suffering, and the frequency of unnecessary wars have made me skeptical about arguments for going to war. Nonetheless, I accept that there are times when the arguments for war are compelling.

Like others, my immediate responses to the September 11 attacks were shock, horror, and fear. While I worried about the possibility of additional attacks against us, however, I also worried about what we Americans or – more accurately – our political leaders would do in response to the September 11 attacks. And, however our leaders might choose to act, what should we, ordinary citizens, want them to do?

It took time to get from the stunned horror and moral confusion that the September 11 attacks generated to a point where I could start to construct a coherent response.[1] While Socrates says that philosophy begins with wonder, I agree more with the American pragmatists William James and Charles Sanders Peirce, who thought that philosophical reflection grows out of feelings of conflict and confusion. Because confusion is an uncomfortable state, it generates a desire for the feeling of stability that we have when our ideas fit together coherently.[2] When confusions are generated by traumatic events, we have to recover before we can think clearly about the meaning of these events and their implications for our beliefs and our actions.

The responses to the September 11 attacks are now history. President George W. Bush and his advisors saw the attacks as acts of terrorism, committed by evil people who sought to destroy the United States, its values, and its way of life. The Bush administration decided that the proper response was a global war against terrorism. Moreover, because they saw the terrorist threat as new and unique, they believed that traditional moral and

---

[1] My first effort was a public talk entitled "Is the War on Terrorism a Defense of Civilization?" This appeared in *Concerned Philosophers for Peace Newsletter*, Vol. 22 (Spring/Fall 2002), 19–27.
[2] For these ideas, see Charles Sanders Peirce, "The Fixation of Belief," Parts III and IV, and William James, "What Pragmatism Means," Lecture II of *Pragmatism*, both reprinted in H. S. Thayer, ed., *Pragmatism: The Classic Writings* (Indianapolis: Hackett Publishing, 1982).

legal restraints on the conduct of war were no longer applicable. They saw the war on terrorism as a no-holds-barred struggle.

These reactions seemed so clearly right to some people that they experienced a feeling of moral clarity about what had happened and how we should respond. The attacks, they thought, showed that evil is real, that evil people must be resisted by military force, and that good people need to stand together to support our leaders in this effort. Because all of this seemed axiomatic, those who experienced moral clarity saw no need to debate, discuss, analyze, or ask questions. The important thing was to oppose the "unmitigated global evil" of terrorism by supporting the Bush administration's global war on terrorism.[3]

The moral clarity response to the September 11 attacks rested on a few main ideas about terrorism: Terrorism is a distinctive type of violence that is always morally wrong. Because terrorism is inherently evil, people who engage in terrorism are evil. Terrorists have no positive moral values and only seek to destroy what is good. Since there can be no compromise or negotiation with evil people, the only proper response to them is global war against terrorism.

Even before the effects of the Bush administration's actions began to play out, it should have been clear that claims to moral clarity about terrorism were illusory and dangerous. They oversimplified complex issues, encouraged support for destructive policies, and created obstacles to achieving security. We can see that claims to moral clarity about terrorism were illusory by noting the serious confusions that lie just below the surface of the moral clarity view of terrorism and the ethics of war. To see these confusions, consider the following puzzling facts.

Consider the fact that, while many people take it as axiomatic that terrorism is wrong, it is widely acknowledged that when people try to say what terrorism is, they generally fail to come up with an acceptable definition. But if we cannot say what features make something a terrorist act, how can we differentiate terrorist acts from other acts of violence? And if we cannot differentiate terrorist acts from other acts of violence, how can we know that terrorist acts are always wrong while other violent acts are sometimes morally right?

Consider the fact that, in spite of the allegedly axiomatic belief that terrorism is wrong, the most famous comment about terrorism is the cynical

---

[3] The idea of moral clarity and its related agenda appear in William J. Bennett, *Why We Fight* (New York: Doubleday, 2002), and in Jean B. Elshtain, *Just War Against Terror* (New York: Basic Books, 2003). The phrase "unmitigated global evil" occurs in "A letter from America," reprinted in ibid., 182–98.

slogan "one man's terrorist is another man's freedom fighter." The slogan's subversive message is that the labeling of people as terrorists is subjective, a matter of taste rather than an objective description. Terrorism, the slogan suggests, is in the eye of the beholder. But how can the wrongness of terrorism be a self-evident moral fact if the concept of terrorism itself is subjective (so that different people apply the terrorist label to different acts)?

Consider this: when we condemn terrorism, we expect all decent people to agree with our condemnation. Yet moral criticisms of terrorism are often turned back against its critics. Instead of seeing denunciations of terrorist acts as evidence of respect for human life, many people see them as hypocritical and self-serving. How can this be? Why do moral condemnations of terrorism often fail to generate sympathy and instead evoke cynical responses to this and other moral judgments?

Consider this: many people who condemn terrorism do so because the victims of terrorist attacks are innocent people who are going about the ordinary business of life. It seems so clearly wrong for innocent people to be killed and injured in this way. At the same time, most people who condemn terrorist acts believe that war is often morally justifiable even though wars generally result in many more deaths of innocent people than terrorist attacks. But how can this be? How can terrorism be wrong because it kills innocent people while war, which generally kills more innocent people, may sometimes be right?

Each of these problems casts doubt on the credibility of moral condemnations of terrorism. How can we confidently and credibly condemn terrorism if we can't say what it is, if terrorism is not an objective category but exists only in the eye of the beholder, and if our judgments about the wrongness of terrorist acts that kill innocent people are inconsistent with our belief that the killing of innocent people in war can be morally right?

My initial aim in this book was to answer these questions by clarifying what terrorism is, what makes it wrong, and what conditions must be met in order to make moral condemnations of terrorism credible. In trying to answer these questions, however, I found that I had to ask and answer other questions about the ethics of war. In particular, I had to ask whether the often-cited prohibition on killing civilians in war (which I myself accepted) is actually justified. And this led to further questions about the justification of moral principles and then to philosophical debates between rights theories and utilitarianism. The result of trying to follow these questions where they led is a longer, more complex, and more theoretical book than I originally intended to write. My hope, of course, is that it is a better book as well.

A PREVIEW OF WHAT'S AHEAD

The book is divided into four main sections.

In Part I, "Terrorism: what's in a name?," I discuss the vexing question of what terrorism is. Which acts of violence should we call "terrorism"? Since attempts to define terrorism have been undermined by political motives and biased moral judgments, I offer a definition that is politically and morally neutral and thus avoids the problems raised by the slogan "one man's terrorist is another man's freedom fighter." One of the distinctive features of terrorism is that it is violence directed against innocent people, and this fact is what best explains why it is condemned so harshly by many people. An important virtue of the definition I defend is that it does not build this negative moral judgment into the definition of terrorism. Even if all terrorist acts are immoral (which is the view I defend), we cannot simply assume that. We need to at least consider whether terrorism can be morally justifiable, and we can only do that by using a definition that leaves open this possibility.

After giving my own definition, I consider several challenges to it. Responding to these challenges requires me to discuss what it means to say that the victims of terrorism are *innocent* and whether actions that kill innocent people *unintentionally* (as side effects or collateral damage) qualify as terrorist acts. It also requires me to criticize the influential view that we should apply the word "terrorism" only to actions carried out by non-governmental groups. An implication of this view, which I shall reject, is that governments cannot engage in terrorism acts.

In Part II, "Why moral condemnations of terrorism lack credibility," I show that many familiar views about the ethics of war imply that terrorism is not always morally wrong. I briefly discuss political realism, common-sense morality, some versions of utilitarianism, and Michael Walzer's theory in his influential book *Just and Unjust Wars*. I argue that people who hold these views cannot credibly condemn all terrorist acts for killing innocent people because these views approve of killing innocent people in at least some circumstances. I also show that traditional just war theory's condemnation of all terrorist acts lacks credibility. The credibility of just war theory is undermined by its reliance on the "principle of double effect" and its overly permissive approach to "collateral damage" killings of civilians (i.e., killings that are not aimed at civilians but that may be foreseen). I will show that some collateral damage killings are morally on a par with terrorism. Because these actions are permitted by just war theory, just war theory's credibility in condemning terrorism is undermined.

In Part III, "Defending noncombatant immunity," I defend the view that it is always wrong to attack civilians in war. In my view, we can only credibly say that terrorism is always wrong if we believe that deliberate attacks on civilians are always wrong. Having described several views that reject an absolute ban on attacking civilians, I show why each of these views is defective. I show why realists are wrong to reject the idea that morality applies to war and why Walzer is wrong in approving attacks on civilians in the circumstances that he calls "supreme emergencies."

In considering how we might justify an absolute ban on killing civilians, I begin with Walzer's claim that noncombatant immunity cannot be justified on utilitarian grounds but must be based on a theory of individual rights. Against this widely held view, I show why rights theories do not necessarily support strong rights of noncombatant immunity. I then challenge the view that no utilitarian theory could justify noncombatant immunity by developing a rule-utilitarian justification for the view that it is always wrong to attack civilians in war.

I respond to several challenges to my rule-utilitarian defense of absolute noncombatant immunity, including the argument that rule utilitarianism itself would support a "supreme emergency" exception to noncombatant immunity and the argument that it would support the view that we should minimize the total casualties of war but give no special status to civilians. Finally, I rebut the charge that the noncombatant immunity principle, when supported by utilitarian reasoning, is a merely conventional rule that cannot support serious moral demands on people engaged in war or political conflict.

In Part IV, "How much immunity should noncombatants have?," I discuss the difficult question of collateral damage. These are harms to civilians that are not intended but that occur as side effects of attacks on legitimate targets. These deaths and injuries of civilians are almost inevitable in any war. The challenge in dealing with this problem is to find a principle that is permissive enough to allow fighting a war while being restrictive enough to provide serious protection to civilians. The standard approach to this problem relies on the principle of double effect. It says that while killing civilians intentionally is wrong, actions that kill civilians may be morally justified when they do not intentionally kill the civilians. I show why this focus on intention is mistaken, in part by drawing on the legal concepts of negligence and recklessness to show that actions that cause bad consequences can be wrong even if the harms caused are not intended.

After rejecting the principle of double effect, I go on to consider three principles, each of which tries to draw the line between unintended civilian deaths that are permissibly caused and those that are wrong. These are the foreseeable harm principle, the precautionary principle, and the proportionality principle. In considering these principles, I discuss the rules of war found in international law, Walzer's views on collateral damage killings, and parts of a Human Rights Watch evaluation of the first stage of the US war in Iraq. I argue that the precautionary principle plays a central role in the ethics of inflicting collateral damage and defend it against both the foreseeable harm principle and the proportionality principle.

In the concluding chapter, I review the answers to the questions I had raised about terrorism and return to the role of utilitarian reasoning in the development of an ethic of war. I defend the utilitarian approach against several important objections and try to strengthen its credibility as a basis for the principle of noncombatant immunity and the condemnation of terrorist acts.

PART I

Terrorism: what's in a name?

CHAPTER I

The problem of defining terrorism

For decades prior to the September 11 attacks, a frustrating debate went on about the definition of terrorism. The mere existence of this debate presents a serious challenge to the claims of moral clarity associated with proponents of the "war on terrorism." How can we know that terrorism is always wrong if we can't say what it is? The confusions generated by the definition debate are nicely captured in remarks by Christopher Joyner. He writes:

Politically, academically, and legally, the phenomenon of terrorism eludes clear and precise definition. In a real sense, terrorism is like pornography: You know it when you see it, but it is impossible to come up with a universally agreed-upon definition. The hackneyed bromide "One man's terrorist is another man's freedom fighter" still remains a truism in international political perceptions. "Terrorism" lies in the eye of the beholder.[1]

Three competing views appear in Joyner's account: the confident claim that we know terrorism when we see it, the distressing idea that it is impossible to agree on a definition of terrorism, and the surprising conclusion that terrorism has no objective reality but exists only "in the eye of the beholder."

The second and third points shake the moral clarity view at its foundations, criticizing its proponents for literally not knowing what they are talking about. But they also challenge anyone who believes that terrorism is wrong to "put up or shut up." Either we should define terrorism or we should keep our condemnations to ourselves. If we can't define terrorism but condemn it nonetheless, we should acknowledge that our condemnations have no moral validity but only express our personal distaste for terrorism.

I will try to show that none of the three views is true. Most important, because it is possible to define terrorism by specifying a set of objective features that all terrorist acts possess, there is no reason to think that it exists

---

[1] Quoted in Charles Kegley, "The Characteristics of Contemporary International Terrorism," in Charles Kegley, ed., *International Terrorism* (New York: St. Martin's, 1990), 11–12.

only in the eye of the beholder. While such a definition makes objective identifications possible, it does not show that we know terrorism when we see it. Given the inflammatory nature of the word "terrorism" and the selective, propagandistic uses of the terrorist label, it is easy to be confused. We may fail to notice terrorism when it is staring us in the face and think we see it when it is not there.

THE DEBATE ABOUT DEFINITIONS

The problem of defining terrorism is not merely academic or theoretical. For years, efforts to oppose terrorism have been stymied by disagreements about how to define it. While there are United Nations resolutions against terrorism, there is disagreement about who and what they apply to. Charles Kegley, after surveying various definitional problems, concludes pessimistically that

> It is not certain that the analytic issues facing the accurate characterization of international terrorism can be satisfactorily overcome. It may be that, as a committee of the French Senate concluded in 1984, "any definition is practically guaranteed to fail."[2]

Even if efforts to arrive at a consensus have failed, however, we should not conclude that terrorism cannot be defined unless we understand why it is indefinable.

Although Kegley tries to explain why terrorism can't be defined, his account fails. Kegley stresses the great diversity of groups that have "waged" terrorism, noting that they have been leftist, rightist, autocratic, liberationist, religious, nationalist, etc. From this, he concludes that terrorist groups share no common feature and explains that our "inability to arrive at a consensus about terrorism's characterization stems from the great variety of aims, actors' motives, and practices that are associated with it."[3]

This diversity of aims, motives, and practices, however, fails to explain the lack of a definitional consensus. Many concepts apply to diverse instances that nonetheless share some common, essential features. We have no trouble defining "theft," for example, even though people who commit thefts have diverse motives, use diverse means, and steal vastly different kinds of things. People steal for money, for the pleasure of possession, to hurt the owner, or to reclaim what they think is rightly theirs.

[2] Ibid., 12.   [3] Ibid., 16.

Their means vary from mugging and breaking and entering to safecracking, picking pockets, and embezzling.

Nonetheless, despite the great variety of "aims, actors' motives, and practices" associated with theft, theft is easily definable. It is a process by which people illegally acquire the property of others. The fact that these illegal acquisitions vary in many ways is no obstacle to agreeing on this definition. Similarly, although instances of terrorism vary in many ways, that does not show that it cannot be defined.

THE POLITICS OF DEFINITION

The main reasons it has been difficult to define terrorism are political rather than theoretical. Many people approach the definition problem with strong vested interests. They know that there are actions, groups, and policies that they support, and they assume that to classify something as terrorism is to condemn it as morally wrong. As a result, they reject any definition that implies that actions, groups, or policies that they themselves support are instances of terrorism. While they are happy to apply the terrorist label to their enemies, they will not apply it to friends. Even though it is false that terrorism is "in the eye of the beholder," it is nonetheless true that the willingness to label acts as terrorism depends on who is beholding them and whose acts they are.[4]

DEFINING TERRORISM AS WHAT TERRORISTS DO

The politics of labeling leads to the idea that whether something is terrorism depends on who carries it out. Some people or groups are called terrorists, and then, by implication, their activities are terrorism because they were done by terrorists. Other people are not labeled as terrorists, and, no matter what they do, they will not merit the terrorist label.[5]

The idea that we should define "terrorism" by who does it leads to absurd results. If we define a "terrorist act" as *an act carried out by terrorists*, an obvious problem is that this definition does not tell us how to identify someone as a terrorist. But even if we could independently identify some people as terrorists, we would still need criteria for identifying terrorist acts

---

[4] On the politics of definition, see Bruce Hoffman, *Inside Terrorism* (New York: Columbia University Press, 1998), 28–40. For the definition debate among social scientists, see Alex P. Schmid and Albert J. Jongman, *Political Terrorism* (New Brunswick, N.J.: Transaction Publishers, 1988), 1–32.

[5] Tomis Kapitan discusses biased labeling in "The Terrorism of 'Terrorism,'" in James Sterba, ed., *Terrorism and International Justice* (New York: Oxford University Press, 2003), 47–66.

because most of the things that terrorists do are not terrorist actions. They wake up in the morning, eat breakfast, drive cars, make phone calls, etc. Even if we add that terrorist actions must be violent, not every violent act by members of a terrorist group is terrorism. If members of a terrorist group are attacked by a rival terrorist group and kill their attackers in self-defense, these self-defensive killings would not be terrorist acts.

And yet, a focus on who does the act is extremely common. Kegley, who seems to have no political axe to grind, mistakenly sees defining terrorism as classifying groups rather than actions. He asks:

Should Palestinian skyjackers, Basque separatists, Irish revolutionaries, and South American kidnappers be seen as similar? Are they properly classified with the insurgents who produced the American, French, and Russian revolutions? Do their actions resemble the tactics of the Red Brigade, the Ku Klux Klan, or big-time drug-trafficking street gangs?[6]

This confusing list may well make us dizzy enough to give up on seeking a definition. We can escape this dizzying confusion by focusing on terrorist acts rather than terrorist groups. Even if some or all of the groups listed engaged in terrorist acts, what makes them terrorists is the nature of the acts themselves, not the group that carried them out.[7]

Identifying terrorist acts as "acts done by terrorists" puts the cart (*who* does the act?) before the horse (*what* kind of *act* is it?). In order to define "terrorism," we need to focus on the idea of a terrorist *act*, directing our attention to *what* is done, not *who* does it.

POPULAR CONCEPTIONS OF TERRORIST ACTS

Popular thinking about the nature of terrorism has been dominated by two radically opposed views. According to the most common view, terrorism is the name of a distinctive class of especially immoral actions. While other violent actions may sometimes be morally justified, it is part of terrorism's essence that it is wrong. This is reflected in Louise Richardson's comment that "The only universally accepted attribute of the term 'terrorism' is that it is pejorative. Terrorism is something that bad guys do."[8]

---

[6] Kegley, *International Terrorism*, 13.

[7] For a contrary view, see G. Wallace, "The Language of Terrorism," *International Journal of Moral and Social Studies* 8 (Summer 1993), 128ff.

[8] Louise Richardson, *What Terrorists Want: Understanding the Enemy, Containing the Threat* (New York: Random House, 2006), xi.

This view is powerfully challenged by the slogan "one man's terrorist is another man's freedom fighter." The slogan says that people call violent acts "terrorism" only when they disapprove of them. When they approve, they call them "freedom fighting" or use some other positive term. Depending on who makes the judgment, the very same action may be labeled as "terrorism" or as "freedom fighting." What this allegedly shows is that whether an act is terrorism depends on subjective facts about the beholder, not on features of the act itself.

In spite of their differences, both of these views assume that "terrorism" is a negative term and that we call an act "terrorism" only when we think it wrong. Each view understands this assumption differently, however. Those who champion the moral clarity view see terrorism as objectively evil while those who use the "one man's terrorist" slogan insist that terrorism has no objective nature. Still, both agree that people who use the word "terrorism" are evaluating actions, not merely describing them.

Both of these views are flawed for the same reason. They fail to distinguish the problem of classifying actions from the problem of evaluating them. As a result, disagreements about whether particular actions are morally right or wrong are transformed into disagreements about whether to classify them as terrorist acts. The debate about defining terrorism becomes impossible to resolve because it mirrors disagreements about contentious moral and political issues. While it is true, as Richardson says, that terrorists are always seen as bad guys, people do not agree about who the bad guys are. These disagreements spill over into disagreements about which actions are right or wrong, which in turn distort the definition debate and undermine efforts to arrive at a consensus on how to define terrorism.

CLASSIFYING VS. EVALUATING

In order to make progress toward a definition, we need to separate the issue of classifying actions as terrorist (or not) from the issue of morally evaluating them. If we could devise a definition that is morally and politically neutral, this would enable us to label acts as terrorist or not independently of our views on whether they are morally justifiable or not.

This strategy will be resisted both by defenders of a moralized definition (one which defines terrorism as morally wrong) and by defenders of the "one man's terrorist" slogan. According to the slogan, the sole purpose of using the word "terrorism" is to make a condemnatory judgment. Stripping "terrorism" of its negative meaning misses the whole point of its use.

Similarly, people who see terrorism as essentially evil may fear that leaving out the evil of terrorism from a definition paves the way for approving of terrorism. Since my aim in this book is to defend the view that terrorism is always wrong, I have no intention of using a definition to block a negative judgment of it. We have to acknowledge, however, that there are widespread differences among people both about the morality of actions that some see as terrorism and about the use of that label. We will not make progress unless we separate the moral question and the classification question.

Even if the word "terrorism" is almost always understood negatively, that does not rule out the possibility of a neutral definition. Many terms with negative connotations can be defined in morally neutral language. Consider the word "lie." When we call a statement a "lie," we are generally characterizing it in a negative way. Nonetheless, we can define a lie neutrally as "a statement that is made by someone who believes the statement is false and asserts it in order to deceive." Using this definition, we can classify statements as lies independently of judging them to be right or wrong. Having done that, we can go on to consider whether a particular lie is right or wrong or whether lies are always wrong or sometimes morally justified.

John Finnis makes this same point about adultery. Finnis, who strongly condemns adultery "as always and necessarily wrongful," nonetheless believes that adultery is "not defined in terms of its wrongfulness ... It is defined as sex by a married person outside marriage."[9] Though Finnis's definition is morally neutral, it does not prevent him from condemning adultery as always morally wrong. Yet the same definition could be accepted by someone who sees nothing morally wrong with adultery.

We can make the same distinction between classification and evaluation in thinking about terrorism.[10] The central classification question is: which actions should we classify as "terrorist" acts? The central moral question is: are the actions that we classify as "terrorist" sometimes morally right or always morally wrong? The first question is answered by a definition and the second by a moral judgment. In order to make progress on the moral question, we need to settle the classification question. Until we know what terrorism is, we cannot know if it is right or wrong.

---

[9] John Finnis, *Moral Absolutes* (Washington, D.C.: Catholic University of America Press, 1991), 8.
[10] Simon Keller supports this view but explains why it seems counterintuitive in "On What Is the War on Terror?," in Timothy Shannon, ed., *Philosophy 9/11: Thinking About the War on Terrorism* (Chicago: Open Court, 2005), 55–8.

"ONE MAN'S TERRORIST ..."

Even though the slogan incorporates the idea that the word "terrorism" is used evaluatively, the point of the slogan is to undermine these negative value judgments. Although the slogan is confused in important ways, it nonetheless encapsulates a number of important ideas. We need to see why these ideas are errors rather than insights.

Before turning to errors, however, we should acknowledge that the slogan expresses a justified protest against the bias and hypocrisy that characterize the use of the term "terrorism." "Terrorism" is frequently used to slander one's enemies, while its non-use is often motivated by a desire to spare one's friends from criticism. The slogan is a legitimate protest against the political rhetoric of terrorism.

The slogan's force in undermining the rhetoric of terrorism derives from its appeal to two philosophical theories: relativism and subjectivism. It invokes relativism by denying that there is any absolute truth about whether something is terrorism. It invokes subjectivism by suggesting that whether acts are terrorism or freedom fighting depends on the attitudes of the person describing them. From an objective perspective, there is no such thing as terrorism. Rather an action that is terrorism to people with negative attitudes toward it is something quite different, such as freedom fighting, to people with positive attitudes.

The aim of people who invoke the slogan is political rather than theoretical. They use it to shield some favored political group from moral criticism by reducing condemnations of terrorist acts to matters of taste. To critics who condemn acts of violence as terrorism, it says: "You call it 'terrorism' only because you don't like it. When you like it, you call it 'freedom fighting.'"

While the slogan uses relativist and subjectivist ideas to block moral criticism, it (perhaps shamelessly) makes a latent appeal to objective values as well. It seeks to elevate the status of a favored group by associating it with the positive connotations of the expression "freedom fighting." Since freedom is widely seen as a lofty goal, attributing this goal to a group is a way to raise its status. The slogan suggests that people who fight for freedom should not be seen as terrorists, even if they do things (such as killing innocent people) that are normally morally wrong.

This reasoning is flawed. It assumes that if the terrorist label can successfully be resisted, then a group and its actions will be immune to moral criticism. This is a mistake. Saying that an act is not terrorism makes a judgment about how to classify it. It so far says nothing about how it should be morally evaluated.

ENDS AND MEANS IN JUST WAR THEORY

People using the slogan make a second mistake. They assume that actions are morally justified if they are done to achieve freedom or other valuable goals. This too is an error. Actions can be morally wrong even if their intended goals are genuinely valuable. This is a central part of commonsense morality. Because some ways of pursuing valuable goals are morally wrong, a valuable end does not by itself justify the means used to achieve it.

This point about ends and means is reflected in the two-part structure of just war theory, a central tradition in the ethics of war. Just war theory divides into two separate parts. The first – usually referred to by the Latin expression *jus ad bellum* – provides criteria for determining when it is morally permissible to enter into a war. The second – *jus in bello* – provides a separate set of criteria for determining whether the means used in fighting a war are morally permissible.[11] The *jus ad bellum* criteria focus in part on the goals of war. They recognize some goals (for example, defending one's territory against aggression) as just causes for going to war. Other goals (for example, acquiring other people's territory) are seen as unjust causes that do not justify going to war.

The distinction between the *jus ad bellum* and *jus in bello* criteria reminds us that evaluating a war requires attention to both the goals for which it is fought and the means used to fight for them. If a group meets the criteria for justifiably going to war, its actions may still be immoral if they violate the rules about permissible forms of fighting. A country fighting in self-defense, for example, acts wrongly if it commits atrocities in the course of defending itself. This is a fundamental point in the ethics of war. Even when people fight for goals of great value, there are moral limits on the means that they may use to achieve victory.

As a device for warding off moral criticism, the "one man's terrorist" slogan misses this important point. It assumes that people who are freedom fighters have such a valuable goal that they are justified in whatever violence they use to achieve it. Moreover, because they are justified in their actions, it is claimed that we should not apply the negative term "terrorist" to them. Both of these ideas are mistaken. Neither the classification problem nor the moral evaluation problem is settled by telling us that an action has been performed for a worthy goal.

---

[11] For a description of the just war criteria, see James Turner Johnson, *Morality and Contemporary Warfare* (New Haven: Yale University Press, 1999), 22–40.

Both of these errors occur in Yasir Arafat's 1974 speech to the United Nations General Assembly. Arafat claimed that

The difference between the revolutionary and the terrorist lies in the reason for which each fights. For whoever stands by a just cause and fights for freedom and liberation of his land ... cannot possibly be called [a] terrorist.[12]

Even though Arafat implicitly rejects the slogan's relativism and subjectivism, he echoes its assumption that people who fight for freedom or other just causes should neither be called terrorists nor condemned for their actions.

Both Arafat and those who use the slogan fail to see that people can be both terrorists and freedom fighters. Calling someone a "freedom fighter" tells us about their goal while calling someone a "terrorist" tells us about their means. It is perfectly possible for people to use terrorist means to fight for the goal of freedom.

TERRORISM AS A MEANS

The lesson to be drawn from these errors is that we should define terrorism in terms of means rather than ends. According to the most plausible definitions, terrorism is best understood as a tactic, a means of fighting.[13] Typical definitions require that terrorist acts must be violent, must deliberately harm innocent people, and must be done for some political or social purpose. In addition, many definitions include the idea that terrorist actions have two targets: the immediate victims of the attack and a second group, an audience, whom the terrorists are trying to influence. Terrorists direct their violence against a smaller group in order to influence the members of a larger group or the leaders who represent them. Brian Michael Jenkins's comment that "terrorism is theatre" stresses this communicative aspect of terrorist violence.[14]

Those who use the slogan to defend groups that they support unnecessarily muddy the debate about what terrorism is. In the interests of clarity, they could agree to accept a neutral definition of terrorism as a means of fighting and still remain free to support whatever political causes or groups they want to.

---

[12] Quoted in Hoffman, *Inside Terrorism*, 26.
[13] C. A. J. Coady defends the "terrorism is a tactic" view in "Defining Terrorism," in Igor Primoratz, ed., *Terrorism: The Philosophical Issues* (Houndsmills: Palgrave Macmillan, 2004), 7.
[14] Haig Khatchadourian calls this the "bifocal" quality of terrorism in *The Morality of Terrorism* (New York: Peter Lang, 1998), 6. Jenkins's comment is quoted in Hoffman, *Inside Terrorism*, 132.

They could adopt one of two approaches. They could acknowledge both that the group they support uses means that are rightly classified as terrorism and that using terrorist tactics is generally wrong. Nonetheless, they could argue, terrorist tactics are morally justified in this case because of the dire conditions against which the group is rebelling or its lack of alternative means of resistance. This approach replaces the idea that terrorism is necessarily wrong with the view that, while terrorism is generally wrong, it can sometimes be morally justified.

Interestingly, Osama bin Laden makes something like this point, distinguishing between "commendable" and "reprehensible" terrorist acts. According to him, terrorist acts are commendable when they target "the tyrants and the aggressors and the enemies of Allah."[15] Otherwise, they are reprehensible. Whatever the merit of this moral criterion, it is compatible with a neutral, objective definition of terrorism.

A second approach that a group's supporters could use is to praise its goal of seeking freedom while condemning its use of terrorist means to achieve this goal. This view is akin to Jenny Teichman's point that the word "terrorism" can apply to a "rebellion which is conducted *for a good aim but in a bad way*."[16] If terrorist methods are a "bad way," then allies of groups that use terrorist means could urge them to use other tactics. They might point out that other successful freedom fighters have avoided terrorism. The Minute Men of the American Revolution used violence but directed it against British army troops, and Mahatma Gandhi, in seeking India's independence from Britain, completely abstained from violent acts. As these examples make clear, freedom fighters need not use terrorist tactics. They can pursue freedom in other ways.

Both of these approaches provide the kind of political defense that the slogan aims for, but they do it more directly and without blurring the distinction between classifying and evaluating. Because they recognize a neutral, non-partisan sense of the word "terrorism," adopting either of them would make it easier to resolve the definition problem.

Clarity is not everyone's goal, however, because confusion can be politically useful. To solve the definition problem, we need either to find ways of stating political views that do not depend on confusions or to put aside partisan motivations and make genuine clarity a serious goal. Impartiality in labeling is essential both for any empirical inquiry into the nature of

---

[15] Quoted in Richardson, *Terrorists*, 7; original source: John Miller's 1998 interview of Bin Laden on ABC News.
[16] Jenny Teichman, "How to Define Terrorism," *Philosophy* 64 (1989), 511.

terrorism and for any attempt to make credible moral judgments about terrorist acts.[17]

MORAL CLARITY AND THE SPECIAL IMMORALITY OF TERRORISM

Those who found moral clarity after the September 11 attacks translated their feelings of horror into moral judgments without seeing that the two are different. By building their moral reactions into the word "terrorism," they made it harder to think about what terrorism is and why it is wrong. Given the history of propagandistic uses of the term, we need to be especially careful about translating gut feelings into classifications of complex terms.

While I agree with the moral clarity view that terrorist acts are wrong, the view not only undermines classification efforts but also distorts our moral judgments by over-inflating the genuine evil involved in terrorism. As Virginia Held has rightly claimed, "terrorism is not uniquely atrocious but is on a continuum with many other forms of political violence."[18] As terrible as terrorism is, many non-terrorist actions are equally or more vile.

To put terrorist violence into perspective, imagine a case in which attackers kill and injure some members of an ethnic or religious group in order to terrorize the whole group and cause its members to flee from a particular area. In this case, terrorist attacks are a means of ethnic cleansing. Their aim is to expel a group from a territory by transmitting a powerful threat to them. These acts would count as terrorism according to most definitions and would surely be worthy of moral condemnation.

Imagine a second case in which ethnic cleansing is achieved by massacring all the members of a group. In this case, the communicative aspect of terrorism – its tactic of harming a relatively small group in order to terrorize, intimidate, or influence the decisions of others – is lacking. Instead, the whole group is attacked, and ethnic cleansing is achieved directly by killing all its members.

According to many definitions, this is not a terrorist act because it lacks the "communicative" aspect of terrorism.[19] It would certainly be a great evil, however, and would be condemned by most people as worse than terrorism.

---

[17] Schmid and Jongman make a plea for an impartial definition in *Political Terrorism*, 3.

[18] Virginia Held, *How Terrorism Is Wrong: Morality and Political Violence* (New York: Oxford University Press, 2008), 9.

[19] Tony Coady is an exception; he defines "terrorism" as a tactic but does not include the "communicative" element in his definition; see his *Morality and Political Violence* (Cambridge: Cambridge University Press, 2008), 161–3.

After all, the terrorist strategy used in the first case kills a smaller number of people and leaves open the possibility for others to flee and build a new life elsewhere. Horrible as it is, it is less dreadful than outright massacre.

The point of these examples is twofold. First, they remind us that terrorist actions are neither the only terrible deeds nor the worst. Second, they show that we don't need to use the terrorist label in order to condemn an action in the strongest terms.

CONCLUSION

At the start of this chapter, I identified three views in Joyner's description of the definition debate:

1. we know terrorism when we see it;
2. it is impossible to agree on a definition of terrorism, and
3. terrorism has no objective reality but exists only "in the eye of the beholder."

I have tried to show that each of these views is wrong. The "we know it when we see it" view is wrong because it cannot account for persistent disagreements about the nature of terrorism and does not acknowledge the obvious bias in many applications of the term. It is the problem of bias that gives rise to the "one man's terrorist" slogan and the apparent impossibility of a definition.

While I have not yet shown the "impossible to define" view to be mistaken, I have suggested a strategy for arriving at a definition. We should look for a definition that focuses on actions rather than people and that contains neutral criteria for determining which actions are terrorist acts. The search for neutral criteria rests on the distinction between defining or classifying acts as terrorism and making moral evaluations of them. The more that we can segregate our classification effort from our moral evaluations, the better are our chances of arriving at a clear, useful definition of terrorism. If this effort succeeds, we will have provided objective criteria for being a terrorist act, and this will refute the claim that terrorism exists only "in the eye of the beholder."

In the next chapter, I will offer a definition of terrorism that I believe provides the clarity we need. I should warn readers that the definition I will propose does not simply describe how the word "terrorism" is used and conflicts with aspects of our ordinary usage of the term. Such conflicts with actual usage are inevitable in any definition because all terms are misused. An inflammatory word like "terrorism" invites misuses that involve applying it both too broadly and too narrowly. Usage is too narrow when, for political reasons, some acts are exempted from the terrorist category even though they strongly resemble acts that are included in it. It is too broad when political motivations lead to including non-terrorist actions under the terrorist label in order to inflame people's feelings toward those who engage in these actions.

A clear definition will conflict with ordinary language because our use of the term "terrorism" is a hodgepodge of different, confusing usages. A clear definition will necessarily differ from this because it will substitute clarity for confusion. Although a good definition is based on the actual use of a term, it does not merely report or describe it.[20]

A philosophical definition is a proposal about how best to understand the core meaning of a term. It proposes that we see certain uses as core and others as deviations from, or distortions of, this core meaning. Because definitions of complex terms are proposals rather than descriptions, they are neither true nor false. For this reason, I will not claim that the definition I give is true or that those I reject are false. The best argument for accepting a particular definition is that it is helpful, that it clarifies things in ways that promote understanding. If the definition I offer is superior, it will be because it accomplishes the goal of helping us to make reasonable, morally credible judgments about terrorism.

---

[20] Schmid and Jongman attempt to define "terrorism" based on scholarly usage in *Political Terrorism*, 1–38. Teichman discusses why definitions of terrorism cannot simply report usage in "How to Define Terrorism," 505–17. Richard Brandt discusses philosophical definitions in *A Theory of the Good and the Right* (New York: Oxford University Press, 1979), 2–10.

CHAPTER 2

Defining terrorism

I now want to propose a definition of terrorism that avoids the defects of the views I have discussed. Unlike biased, propagandistic ideas about terrorism, it provides neutral criteria for classifying actions as terrorist acts. These criteria describe features of actions themselves and omit any reference to the groups that carry them out. Unlike the "one man's terrorist" slogan, the definition identifies objective features as the essential characteristics of terrorism and thus avoids seeing terrorism as subjective or relative to observers.

Definition: Terrorist acts:

1. are acts of serious, deliberate violence or credible threats of such acts;
2. are committed in order to promote a political or social agenda;
3. generally target limited numbers of people but aim to influence a larger group and/or the leaders who make decisions for the group;
4. intentionally kill or injure innocent people or pose a threat of serious harm to them.

The definition has several parts which, together, differentiate terrorist acts from other actions. Each part highlights a type of feature and then specifies the form of that feature that characterizes terrorist acts. These features are:

1. the general type of action: violent;
2. the general type of goal: promoting a political/social agenda;
3. the strategy behind the action: harming some people to influence others;
4. the nature of the victims: innocent people.[1]

In order to evaluate this definition, we should consider several questions. Does it avoid the pitfalls of subjectivism and political bias? Could it be accepted by people who have different political and moral aims? How well does it fit with our common understanding? Do its departures from ordinary language clarify the discussion of terrorism?

---

[1] Boaz Ganor proposes a similar definition in "Defining Terrorism," http://www.ict.org.il/Research Publications/tabid/64/Articlsid/432/Default.aspx.

We can see if it satisfies these criteria by considering each part of the definition.

1. *Serious, deliberate violence or destruction or credible threats of these.* This condition seems quite uncontroversial. While there are debates about the definition of violence, people are generally clear that typical cases of terrorism are violent, destructive actions that cause injury and death to people.[2] Virtually no one would think that non-violent, non-destructive acts should be classified as terrorism. In some cases, mere threats can be terrorist acts, but they must be credible threats, and this generally requires that those who make the threats have previously carried out actual attacks.

2. *Committed in order to promote a political or social agenda.* Terrorist acts are meant to advance a political or social agenda. Sometimes terrorists make political demands and threaten more violence if the demands are not met. Or they engage in violence to publicize their cause. Sometimes they act out of revenge – both to make others suffer and to let them know that continued suffering is the price they will pay for resisting the terrorists' agenda. Whatever the goals of a specific attack may be, it must be connected to a political agenda. Violence that is unconnected to such an agenda is generally not called "terrorism," even if it causes widespread fear.

Some people see this condition as too restrictive. Igor Primoratz, for example, has argued that the goals of terrorism need not be political but can be religious or criminal. In a similar spirit, Alex P. Schmid defines terrorism so broadly that it includes violent actions done for "idiosyncratic, criminal, or political reasons."[3]

I don't disagree with Primoratz that terrorism may have religious goals, but I understand the word "political" in a broad sense that includes this. People who seek to make a society adhere to particular religious practices or values, for example, have a political goal in this sense. It is political because it aims to make the organization of social life conform to religious ideals.

Primoratz and Schmid both think that the goals of terrorist acts can be criminal. Here, we need to distinguish different kinds of criminal activities. We generally see people who engage in violence for personal gain as different from terrorist attackers. Kidnappers and extortionists, for example,

---

[2] Tony Coady discusses debates about the definition of violence in *Morality and Political Violence*, chapter 2.

[3] Igor Primoratz, "What Is Terrorism?," in Igor Primoratz, ed., *Terrorism: The Philosophical Issues* (Houndsmills: Palgrave Macmillan, 2004), 22. Schmid and Jongman, *Political Terrorism*, 28.

threaten violence but generally seek to make a profit for themselves and have no interest in social or political change. These are apolitical crimes. In some cases, however, a criminal organization may use violence to alter the institutional life and practices of a society so as to make it a better setting for their criminal activities. Such goals, like the religious goals just mentioned, are in fact political rather than merely personal.

Can "idiosyncratic" acts of violence that have no further purpose be terrorism? Walter Sinnott-Armstrong suggests that a person who "bombs buses simply in order to terrify people" could be considered a terrorist.[4] I don't think that we do or should view such acts as terrorism. While "idiosyncratic" perpetrators of violence like the bus bomber may mimic terrorist techniques, their actions flow from individual goals or pathology and thus differ from paradigmatic cases of terrorism. Like war, terrorism is a political phenomenon and is typically carried out by organized groups rather than individuals. When two men killed ten people in the Washington, D.C. area in 2002, their sniper attacks terrorized the city for weeks. Because these killings were not connected to a political agenda, the men were not referred to as terrorists. While we could broaden the definition to include such cases, this would not help to clarify our thinking about terrorism.

3. *Generally target limited numbers of people but aim to influence others, either a larger group and/or the leaders who make decisions for the group.* In many cases, terrorists commit relatively small-scale violence against members of a larger group that they want to influence. This is the communicative aspect of terrorism. Its success depends on publicity and on people's tendency to identify with victims who are like themselves in order to magnify the psychological effects of the attacks.[5]

Terrorists sometimes use this communicative strategy because they lack access to the powerful weapons that states possess. That is why terrorism has sometimes been called the "poor man's war." An important change in recent years is that non-governmental groups have acquired or seek powerful weapons that can increase the amount of damage they can create. The September 11 attackers certainly upped the ante in death and destruction by using large passenger airplanes as explosive missiles and hitting large, heavily populated targets. There is now considerable concern about nuclear

---

[4] Walter Sinnott-Armstrong, "On Primoratz's Definition of Terrorism," *Journal of Applied Philosophy* 8 (1991), 118.
[5] On the role of publicity, see Held, *How Terrorism Is Wrong*, chapter 6, "The Media and Political Violence."

weapons as instruments of terrorism. When terrorist attacks increase in scale and destructiveness, they look more like the wartime attacks we associate with governments.

The communicative feature is not unique to terrorist violence. The usual goal in wars between states is to inflict enough damage to convince an enemy that it should surrender or otherwise comply with one's demands. The goal is submission, not extermination. As Clausewitz notes in his classic *On War*:

> If we attack the enemy's Army, it is a very different thing whether we intend to follow up the first blow with a succession of others, until the whole force is destroyed, or whether we mean to content ourselves with a victory to shake the enemy's feeling of security, to convince him of our superiority, and to instill into him a feeling of apprehension about the future. If this is our object, we only go so far in the destruction of his forces as is sufficient.[6]

Attacks in war, like terrorism, often have both a target and an audience. The target consists of weapons or military personnel, but the attack sends a message, telling the enemy that it cannot win, that continuing to fight will only lead to greater losses, and that surrender is their best option.

While people often contrast war and terrorism, this blurring of the distinction between them shows that war and terrorism are not mutually exclusive ideas. Wars are typically extended campaigns of organized violence to achieve political goals. Terrorism carried out over time can constitute a war. Similarly, wars between states can involve terrorist tactics, i.e., attacks that have the features listed in the definition. Although people often contrast war and terrorism, the two terms overlap in their application. It is not surprising that the September 11 attacks were seen both as terrorist attacks and acts of war.

Some people may be surprised that my description of terrorism's communicative function says nothing about terrorizing people. I have used a broader description, saying that the violent attacks on some people are meant to "influence" a broader audience. But it may seem odd that a definition of terrorism would not specify terrorizing people as the specific form of communication. Robert Goodin, discussing the aims of terrorist attacks, says that the "aim by virtue of which they earn the designation 'terrorist' is the production of terror among the target population …"[7] The aim of producing fear, he thinks is central to terrorism's nature.

---

[6] Carl von Clausewitz, *On War*, edited and abridged by A. Rappaport, translated by J. J. Graham (New York: Penguin Books, 1968), 126.
[7] Robert Goodin, *What's Wrong With Terrorism?* (Cambridge: Polity Press, 2006), 45.

I believe that this description is too restrictive. Terrorists may have many types of immediate aims in launching an attack on innocent people. Terrorizing people may be one of them, but there are others. The killing of Israeli athletes at the Munich Olympics is widely seen as an attempt to put the Palestinian cause on the map, i.e., to make it known to a broader audience so that Palestinian interests would not be ignored. Similarly, one might see the September 11 attacks as a way of saying "We are here; you can't ignore us." Reducing the message of terrorist attacks to the production of terror over-simplifies its communicative function.[8]

5. *They intentionally kill or injure innocent people or pose a serious threat of harm to them.* The key point here is that in paradigmatic cases, the victims of terrorist acts are innocent people. Terrorists attacks are not aimed at members of an army in conditions of combat. Rather, they target ordinary people riding on a bus, shopping in a market, or going to work. Why is this? One reason is that civilian targets are both plentiful and vulnerable. It is easier to kill and injure defenseless civilians than well-protected members of the military. Sometimes, civilian targets are attractive to national military planners for the very same reason. In World War II, military planners took advantage of the fact that it was easier to bomb whole cities than to bomb a military facility within a city.[9]

The word "terrorism" is sometimes used to describe attacks on military personnel, and some writers take this as evidence that terrorism should not be defined as attacks on civilians or innocent people. Virginia Held takes this view, noting that the 1983 attacks on US Marines in Lebanon and the 2000 attack on the USS *Cole* in Yemen are "routinely offered as examples of terrorism."[10] This is a case where ordinary language is, I believe, distorted by political aims and by the tendency to classify actions as terrorism if they are carried out by groups that we call terrorists. My view is that this is a politically biased misuse of the term that confuses rather than clarifies our thinking.

In fact, of the four features that make up the definition, it is number 4 that best accounts for the sharp distinction between terrorism and other

---

[8] Jeremy Waldron develops an account of the communicative functions of terrorism that distinguishes between the impact of terrorist attacks on the general public and its impact on political leaders in "Terrorism and the Uses of Terror," *The Journal of Ethics* 8 (2004), 5–35. Tony Coady rejects the terror-focused view in "Defining Terrorism," 6.

[9] On the reasons why states at war target civilians, see Alexander Downes, *Targeting Civilians in War* (Ithaca, N.Y.: Cornell University Press, 2008). Hugo Slim investigates rationales for targeting civilians by both states and non-state groups in *Killing Civilians* (New York: Columbia University Press, 2008), chapters 4 and 5.

[10] Held, *How Terrorism Is Wrong*, 17.

forms of political violence. While we expect soldiers to be attacked in war, we do not expect civilians – people who are typically not engaged in fighting and who are going about the ordinary activities of daily life – to be attacked for political purposes. That is what makes terrorist attacks so shocking.

CONCLUSION

The four-part definition of terrorist acts can, I believe, help us to avoid many of the problems that have made defining terrorism difficult. The definition makes clear why we can ignore many factors in classifying actions as terrorism. We can ignore differences in the specific political goals of attackers, their ethnic makeup or ideology, and differences in the weapons they use. Likewise, it is irrelevant whether the attacking group has lofty or base goals or whether they are friends or enemies. All that matters are these four features. Acts that have them are terrorist acts; acts that don't have them are not, though they may still be morally reprehensible.

None of these points is novel or original. The key elements in my definition can be found in many other definitions of terrorism.[11] This overlap supports the definition because striking originality would suggest too great a departure from ordinary usage. Though definitions cannot mirror actual usage, they should reflect it as much as possible while departing from it only when necessary to achieve greater clarity.

In the next chapter, I will show that this definition has two important virtues. First, it is morally neutral and thus classifies actions without evaluating them. Second, in spite of its neutrality, it allows us to explain why terrorist acts are morally wrong.

---

[11] For extensive lists of definitions, see Schmid and Jongman, *Political Terrorism*, 32–8; and http://www. answers.com/topic/terrorism.

CHAPTER 3

What makes terrorism wrong?

Now that we have a definition of terrorist acts, it should be possible to pinpoint why it is so widely believed that terrorist acts are wrong and why they are often condemned with special vehemence. The definition specifies four essential features of terrorist acts.[1] Obviously, individual terrorist acts differ from each other in many ways, including where and when they occurred, who carried them out, what weapons were used, and what agenda motivated it. But the general features cited in the definition are features of all terrorist acts. If all terrorist acts are morally wrong, their wrongness must be the result of some or all of these features.

MORAL VS. PSYCHOLOGICAL REASONS FOR CONDEMNING TERRORISM

It is quite natural to see an explanation of the special immorality of terrorism as an answer to the following questions.[2] What makes terrorism so terribly wrong? Why do people condemn terrorist acts with a special vehemence? It is important to see, however, that these questions are not identical. The first is a moral question about the wrong-making features of a type of action. The second is a psychological question about what provokes certain responses in people. In an ideal world, the answers to both questions would be the same. The features that make terrorism wrong would be the same features that explain why people view it so negatively.

---

[1] They are: 1) acts of serious, deliberate violence or destruction or credible threats of such acts; 2) acts committed as part of a campaign to promote a political or social agenda; 3) acts that generally target limited numbers of people but aim to influence a larger group and/or the leaders who make decisions for the group; 4) acts that intentionally kill or injure innocent people or pose a serious threat of such harms to innocent people.

[2] While this statement assumes that terrorism is wrong, I mean to assume this only provisionally. As will become clear, I oppose prejudging the issue and will later defend this negative evaluation of terrorism.

30

It is possible, however, for an act to be wrong for one reason while it is condemned by people for some other reason. Suppose, for example, that some people condemned the September 11 attacks because the victims were (mostly) Americans. The fact that the victims were Americans might explain why many Americans so strongly condemned the attacks. Because people often react with greater horror when they identify with the victims of violent attacks, it would not be surprising for Americans to react more strongly when their fellow citizens are injured and killed.

Nonetheless, the identity of the victims does not explain what made the acts morally wrong. "Because the victims were Americans" is not the reason why the September 11 attacks were wrong. When Pope John Paul II called the attacks an "unspeakable horror," it was because the victims were human beings, not because they were Americans.[3] In fact, the attacks were widely condemned by people around the world, and Americans expected others to take this universalist perspective. By implication, if the attacks had been against people in other countries, Americans should have condemned the attacks even though the victims were not fellow countrymen and women. If there are people who condemned the attacks only because the victims were Americans, then the explanation of their condemnation of the attacks would differ from the explanation of the attacks' wrongness.

It remains to be seen whether the reasons that make terrorism wrong and the reasons that motivate condemnations of terrorism are the same. In considering possible grounds for believing that terrorism is wrong, I will look for reasons that are widely accepted, and if widely accepted reasons explain its wrongness, then the answers to the two questions will converge.

THE WRONGNESS OF TERRORISM

Which of the features of terrorism cited in the definition best explain the idea that terrorist acts are always wrong?

1. Condition 1 says that terrorist acts are *acts of serious, deliberate violence or destruction*. Because acts of serious violence injure and kill their victims, commonsense morality generally condemns them. Nonetheless, such acts are not regarded as always being wrong. Most people believe that some acts of serious violence can be morally justified, and this is a reasonable belief.

We can see that some acts of serious, deliberate violence are morally justified by considering cases in which people act in self-defense. It is an

---

[3] The Pope's remark is cited in Elshtain, *Just War Against Terror*, 9.

important part of commonsense morality that if a person's life is unjustifiably threatened by an attacker, the victim has a right to injure or kill the attacker in self-defense. The same is true in cases where a person uses violence to defend someone else against a serious, wrongful attack. While the attacker's violence is not morally justified, almost everyone would see the defender's use of violence as morally permissible. Acts of serious violence, then, are sometimes morally permissible. They are not inherently or universally wrong.

One way to understand why defensive violence is morally permissible is to appeal to the victim's right to life. The fact that the victim has a right to life implies that no one has a right to threaten the victim's life without special justification. In addition, the right to life includes a right to defend oneself. The right to life, then, includes both a prohibition on others attacking us and a permission to use violence to protect ourselves against wrongful attack. These are familiar ideas, and they make us feel justified in criticizing the attacker's violence while approving acts of serious violence used by victims of wrongful attacks to defend themselves.[4]

If these serious acts of violence are morally justified, then it cannot be that what makes terrorist acts always wrong is that they are acts of serious violence. Terrorist acts share this feature with other actions that are morally justified. Most people do not condemn terrorist acts simply because they are acts of serious violence. They do not do this because they reject the idea that all acts of serious violence are wrong. This feature explains neither the wrongness of terrorism nor its widespread condemnation.

2. The same point applies to condition 2, the idea that terrorist acts are *committed as part of a campaign to promote a political or social agenda.* Clearly, there is nothing necessarily wrong about politically motivated acts. If there were, it would be immoral to vote or run for office. But even if we combine this feature with condition 1 and focus only on politically motivated acts of violence, this still will not account for the wrongness of terrorism. Why not? Because most people believe that some acts of serious, politically motivated violence are morally justified. The clearest case is war.

Although pacifists condemn all war, pacifism is very much a minority view. Most people believe that war is sometimes morally justified. War, however, is simply an organized form of serious violence that is carried out to promote a political or social agenda (which may be just or unjust, defensive or aggressive). If war is sometimes morally justified even though

---

[4] For a careful analysis of the right of self-defense, see David Rodin, *War and Self-Defense* (Oxford: Oxford University Press, 2002), chapter 2.

it is serious violence to promote a political agenda, then terrorism cannot be condemned because it possesses these very same features.

Of course, people who approve of some wars often disapprove of others. Their judgment about whether a war is justified often depends on the type of political goals that a war is meant to promote. The idea that the goals and purposes of a war matter to its justification is found in both commonsense morality and just war theory. Each of these views accepts the idea that going to war is sometimes morally justified and sometimes not.

This differs from the usual ways of thinking about terrorism. The usual view is that terrorism is always wrong and thus can never be morally justified. That is why people resist applying the term "terrorism" to groups or causes that they support. Unlike "war," which is a neutral term, "terrorism" is often understood in a way that rules out approval under any circumstances. Neither of the first two features explains why this is so.

3. Condition 3 says that terrorist acts *generally target limited numbers of people but aim to influence a larger group and/or the leaders who make decisions for the group*. This feature also fails to explain either the wrongness of terrorism or people's condemnation of it. It fails because it too is a feature of war, and most people approve of at least some wars.

Wars typically consist of battles between opposing military forces, and the most immediate goal in these battles is to destroy or disable enemy soldiers, weapons, or other military resources while also protecting one's own troops, weapons, and military resources. The overall aim of these battles, however, is to convince the enemy that it cannot prevail and that continued fighting is not in its interest. War, like terrorism, employs violence for a communicative purpose. This feature, then, cannot be our basis for condemning terrorism.

THE HEART OF THE MATTER

This brings us to condition 4, the idea that terrorist acts *intentionally kill or injure innocent people or pose a serious threat of such harms to innocent people*. Unlike the first three features, it seems to provide a plausible basis for understanding both why terrorist acts are wrong and why people condemn terrorism with special vehemence. It does this because there seems to be something especially terrible about targeting innocent people.

Most people believe that traditional warfare, dreadful and destructive as it is, can sometimes be morally justified, but terrorism often strikes people as different because it targets innocent people. Ideally, in a war, the targets are military personnel and objects of military value. Innocent people lack this type of military value and are not seen as legitimate targets of attack. According to condition 4, however, terrorism always and necessarily picks out innocent people to be its targets. This is what makes it plausible to believe that terrorism is always wrong. It also differentiates terrorism from war, since, at least in theory, a war could be fought in which only soldiers are targeted and civilians are never attacked.

Condition 4, then, appears to identify the heart of the matter. It provides answers to two central questions: What makes terrorism wrong? And, Why do people condemn terrorism so vehemently? We can answer both questions if we a) define "terrorism" as always involving the intentional killing and injuring of innocent people, and b) accept the belief that intentionally killing innocent people is always wrong.

Both of these views, however, have been attacked by scholars who appear to lack political motives. In the rest of this chapter, I will briefly consider two objections and will move to more substantial discussions of other criticisms in chapters 4 and 5. Responding to these objections will provide the opportunity both to test my view and to clarify other issues about the nature of terrorism.

SHOULD WE DEFINE TERRORISM AS ATTACKS ON INNOCENT PEOPLE?

Angelo Corlett challenges a central part of my view by arguing that we should not include the killing of innocent people in the definition of terrorism. Corlett raises this criticism against philosophers like Tony Coady and Igor Primoratz who claim that the "targeting of the innocent is the essential trait of terrorism, both conceptually and morally."[5] Corlett thinks that defining "terrorism" in this way makes it impossible even to ask whether terrorism might be morally right. Because he thinks this is an important question, Corlett favors a definition that leaves open the possibility of morally justified terrorist acts, and, he believes, any definition of terrorism that refers to targeting innocent people closes off this possibility. If he is right, then his argument provides a reason to reject both my definition and my explanation for the wrongness of terrorism.

Corlett believes that "innocent victim" definitions have this flaw because, he says, attacking innocent people "violates the fundamental moral intuition that innocent people ought not to be targets or victims of violent

---

[5] The quote is from Igor Primoratz, "What is Terrorism?," *Journal of Applied Philosophy* 7 (1990), 133; it appears in J. Angelo Corlett, *Terrorism: A Philosophical Analysis* (Dordrecht: Kluwer, 2003), 115.

physical attack."[6] Because attacks on innocent people violate this "funda-mental moral intuition," Corlett believes that any definition of terrorism that includes this feature necessarily implies that terrorism is wrong. And if terrorism is wrong by definition, then we cannot even conceive of it being morally justified.

Corlett is correct in thinking that we should not accept a definition that makes it impossible to ask whether terrorism could be morally justified. He is wrong, however, in thinking that a definition that refers to the innocence of terrorism's victims blocks us from asking whether terrorism could be morally justified. To see where Corlett goes wrong, recall that I appealed to two distinct beliefs to explain the belief that terrorism is always wrong.

1. Terrorism always involves the intentional killing (injuring, etc.) of innocent people.
2. Intentionally killing innocent people is always wrong.
3. Therefore, terrorism is always wrong.

While the first statement is part of the definition of terrorism, the second is a moral principle that is completely distinct from the definition. Because these statements are independent of one another, it is possible to accept either one and reject the other. Most important, a person can accept: 1. the definitional claim that terrorism intentionally kills innocent people while rejecting both 2. the moral principle that killing innocent people is always wrong and 3. the moral conclusion that terrorism is always wrong. Corlett is simply mistaken that accepting 1 commits one to accepting either 2 or 3. For this reason, accepting the definition does not require the condemnation of terrorism and does not preclude serious thinking about the morality of terrorism.

Corlett is also mistaken in thinking that the wrongness of killing inno-cent people is a "fundamental moral intuition," a self-evident moral belief that needs no justification. Although the belief in the wrongness of killing innocent people is widely regarded as obviously true, it has in fact been rejected by many people. As Hugo Slim notes in his book *Killing Civilians*,

> there has never been unanimity about this moral ideal and its ethic of protection in war … [M]arking out a special category of people called civilians from the wider enemy group in war … is not, and never has been, either clear, meaningful or right for many people … Most political and military leaders and many of their spearing, hacking, shooting, bombing and burning subordinates have not usually valued this ethic of mercy and protection as an important priority in war. Normally, they have rejected it.[7]

---

[6] Ibid., 115.   [7] Slim, *Killing Civilians*, 2.

It would be good if Corlett were right that the inviolability of the innocent was a fundamental moral intuition, but as we shall see, even thoughtful, morally conscientious people have often rejected this view. I agree with Corlett that there is a widespread belief in the wrongness of killing innocent people, but that belief, as I will show later, exists alongside competing beliefs that allow for killing innocent people under certain conditions. That is why it is a mistake to call it a "fundamental moral intuition."

Corlett's attack on victim-focused definitions of terrorism fails to show that they are defective. He does not show that the definition by itself implies a moral judgment or that it makes it impossible to ask whether terrorism could be justified. And, he is wrong to assume that the moral wrongness of killing innocent people is a self-evident moral truth.[8]

IS TERRORISM DISTINCTIVELY WRONG?

In a probing essay, Lionel McPherson criticizes what he calls the "dominant view" of terrorism. The dominant view includes two beliefs: that terrorism is by definition wrong and that terrorism is in some way worse than war. McPherson rejects both of these views and thereby gives a "no" answer to the question posed by his title, "Is Terrorism Distinctively Wrong?" While McPherson does think that non-state terrorism differs from state terrorism regarding legitimate authority, this particular distinctiveness, he writes, "does not support the dominant view that terrorism is necessarily wrong and intrinsically worse than conventional war."[9]

If terrorism's being "necessarily wrong" is understood to mean that the definition of terrorism includes the idea of wrongness, then, as I have stressed in replying to Corlett, I agree with McPherson that terrorism is not "necessarily wrong." I do, however, defend the idea that there is something especially wrong about terrorism and that this special wrongness is related to the nature of its victims. So I would answer the question "is terrorism distinctively wrong?" with a "yes." In giving this answer, I appear to fall into the category of people who think that "terrorism is ... intrinsically worse than conventional war" and join them in being a target of McPherson's criticisms.

---

[8] For criticisms of Corlett and other contributors to the definition debate, see Uwe Steinhoff, *On the Ethics of War and Terrorism* (Oxford and New York: Oxford University Press, 2007), 109–22.

[9] Lionel McPherson, "Is Terrorism Distinctively Wrong?," *Ethics* 117 (April 2007), 546. I discuss the question of legitimate authority to use political violence in chapters 5 and 9.

McPherson's discussion contains many valuable points. In particular, he is right that people are generally too complacent about the non-terrorist killings of civilians in conventional wars. I raised this issue at the start of the book, where I noted that the credibility of people's condemnations of terrorism is often undermined by their casual acceptance of killings of civilians in war. McPherson, too, is disturbed by these inconsistencies and tries to expose them. He tries to force people "to adopt either a more critical attitude toward conventional war or a less condemnatory attitude toward terrorism."[10]

By putting his point in this way, McPherson suggests the wrong lesson for readers to take from his rejection of the distinctiveness of terrorism. He seems to be arguing that we have a choice between being either more critical of war *or* less critical of terrorism. There are two immediate problems with this. First, it is clear that McPherson himself makes no such choice and is in fact both more critical of conventional war than most people and less condemnatory of terrorism. Second, I believe that the right view is that we need to be more critical in our judgments about conventional war while maintaining a strongly condemnatory attitude toward terrorism.

There are also problems with the way that McPherson compares war and terrorism. This comparison is confused in a "comparing apples and oranges" way. Terrorism, as we have seen, is a specific tactic. War, however, is generally a form of organized violent activity that goes on for some time and that can include many types of tactics. Because a particular war may include the use of terrorist tactics, it does not make sense to ask: which is worse, war or terrorism?

Terrorism is a tactic that has some features that distinguish it from other tactics. It makes sense to compare these different tactics to determine whether some are morally better or worse than others. But that quite reasonable comparison is very different from comparing these tactics with warfare in general. The use of poison gases in war, for example, has been seen as a distinctive tactic that is worthy of special condemnation, but we do not ask which is worse: war or poison gas attacks? The same point can be made about rape, ethnic cleansing, killing children, and using nuclear weapons as tactics of war. We can compare these tactics with one another or with other means of fighting. We cannot compare them with war itself because wars differ so much from one another. They can be long or short, high casualty or low, nuclear or non-nuclear, terrorist or non-terrorist, fought for just or for unjust causes.

---

[10] Ibid., 546. For a similar view, see Held, *How Terrorism is Wrong*, chapter 1.

McPherson seems to confuse two different questions: a) whether terrorism as a tactic has distinctive features that make it wrong in a special way, and b) whether terrorism as a tactic is "intrinsically worse than conventional war." The first makes sense, but the second does not. The better way to put his point would be to say that people who condemn terrorism as a tactic ought to condemn other tactics of warfare that have equally serious moral defects.

The correct moral of McPherson's story is that people should be as prepared to criticize the tactics of "conventional war" as they are to criticize the tactics used by terrorists. This point is fully consistent with the view I have defended: that terrorist acts are distinctively wrong because they intentionally attack innocent people in order to promote a political goal. One can make that claim without claiming that terrorism is worse than warfare.

WHERE ARE WE NOW?

I began my discussion of definitions with several problems in mind. The first was a lack of clarity about what terrorism is and the impact of this lack of clarity on the credibility of moral condemnations of terrorism. Having put forward a definition of terrorism, I think we are in a position to avoid important sources of confusion about terrorism.

By defining terrorism as a tactic, we can avoid the problems that arise when terrorism is defined either by the specific goals that motivate it or by the identity of those who carry out terrorist acts. Because the definition is politically neutral, it can be accepted by people with different political interests and alliances. Because it is morally neutral, it can be accepted both by people who think terrorism is always wrong and by those who believe it can sometimes be justified. This should allow people to commit to "truth in labeling" when it comes to calling or refraining from calling particular acts "terrorism." To call an act "terrorism" is to label it and not necessarily to judge it morally.

While I believe that the definition helps to clarify what terrorism is and what are the key moral issues it raises, there are important objections against this type of definition. I have already tried to show why two objections fail, but there are other objections that cannot be ignored and that require greater attention. I will discuss the following three objections in the next two chapters.

Objection 1: The definition fails to explain what is meant by an "innocent" person in condition 4. If we can't define "innocence," we have made no progress in clarifying "terrorism." Moreover since the word "innocent" expresses a value judgment, including it in the definition of "terrorism" undermines the goal of providing a morally neutral definition.

Objection 2: The definition is too narrow because it restricts terrorist acts to attacks that *intentionally* kill and injure innocent people. This wrongly excludes acts that kill and injure innocent people as "collateral damage," side effects of attacks on other targets. In order to recognize some unintentional killings of innocent people as terrorist acts, the definition should be revised by deleting the word "intentional" from condition 4.

Objection 3: The definition is too broad because "terrorism" only applies to violent acts carried out by non-governmental groups (non-state actors). This is how terrorism is widely understood, not only in the media but also by government officials and academic experts on terrorism. No definition can succeed without specifying that terrorism is a tactic of non-state groups rather than a means used by established governments.

The first two of these objections will be the subject of chapter 4 while answering the third objection will occupy chapter 5. This may seem like a lot of time to spend on defining a single term. How we define "terrorism," however, has a large impact on how we understand the problem of terrorism and on the credibility of our moral judgments about terrorism. Moreover, in the course of considering definitional issues, many other important issues emerge. The definition debate is not "merely semantic."[11]

---

[11] Jeremy Waldron notes the ways in which definitional questions about terrorism connect with broader issues in "Terrorism and the Uses of Terror."

CHAPTER 4

Innocence and discrimination

Terrorist acts, I have argued, have the following feature: they *intentionally kill or injure innocent people or pose a serious threat of such harms to innocent people*. One aspect of this feature, indicated by the word "intentionally," involves the manner in which the killing or injuring occurs. The harms that terrorist acts produce are not side effects; they are exactly what the attackers aim to produce. A second aspect, indicated by the word "innocent," identifies a feature of terrorism's victims. The victims are not targeted for reasons that relate specifically to them as individuals. Sometimes this feature is suggested by use of the word "random," as in Michael Walzer's description of terrorism as "the random murder of innocent people."[1] While "random" is not quite the right word, Walzer is right to suggest a certain indiscriminateness in the relationship between the attack and the individual victims. Which specific individuals suffer is random even if other things about them are not.

Both of these ideas are open to criticism. Some critics want to delete the word "intentional" from the definition so that "terrorism" can apply to attacks that cause collateral damage to innocent people. A second criticism is that the word "innocent," which plays a central role in the definition, is neither clear nor morally neutral. If it is not clarified, the definition is useless; if it is clarified, it will cease to be morally neutral. In this chapter, I address these criticisms by answering two questions: What do we mean by *innocent* people? And, must terrorist actions *intentionally* harm their victims?

MORAL INNOCENCE

The most intuitively plausible understanding of innocence is the idea of moral innocence. People are innocent if they are not guilty of wrongdoing. Innocence and guilt are generally understood as particular rather than

[1] Michael Walzer, *Just and Unjust Wars* (New York: Basic Books, 1977), 198.

holistic ideas. Even if the doctrine of original sin is true and no one is completely innocent, we can still distinguish innocent from guilty people in specific contexts. People guilty of original sin may still be innocent of embezzling money, and people who are guilty of embezzlement may be innocent of murder or jay-walking. Guilt and innocence are connected with responsibility for particular actions, and how we treat people is supposed to be governed in part by their guilt or innocence with respect to particular actions. Different actions are relevant in different contexts.

How do we determine what kinds of guilt and innocence are relevant when we describe the victims of a terrorist attack? According to feature 2 of the definition, terrorist acts *are committed as part of a campaign to promote a political or social agenda.* Terrorists seek to influence the ways that societies operate or relate to one another. Typically, terrorists are motivated by a sense of grievance or hostility. They believe that groups that they identify with have been treated badly or that things that they value are not properly respected. For terrorists who seek self-rule for a particular group, the group's lack of political independence is an evil that they want to eliminate. Terrorists who seek to overthrow a particular regime or institution see it as evil and want to replace it.

If terrorist attacks are part of a campaign against perceived evils, then people are innocent (in this context) if they are not responsible for these evils. While some people may be responsible for these evils and thus guilty (assuming that these are genuine evils), the victims of terrorist attacks are not these people. The victims are seen as innocent because they are not morally responsible for the alleged evils that the terrorists oppose.

IS THE "MORAL INNOCENCE" VIEW NEUTRAL?

This "moral innocence" view is plausible because it matches our common understanding. Because it is explicitly moral, however, it seems inconsistent with my goal of providing a neutral definition that can be objectively applied. This is a mistake. It wrongly assumes that it is impossible to have objective, factual criteria for applying a value-laden term.

To see this, consider the concept of "murder." *Murder*, unlike *killing*, is not a neutral concept. We only classify killings as murders if we judge them to be wrong. These value judgments, however, are based on objective features that differentiate murders from other homicides. For example, murders are intentional rather than accidental killings. Similarly, among intentional killings, we differentiate defensive killings from killings done for non-defensive reasons like hatred or the desire for private gain. If a particular homicide was either accidental or a defensive response to an unprovoked attack, then we can use these criteria and objectively decide that a particular killing was not murder. While this account is incomplete, it shows how we can use factual, objective criteria to apply an evaluative, non-neutral concept. Similarly, if there are factual criteria for moral innocence, we can make objective determinations of whether people are morally innocent with respect to the conditions that motivate terrorist acts.

Haig Khatchadourian, a defender of the moral innocence view, explains the idea of a "perfectly innocent person" in the context of terrorism. A morally innocent person, he says, is someone who "has no share in the *moral responsibility* … [and] no *causal responsibility* at all" for the wrongs, if any, that "give rise to" the terrorist act.[2] Although the two factors that Khatchadourian mentions – *moral* responsibility and *causal* responsibility – are different, they are not unrelated. Causal responsibility is often the basis for judgments of moral responsibility. We see someone as morally responsible for and thus guilty of a certain crime because that person was causally responsible for it. A person guilty of arson, for example, is morally responsible because he or she caused the fire. People who did not cause the fire are not morally responsible for it.[3]

Using this model, we can say that victims of terrorist attacks are innocent if they did not cause – and are therefore not morally responsible for – whatever conditions the terrorists oppose. By contrast, a non-innocent person is someone who is causally responsible for the (alleged) wrongs that give rise to an attack. For this reason, if a group kills a government official who initiates policies that severely violate people's rights, this would not be a terrorist act because the official is not innocent. An official may be responsible for a perceived evil in several ways. He or she may a) initiate the policy or action, b) implement an already existing policy, or c) have the power to stop the policy but fail to do so. In the last case, it is an omission rather than an action that generates guilt.

According to this view, whether people are morally innocent or not depends on what they cause to happen or fail to prevent.[4] People who neither create nor continue an evil policy and who lack the power to end it are not responsible for it. These are the criteria for innocence, and victims of terrorists attacks are innocent in this sense.

---

[2] Haig Khatchadourian, "Terrorism and Morality," *Journal of Applied Philosophy* 5 (1988), 135.
[3] While causal responsibility may be a necessary condition for guilt, it is not a sufficient condition. Someone who accidentally causes a fire is not an arsonist.
[4] For further discussion of innocence, see Primoratz, "What is Terrorism?," 17–21.

An implication of this view is that assassinations are not necessarily instances of terrorism. While assassination is often cited as a terrorist act, the moral innocence definition implies that this is a mistake. Whether an assassination is a terrorist act depends on whether the official who is assassinated had a direct role in creating or continuing the policies being opposed. If an official had no role in these policies, then the assassination would be terrorism (assuming that it is done to advance a political agenda, send a message to a broader audience, etc.).

In saying that assassinations are not necessarily instances of terrorism, I am making a point about classifying actions. I am not suggesting that non-terrorist assassinations are morally justified. Even if a public official is guilty of terrible crimes, it might still be wrong to assassinate him. Why? Perhaps because no one should be punished without a trial. People who engage in vigilante justice may be mistaken about what a particular official did or did not do. Likewise, even if an official is morally responsible for certain acts or policies, death may be too severe a punishment. The fact that a person is morally guilty does not automatically justify others in killing or injuring that person.

The moral innocence view fits very well with ordinary beliefs about innocence and the wrongness of terrorism. One of the shocking things about terrorist acts is that the victims have no control over the conditions that thwart the political goals of the attacking group. The victims of the attack do not deserve to suffer for actions or policies that they did not initiate, did not carry out, and had no power to change.[5]

DEGREES OF RESPONSIBILITY

After defining "perfect innocence," Khatchadourian points out that innocence and guilt are often matters of degree. The fact that people can be partially responsible for conditions that terrorists oppose complicates the problem of determining whether victims of attacks are innocent or not.

Consider person A, who works in a government bureaucracy that implements policies. Such a person will have a small fraction of causal responsibility for these policies. How can we determine A's degree of responsibility? To simplify, if A is one of a group of 1,000 people who implement a policy, we could say that A's amount of causal responsibility is 1/1,000 of the total.

---

[5] Jeff McMahan argues that the moral innocence view undermines many ordinary beliefs about the ethics of war in "Innocence, Self-Defense, and Killing in War," *The Journal of Political Philosophy* 2 (1994), 193–221.

Whether this makes sense depends on the type of task that each person performs. If A's department has the task of exterminating another group of 1,000 people and if each person's task is to kill one, the fact that A only kills 1/1,000 of the victims will not make A largely innocent. In this case, A is completely responsible for the death that he or she directly causes and is clearly not innocent.

Consider person B, who is a "paper pusher" in the same bureaucracy. B never harms anyone directly. Still, if B knows that his filing papers plays a role in the extermination of a group, B would bear some responsibility for the part that his work plays in the extermination project. Here, the idea of fractional responsibility appears to make sense. If B is wrong to take part in this activity, then B is at least partially guilty. (Other facts about the consequences of B's not doing this work might be relevant to the degree of guilt.)

Consider C, who is also a government bureaucrat. B's department has no direct involvement in this particular evil. Suppose C works in tax collection. Even though raising taxes may be necessary to implement evil policies, tax collection is also connected to a multitude of government policies that are not evil and that may have important, beneficial effects. While B's work does contribute to evil policies, C's fraction of causal responsibility for them is so small that it would be odd to attribute any significant guilt to C. Such a person would be almost entirely morally innocent with respect to the evils carried out by the government because he or she is only very indirectly causally responsible for them.

If an opposition group acting in defense of the victims of government policies of oppression or extermination attacks the government offices in which A and B work, this group would be attacking an agency with direct responsibility for the policies being opposed. This would not be a random attack and could be seen as similar to assassinations since the target is the agency carrying out the evil policies. Hence, it would not be a terrorist attack. In the case of the taxation bureau for which C works, its overall role is more general and diffuse, and its responsibility for the evils is much smaller. An attack on it and the people working for it would more plausibly be described as a terrorist attack on largely innocent people.

This same point holds even more strongly for ordinary citizens whose causal role is limited to paying taxes. As long as the taxes paid are for general governmental functions, it would be wrong to say that these individuals are significantly responsible for whatever evils the government may do. Their payment of taxes did not create the evil policies and plays only a tiny role in their continuation. Moreover, ordinary tax payers lack the power to alter the government's actions. Even if they hold back their taxes, this would be a largely symbolic act and would not end the policies.

Even if people can be partly innocent or guilty, average citizens in a society are not sufficiently responsible to justify labeling them as non-innocent. If we imagine a scale that indicates amounts of responsibility and a point on the scale at which people are sufficiently "non-innocent" so that an attack on them would not be terrorism, most people will be well below that point. They would qualify as innocent victims of a terrorist attack.

ARE AVERAGE CITIZENS REALLY INNOCENT?

Would terrorists and their supporters accept the judgment that ordinary, tax-paying citizens are innocent? They might. They could agree that the victims of their attacks are innocent but add that they do not care about this fact. They might believe that the cause they are fighting for is so important that it justifies them in attacking innocent people. So, believing that terrorist acts are justified is compatible with accepting the idea that ordinary citizens are morally innocent.[6]

Other terrorists and their supporters, however, might well reject the view that their victims are innocent. As Khatchadourian notes, "[T]errorists, driven by passion or paranoia, often baselessly enlarge, sometimes to a tragically absurd extent, the circle of alleged non-innocents."[7] Terrorists may classify large classes of people as automatically guilty, even if their connection to evil actions and policies is minimal or nonexistent. They may have a concept of collective guilt that allows them to attribute guilt to all members of a particular group. In this case, they might believe that all members of a group – including individuals who did not create, do not sustain, and could not change these policies – share responsibility for the conditions being opposed.

To believe that group membership by itself is grounds for moral responsibility and guilt is, as Khatchadourian says, both tragic and absurd. It would be a selective version of original sin that would apply only to certain groups. They would be guilty for things over which they had no

---

[6] For an account of why terrorists might see attacks on innocent people as justified, see Aleksandar Pavkovic, "Towards Liberation: Terrorism from a Liberation Ideology Perspective," in Tony Coady and Michael O'Keefe, eds., *Terrorism and Justice* (Melbourne: Melbourne University Press, 2002), 58–71.

[7] Khatchadourian, "Terrorism and Morality," 135. For a defense of an "expansive" conception of guilt and its relevance to terrorism, see Burleigh T. Wilkins, *Terrorism and Collective Responsibility* (London: Routledge, 1992).

control, and this unearned guilt would allegedly justify imposing severe punishments on them. This view completely rejects the idea that guilt and responsibility depend on what people do. The view also rejects the idea that punishment should be proportionate to crimes. The idea that ordinary citizens who are virtually powerless with respect to their country's policies could be sufficiently responsible to merit death or severe injury is extremely implausible. Even if members of a society bear some fraction of moral responsibility for their society's deeds, their minimal role and slight degree of guilt would not merit serious injury or death as the appropriate punishment.

BROADENING THE SCOPE OF RESPONSIBILITY

While these harsh ideas about moral responsibility sound quite fanatical, it is worth noting that similar views have played a role in justifying policies that are often seen as morally justified. One area in which they appear is in debates about the morality of nuclear deterrence strategy. The strategy of nuclear deterrence attempts to prevent a nuclear attack on one's own country or its allies by saying that, if an enemy launches a nuclear attack, the victim country will respond with nuclear retaliation against the attacker. In so-called counter-value attacks, cities would be the targets of retaliatory attacks, and the primary victims of these attacks would be ordinary citizens who live in or near cities. These are the same types of people we consider innocent when discussing terrorism.

Some critics have charged that nuclear retaliatory attacks are immoral because the victims would be innocent people. In response, Gregory Kavka defended nuclear deterrence by appealing to an expanded notion of responsibility. In this context, he argued, it is permissible to "loosen the conditions of liability" so as to justify threats against a country's civilians. Even though ordinary citizens are not individually responsible for the threat posed by their country, Kavka argued that they are "partially responsible and thus partly liable."[8] In his view, ordinary citizens have enough responsibility for their country's policies to render them non-innocent and thus sufficiently liable to make them legitimate targets of a nuclear attack.

Kavka's claims about individual moral responsibility are not reasonable. Ordinary citizens, especially in an undemocratic country like the Soviet Union, did not create or implement the threatening policies and could not alter them. Attributing even partial responsibility to them is just as

[8] Gregory Kavka, *Moral Paradoxes of Nuclear Deterrence* (New York: Cambridge University Press, 1987), 91.

unreasonable as the claims by terrorists that all members of a national, ethnic, or religious group are guilty simply by virtue of their group membership. These conceptions of moral responsibility are unreasonable because the causal role of most members of the group in creating and sustaining the policies of their government is minimal to nonexistent.

What about citizens of democracies? Virginia Held has suggested that they may not be innocent and may be legitimate targets of attacks.

Especially in the case of a democracy, where citizens elect their leaders and are ultimately responsible for their government's policies, it is not clear that citizens should be exempt from the violence those policies lead to while the members of their armed services are legitimate targets.[9]

Even in democracies, this description vastly overstates both the causal role and the moral responsibility of ordinary citizens for their country's actions and policies. Individually, as voters, their fractional power is minimal. Moreover, important government decisions, especially about war, are often made secretly, and even when they are made publicly, citizens often must rely on the decision-making officials for their information. These officials often believe that lying is justified as a means of obtaining or sustaining support for their policies. Even if attacks on ordinary citizens can somehow be justified, they cannot be justified by the claim that these people are causally or morally responsible for their government's actions.[10]

A PROBLEM FOR THE MORAL INNOCENCE VIEW

The moral innocence view is appealing because it explains the idea of innocence in a way that connects with ordinary understandings. It also preserves the neutrality of the definition by providing causal criteria of responsibility, and it explains why almost all ordinary citizens and most government officials are innocent.

In spite of these virtues, the moral innocence view faces a difficult problem. It implies that many soldiers are also morally innocent and, therefore, are not permissible targets in war. But if soldiers are not permissible targets, then there is no difference between soldiers and civilians.

---

[9] Held, *How Terrorism Is Wrong*, 20. For further defense of this expansive view of responsibility by Held, see chapter 6, "Group Responsibility for Ethnic Conflict."

[10] On the lack of responsibility of citizens in a democracy, see Robert Sparrow, "Hands Up Who Wants to Die?: Primoratz on Responsibility and Civilian Immunity in Wartime," *Ethical Theory and Moral Practice* 8:3 (2005), 299–319. For a vivid account of the role of both secrets and lies, see Daniel Ellsberg, *Secrets: A Memoir of Vietnam and the Pentagon Papers* (New York: Penguin, 2003).

This result follows because the features that make most civilians innocent are shared by many soldiers as well. Ordinary soldiers did not start the war in which they fight, lack the ability to prevent or end the war, and bear only a small fraction of causal responsibility for the conduct of the war. A single soldier's causal responsibility is so small that it seems very much like that of the paper-pushing bureaucrat or the ordinary citizen who votes and pays taxes. This application of the moral innocence criterion suggests that attacking soldiers is morally comparable to attacking civilians.

This argument attacks the traditional, generally accepted view that soldiers in war are legitimate targets of attack. It is a problem for my explanation of the wrongness of terrorism because my account assumes the traditional view that there is a moral difference between attacking soldiers and attacking people who are not in the military. If most soldiers are morally innocent, however, then there is no way to make a distinction that puts most civilians in the innocent category and most soldiers in the non-innocent category. Without this distinction, the special feature of terrorism as attacks on innocent civilians disappears.

George Mavrodes makes a similar point to show that the moral innocence view cannot account for the legitimacy of attacking soldiers. Mavrodes asks us to imagine a young man of "limited mental ability and almost no education" who is drafted and sent off to fight.

He may have no understanding of what the war is about ... [and] might want nothing more than to go back to his town and the life he led before. But he is ... without doubt a combatant, and "guilty," a fit subject for intentional slaughter.[11]

Mavrodes's point is that, while the traditional ethic of war makes all soldiers permissible targets, the moral innocence criterion contradicts this view. To make matters worse, civilians who enthusiastically support a war seem less innocent than ignorant, immature soldiers who are drafted to fight. Even if the hawkish, war-supporting civilians have only a minimal degree of responsibility, it seems more morally fitting to attack them than to attack soldiers who have no desire to fight.

One possible reply is that when soldiers take up weapons, they lose their innocence by becoming a threat to others. Soldiers on both sides have a moral right to act in self-defense by killing or injuring enemy soldiers who are attacking them. In addition, by becoming a soldier and actually killing

---

[11] George Mavrodes, "Conventions and the Morality of War," in Charles Beitz *et al.*, eds., *International Ethics* (Princeton: Princeton University Press, 1985), 80–1; originally published in *Philosophy and Public Affairs* 2 (1975). Colm McKeogh discusses St. Augustine's view of the guilt and innocence of combatants in *Innocent Civilians* (New York: Palgrave, 2002), chapters 2–3.

or wounding others, a person carries out serious acts of violence against others and is causally responsible for the harms he inflicts.[12]

This answer overlooks the fact that many members of the military never harm or threaten anyone. They prepare food, carry supplies, build bases, repair trucks, and play other support roles. Because they never threaten anyone directly, no one could claim a right to kill them in self-defense. Yet the traditional principle of discrimination classifies them as legitimate targets.

While Mavrodes criticizes the moral innocence criterion to show that we need a better basis for discriminating between soldiers and civilians, Jeff McMahan takes the opposite view. He uses the moral innocence criterion to criticize the standard view that all soldiers are legitimate targets. According to McMahan, soldiers whose country is fighting a just war of defense are morally innocent because they do no wrong in fighting. For this reason, they are not legitimate targets. According to McMahan, only those soldiers who fight for an unjust cause are non-innocent, and only they may legitimately be attacked.[13]

In spite of their differences, Mavrodes and McMahan agree that the moral innocence criterion does not support the standard view that all soldiers are non-innocent and thus legitimate targets and that all civilians are innocent and thus may not be attacked. In addition, the view that there is something especially wrong about targeting civilians does not seem to be supported by the moral innocence view. For these reasons, we need to consider an alternative view of innocence, one that provides a different basis for distinguishing military from civilian victims.

THE STATUS CONCEPTION OF INNOCENCE

According to a second account of innocence, whether people are innocent in the context of war depends on their role or status rather than their actions. This status-based definition can be found in just war theory and in international law, both of which permit intentional attacks on soldiers while prohibiting them against civilians. Instead of using the language of moral innocence and guilt, the status conception contrasts the roles played by soldiers in war with the roles played by civilians.

Using the status conception of innocence, we can clarify condition 4 of my definition by saying that terrorist acts intentionally kill and injure

---

[12] Michael Walzer makes this argument in *Just and Unjust Wars*, 145.
[13] McMahan, "Innocence, Self-Defense, and Killing in War."

people who are civilians or noncombatants. (I use these terms interchangeably.) Terrorist attacks target people who are neither members of the military nor public officials who play direct roles in carrying out a war. Although soldiers may not be morally or causally responsible for whatever the attackers oppose, they occupy a role or status that connects them with military activity. By wearing a uniform and serving in the military, soldiers lose their immunity and become permissible targets. Civilians, however, retain their status and remain innocent in this sense.[14]

Since the status-based conception derives from moral and legal views that were designed to apply to wars between states, someone might object that it cannot be applied to terrorist campaigns by non-governmental groups. In fact, many wars and much political violence have been conducted by non-governmental groups. This makes it both natural and useful to extend ideas from the ethics of war to the ethics of political violence more generally, and most writers on this subject have done so.[15] It would be foolish to ignore the rich tradition of ethical thinking about war between states when we consider problems about violent conflict involving non-state groups. In fact, as we will see, the questions raised by war and by terrorism are identical.

VIRTUES OF THE STATUS-BASED CONCEPTION OF INNOCENCE

The status-based conception has two advantages over the moral innocence view. First, it is generally easier to apply. We can determine whether a person is in the military or is a civilian official engaged in military-related activities. People who are not members of either group are innocent in the relevant sense. We do not have to know their attitudes or thoughts. When attacks are directed at people who are not members of either of these groups, then (assuming that the attacks have the other features of terrorist acts) they are terrorist acts.

A second virtue of the status conception is that it can play a role in diminishing the horrors of war. Since most people are civilians, recognizing civilians as innocent people who are not legitimate targets of attack can help to reduce the human costs of war and political violence. The doctrine of noncombatant immunity – the principle that prohibits attacking people

---

[14] Walzer, *Just and Unjust Wars*, 135.
[15] Tony Coady defends this extension in *Morality and Political Violence*, 3–8.

who are not members of the military – is an important device for lessening war's damage to human life.[16]

This humanitarian defense of the status view is a moral argument since it appeals to the desirability of minimizing human suffering and loss. While this is not a morally neutral argument, this need not undermine my aim of producing a neutral definition. This is because the goal of minimizing suffering does not coincide with any specific political agenda or the interests of any particular groups. In this sense, it is politically neutral even if it is not fully morally neutral. (Neutrality is complex; it may be a matter of degree, and a view may be neutral with respect to one issue but non-neutral with respect to another.) Second, even if someone rejects the idea that it is always wrong to attack civilians, they might still use the status conception to classify actions as terrorist or not. Conventional war attacks would be against soldiers while terrorist attacks would target civilians.[17]

WHICH IS RIGHT – THE STATUS VIEW OR MORAL INNOCENCE?

Because both of these conceptions of innocence play important roles in our thinking, my view is that we should combine them rather than choosing one and rejecting the other. In many cases, these views of innocence overlap and reinforce one another. People who are civilians generally lack causal and moral responsibility for war-fighting or for policies that provoke political violence. Children, for example, readily qualify as innocent in both senses, while soldiers and government officials with military status play a larger, more direct causal role in government actions.

The two views of innocence sometimes give conflicting answers. Mavrodes's draftee seems morally innocent but is not a civilian while some civilians seem guilty by virtue of their enthusiasm for war. McMahan's just warriors have the status of soldiers, but because they fight in self-defense, they are morally innocent. In these cases, the moral innocence and status conceptions generate conflicting answers.

We can resolve these conflicts by requiring that people satisfy both criteria of innocence in order to count as innocent victims when we are classifying attacks as terrorist or not. The resulting view tells us what

---

[16] George Mavrodes defends this view in "Conventions and the Morality of War." I defend related ideas in chapters 14–15 below.

[17] For the use of the status-based distinction in international law, see Frits Kalshoven, *Constraints on the Waging of War*, 2nd edn (Geneva: International Committee of the Red Cross, 1991), 88–91.

innocence is in the context of war and political violence. To be classified as innocent in this context, people must satisfy *both* the moral innocence criterion and the status criterion of innocence.

Mavrodes's unwilling draftee and McMahan's just warriors are not innocent because they satisfy only the moral innocence criterion but fail to meet the status criterion. Civilians directly involved in war efforts or the implementation of allegedly evil policies satisfy the status criterion but not the moral innocence criterion. Civilians who support a war but play no direct role in it are innocent because they satisfy both criteria. They satisfy the status criterion because they are civilians and the moral innocence criterion because their degree of causal responsibility is too small to make them morally responsible for the war.

AN OBJECTION: SOME TERRORIST ACTS TARGET NON-INNOCENT PEOPLE

Seumas Miller challenges the view that we should define terrorism as attacks on innocent people in his book *Terrorism and Counter-Terrorism*. Miller uses several counter-examples to show that terrorist attacks can be directed against non-innocent people. His examples are especially relevant because they attack the role of innocence, whether it is understood as moral innocence or in terms of a status conception. According to Miller, the examples that he describes are plausibly labeled as terrorism even though they target people who are not innocent. I will try to show why the examples he gives are not examples of terrorist attacks.

Miller's first example is based on the 1984 disaster in Bhopal, India. This disaster at a Union Carbide plant caused more than 10,000 deaths and left hundreds of thousands of people with injuries and serious health problems. Miller's example involves a group that attacks Union Carbide officials who were responsible for the 1984 disaster in Bhopal, India. Miller writes:

> By the lights of the definition of terrorism in terms of innocents, a political group that killed members of the Union Carbide management ... [or] members of the US or Indian government in order to cause their respective governments to redress the injustice of inadequate compensation, would not be a terrorist group; for these victims are not innocent.[18]

---

[18] Seumas Miller, *Terrorism and Counter-Terrorism: Ethics and Liberal Democracy* (Oxford: Blackwell Publishing, 2009), 37.

Miller, however, thinks it is obvious that this would be a terrorist attack, even though the victims are not innocent. He concludes that there can be terrorist attacks against non-innocent people.

Miller's example certainly has some features of a terrorist act: it is violent, has a political goal, and attacks some people to influence others. But is it a terrorist act? Recall that Walzer defined terrorism as "random murder" in order to draw attention to the fact that terrorism is indiscriminate with respect to individuals. Yet, the attack that Miller describes is not indiscriminate. It is targeted at people who are directly responsible for serious evils.

If we focus on the Union Carbide management and assume that the people targeted were directly responsible either for actions that caused huge numbers of deaths and serious injuries or for the failure to provide adequate compensation to the victims, then an attack against them is best seen as a case of vigilante justice. While vigilante justice has its liabilities, it is very different from terrorism. Terrorist attacks strike people irrespective of their individual culpability while vigilante justice seeks to punish individuals for their misdeeds. For this reason, Miller is wrong to call this a case of terrorism.[19]

One reason that Miller's case seems plausible is that he adds other features that differentiate it from vigilante justice. He tells us that the attacks are also against US and Indian government officials, but he does not specify the role these officials played and whether they are responsible either for the disaster or for the failure to compensate victims. If they are responsible, then they too are victims of vigilante justice. If, however, their work was unconnected to Union Carbide and they had no power to order compensation, then they would be innocent victims, and attacks against them would be terrorism, especially because the goal was to influence the actions of Union Carbide and the two governments. When we stress these elements, the terrorist label is appropriate, but, contrary to Miller's view, the victims are innocent.

A similar problem weakens Miller's second example. Drawing on the early years of ANC resistance to South African apartheid, Miller imagines a group that uses non-violent methods in an attempt to overthrow an oppressive government regime. The government responds with

a campaign of killings ("disappearances") and torture of opposition elements in order to instill fear in the opposition forces as a whole, and thus put an end to the "insurrection". Surely, this is state terrorism ...[20]

---

[19] Jeff McMahan uses a similar example to argue that terrorist attacks against civilians can be morally permissible in "The Ethics of Killing in War," *Ethics* 114 (2004), 725–9. I believe that McMahan, like Miller, fails to distinguish terrorism from vigilante justice.

[20] Miller, *Terrorism and Counter-Terrorism*, 38.

Miller is correct that the victims are not innocent in the sense that they are causally responsible for the actions that provoke the government's harsh response. Because the leaders of the insurrection used non-violent means, we may find the government's actions to be despicable, but that is not the issue. The question is whether we should classify the government's response as terrorism.

This example faces the same problems as Miller's first case. If the government focuses only on leaders who are responsible for the insurrection, then the attacks lack the random, indiscriminate aspect of terrorist violence and are not terrorism. Miller also talks about the government killing and torturing "opposition elements," and this suggests that the government may have widened the net and killed people who played at best a minimal role in the movement. (Perhaps they attended rallies or meetings.) If that is the case, their causal responsibility was too slight to render them non-innocent, and attacks on them would be terrorism.

The example, then, is ambiguous. If the government targeted non-innocent leaders, this is not a case of terrorism. If it indiscriminately attacked large numbers of minimally involved people in order to create widespread fear, then it is terrorism. Either way, the example does not damage the claim that terrorist attacks are always directed against innocent people.

Miller tries to show that his argument works equally well when the definition uses a status-based conception of innocence and sees terrorism as attacks on non-combatants. He tries to show that there can be terrorist attacks against combatants by describing a case in which "[w]idespread torture of armed insurgents" is used to "to instill fear in a target population ..." This, he says, "is an instance of terrorism, and yet the victims of the torture are combatants." Therefore, "it is possible to use some of the methods of terrorism against combatants."[21]

In this case the tortured insurgents are neither morally innocent nor civilians (in the sense of non-fighters). Miller says that torturing them for the purpose of instilling fear is terrorism. Since the victims are not innocent, however, it is not clear why he says that. Perhaps he is misled by the wording of his conclusion, which says that it is possible to use "some of the methods of terrorism" against victims who are combatants. If the method referred to is using violence against some people to influence others, then, as we have seen, this is also a characteristic of non-terrorist forms of war. No doubt traditional armies sometimes carry out attacks in particularly fearsome ways so as to terrorize the enemy army. As long as they target armed forces and

---

[21] Ibid., 42.

not innocent civilians, however, their actions do not qualify as terrorism. My conclusion, then, is that Miller's counter-examples fail to undermine the view that attacking innocent people is a defining feature of terrorism.

MUST TERRORIST HARMS TO CIVILIANS BE INTENTIONAL?

The final criticism that I will consider here accepts the view that terrorism's victims are innocent. In fact, it takes the innocence of victims so seriously that it aims to broaden the definition of terrorism to include many acts that kill or injure civilians unintentionally. It rejects the view that terrorist acts must *intentionally* kill or injure innocent people.

Supporting this broader view, David Rodin writes that "Some harms inflicted unintentionally on noncombatants – so called collateral damage – may indeed be properly categorized as terrorist." He defines "terrorism" in part as "the deliberate, negligent, or reckless use of force against noncombatants ..."[22] For Rodin, intentional harm to civilians is but one form of terrorism. Harms inflicted negligently or recklessly are also terrorism, even though they are not intended.

Tony Dardis attacks the "intentional attack" requirement by describing the case of an insurgent who plants a bomb in a police officer's car, knowing that it could kill or injure the officer's wife and children.[23] While the attacker intends to kill the police officer, he does not care that others may be killed. Dardis sees this as a terrorist act, even though the officer's wife and children are not intentionally targeted. The attack is indiscriminate and shows an indifference to the lives of innocent people.

Should we classify this as a terrorist act? To answer this, we need first to consider whether it would be a terrorist act if only the police officer is killed. Police officers are civilians, but if they are used to put down groups that violently oppose the government, they play a quasi-military role. Even if some officers play this role, others may be involved in directing traffic or other activities unrelated to this quasi-military role. In such cases, the officer should be seen as a civilian, and directly attacking him would be a terrorist act. Dardis appears to treat the officer as someone with a quasi-military role. If that is so, attacking him would not be terrorism.

Suppose that the bomb does kill members of the officer's family. Dardis favors classifying this unintended killing as a terrorist act because it is

---

[22] David Rodin, "Terrorism Without Intention," *Ethics* 114 (2004), 752, 755.
[23] Tony Dardis, "Primoratz on Terrorism," *Journal of Applied Philosophy* 9 (1992), 97.

indiscriminate and reveals indifference to the possibility of innocent victims. Using Rodin's definition, we can say that Dardis's car bomber acts recklessly; he knows that the bomb may kill or injure innocent people and plants it nonetheless. This argument has some persuasive force. If attackers show callous disregard for the lives of civilians, isn't this enough to make them terrorists?

WHY THIS ISSUE IS IMPORTANT

This might seem like a trivial issue, but our response to it has important implications for how we think about many acts of war. If we see the car bombing as a terrorist act, then we might view the use of cluster bombs and land mines as forms of terrorism. These weapons are indiscriminate. People who use them cannot control who the victims will be.[24] Land mines are often placed in locations that are used by both soldiers and civilians, and the longer they remain undetonated, the less it can be predicted who the victim will be. Similar problems arise with cluster bombs, which spread large numbers of bomblets over an area. Because these bomblets often fail to explode immediately, they too are indiscriminate weapons. If we accept Dardis's view, that strongly suggests that we should see these military tactics as terrorist acts (assuming that their use has the other features included in the definition).

In some cases, unintentional killings of civilians are not reckless or negligent. Suppose that Dardis's car bomber makes a serious effort to avoid killing innocent people. He discovers the officer's regular routines and carefully places the bomb in the car when the officer regularly uses it. If these factors show the bombing to be neither reckless nor negligent, then the Dardis/Rodin view would not pronounce it a terrorist act.

SHOULD WE DELETE "INTENTIONAL" FROM THE DEFINITION OF TERRORISM?

Should we broaden the definition to include some acts that are not intended to harm civilians as terrorism? There are several possible responses to this proposal. Most obviously, we can accept or reject it, deciding either to maintain the original definition or to revise it by including some unintended killings of civilians.

---

[24] On the use of these weapons, see Human Rights Watch, "Cluster Bombs in Afghanistan," http://www.hrw.org/backgrounder/arms/cluster-bck1031.htm.

These are not the only possible options, however. A third response would be to classify the cases that Rodin and Dardis emphasize as borderline cases. We could decide that while intentional attacks on civilians are paradigm cases of terrorism, unintended killings share some features of terrorism but lack others. If they are borderline cases, then there is no definitive answer as to whether or not they are terrorist acts. Accepting this view would not mean that the word "terrorism" is completely unclear. We could still classify intentional killings of civilians as clear cases of terrorist acts even if we are unsure about how to classify unintended killings of civilians.

Finally, we could decide that this debate involves a merely verbal issue that is ultimately unimportant. Even if we are unsure how to classify the car bomber's act, we may still be certain that it is an immoral act. We can often know that an act is right or wrong even if we don't know how to classify it. We know, for example, that massacring a large fraction of a group is immoral even if we are unsure whether these killings constitute genocide.

While I find some merit in all these options, I am going to reject the Rodin/Dardis proposal and retain the view that terrorist acts *intentionally* harm civilians. There are several reasons for doing this. Intentional attacks on civilians are the clearest, least controversial instances of terrorism. For this reason, retaining the requirement of intentional targeting keeps the definition closer to ordinary usage and avoids needless controversy.

Second, retaining the word "intentional" preserves a parallel between the definition and the language of just war theory. The just war theory "principle of discrimination" prohibits intentional attacks on civilians but recognizes that some collateral damage killings may be morally legitimate. I will later argue that just war theory exaggerates the moral significance of the distinction between intended and unintended harms. Nonetheless, for classification purposes, it is worth retaining this distinction.

Retaining the requirement of intentional targeting also fits well with the idea that terrorism has a communicative function. Terrorist acts kill and injure innocent people in order to send a message to an audience that terrorists want to influence. Collateral damage killings lack this feature. They are not intended and thus are not a means of communicating with others.

Finally, the main motivation for classifying unintended killings as terrorism is a desire to condemn these acts as strongly as terrorist acts are condemned. People think that if we classify collateral damage killings as terrorism, they will be strongly condemned, while if we don't call them "terrorism," people will complacently accept them as legitimate. I am sympathetic with this motivation, but we can (and should) strongly condemn collateral damage deaths and injuries that reveal callous indifference to human life even if we do not call them "terrorism." Once we separate classification from moral evaluation, we can see that deciding not to classify an act as terrorism leaves us free to condemn it as strongly as it merits. Once that is clear, the motivation to change the definition should diminish.

CONCLUSION

In this chapter, I have replied to three criticisms of the definition of terrorism. I have clarified the idea of innocence, shown that we should not include attacks on non-innocents as terrorism, and explained why we should not expand the concept of terrorism to include unintended harms to civilians.

CHAPTER 5

"Who dun it" definitions of terrorism

If I have succeeded so far, readers should now accept the definition I have defended. Before fully accepting it, however, readers should understand that the definition differs from the definitions given by many experts on terrorism and clashes with widespread beliefs about terrorism. In this chapter, I will show why the definition should be accepted in spite of these clashes and departures.

AGENT-FOCUSED DEFINITIONS

I claim that terrorist acts have four features. They:
1. are acts of serious, deliberate violence or credible threats of such acts;
2. are committed in order to promote a political or social agenda;
3. generally target limited numbers of people but aim to influence a larger group and/or the leaders who make decisions for the group;
4. intentionally kill or injure innocent people or pose a threat of serious harm to them.

Someone could accept all the features on the list as defining characteristics of terrorism but reject the definition because it fails to include a crucial feature of terrorist acts. According to both ordinary usage and the language of scholars, the word "terrorism" only applies to actions done by certain types of people or groups. This "agent-focused" conception of terrorism takes different forms. The crudest, most blatantly biased form defines "terrorism" as violence by groups who are "our" enemies. A less crude but still biased form limits terrorist acts to violence carried out by non-governmental groups. This view implies that the word "terrorism" cannot be applied to violence carried out by governments. Because these agent-focused views pervade ordinary speech, media reports, and scholarly works, most of us think of various "non-state actors" when we think about terrorists. We do not tend to think of government officials. If terrorism is defined as a means or tactic, however, it is hard to see why actions by governments cannot be terrorism. Yet, this is a common view.

THE LANGUAGE OF TERRORISM EXPERTS

The agent-focused view can be found in Louise Richardson's *What Terrorists Want*. Richardson begins by characterizing terrorism very much as I do. "Terrorism," she says, "simply means deliberately and violently targeting civilians for political purposes."[1] She also notes the communicative aspect of terrorism and strongly affirms that the "most important defining characteristic of terrorism is the deliberate targeting of civilians."[2] Richardson does not stop there, however. She adds to her definition the idea that "terrorism is the act of sub-state groups, not states."[3]

While Richardson says that including this reference to non-state groups is necessary for "analytical clarity," she does not explain how it does this. In fact, it immediately leads her into confusions and contradictions. Having limited "terrorism" to acts by "sub-state groups, not states," she then makes the confusing disclaimer that "This is not to argue that states do not use terrorism as an instrument of foreign policy."[4] This statement, however, contradicts Richardson's definition. If "terrorism" applies only to actions by non-state groups, then it cannot be that states "use terrorism as an instrument of foreign policy." But if states do "use terrorism as an instrument of foreign policy," then Richardson must be mistaken in saying that "terrorism is the act of sub-state groups, not states."

Robert Pape briefly discusses definitional issues in *Dying to Win*, his study of "suicide terrorism." Terrorism, he says, "signifies, principally, violent acts against innocents that are committed by non-governmental actors …"[5] Pape acknowledges that some people reject the idea that terrorist acts must be "committed by non-governmental actors." Governments, he says,

have sometimes been accused of terrorism, either against their own people, to suppress dissent (Soviet show trials in the 1930s), or against enemy states, to compel their surrender in war (British fire-bombing of German cities in World War II).[6]

Pape disagrees and rejects the proposed expansion of the definition to include violent acts against civilians that are committed by governments, saying that it

[1] Louise Richardson, *What Terrorists Want*, 4.   [2] Ibid., 6.   [3] Ibid., 5.   [4] Ibid., 5.
[5] Robert Pape, *Dying to Win* (New York: Random House, 2005), 297 n1.   [6] Ibid.

would distract attention from what policy makers would most like to know: how to combat the threat posed by non-state actors to the national security of the United States and our allies.[7]

Pape's argument against allowing for the possibility of governmental terrorism is that this would not fit the interests of governmental policy-makers.

This argument explicitly adopts a biased, partisan perspective on terrorism and supports tailoring the definition of "terrorism" to serve the interests of government. It should be rejected because it exhibits exactly the kind of biased usage that gives rise to the slogan "one man's terrorist is another man's freedom fighter" and that ensnares the definition effort in political conflict.

Not all scholars accept biased, agent-focused definitions. Alex Schmid and Albert Jongman strongly criticize researchers for failing to study governmental terrorism. They write: "Given the ubiquity of rule by terror, the uneven attention given by social scientists to regime terrorism in contrast to insurgent terrorism is depressing."[8] Writing prior to the September 11 attacks, Schmid and Jongman criticize scholars for focusing on "non-state, mainly left-wing and minority group opponents," and deplore the "conspicuous absence of literature that addresses ... the much more serious problem of state terrorism."[9] Since the September 11 attacks, terrorism studies have shifted from left-wing radicals to Islamic groups, but the overall focus remains on non-state, insurgent groups.

TERRORISM BY GOVERNMENTS

The definition I defend contains no reference to the nature of the agents who carry out terrorist acts. This omission is intended to avoid any bias in favor of or against particular types of groups. Once we omit biased references to particular types of agents from our conception of terrorism, our picture of terrorism changes. If terrorist acts deliberately target innocent people for political purposes, then any acts of this sort are terrorist acts, no matter who commits them.

How might governments engage in terrorism? One form of state terrorism attacks innocent people in order to maintain political power through fear and intimidation. While some people are attacked for being opponents of the government, other people are indiscriminately injured and killed in

[7] Ibid., 298 n2.　[8] Schmid and Jongman, *Political Terrorism*, 72.
[9] Schmid and Jongman, *Political Terrorism*, 179.

order to send the message that the regime can target anyone it wants to. By creating fear, they discourage even the mildest criticism of the regime.[10]

Governmental terrorism also occurs in the course of wars. In addition to attacking military targets, government forces often attack civilians when they believe that this will be strategically valuable. By launching attacks against civilians, they think that they can hasten their own victory or prevent defeat.

In both cases, terrorist attacks on innocent people are a tactic for achieving political goals. The fact that the victims are sometimes citizens of the government's own country and sometimes citizens of other countries is irrelevant to whether the attacks are terrorism or not. Similarly, the fact that the attacks are carried out by governments rather than insurgents is also irrelevant.[11]

A DEFENSE OF AGENT-FOCUSED DEFINITIONS

Like many terrorism experts, Bruce Hoffman focuses almost entirely on violence by non-governmental groups in his book *Inside Terrorism*.[12] He pays virtually no attention to political violence by governments. To his credit, however, Hoffman devotes a whole chapter to the definition debate and vigorously defends the view that only acts carried out by non-governmental groups should be classified as terrorism.

Hoffman's description of the nature of terrorism contains both a list of features and a definition. Terrorist acts, he says, are

- designed to have far-reaching psychological repercussions beyond the immediate victim or target;
- conducted by an organization with an identifiable chain of command or conspiratorial cell structure (whose members wear no uniform or identifying insignia); and
- perpetrated by a subnational group or non-state entity.
- We may therefore … define terrorism as the deliberate creation and exploitation of fear through violence or the threat of violence in the pursuit of political change.[13]

---

[10] Samuel Scheffler discusses this function of state terrorism in "Is Terrorism Morally Distinctive?," *Journal of Political Philosophy* 14 (2006), 1–17.

[11] For discussions of state terrorism, see Jonathan Glover, "State Terrorism," in R. G. Frey and C. W. Morris, eds., *Violence, Terrorism, and Justice* (Cambridge: Cambridge University Press, 1991), 256–75; Igor Primoratz, "State Terrorism," in Primoratz, ed., *Terrorism*, 113–27; Edward Herman, *The Real Terror Network: Terrorism in Fact and Propaganda* (Boston: South End Press, 1982); and Alexander Downes, *Targeting Civilians in War* (Ithaca, N.Y.: Cornell University Press, 2008).

[12] Hoffman, *Inside Terrorism*.   [13] Ibid., 43.

Although Hoffman's definition does not match the list of features that precedes it, we can see what he has in mind by combining the list and the definition. This gives us the view that terrorist acts:

1. are violent;
2. are motivated by political goals;
3. aim to create fear and other psychological effects beyond the immediate victims;
4. are carried out by non-state groups that do not wear uniforms or identifying insignia.

While the first three features of Hoffman's definition overlap with my definition, his definition differs from mine in two ways. First, his definition does not specify that terrorist attacks target innocent people. Second, like the definitions of Richardson and Pape, Hoffman's definition requires that terrorist acts must be carried out by *non-governmental groups*.

DOES THE DEFINITION CLARIFY THE WRONGNESS OF TERRORISM?

While Hoffman himself does not directly examine moral issues, one might expect a good definition of terrorism to help us understand moral condemnations of terrorism. Victim-focused definitions highlight the fact that terrorist acts intentionally kill and injure innocent people, and this helps to explain why terrorism is often seen as especially wrong. Hoffman, however, rejects the inclusion of any reference to innocent victims in his account. The question, then, is whether his definition sheds any light on the basis for condemning terrorism.

According to Hoffman, terrorist acts are a) violent, b) "ineluctably political in aims and motives," and c) "designed to have far-reaching psychological repercussions beyond the immediate victim or target." I have shown earlier why none of these features explains the wrongness of terrorism. All of these features are characteristics of actions that most people believe can be morally right. Anyone who thinks that war can sometimes be morally justified must believe that acts of violence that are politically motivated and aim to have a psychological impact (such as inducing surrender) are sometimes morally justified.

The fourth feature in Hoffman's definition is that terrorism is "carried out by non-state groups that do not wear uniforms or identifying insignia." Does this provide a basis for condemning terrorism? Could actions that are right if carried out by government officials be wrong when carried out by non-state groups who do not wear uniforms or insignia?

This feature, unlike the others Hoffman cites, might be morally relevant because the rightness or wrongness of an action sometimes depends on *who* carries it out. For example, while it is morally permissible for me to sign a check in my checkbook, someone else who signs my name on the check is committing the double wrong of forging my signature and stealing money from my account. Although the two acts of signing a name are physically similar, we classify and evaluate them differently because I have the authority to draw funds from my account by writing a check, and the forger does not.

Similarly, government officials often have legal and moral authority to do things that ordinary citizens have no right to do. Prison wardens or guards, for example, can lock someone in a cell, but ordinary citizens may not. It is not absurd, then, to believe that who carries out an action is morally relevant. Hoffman might claim that people condemn terrorism with special vehemence because the perpetrators of terrorist acts lack the authority to perform these actions.[14]

The problem with this view is that, while official status affects the moral status of actions in some cases, there are many cases in which it does not. The legitimate authority of government officials is limited. While police officers have the authority to carry guns in public places, they have no right to shoot people simply because they dislike them. Tax officials have no right to collect money from citizens for their own personal use. Similarly, although government officials have the authority to use violence to win a war or maintain public order, it does not follow that they have the right to achieve these goals by killing or injuring innocent people.

In most cases, our moral vocabulary applies equally to acts by government officials and private individuals. A lie by a government official is still a lie, a theft is a theft, and a murder a murder. If we can classify the intentional killing of innocent people by government officials as murder, it is hard to see why we cannot call such actions terrorism when they are politically motivated and aim to influence other people.

HOFFMAN'S DEFENSE

Hoffman insists that it matters greatly whether acts of violence are carried out by governments or non-state groups. He explicitly criticizes definitions

---

[14] Janna Thompson uses this argument in "Terrorism and the Right to Wage War," in Coady and O'Keefe, eds., *Terrorism and Justice*, 87–96. For criticisms, see Steinhoff, *On the Ethics of War and Terrorism*, chapter 1. Lionel McPherson considers the view that lack of legitimate authority makes terrorist acts distinctively wrong but ultimately argues that non-state groups can have a form of legitimate authority in "Is Terrorism Distinctively Wrong?," 524–46.

that focus on victims for failing "to differentiate clearly between violence perpetrated by states and by non-state entities, such as terrorists." A victim-focused definition (like mine), he argues,

plays into the hands of terrorists and their apologists who would argue that *there is no difference between* the "low-tech" terrorist pipe-bomb placed in a rubbish bin at a crowded market that wantonly and indiscriminately kills or maims everyone within a radius measured in tens of feet and the "high-tech" precision-guided ordinance dropped by air force fighter-bombers ... that achieves the same wanton and indiscriminate effects on the crowded marketplace far below. This rationale thus *equates the random violence inflicted on enemy population centres by military forces* – such as the Luftwaffe's raids on Warsaw and Coventry, the Allied fire-bombings of Dresden and Tokyo, and the atomic bombs dropped by the United States on Hiroshima and Nagasaki during the Second World War, and indeed the countervalue strategy of the post-war superpowers' strategic nuclear policy, which deliberately targeted the enemy's civilian population – *with the violence committed by substate entities labeled "terrorists"*, since *both involve the infliction of death and injury on non-combatants.*[15] (Italics added.)

This passage contains four objections to definitions of terrorism that do not distinguish governmental actions from attacks by non-state groups. The objections are that such definitions:

1. "play into the hands of terrorists and their apologists";
2. mistakenly equate a) attacks by non-governmental groups that use low-tech weapons to kill innocent people with b) attacks by governmental air forces that kill innocent people using high-altitude bombings;
3. misclassify the city bombings by both German and Allied forces in World War II as terrorist acts;
4. misclassify the strategy of nuclear deterrence (which targeted enemy civilian populations in order to deter a nuclear attack) as terrorism.

The last three points have the same logic. Each charges that definitions that focus on victims rather than agents misclassify actions. The first argument makes a different charge. None of them, however, provides an effective defense of Hoffman's view.

THE "PLAYING INTO THE HANDS" ARGUMENT

Hoffman's charge that victim-based definitions play into the hands of terrorists is false if "playing into the hands" of terrorists means approving of their acts. Even if a definition implies that both the low-tech, market

---

[15] Hoffman, *Inside Terrorism*, 33.

bombing and the hi-tech, air force bombing are terrorist acts, this does not imply the approval of either act. If all terrorist acts are wrong and both acts are terrorism, then both attacks are wrong.

Non-state groups often reject victim-based definitions for the same reason that governments do. They want to avoid the moral condemnation that usually goes with the "terrorist" label. Accepting the victim-based definition does not play into their hands because it does not shield them from moral condemnation. Moreover, even if we "equate" the low-tech and hi-tech bombings by classifying both as terrorist acts, we need not equate them morally. There may be special reasons that morally justify one but not the other.

Hoffman's overtly political, "playing into hands" argument seems crudely partisan and out of place in a serious investigation of terrorism. Such an investigation should be politically neutral. It should consider what is the best way to define terrorism and let the chips fall where they may. If our own country or its allies have attacked civilians to advance political goals and if this is the essence of terrorism, it follows that they have committed terrorist acts. This conclusion may be distasteful, but it does not show that the definition is defective.[16]

THE PROBLEM OF BIASED DEFINITIONS

The strongest argument against agent-focused definitions is that they inevitably generate biased labeling and biased evaluations. Connor Cruise O'Brien makes this point very effectively, writing that:

Those who are described as terrorists, and who reject the title for themselves, make the uncomfortable point that national armed forces, fully supported by democratic opinion, have in fact employed violence and terror on a far vaster scale than what liberation movements have as yet been able to attain. The "freedom fighters" see themselves as fighting a just war. Why should they not be entitled to kill, burn and destroy as national armies, navies and air forces do, and why should the label "terrorist" be applied to them and not the national militaries?[17]

In this mirror image of Hoffman's argument, O'Brien describes the frustration of those who think that governments are allowed to "kill, burn and destroy" while insurgent groups are called terrorists and condemned for the very same actions. If governments engage in such violence and escape the

---

[16] On the need for neutral definitions in terrorism research, see Schmid and Jongman, *Political Terrorism*, 1–4, 25–8.
[17] Connor Cruise O'Brien, quoted in Kegley, *International Terrorism*, 12–13.

terrorist label, why, they ask, can't non-governmental groups do the same? This is a powerful challenge to the idea that the term "terrorism" should apply only to violent acts by some groups but not to similar acts by others.

While agent-focused definitions inevitably lead to biased views, victim-focused definitions escape the charge of inconsistent labeling. They do this by labeling any political violence that targets innocent people as terrorism, no matter who carries it out. Focusing on victims leads to truth in labeling while focusing on agents leads to hypocritical inconsistency. This is one of the strongest arguments for victim-focused definitions.

THE MISCLASSIFICATION ARGUMENT

Hoffman argues that victim-focused definitions misclassify acts of violence. He finds it obvious that the insurgent's pipe-bombing in the market is terrorism while the bombing of the same market by governmental air forces is not. Likewise, he finds it obvious that the bombings of cities by governments in World War II were not terrorist acts, even though they intentionally killed innocent people in order to send a message to an enemy and promote a political agenda (victory). Similarly, he finds it obvious that the nuclear deterrence strategy of targeting civilian populations is not terrorism even though it threatens to kill millions of civilians.

Hoffman does not argue for these claims. He simply assumes that readers will agree with him. Even without argument, however, Hoffman's view has a certain plausibility because it reflects common usage. While the word "terrorism" is frequently applied to attacks by non-governmental groups, it is seldom applied to violence by government forces. This fact about usage is not strong evidence for Hoffman's view because the word "terrorism" is generally used in a biased, inflammatory, and propagandistic manner. If we seek analytic clarity, we must either stop using the word "terrorism" or devise a definition that strips it of its biased, inflammatory, propagandistic connotations.

Viewed in an impartial way, is there any reason to classify the acts on the following list differently?
1. the low-tech, pipe-bombing in a market by an insurgent group;
2. the air force bombing of a market by governmental forces;
3. the bombing of cities in World War II by German and Allied air forces;
4. the threats by nuclear powers to destroy an enemy's civilian population in response to a nuclear attack.

To answer this question, we need to look at these actions more carefully.

According to Hoffman, of all the items listed, only the pipe-bombing is a terrorist act. In fact, he fails to describe either of the market bombings fully enough for us to know if they are terrorism. He never says, for example, whether the pipe-bombing is intended to kill civilians. If killing civilians is the goal of the attack, then the definition I support would classify it as terrorism (assuming that the goals are political, etc.). If the attack is aimed at soldiers or military equipment in the market, then the civilian deaths would be collateral damage, and the act would not be terrorism.

Similar points apply to the attack on the market "by air force fighter-bombers." If the civilian deaths are intended, have a political goal, and are meant to send a message to others, then the definition implies that the air force bombing is a terrorist act. If the deaths are unintended side effects of an attack on armed fighters near the market, then the attack is not terrorism. It is hard to see why we should classify or evaluate these acts (both of which Hoffman calls "wanton and indiscriminate") differently simply because they are carried out by different types of agents. Although we don't know enough to classify either example, if they are similar in relevant ways, we ought to label them in the same way.

What about the World War II bombings? In one way, these are easier to deal with because we know the actual facts about them. Writing about the British bombings of German cities, the historian Stephen Garrett tells us that

By the end of 1944, around 80 percent of all German urban centers with populations of 100,000 had been devastated or seriously damaged ... It is estimated that overall some 500,000 German civilians lost their lives as a result of the area offensive, and perhaps another 1,000,000 received serious injury.[18]

This gives us a picture of the results of these bombings. In addition, we know why these attacks were launched. As Garrett notes:

The ... shattering of the German people's morale, and thus of Germany's will or ability to continue the war, was ... one of the guiding premises of British bombing policy.[19]

Based on these facts, we can see that these bombings have the same features identified in the definition of terrorism. They were serious acts of violence. They were part of a political campaign to achieve victory in war. Many of the bombings were intended to kill civilians in order to break the will of the German people and force their leaders to surrender. (Some were intended to

---

[18] Stephen Garrett, "Terror Bombing of German Cities in World War II," in Primoratz, ed., *Terrorism*, 142.
[19] Ibid., 144.

destroy objects of military value.) These attacks had the same communicative function characteristic of terrorism, killing and injuring some people in order to create a psychological effect on other people.

It is odd that Hoffman does not see these attacks as terrorism since he describes them as "random violence inflicted on enemy population centres by military forces."[20] But he is not alone in his reluctance to label the Allied bombings of cities as terrorism. Most people see the Allied bombings as a response to a terrible enemy and believe that the people who ordered and carried out these attacks acted with the best motives. They find it hard to think of these people as terrorists and would resist applying the "terrorist" label to them.

Nonetheless, as we saw in discussing terrorists and freedom fighters, the value of the goal for which people are fighting is not relevant to the classification of their actions. Terrorism is a tactic. It can be employed either for lofty goals or for vile ends. Though defeating Nazism was a lofty goal, the bombings were a tactic, and they have the features that justify us in classifying them as terrorism.[21]

Hoffman's last example, the case of nuclear deterrence threats, differs from the others because these threats of retaliation were (fortunately) never carried out. Recall, however, that the first condition in my definition is that terrorist acts are "acts of serious, deliberate violence or credible threats of such acts." Many people, in fact, called the threat of mutual assured destruction a "balance of terror." While the fact that these threats were never carried out might be a reason not to call them terrorism, the fact that the threats were made by governments is not.[22]

A FINAL ARGUMENT FOR THE STATE/NON-STATE DISTINCTION

Hoffman's final argument for restricting the word "terrorism" to violence by non-state groups concedes that governments have caused "far more death and destruction" than non-state groups. Nonetheless, he claims that

---

[20] Hoffman, *Inside Terrorism*, 33.

[21] For accounts of the Allied bombing campaigns, see Stephen Garrett, *Ethics and Airpower in World War II: The British Bombing of German Cities* (New York: St. Martin's Press, 1993); Ronald Schaffer, *Wings of Judgment: American Bombing in World War II* (New York: Oxford University Press, 1985).

[22] Steven Lee discusses parallels between nuclear deterrence and terrorism in *Morality, Prudence, and Nuclear Weapons* (Cambridge: Cambridge University Press, 1993), 49–53, 69. Louise Richardson discusses threats of nuclear, biological, and chemical terrorism in *What Terrorists Want*, 159–68.

there is "a fundamental qualitative difference" between the violence carried out by these two types of groups.

> Even in war governments recognize rules and accepted norms of behaviour that prohibit the use of certain types of weapons ... proscribe various tactics and outlaw attacks on specific categories of targets. Accordingly, in theory, if not always in practice, the rules of war ... grant civilian non-combatants immunity from attack .... By comparison, one of the fundamental *raisons d'être* of international terrorism is a refusal to be bound by such rules of warfare and codes of conduct.[23]

The contrast Hoffman makes would be decisive if governments never violated the rules of war by intentionally attacking civilians. But, he acknowledges, "the armed forces of established states have also been guilty of violating some of the same rules of war."[24] What then is the qualitative difference between violence by governments and by the groups that Hoffman calls terrorists? There are two, he says. First, governments publicly acknowledge the rules of war, and second, governments prosecute their own forces for war crimes when they "deliberately and wantonly" violate these rules. Terrorist groups do neither.[25]

While Hoffman is correct that many governments publicly express respect for laws of war, the significance of this is seriously weakened by the frequency and number of civilian deaths caused by government forces. When this repeatedly occurs, public affirmations of the rules of war begin to look like lip service and hypocrisy.[26]

Hoffman's claim about governments prosecuting their own military personnel for war crimes is an attempt to fend off the charge of hypocrisy. His argument would have some force if governments did regularly prosecute members of their own forces for violating the rules of war. Such prosecutions, however, are extremely rare. Many attacks on civilians are not labeled as war crimes at all. At the end of World War II, only German and Japanese military leaders were prosecuted for killing civilians. During the Vietnam War, only extreme atrocities like those at My Lai were prosecuted while many actions and policies that routinely took civilian lives were accepted as necessary in war. In the United States' War in Iraq,

---

[23] Hoffman, *Inside Terrorism*, 34–5.   [24] On this, see Alexander Downes, *Targeting Civilians in War*.
[25] Hoffman, *Inside Terrorism*, 35–6.
[26] For discussion of this phenomenon, see Sahr Conway-Lanz, *Collateral Damage: Americans, Noncombatant Immunity, and Atrocity after World War II* (New York: Routledge, 2006). George Lopez discusses US compliance with the laws of war in the 1991 Gulf War in "The Gulf War: Not So Clean," *Bulletin of Atomic Scientists* 47:6 (1991). Colin H. Kahl reviews the War in Iraq in "How We Fight," *Foreign Affairs* 85:6 (November–December 2006) and "In the Crossfire or the Crosshairs? Norms, Civilian Casualties, and U.S. Conduct in Iraq," *International Security* 32 (Summer 2007), 7–46.

there have been some prosecutions of soldiers for murdering Iraqi civilians and torturing detainees, but the number of prosecutions is small, and many have resulted in acquittals or light punishments. And, those who have been prosecuted tend to be lower-level soldiers rather than the upper-level officers and civilian officials who countenanced and encouraged these actions.

The bottom line is that both insurgents and governments sometimes target civilians and violate laws of war. While some governments sometimes prosecute their own forces for war crimes, this is the exception not the rule. As David Kretzmer notes, "Experience shows that states are not exactly over-zealous in prosecuting members of their own forces suspected of violations" of civilian immunity.[27]

The only real difference cited by Hoffman is that many governments publicly acknowledge rules that forbid attacking civilians while many insurgent groups do not. The weakness of this claim is evident, however. Suppose that terrorist groups publicly embraced the rules of war but continued to violate them and seldom if ever punished their members for violations. If a group did this, no one would take seriously their commitment to the rules of humane warfare. The same view should be taken of established states.

Only late in his book does Hoffman display this kind of even-handedness. In a section on "state-sponsored" terrorism, he writes:

Certainly, governments have long engaged in various types of illicit, clandestine activities – including the systematic use of terror – against their enemies, both domestic and foreign.[28]

This passage is correct, but it is clearly inconsistent with the view that he fervently defends earlier in his book.

Hoffman's late comment on terrorism by governments suggests a final problem with the agent-based view. In noting that governmental terrorist acts are often "clandestine," Hoffman reminds us that we are sometimes unsure who has committed a particular act of violence. It follows from his main view that if we were to discover that the September 11 attacks had been carried out by agents of an established government, then, according to the definition supported by Hoffman, Pape, and Richardson, we would have to conclude that these attacks were not terrorism after all. It is hard to imagine that we would do this.

---

[27] David Kretzmer, "Civilian Immunity in War: Legal Aspects," in Igor Primoratz, ed., *Civilian Immunity in War* (Oxford: Oxford University Press, 2007), 112.
[28] Hoffman, *Inside Terrorism*, 186.

CONCLUSION

Two important ideas come out of this chapter. The first is that governments can be agents of terrorism as well as non-governmental groups. The second is that, when we understand this, we can see that any inquiry about the moral status of terrorism must widen its scope to include traditional wars. To understand the moral status of terrorist acts, we must investigate the moral status of intentional attacks on civilians for political purposes, whether they occur in wars carried out by states, in intimidation efforts carried out by states against their own people, or in campaigns of political violence by non-state agents.

At the start of this book, I suggested that the notion of moral clarity about terrorism was an illusion. In this chapter, it has emerged that attacks on civilians by states, such as the Allied city bombings in World War II, satisfy the criteria for being instances of terrorism. Since most people never think of these well-known attacks as terrorism, it is clear that we can be familiar with acts of terrorism and fail to see that they are terrorism. This is because our actual use of the term "terrorism" is both unclear and politically biased. We should not be surprised that attempts to apply a clear, unbiased definition lead to unexpected results.

The moral clarity view also assumes that the wrongness of intentionally killing innocent people is a self-evident moral truth. The lack of self-evidence emerges, however, when we think about the World War II Allied bombings. Many people believe that these attacks were morally justified. Since these bombings intentionally killed innocent people, however, people who approve of them must reject the belief that it is always wrong to attack innocent people in war.

Thinking about this case might make people feel confused and uncertain about the killing of innocent people. This uncertainty results from a clash between their desire to affirm the moral idea that intentionally killing civilians is always wrong and their desire to approve whatever is necessary to defeat a truly evil enemy in war. This uncertainty is not foolish. It is, however, incompatible with the idea that the wrongness of killing civilians is self-evident. Self-evident statements do not allow for uncertainty.

I believe that confusion and uncertainty are appropriate. In order to know whether to condemn all terrorism, we need to answer difficult questions in the ethics of war and violence. Does the justice of a cause legitimate the intentional killing of innocent people? Or is the intentional killing of innocent people so grievous a violation of fundamental values that it is forbidden even in the direst circumstances and for the strongest of reasons?

Conclusion: taking stock

I have spent a lot of time (yours and mine) trying to clarify the word "terrorism." This is important to do because confusions about what "terrorism" means make it impossible to think clearly about it. "What is terrorism?" was the first question on my agenda at the start of this book. I have now answered this question with a definition. The definition leads to an answer to the second question: what is it that makes terrorism especially wrong? When we examine the features of terrorist acts, the one that most plausibly explains why terrorism is especially wrong is that it intentionally kills and injures innocent people.

I have also partly answered the third question: If terrorism is so obviously wrong, why do moral condemnations of terrorism often lack credibility? These condemnations often lack credibility because they rely on biased definitions of terrorism. As a result, actions that are labeled as "terrorism" when carried out by some people escape the "terrorist" label when carried out by others.

The answer to question 3 provides a partial answer to question 4: What requirements must be met in order to make condemnations of terrorism morally credible? The first requirement is that the labeling of acts as terrorism must be unbiased and impartial. A second requirement is that moral condemnations of terrorism must be based on credible moral principles that are applied in an unbiased, impartial way. For example, if the principle underlying our condemnation of terrorism is that it is always wrong to intentionally kill innocent people, then this principle must be applied to all such acts, whoever does them. If we only condemn intentional killing of innocent people when it is done by non-governmental groups who are our enemies, it will be clear that it is not *intentionally killing innocent people* that we object to. Rather, what we object to is *intentional killing of innocent people by non-governmental, enemy groups*. Someone who condemns intentional killings of innocent people by enemy groups but does not condemn such killings by governments or allies is not a credible moral judge.

73

In addition, if we want to make credible moral judgments about terrorism, we need to broaden our focus to other acts that kill and injure civilians. If we only care about terrorist killings but do not care about other killings of innocent people, then our moral judgments about terrorism are morally arbitrary.

Having answered or partly answered the first four questions, I can now consider question 5: is terrorism always wrong, or can terrorism be morally justified in some circumstances? The most plausible basis for believing that terrorism is always wrong is the moral principle that intentionally killing innocent people is always wrong. This principle has seemed axiomatic to many people, but consideration of the Allied bombings in World War II shows that it is not axiomatic and raises the question of whether this principle is even true.

My focus for much of the rest of this book will be on the question: is it always wrong to intentionally kill innocent people? If it is, then we can cite this simple principle to justify condemning all acts of terrorism. If it is not, then we cannot condemn terrorism simply because it intentionally kills innocent people.

In calling this book *Terrorism and the Ethics of War*, I want to suggest that we cannot make credible moral judgments about terrorism unless we have a consistent, credible set of moral principles about war and political violence. Without this, we cannot make sound judgments ourselves, and the judgments that we make will not be credible to others, especially those who do not share our loyalties and sympathies. For this reason, the key moral questions are not simply about terrorism but instead are about the ethics of permissible killing in war and political conflict.

PART II

Why moral condemnations of terrorism lack credibility

Introduction: toward morally credible condemnations of terrorism

While having an unbiased definition of terrorism is the first step toward moral credibility, the second step is to base our condemnation of terrorism on the impartial application of a general moral principle. The simplest, most plausible moral principle for this purpose is one that forbids all intentional killings of innocent people. This is what the principle of noncombatant immunity does in the context of war and political violence.

The principle of noncombatant immunity is one half of the principle of discrimination. The first half is a permission that allows soldiers to attack enemy soldiers in war while the second prohibits soldiers from attacking civilians. Terrorism violates this prohibition by intentionally directing its attacks against civilians.[1]

If noncombatant immunity is an absolute principle that permits no exceptions, then it will follow that terrorism is always wrong. The argument would be simple and direct.

1. Terrorist acts always intentionally kill or injure innocent people.
2. It is always wrong intentionally to kill or injure innocent people.
3. Therefore, terrorist acts are always wrong.

In this argument, the view that terrorism is always wrong is not a necessary truth. It is an inference from the definition of terrorism and the moral principle that condemns all attacks on innocent people. Since the idea of intentionally killing innocent people often strikes people as morally repellent, we might think that statement 2, the principle of noncombatant immunity, needs no justification. In fact, however, this principle has been doubted, criticized, and rejected by many people.

In the next two chapters, I will briefly discuss five philosophical perspectives on the ethics of war: political realism, commonsense morality, Michael

---

[1] The international law prohibition is broader. It forbids attacks on some military personnel (e.g., chaplains and medical corps), on civilian objects such as hospitals and schools, and on cultural and religious buildings. *Protocol 1 Additional to the Geneva Conventions*, 1977, part IV, articles 48–56.

Walzer's theory, utilitarianism, and traditional just war theory. I will show that the first four sometimes permit intentional attacks on innocent people and thus cannot credibly condemn all terrorist acts. The fifth view, traditional just war theory, does prohibit all intentional killings of civilians, but its overly permissive approach to collateral damage killings undermines the credibility of its condemnation of terrorist acts. While some acts that kill and injure civilians as side effects of attacks on military targets are morally permissible, others are not. Just war theory approves of some acts that fail to show sufficient regard for civilian lives and, in this way, are morally similar to terrorism. As a result, it seems hypocritical to condemn one while allowing the other.

As I will show, none of these five views provides a plausible basis for condemning all terrorist acts. Either these views are false or attacking civilians is sometimes morally permissible.

CHAPTER 6

Why standard theories fail to condemn terrorism

Contrary to what we might expect, standard views about the ethics of war permit terrorist acts under some circumstances. People who accept these views face a difficult choice. They must either acknowledge that terrorist acts can sometimes be morally justified, or, if they want to condemn terrorism absolutely, they must reject whichever of these views they have held.

If we decide that terrorist acts can sometimes be morally justified, we would view terrorism in the way that most of us view war. Although war is brutal and destructive, most of us believe that it is sometimes morally right to engage in warfare. That is why we distinguish between just wars and unjust wars. We do not generally distinguish between just and unjust terrorism, however.[1] But if there are permissible violations of noncombatant immunity, we will have to start making this distinction.

The history of warfare shows that the deliberate killing of innocent people has been hard to resist in practice. I have already mentioned the "terror bombings" of World War II, but there are many other cases.[2] In a recent study of "civilian victimization" in war, Alexander Downes examined 100 wars involving 323 countries between 1816 and 2003. Of the 175 countries that had the option of attacking civilians, almost a third, 52 countries, chose to do so.[3] According to Downes, whether countries choose to attack civilians depends on the type of war being fought and the requirements for victory. In wars to gain territory, attacks on civilians occur 81 percent of the time, often as instruments of ethnic cleansing.[4] When wars bog down into wars of attrition, civilian victimization occurred 62 percent

---

[1] See, however, Ron Hirschbein, "Just Terrorism Theory," *Concerned Philosophers for Peace Newsletter* 21 (Spring and Fall 2001), 13–17. Hirschbein's title is sardonic rather than approving.

[2] Caleb Carr surveys the history of wartime attacks on civilians in *The Lessons of Terror* (New York: Random House, 2002). For description and analysis of such attacks, see Slim, *Killing Civilians*.

[3] Alexander Downes, "Desperate Times, Desperate Measures: The Causes of Civilian Victimization in War," *International Security* 30 (Spring 2006) and *Targeting Civilians in War*.

[4] Downes, "Desperate Times, Desperate Measures," 170, 174, 176.

of the time. Even in cases when states won quick victories, however, civilians were attacked 16 percent of the time. Downes also shows that when liberal democratic states were involved in wars of attrition, they adopted civilian victimization strategies 81 percent of the time.

Since it is a commonplace that "war is hell," these facts may be shocking but not really surprising. What is perhaps surprising is that support for deliberate attacks on civilians has been hard to resist in theory as well as practice. In what follows, I will briefly discuss political realism, commonsense morality, the rights-based theory of Michael Walzer, and utilitarianism. I will show that none of these views categorically condemns deliberate attacks on civilians. As a result, none of them can categorically condemn terrorist acts.

POLITICAL REALISM

Political realism has long been an influential perspective in thinking about war and international relations. Realists trace their key ideas to Thucydides, Machiavelli, and Hobbes.[5] As the name "realism" suggests, realists pride themselves on seeing things as they are. They have no illusions about human goodness and reject idealist hopes for getting nations to adhere to moral principles as wishful thinking. Although individual realist thinkers differ, realism is widely understood as the view that a nation's conduct in war and international relations both is and should be determined by its interests. In opposition to idealists and moralists, realists assert that traditional morality does not apply to this sphere of human conduct.[6]

It is worth distinguishing between an amoral form of realism and a moralized form, even though they lead to the same actions in practice. While amoral realism completely rejects the idea that moral principles apply to war and international affairs, moralized realism does not reject the relevance of morality, but it sees political leaders as having only one moral duty, to promote the interests of their nation or group. For both types of realists, "Do what is in your nation's interest" is the key rule for political leaders.

Amoral realists claim that applying the rules of morality to the practice of war makes no more sense than applying the rules of checkers to chess. Even if one wanted to do this, it is impossible. George Kennan makes this point

---

[5] For analytic overviews of the realist tradition, see Steven Forde, "Classical Realism" and Jack Donnelly, "Twentieth-Century Realism," both in T. Nardin and D. Mapel, eds., *Traditions of International Ethics* (New York: Cambridge University Press, 1992); and Michael Doyle, *Ways of War and Peace* (New York: W. W. Norton, 1997).

[6] This common interpretation is the target of realism's critics. See, for example, Robert Holmes, *On War and Morality* (Princeton: Princeton University Press, 1989), chapters 2–3.

when he says that "there are no internationally accepted standards of morality to which the U.S. government could appeal if it wished to act in the name of moral principles."[7] Though Kennan is speaking about US foreign policy, his view is entirely general and applies to any government. Even if a country's leaders wanted to act according to universal moral principles, they cannot do this because such principles do not exist.

Kennan's writings also contain statements of the moralized version of realism, as when he writes that:

Government is an agent, not a principle. Its primary obligation is to the interests of the national society it represents, not to the moral impulses that individual elements of that society may experience.[8]

In saying that government "is an agent, not a principle," Kennan means that governments have no interests of their own but instead represent the interests of their citizens. Hence, they have a duty to act on behalf of their citizens' interests and no right to act against them. Even if government leaders might personally support an altruistic morality, as public officials, their sole duty is to defend the interests of their country and its citizens. Although this is a moral principle, it narrows the scope and content of morality very severely. It is the national equivalent of ethical egoism, the view that each individual person's sole moral duty is to look out for himself or herself.

In practice, both views express a *realpolitik* perspective that affirms the national interest as the only proper standard of behavior in the realm of war and international relations. They reject universal moral principles that protect the interests and rights of all people.

REALISM, TERRORISM, AND NONCOMBATANT IMMUNITY

Since realists evaluate all actions by their effect on the national interest, they reject any constraints on the means or tactics that may be employed in pursuing the national interest. In their view, "all's fair in love and war." If harming other countries promotes one's own country's interests, that is what political leaders ought to do. If "civilian victimization" is a good strategy for winning a war, that is the policy that should be pursued.

[7] George Kennan, "Morality and Foreign Policy," *Foreign Affairs* 64 (Winter 1985–6), reprinted in *Morality and Foreign Policy* (Washington, D.C.: US Institute of Peace, 1991), 61.
[8] Ibid., 60.

To refrain on moral grounds would be to misunderstand the nature of war and international relations.

Once we understand what realism is, it is obvious that realists must reject the principle of noncombatant immunity and thus have no moral basis to condemn all terrorism. If terrorist attacks benefit a particular nation or group, that group has good political realist reasons to engage in terrorism and no moral reasons not to. The principle of noncombatant immunity, since it imposes a moral duty not to attack enemy civilians, has no force for realists except when abiding by it would promote the national interest. (For example, leaders might believe that attacking enemy civilians will provoke attacks on their own citizens.)

Since direct concern for enemy noncombatants is both foolish and inappropriate, it follows that if the national interest can be promoted by terrorist tactics, then realists would support these tactics. If realism is adopted as a perspective for one's own nation or group, then other nations or groups cannot credibly be condemned for adopting the same perspective and feeling free to use any tactics whatsoever in the conduct of war or international relations.

The realist view is slightly complicated by the fact that in some circumstances it may be in a country's interests to support international rules that forbid terrorism. Nonetheless, realists will never take these rules to be binding and will support violating them when it promotes their country's interests.

Similarly, realists will condemn terrorism when such condemnations advance their nation's interests. But these condemnations will only appear credible to people who are ignorant of their basis. Once it is known that realists condemn terrorism for self-serving reasons and would support terrorist tactics if they benefited their own nation, then the realists' condemnations of terrorism will lose all credibility.

Though realism has been espoused by influential thinkers and is sometimes invoked by political leaders, its inability to support any condemnations of terrorism is an embarrassment in our post-September 11 world. No one takes it seriously when moral denunciations of terrorism emerge from the lips of people who see their own nation's interest as the supreme good and who reserve the right to engage in terrorist acts when these acts would benefit their own nation.

COMMONSENSE MORALITY

We don't generally think of commonsense morality as a moral theory. Indeed, given the diversity of moral beliefs both between and within societies, one may wonder whether such a thing as commonsense morality even exists.[9] Nonetheless, there are moral beliefs on which there is a widespread, fairly stable consensus, and some philosophers suggest that our ordinary moral beliefs are, in a sense, the final appeal in trying to justify particular moral opinions.

Michael Walzer supports this view in *Just and Unjust Wars* and other works. According to Walzer, there is a set of moral ideas about warfare that runs through much of history and many different societies. In his view, when we examine how people try to justify actions in war, we discover that their "justifications and judgments reveal ... a comprehensive view of war as a human activity and a more or less systematic moral doctrine." According to Walzer, commonsense morality contains a coherent set of "shared understandings" that guides us when we make moral judgments about war. When we engage in debate about these issues, we proceed by interpreting and appealing to these shared understandings.[10]

Walzer's perspective gains plausibility from the difference between our responses to views that command a consensus and views that are out of the mainstream. For example, a key part of our commonsense ethic of war is the belief that war is sometimes morally justified. That is why pacifism plays almost no role in public discussions about war. It lies outside the moral consensus. Another part of commonsense morality tells us that soldiers have a right to kill other soldiers and thus should not be seen as murderers. Soldiers are not supposed to attack and kill innocent people, however, because civilians are not legitimate targets in war. If this interpretation is correct, then we can conclude that commonsense morality condemns terrorism because terrorism always attacks innocent people.

According to this view, terrorism is wrong because it violates the shared understanding that it is wrong to attack innocent people. The vehemence with which terrorism is generally condemned arises from the fact that the immunity of civilians to attack is central to our common understandings of the ethics of war.

THE PROBLEM WITH THE COMMONSENSE MORALITY OF WAR

Walzer's depiction of the commonsense ethic of war is half right. Commonsense morality does contain ideas about war and violence that

---

[9] For a philosophical interpretation of commonsense morality, see Bernard Gert, *Common Morality* (New York: Oxford University Press, 2004).

[10] Walzer, *Just and Unjust Wars*, xiii. The phrase "shared understandings" comes from Walzer's *Spheres of Justice* (New York: Basic Books, 1983). He defends his philosophical method in *Interpretation and Social Criticism* (Cambridge, Mass.: Harvard University Press, 1987).

provide a basis for condemning terrorism. Commonsense morality differs from realism. Unlike amoral realism, it recognizes that morality applies to war and international relations. In addition, commonsense morality is less nationalistic than moralized realism. It contains an apolitical, humanitarian strand that recognizes the moral rights and the humanity of people who are not citizens of one's own country. This humanitarian strand of commonsense morality strongly supports the principle of noncombatant immunity and leads most people to condemn terrorist attacks in a sincere and genuine way.

Nonetheless, commonsense morality does not provide a firm basis either for an absolute principle of noncombatant immunity or for condemnations of all terrorist acts. The reason is that the commonsense ethic of war lacks the unity that Walzer attributes to it. Instead, commonsense morality is a hodgepodge of deeply conflicting beliefs, ideals, and principles.

It is not that commonsense morality has no structure and is a merely random collection of beliefs. Instead, it is a network of many different strands, each of which has some structure and unity. Unfortunately, these strands do not fit together in a consistent way. While the humanitarian strand takes seriously the value of all people and supports efforts to avoid civilian deaths in wartime, commonsense morality also contains nonuniversalist strands that compete with humanitarianism. A competing "patriotic" strand exhibits a strong degree of national partiality. Commonsense morality allows us to accord more value to people who are "near and dear" to us and to give priority to members of groups that we identify with. When the interests of our personal or national groups conflict with the interests of distant strangers, commonsense morality permits us to give priority to our own groups.[11] In wartime, the humanitarian protections that extend to enemy civilians often give way to the patriotic, nationalist strand of commonsense morality, resulting in the approval of attacks on civilians if they are necessary for victory or the protection of one's own soldiers.

Under the pressures of war, the humanitarian strands of commonsense morality weaken and give way to narrower, more intensely felt concerns. Attacks on civilians that would ordinarily be condemned come to be seen as morally acceptable. Writing about World War II, Alexander Downes describes this shift in moral opinion in the United States.

---

[11] Thomas Nagel discusses tensions between partial and universal aspects of morality in *Equality and Partiality* (New York: Oxford University Press, 1991). I discuss different forms of patriotism in *Patriotism, Morality, and Peace* (Lanham, Md.: Rowman and Littlefield, 1993).

Most Americans abhorred bombing civilians before the war, and lurid press descriptions of such attacks by Axis countries provoked widespread outrage. But Germany's invasion of Western Europe in the spring of 1940 helped spark a dramatic reversal in opinion … In the immediate aftermath of Pearl Harbor, an opinion poll showed that 67 percent favored aerial bombardment of Japanese cities.[12]

As a result, government leaders came to order types of attacks that they themselves had earlier condemned. As the historian John Dower notes,

Allied air raids were widely accepted as just retribution as well as sound strategic policy, and the few critics who raised ethical and humanitarian questions about the heavy bombing of German cities were usually denounced as hopeless idealists, fools, or traitors.[13]

War is a brutalizing process, and the humanitarian strands in commonsense morality are among its victims.

We can see the nationalist strand of commonsense morality at work in a famous defense of the atomic bombings of Japan by the United States. In a 1947 article, Henry Stimson, Secretary of War under Presidents Roosevelt and Truman, explained why he supported using atomic weapons against Japan.

My chief purpose was to end the war in victory with the least possible cost in the lives of the men in the armies which I had helped to raise … I believe that no man, in our position and subject to our responsibilities, holding in his hands a weapon of such possibilities for accomplishing this purpose and saving those lives, could have failed to use it and afterwards looked his countrymen in the face.[14]

Stimson's statement is illuminating in several ways. First, it is an explicit, public attempt to justify a massive attack on a primarily civilian target. Second, it justifies the attack by citing its positive consequences for Americans: attaining victory over Japan and minimizing American military casualties. The statement shows, too, that Stimson did not reject morality but saw using the atomic bombs as a moral duty. Finally, it shows that Stimson believed that not using the atomic weapons in this situation would have been strongly condemned by the American people.

Although there is debate about the historical accuracy of Stimson's account, his interpretation of the commonsense ethic of war (as understood

---

[12] Downes, *Targeting Civilians in War*, 136–7. See, too, George E. Hopkins, "Bombing and the American Conscience During World War II," *Historian* 28 (May 1966), 451–73.

[13] Quoted in Downes, *Targeting Civilians*, 136.

[14] Henry Stimson, "The Decision to Use the Atomic Bomb," *Harper's Magazine* 194 (February, 1947), 106–7.

in the United States) seems be correct.[15] His defense of the atomic bombings was widely accepted, and Harry Truman, who authorized the bombings and said that he never lost a night's sleep over them, remains a much
admired president.[16]

The atomic bombings of Hiroshima and Nagasaki were direct attacks on
cities and produced hundreds of thousands of civilian casualties. If we apply
the definition of terrorism to them, it is clear that they were acts of
terrorism – direct attacks on civilians for the sake of achieving political
goals (defeating Japan and minimizing American military losses). Like other
terrorist acts, the bombings had a communicative function. They targeted a
city and its civilian inhabitants, but the audience for the attacks was the
Japanese leaders, and the message they conveyed was that Japan ought to
surrender unconditionally.

The idea that these attacks – which were ordered by respected officials
and accepted by a public of ordinary, decent people – were terrorist acts may
be hard to swallow, and some may think we should reconsider the definition
of terrorism. Recall Hoffman's claim that we should not equate the World
War II bombings by governments with acts of terrorism and his proposal
that we limit the word "terrorism" to acts by non-governmental groups.[17]
But if we think that what most matters about terrorist attacks is that they
target innocent people and not that they are carried out by non-
governmental groups, then we have to accept that the word "terrorism"
applies to actions that we don't usually associate with this word.

Once we recognize that the victimization of innocent people for political
purposes is at the heart of terrorism and that this kind of victimization has
been authorized by respected government officials, we may be forced to
rethink our beliefs about terrorism, including the widespread view that
terrorist attacks are only launched by insane, barbaric, or evil people. While
I do count terrorist acts as barbaric, it turns out that barbaric acts can be
carried out by people we regard as civilized human beings.[18]

Moreover, under certain circumstances, barbaric acts are approved by
commonsense morality, which is deeply conflicted on these issues. While
parts of commonsense morality categorically condemn these types of

---

[15] For the history of Stimson's essay, see Robert Jay Lifton and Greg Mitchell, *Hiroshima in America: A Half Century of Denial* (New York: Avon Books, 1995), chapter 7; and Kai Bird, *The Color of Truth* (New York: Simon and Schuster, 1998), chapter 5.

[16] Lifton and Mitchell discuss Truman's attitudes in *Hiroshima and American Memory*, part II.

[17] Hoffman, *Inside Terrorism*, 33.

[18] Louise Richardson challenges the idea that terrorists must be "evil monsters" in *What Terrorists Want*, xi–xxii.

actions, other parts approve of them in some circumstances. It is for this reason that commonsense morality fails to provide a solid basis for condemning all acts of terrorism. Its commitment to universal human values and noncombatant immunity is seriously weakened by its commitment to the national interest and the lives of one's own soldiers in time of war.

These shifts should not surprise us. War is morally confusing because it suspends many of the most central rules of commonsense morality. From the perspective of commonsense morality, acts of violence are among the worst things that people can do to one another. Morality, if it forbids anything, almost always forbids killing people, injuring them, disabling them, and inflicting pain on them.[19] In war, these prohibitions are lifted. Soldiers have a general permission to kill, injure, disable, and inflict pain on other human beings who constitute the enemy military force. Given this transvaluation of moral values in war, it is not surprising that people find it hard to preserve constraints on what is done in war. Because the morality of war is so much more permissive than the morality of everyday life, people may not see how basic moral concerns for enemy civilians can be preserved.

Realists conclude that none of our ordinary morality is preserved in war and that anything goes in the quest for victory. Unlike realism, commonsense morality never fully accepts the logic of national interest and continues to embrace clashing, competing concerns. In wartime, however, commonsense morality moves in the direction that realists wholeheartedly embrace from the start.[20] This wartime embrace of national partiality undermines commonsense morality's role as a credible basis for condemning terrorism.

UTILITARIANISM

The utilitarian theory of ethics has been the object of vigorous attacks and vigorous defenses. The pioneers of utilitarian morality – Jeremy Bentham, John Stuart Mill, and Henry Sidgwick – are among the most significant figures in the history of modern moral philosophy. In addition to its distinguished pedigree, utilitarianism expresses an attractive, powerful concern for promoting human well-being. This appealing goal sustains it in spite of numerous attacks by critics.

---

[19] Bernard Gert stresses the centrality of these prohibitions in *Common Morality*.
[20] Daryl Glaser discusses a similar process in "Partiality to Conationals or Solidarity with the Oppressed? Or, What Liberal Zionism Can Tell Us about the Limitations of Liberal Nationalism," *Ethnicities* 5 (2005), 486–509.

Utilitarianism's basic idea is that what makes actions morally right and wrong is their impact on the well-being of human beings. According to "act utilitarianism," the theory's most familiar and most radical form, any action is right if it produces better consequences in a particular situation than any alternative actions would produce. Reacting against both custom and taboo moralities that judge the morality of actions independently of their effects, utilitarianism tells us to look to the consequences of actions. Nothing else matters.

In spite of its promise, utilitarianism is open to the criticism that it permits even the most vile actions when those actions would yield better effects than alternative actions. The theory's opponents claim that utilitarianism would permit the punishment of innocent people if that would deter terrible crimes or calm an enraged populace. Others suggest that sadistic acts are justified when the pleasures of the sadists exceed the pains of their victims. Even slavery might be justified if it resulted in significant enough benefits for the rest of the population. Indeed, there seems to be no limit to what might be approved if the overall effects were good enough.

UTILITARIANISM AND WAR

In developing an ethic of war, utilitarians have generally argued that attacks in war are only justified if they have military value and do not cause gratuitous, excessive harm. To avoid qualifying as gratuitous, attacks must have genuine military value. To avoid being excessive, the benefits of an attack must outweigh the harms that it inflicts.

Although utilitarianism supports these constraints on the use of military force, it does not appear to support other widely accepted restrictions that are associated with human rights. Torture, for example, is widely condemned as an extreme violation of fundamental human rights, but torture appears to be justifiable in utilitarian terms if the pain inflicted on its victims is outweighed by the benefits it produces for a larger body of people. A popular example that is used to make this point involves a situation in which torturing one person might save an entire city from nuclear destruction.[21]

Given this mode of reasoning, it is easy to see the implications of utilitarianism for the principle of noncombatant immunity and the evaluation of terrorism. An absolute prohibition of attacks on civilians does not seem to be supported by utilitarian morality. If there are circumstances in

---

[21] For powerful criticisms of this argument, see David Luban, "Liberalism, Torture, and the Ticking Bomb," in Steven Lee, ed., *Intervention, Terrorism, and Torture* (Dordrecht: Springer, 2007), 249–62.

which attacking civilians causes better overall effects than not attacking them, then utilitarianism would favor attacking civilians. Since terrorist acts are attacks on civilians, utilitarianism appears to justify terrorist acts when they yield the best overall results.

This is not to say that utilitarians would approve of all terrorist attacks. Rather, utilitarians will avoid any general stand on terrorist acts as a whole. Because we cannot know in advance that no terrorist act could possibly have better overall consequences than available alternatives, act utilitarians will not say that all terrorist acts are wrong. If particular terrorist attacks maximize utility, then these attacks would be permitted – or even required – by utilitarian morality.

WALZER'S THEORY

Michael Walzer's *Just and Unjust Wars* is widely regarded as a modern classic on the ethics of war. One of Walzer's main aims in the book is to defend the central place of noncombatant immunity in the ethics of war. In defending this principle, Walzer appeals to the idea of human rights. He does this in part because he believes that utilitarianism cannot provide a solid basis for prohibiting attacks on civilians. A rights-based approach, however, can give noncombatant immunity the kind of grounding it needs.

Walzer states his central ideas as a reply to the question "what actions are legitimate in wartime?" His answer is that:

A legitimate act of war is one that does not violate the rights of the people against whom it is directed … [N]o one can be threatened with war or warred against, unless through some act of his own he has surrendered or lost his rights. *This fundamental principle underlies and shapes the judgments we make of wartime conduct.*[22] (Emphasis added.)

When people become soldiers in a military organization, two changes occur in their moral status. First, they gain a right to attack enemy soldiers, and, second, because enemy soldiers gain the same right against them, soldiers lose their immunity to attack. For this reason, all soldiers are legitimate targets. This is sometimes called the principle of combatant *non*-immunity.

Civilians, however, have done nothing to change their moral status. Therefore, unlike soldiers, civilians have no right to attack enemy soldiers. And, unlike soldiers, civilians are not permissible targets. According to Walzer, every person starts with a natural immunity, i.e., a right not to be

---

[22] Walzer, *Just and Unjust Wars*, 135.

attacked, and unless they do something to lose this right, they remain immune to attack. The fact that civilians have not relinquished their natural right to immunity from attack is the basis for the principle of noncombatant immunity.

Given Walzer's strong affirmation of noncombatant immunity and his definition of terrorism as "the random murder of innocent people" in order to "destroy the morale of a nation or class," it is not surprising that Walzer strongly condemns terrorism. In a later essay, he states categorically: "I take the principle for granted: that every act of terrorism is a wrongful act."[23]

As described to this point, Walzer's view appears to provide a solid moral basis both for noncombatant immunity and for the condemnation of all terrorist acts. In addition, because he applies the principle of noncombatant immunity in an unbiased way throughout much of his book, his criticism of terrorism satisfies some of the key requirements for moral credibility.

THE EXCEPTION THAT DISPROVES THE RULE

Late in *Just and Unjust Wars*, however, Walzer undermines this solid basis for condemning terrorism. He does this by conceding that there are circumstances in which intentional attacks on innocent people are justified. Walzer concedes this because he believes that during the early years of World War II the British were justified in bombing German cities, even though these bombings were direct attacks on German civilians. Walzer's defense of these attacks has two parts: first, he describes the dire situation that Britain faced when it launched these attacks, and second, he revises his ethic of war to permit attacks on civilians in situations like the one that the British faced.

Walzer argues that there are special circumstances in which the principle of noncombatant immunity is no longer binding on parties to a war. He calls this special, extraordinary circumstance a "supreme emergency" and claims that Britain faced a supreme emergency in 1940.[24] While Walzer believes that noncombatant immunity is absolutely binding in ordinary wars against ordinary enemies, he claims that it ceased to bind the British in 1940 because they were not fighting an ordinary war against an ordinary enemy. Germany under the Nazis posed an extraordinary threat. Nazism, he says,

---

[23] Ibid., 197; the second quote is from "Terrorism: A Critique of Excuses," reprinted in Walzer, *Arguing About War* (New Haven: Yale University Press, 2004), 52.

[24] Walzer, *Just and Unjust Wars*, 251–62.

was an ultimate threat to everything decent in our lives, an ideology and a practice of domination so murderous, so degrading … that the consequences of its final victory were literally beyond calculation, immeasurably awful … Here was a threat to human values so radical that its imminence would surely constitute a supreme emergency.[25]

The threat to Britain in 1940 was not only extraordinary, it was also imminent. Britain's allies in Europe had fallen, the United States and the Soviet Union had not yet entered the war, and a German invasion was expected at any time. The threat of defeat by this extraordinary enemy appeared imminent. Finally, Walzer believes, Britain possessed only one effective means of damaging Germany, the aerial bombardment of German cities – not with the aim of destroying specific military targets but rather with the aim of attacking the German population itself. In this special circumstance, Walzer believes that the British were justified in bombing the civilian populations of German cities.

This case leads Walzer to make a "supreme emergency" exception to the prohibition on attacking civilians. According to this exception, direct attacks on civilians are permissible if one's enemy is evil enough, if the threat it poses is imminent, and if there are no other effective means of military resistance against that enemy. In a supreme emergency, Walzer writes, "one might well be required to override the rights of innocent people and shatter the war convention."[26]

Although Walzer categorically condemns all terrorist acts in *Just and Unjust Wars* and later writings, the supreme emergency exception permits terrorist attacks. As he himself writes, "The intention of the British leaders … was to kill and terrorize the civilian population" of Germany.[27] The aim was to attack the civilian population so as to influence the German population and their leaders. Perhaps Walzer is right about the supreme emergency exception, but if he is, then terrorism is sometimes justified. On the other hand, if his condemnation of terrorism is correct, then attacks on civilians in supreme emergencies are not justified. While each of Walzer's views on these issues is plausible, his overall view is clearly inconsistent.

One of Walzer's main aims in *Just and Unjust Wars* is to fortify non-combatant immunity, but the "supreme emergency" exception provides a formula for permitting attacks on civilians and a model for justifying

---

[25] Ibid., 253.
[26] Ibid., 259. By the "war convention," Walzer here refers to the principle of discrimination.
[27] Michael Walzer, "Emergency Ethics," in *Arguing About War*, 34.

terrorism. As a result, the credibility of Walzer's categorical criticism of terrorism is severely weakened by his approval of some terrorist acts.[28]

CONCLUSION

My aim in this chapter has been to show that the belief that it is always wrong to kill innocent people has been rejected by realists, commonsense morality, act utilitarians, and by Walzer. And, because it is rejected, categorical condemnations of terrorism are inconsistent with these views. This is unsettling because we often assume that all right-thinking people condemn the killing of innocent people. Perhaps there is an element of self-deception here. We tell ourselves that we hold humane, lofty views while in fact these are not the beliefs that we act on.

It is not merely the hypocrisy of public officials that undermines condemnations of terrorism. The ethical views about war that many people hold fail to provide a credible basis for condemning all terrorism because none of them condemns all violations of noncombatant immunity. Of course, it is possible that there is no credible way to condemn all terrorist acts. Perhaps terrorist acts can sometimes be morally justified. If this is true, then it is no fault of standard theories that they do not categorically condemn all terrorist acts. Perhaps the principle that civilians may never be attacked is not correct.

In part III, I will respond to these doubts by providing a justification for an absolute version of noncombatant immunity that rules out all terrorist acts. This will require two things. First, I will have to show why the theories I have discussed are mistaken and why we should reject their arguments against noncombatant immunity. Second, I will have to provide positive arguments to show that violating noncombatant immunity is always wrong and therefore that terrorism is always wrong.

While this chapter has been negative and critical, we can learn some positive lessons from the failures of the theories I have discussed. These failures indicate the features that a view requires if it is to be a credible basis for condemning all terrorist acts.

Since the problem with realism is that it considers only the national interest, a credible view must take into account the interests and rights of all people, not just the interests and rights of citizens of one's own country or group. Since the problem with commonsense morality is that it is

---

[28] For a model of this type of evaluation of terrorism, see Saul Smilansky, "Terrorism, Justification, and Illusion," *Ethics* 114 (July 2004), 790–805.

inconsistent and in times of stress permits attacks on enemy civilians, a credible theory must prohibit attacks on civilians even if such attacks will lead to victory and minimize military losses on one's own side. The problem with utilitarianism (in the form so far discussed) is that it approves of terrorism when it produces beneficial effects. A credible theory will not approve of violating noncombatant immunity simply because it appears to generate better consequences in particular situations. Finally, since Walzer's defense of noncombatant immunity and criticism of terrorism are undermined by his acceptance of a supreme emergency exception, a credible view will have to show why permitting such exceptions is wrong.

Although I believe that the four views I have discussed are mistaken, it is important to acknowledge that there are powerful reasons why these views have been attractive to thoughtful people. It would be a mistake to reject them as obviously wrong.

CHAPTER 7

Just war theory and the problem of collateral damage

Just war theorists share some ideas but differ among themselves on many issues. I will focus on a version of just war theory that prohibits all intentional attacks on civilians and thus condemns all terrorist acts. If we are looking for a view that credibly condemns all terrorism, then this form of just war theory is superior to realism, commonsense morality, (act) utilitarianism, and Walzer's view. Nonetheless, it, too, fails to provide sufficient support for noncombatant immunity, and, because of this, its condemnation of terrorism also lacks credibility.

A BRIEF OVERVIEW OF JUST WAR THEORY

Just war theory has two parts. The first part – *jus ad bellum* – answers the question "under what conditions is a nation or other group morally justified in going to war?" It does this by providing a set of criteria for judging when going to war is morally justified. Among the criteria that are generally cited are having a just cause, legitimate authority to fight a war, reasonable probability of success, fighting as a last resort, and having a cause for fighting that is weighty enough to make war a proportionate response.[1]

The second part of just war theory – *jus in bello* – answers the question "what means of fighting a war are morally permissible?" It contains two principles: discrimination and proportionality. The principle of discrimination requires people fighting a war to distinguish soldiers from civilians, and it prohibits attacks on civilians. The principle of proportionality requires that the damage done in achieving a military objective must match the value of the military objective in an appropriate way. For example, an attack that is expected to cause large-scale casualties is permissible only if the military objective is extremely valuable. If it has little value,

---

[1] For a brief statement and explanation, see United States Catholic Conference, *The Harvest of Justice Is Sown in Peace*, 1993; http://www.usccb.org/sdwp/harvest.shtml.

then the damage caused by the attack would be not be proportionate, and the attack would be wrong.

An important feature of just war theory is that the *jus in bello* rules on fighting a war apply equally to all sides in a war. Even if a country is fighting a just war against an unjust aggressor, the country that is justly defending itself is required to obey the limits on fighting set out by just war theory.

The version of just war theory that I will consider satisfies the four conditions I listed at the end of the last chapter. It considers the rights and interests of all people, prohibits attacks on civilians even when such attacks will lead to victory and minimize one's own military losses, forbids attacking civilians in order to generate better consequences, and does not contain a supreme emergency exception to the ban on attacking civilians.[2] In spite of these virtues, just war theory's Achilles' heel is its too-permissive approach to attacks that kill and injure civilians unintentionally as side effects or collateral damage.

DISCRIMINATION AND DOUBLE EFFECT

In an important statement of the just war principles, the National Conference of Catholic Bishops strongly affirmed noncombatant immunity in a form that allows no exceptions:

[T]he lives of innocent persons may never be taken directly, regardless of the purpose alleged for doing so … Just response to aggression must be discriminate; it must be directed against unjust aggressors, not against innocent people caught up in a war not of their making.[3]

While the word "never" in the opening sentence appears to forbid any actions that kill innocent people, this is a misinterpretation. If this principle prohibited all acts of war that kill innocent people, it would forbid not only terrorism but almost all forms of modern warfare. The reason is that the nature of modern warfare makes it virtually certain that civilian deaths will occur. Anyone entering into a war knows that fighting the war will cause civilian deaths. But if we are forbidden to do anything that causes civilian deaths, it appears that we are forbidden to fight a war. This is the conclusion

---

[2] Walzer is not the only just war theorist who rejects the absolutist interpretation of noncombatant immunity. For others, see William V. O'Brien, *The Conduct of Just and Limited War* (New York: Praeger, 1981), 45; and Johnson, *Just War Tradition*, 219–28.

[3] National Conference of Catholic Bishops, *The Challenge of Peace* (Washington, D.C.: United States Catholic Conference, 1983), section 104, page 33.

reached by some pacifists, who argue that the inevitability of civilian deaths implies the wrongness of all modern war.[4]

Just war theory, however, is not a pacifist theory. Because it assumes that just wars are possible, it interprets the principle of discrimination in a way that allows wars to be fought. It does this by using the "principle of double effect" to explain how acts of war that kill innocent people may be morally permissible. The principle of double effect emphasizes the moral importance of the difference between acts that *intentionally* cause deaths and injuries and acts that cause these harms *unintentionally*. According to double effect, actions that would be wrong if the harms are intended may be right if the harms are not intended. This distinction is signaled in the Bishops' statement by the word "directly." When they say that the lives of innocent people "may never be taken directly," they mean to forbid only intentional killings and to leave open the possibility that actions that kill innocent people "indirectly" (unintentionally) may be permissible.

This idea is part of commonsense morality. We commonly distinguish, for example, between murdering people and designing highways, even though both activities cause the deaths of innocent people. The difference is that murderers intend to kill people while highway designers intend to create effective means of transportation that facilitate travel and enhance people's lives. Highway designers can predict that fatalities will occur on the highways they design, but we judge their actions by the intended results, not by their foreseen but unintended side effects. Adapting the Bishops' language, we can say that improved transportation is the direct effect of the highway designer's work while traffic fatalities are indirect effects. Highway designers do no wrong, even though they know that people will die as a result of their work.

Applying these ideas to war, the principle of double effect tells us that fighting a war may be morally permissible as long as innocent people are not killed or injured intentionally. Attacks that kill civilians may be permissible if they are directed at military targets. What is crucial is that the attackers have no intention to harm the civilians.

DOUBLE EFFECT AND TERRORISM

The principle of discrimination, interpreted through the filter of double effect, absolutely prohibits attacks that deliberately kill innocent people and thus absolutely prohibits terrorist acts. A problem arises, however,

---

[4] This defense of pacifism is developed by Holmes in *On War and Morality*.

because these principles permit actions that are morally equivalent to terrorism. To see this, consider a variation of the September 11 attacks. While the actual September 11 attackers intended to kill large numbers of civilians, it is worth asking how we would judge their actions if they had not. Suppose that the September 11 attackers had intended only to damage or destroy the World Trade Center and the Pentagon buildings. Suppose that while they knew that many innocent people would die as a result of the attack, these deaths were not part of their goal. In this case, these deaths would have been "collateral damage," unintended but foreseen effects of the attack. Imagine that tapes of Osama bin Laden after the attacks showed him saying that he had only intended to attack the buildings and deeply regretted the deaths of innocent people, and suppose that there was evidence that he was sincere.

If we use the Bishops' language to describe these imagined attacks, we would say that the victims were "indirectly" rather than "directly" killed. In this case, they might be permitted by the principle of double effect. I very much doubt, however, that many of us would alter our condemnation of these attacks in the light of this distinction. Even if innocent people had not been the intended targets, the attacks would have shown such a high degree of callous disregard for human life that we would still judge them to be morally indefensible. Nonetheless, they might pass the "double effect" test for permissibility. What this shows is that the principle of double effect could allow actions that are morally indistinguishable from terrorism.

To cite a real case, Timothy McVeigh apparently claimed that he sought only to destroy the federal building in Oklahoma City, and he described the hundreds of people inside the building who were killed by his act as "collateral damage." Even if his claim is true, we do not regard this as possibly justifying or excusing his terrible crime.

INTENTIONS DON'T ALWAYS MATTER

The idea that causing unintended deaths may be permissible or excusable gains plausibility from common misconceptions about the law of homicide. It is widely believed that intentionally killing a person counts as first- or second-degree murder, while unintentionally killing someone is always the lesser crime of manslaughter. But this is not correct. The law sometimes judges unintentional killings to be as bad as intentional killings.

While intentional killings are paradigms for first-degree murder, the category of first-degree murder called "depraved heart" murder does not require the intention to kill. In such cases, the accused does not intend to kill, but malice is implied because there is a wanton and willful disregard of the likelihood that the natural tendency of [the] defendant's behavior is to cause death or great bodily harm.[5]

If it should be obvious that the "natural tendency" of an act is to cause death, then even if death is not the intended result, a person's conduct can be as bad as a deliberate murder. In this case, the act "manifests such a high degree of indifference to the value of human life that it may fairly be said that the actor 'as good as' intended to kill his victim."[6] Both law and morality condemn such unintended deaths very strongly and in a way that is incompatible with the principle of double effect.

Collateral damage deaths are very common in warfare. Although they sometimes result from accidents or mistakes in the heat of battle, they often result from prior decisions about what tactics to use. These decisions may then be written into rules of engagement or battle plans. Similar decisions may also be made to develop and use weapons that are inherently indiscriminate, such as cluster bombs and land mines. Though these actions are often wrong, they appear to be permitted or excused because of the way that the principle of double effect is generally understood. As long as killings and injuries are not intended, they are thought to pass an important moral test. Yet, this view is clearly too permissive. When people engage in or accept unintended killings that show callous disregard for their victims, it makes a mockery of their condemnations of terrorism.

In his discussion of double effect, Michael Walzer describes a tactic used by American forces in the Korean War. Summarizing an account by the British journalist Reginald Thompson, Walzer says that American ground troops would proceed into an area until they drew hostile fire. When this occurred, air attacks would be launched against the area from which the shots came. Only afterward would the troops move forward. Walzer writes:

This is the new technique of warfare, writes the British journalist … "the cautious advance, the enemy small fire, the halt, the close support air strike, artillery, the cautious advance, and so on." It is designed to save the lives of soldiers, and it may or may not have that effect. "It is certain that it kills civilian men, women, and children, indiscriminately and in great numbers, and destroys all that they have."[7]

While this tactic causes many foreseeable civilian deaths, none of them is directly intended. The intention is to kill enemy troops and save American

---

[5] Joshua Dressler, *Understanding Criminal Law*, 3rd edn (New York: Lexis Publishing, 2001), 513.
[6] Ibid., 513. For an analysis, see Samuel H. Pillsbury, *Judging Evil: Rethinking the Law of Murder and Manslaughter* (New York: New York University Press, 1998), chapter 9, "Crimes of Indifference."
[7] Walzer, *Just and Unjust Wars*, 154, quoting from Reginald Thompson, *Cry Korea* (London, 1951), 54, 142–3.

soldiers' lives. But the method is indiscriminate. The area attacked is likely to contain both enemy troops and civilians, and no steps are taken to discriminate between them.

While the tactic that Walzer criticizes does not intentionally target innocent people, it shows complete indifference toward them by firing indiscriminately into an area that they are likely to inhabit. The principle of double effect does not handle such cases properly, and, for this reason, it undermines just war theory's credibility as a basis for condemning terrorist acts. If people deplore terrorist acts because they kill innocent people but approve collateral damage attacks that are equally callous, we would wonder how much the deaths of civilians actually matter to these people.

A DEFENSE OF DOUBLE EFFECT

I have so far spoken as if the principle of double effect judges actions solely on the basis of whether a bad result was intended or not. This is an over-simplification, however. As A. J. Coates writes in rejecting this interpretation of double effect,

> it would be a gross and highly misleading simplification to equate the principle [of double effect] with the view that "it is the *intention* that informs the act that counts" … [To] reduce morality to a matter of intention is to suppress other essential elements to which the theory of double effect draws attention. Right intention is a necessary but not a sufficient condition, an important part but not the whole of moral action.[8]

Coates would no doubt challenge my claim that double effect could permit actions like the imaginary version of the September 11 attacks. Although he is right that the traditional principle of double effect contains additional criteria for evaluating actions, I will show that the versions of double effect that include these criteria are also too permissive and remain vulnerable to my criticism.

The principle of double effect was developed to evaluate actions that are aimed at producing a good effect but will foreseeably produce a bad effect as well. Double effect tells us that the action is wrong unless it can meet four conditions.

1. The action must be morally good or at least indifferent.
2. The agent may not positively will the bad effect.

---

[8] A. J. Coates, *The Ethics of War* (Manchester: Manchester University Press, 1997), 240–1. For debates about double effect, see P. A. Woodward, ed., *The Doctrine of Double Effect* (Notre Dame: University of Notre Dame Press, 2001).

3. The bad effect must not be the means for producing the good effect.
4. The good effect must be "proportionate to" the bad effect; that is, it must be sufficiently valuable to compensate for the bad effect.[9]

In order for double effect to condemn my imagined version of the September 11 attacks, the attack would have to fail to meet one or more of these criteria. I believe that the imagined attack can pass all of these tests and thus cannot be condemned by double effect.

APPLYING THE COMPLEX VERSION OF DOUBLE EFFECT

Condition 1 says that the action must be "morally good or at least indifferent." While we do not usually regard flying airplanes into crowded buildings as "good or indifferent," we know that in war buildings are routinely attacked and destroyed, and we think that such actions are sometimes permissible. If this is true, then this type of act is not inherently wrong.

If the attack was intended to kill innocent people in the building, then it would be inherently wrong because – in the view of traditional Catholic moral thought – intentionally killing innocent people is inherently wrong. In my imagined example, however, the aim of the attackers is to destroy buildings, not to kill innocent people. Condition 1, then, does not prohibit the attack.

What about condition 2, that the agent may not positively will the bad effect? This condition is met because, in the case I have described, the killing of innocent people is not intended and thus not "positively willed." Indeed, this condition is automatically met in all cases in which bad effects are side effects or collateral damage.

Condition 3 says that the bad effect must not be the means by which the good effect is produced. In terrorist attacks, innocent people are attacked in order to influence a broader audience and promote a political agenda. Because killing and injuring them is a means of achieving something, their deaths clearly are intended, and the terrorist attack violates condition 3. In collateral damage cases, however, the bad effect is not a means of achieving a goal. In my imaginary case, the attackers would have been

---

[9] Here I draw on the articles on double effect by F. J. Connell, "Double Effect, Principle of," in *New Catholic Encyclopedia*, 2nd edn (Detroit: Thomas Gale, 2003), vol. IV, 880–8, and William David Solomon, "Double Effect," in Lawrence and Charlotte Becker, eds., *Encyclopedia of Ethics*, 2nd edn (New York: Routledge, 2001), vol. I, 418–20.

content to damage or destroy the World Trade Center and the Pentagon even if these buildings had been empty of people. For this reason, the imaginary case satisfies condition 3.

Condition 4 is a proportionality test. It says that in order for an act to be permissible, its intended good effects must be sufficiently valuable to justify the unintended, bad effects that the act causes. Recall the highway example. If the benefits of building a highway are trivial and the highway's construction will lead to many traffic fatalities, it would be wrong to build the road. We commonly think that building highways is justified because we believe (perhaps unthinkingly) that the benefits of increased mobility for many people are sufficiently valuable to justify the bad effects. Similarly, in war, collateral damage killings and injuries are acceptable only if the military benefit of the attack that causes them is very substantial. The more civilian deaths and injuries that are expected, the higher the benefit has to be to justify the attack.

What does the proportionality requirement tell us about my imaginary version of the September 11 attacks? Someone might say that both the imagined attack and the real one fail the proportionality test because neither one produced any good at all. Even if the amount of harm that the attacks caused had been small, they would still be wrong because no good was achieved to offset it.

One thing to notice about this reply and about the proportionality requirement itself is that neither of them has anything to do with the distinction between intended and unintended consequences. One need not accept the principle of double effect in order to believe that it is wrong to create a great evil in order to produce a lesser good. So, if my imaginary case is wrong because of a failure of proportionality, its wrongness has nothing to do with the principle of double effect.

Second, recall that the *jus in bello* rules on how to fight a war are supposed to apply equally to all sides of a conflict. If one side has evil goals and another has good goals, this has no bearing on whether certain means of fighting are legitimate or not. Just war theory, then, is not generally understood in a way that makes it impossible for unjust fighters to satisfy the principle of proportionality. For this reason, the actual worthiness of the goals is not really relevant to whether an act satisfies the proportionality test.[10]

---

[10] Thomas Hurka challenges this view and argues that no actions by the unjust side in a war can meet the proportionality criterion because none of their actions do any good. See his "Proportionality in the Morality of War," *Philosophy and Public Affairs* 33 (2005), 36–9, 44–5.

One reason why the worthiness of the goals is not relevant is that in war and other conflicts, all sides think that they are fighting for valuable goals. We do not think that the September 11 attackers had a just cause, but Osama bin Ladin and others have explained why they felt justified in launching attacks on the United States and its allies.[11] Moreover, from Al Qaeda's perspective, the September 11 attacks were a success. Not only did they damage and destroy American buildings of great symbolic importance and temporarily paralyze important aspects of American society, they also succeeded in inducing the United States to initiate two difficult wars in Muslim countries. These wars increased support for Al Qaeda among many Muslims. From Al Qaeda's perspective, the attacks were a great victory whose gains may well have been great enough to satisfy the principle of proportionality.

Overall, then, if we use the complex version of double effect to evaluate the imaginary version of the September 11 attacks, we still get the result that these attacks are justified. If the planners of the September 11 attacks had wanted to comply with the principle of discrimination as it is interpreted in the light of the principle of double effect, they could have concluded that the attacks were permissible by reasoning in the following way:

1. Their aim was to damage or destroy buildings.
2. They did not intend to kill or injure innocent people.
3. Although they knew that large numbers of innocent people were likely to die as collateral damage, they believed that the attack was proportional because the gains for their cause would be large enough to offset the evils of the collateral damage.

With these beliefs as background, they could well conclude that their attacks met the requirements of the principle of double effect because they did not "directly" kill civilians. For this reason, the attacks did not violate the principle of discrimination and were in compliance with the *jus in bello* rules of just war theory.

My point in constructing these arguments is emphatically not to justify either the actual or the imaginary version of the September 11 attacks. I believe that both versions of the attack are wrong. My point is that just

---

[11] Bin Ladin, Osama, *et al.*, "Jihad Against Jews and Crusaders: World Islamic Front Statement," February 1998; http://www.fas.org/irp/world/para/docs/980223-fatwa.htm. Michael Scott Doran discusses the motivations for the September 11 attacks in "Somebody Else's Civil War: Ideology, Rage, and the Assault on America," in J. Hoge, Jr. and G. Rose, eds., *How Did This Happen? Terrorism and the New War* (New York: Public Affairs, 2001). For Islamic criticisms of the bin Ladin call for jihad, see Abdullah Saeed, "Jihad and Violence: Changing Understandings of Jihad Among Muslims," in Coady and O'Keefe, eds., *Terrorism and Justice*.

war theory's use of the principle of double effect makes the theory too permissive. It is a defect of just war theory that, while it can condemn the actual September 11 attacks, it cannot condemn an imaginary version which shows the very same indifference to killing innocent civilians.

CONCLUSION

In this chapter, I have tried to show that traditional just war theory fails to provide sufficient protection for civilians and lacks credibility for criticizing terrorism. While just war theory strongly forbids intentional attacks on civilians, it is too permissive with respect to collateral damage killings that are close cousins to terrorism. If the point of the principle of discrimination is to protect the lives of noncombatants, then it must be interpreted in a way that is more restrictive than the double effect interpretation.

In the chapters that follow, I will focus again on the question of whether intentional attacks on civilians can ever be justified. Only in part IV will I return to the difficult problem of collateral damage and ask what principles governing collateral damage attacks are restrictive enough to protect civilians while being permissive enough to allow for warfare.

Conclusion: categorical vs. conditional criticisms of terrorism

While terrorism has been widely condemned in the strongest, most categorical terms, we have seen that this judgment is not supported by standard approaches to the ethics of war. If we ask whether terrorism can ever be morally justified, we find a "yes" answer implicit in political realism, commonsense morality, Michael Walzer's theory, and utilitarianism. None of these views, however, gives a blanket permission to engage in terrorism. Each forbids and criticizes terrorism under some circumstances.

The chart below shows the conditions under which these views approve or disapprove of terrorist acts.

Theory	Conditions Under Which Attacking Civilians is Justified	Conditions Under Which Attacking Civilians is Not Justified
Realism	It promotes "our" national/group interests	It harms "our" national/group interests
Commonsense Morality	It helps us to win wars or minimize "our" casualties	It does not help us to win wars or minimize "our" casualties
Act Utilitarianism	It maximizes overall utility, perhaps by minimizing casualties or achieving valuable goals	It fails to maximize overall utility, perhaps by increasing casualties or failing to achieve valuable goals
Walzer's theory	In a supreme emergency when attacking civilians is a last resort and has some chance of success	In a war against an ordinary enemy or in supreme emergencies when there are alternatives to attacking civilians or doing so has no chance of success

Each view, then, provides criteria for condemning some terrorist acts, but none can categorically condemn them all. For this reason, people who hold these views cannot invoke what I will call "the simple argument against terrorism." The simple argument says: This is an act of terrorism; terrorism is always wrong; therefore, this act is wrong. None of these views can invoke this argument. Instead they will have to show that a particular terrorist act is not in our interests, is or is not a response to a supreme emergency, etc. No one who is committed to the simple argument against terrorism can look to these theories for support of the view that killing civilians intentionally is always wrong.

The key question is whether it is possible to justify noncombatant immunity as an absolute prohibition. According to these established views on the ethics of war, no reasonable morality will require an absolute prohibition on intentionally killing civilians, especially from people who face serious threats in a violent and often cruel world. My aim is to show that morality does prohibit all attacks on civilians and that the views I have discussed fail to show that this principle is misguided or unreasonable.

PART III

Defending noncombatant immunity

Introduction: the ethics of war-fighting: a spectrum of possible views

There are two central questions about the principle of noncombatant immunity. First, should we accept it at all? That is, should we believe that it is wrong to attack civilians? Second, if we do accept it, should we accept it as an absolute principle or as a principle that permits some justifiable exceptions? These questions focus on issues about who or what are permissible targets of attack. These are only some of the many questions that a full ethic of war will answer.

Some people may wonder whether it makes sense to apply ideas about the ethics of war to questions about terrorism. They may think it is not appropriate to apply ethical principles about warfare to violent attacks conducted by non-governmental groups. I have argued in several places (and will continue to do so) for the applicability of ethics of war principles to terrorist actions. One reason for this is that terrorist acts can be carried out by states as well as non-state groups. Another is that there are general problems about the ethics of violence, no matter who carries it out and what their reasons might be. The ethics of war between states is a subset of these broader issues. Nonetheless, when I speak of the ethics of war, I generally assume that the principles that are relevant to war apply to organized violence by governments and non-governmental groups alike, including the groups usually identified as terrorists.[1]

A SPECTRUM OF RULES

To this point, I have looked at noncombatant immunity from the perspective of various prominent theories. Another useful approach is to list a spectrum of possible rules that we might include in an ethic of war. Seeing the array of possible rules can help us to see individual principles in

---

[1] For a similar understanding, which is reflected in his book title, see Coady, *Morality and Political Violence*, 3ff.

perspective. The table below describes a variety of possible war-fighting principles and arranges them in order from the most permissive to the most restrictive.

Degree of Permissiveness/ Restrictiveness	Type of Theory or Principle	Possible *Jus in Bello* Rules
Most permissive	Extreme realism	Anything goes
	Moderate realism	Any attack that has military value is permissible
	Necessity	Any militarily necessary attack is permissible
	Proportionality	Any attack that is militarily valuable and whose negative effects are proportional to the positive value of the military goal is permissible
	Limited noncombatant immunity	Combatants may be attacked, but non-combatants may not be intentionally killed or injured unless doing so has significant military value
	Noncombatant immunity with a supreme emergency exception	Combatants may be attacked, but non-combatants may not be intentionally killed or injured except in supreme emergencies
	Strong noncombatant immunity	Combatants may be attacked, but non-combatants may not be intentionally killed or injured
Most restrictive	Pacifism	Neither combatants nor noncombatants may be intentionally killed or injured

LOOKING AT THE OPTIONS

Anything goes. This is the most permissive possible rule. I call it "extreme realism" because it places no constraints on what may be done by a nation at war, and the amoral realist view is sometimes understood in this way. This principle does not forbid anything. By implication, even acts that have no military value but are motivated by anger or hatred would be permissible under this rule.

Any attack that has military value is permissible. Although this rule is extremely permissive, it is more restrictive than its predecessor. It requires that an attack do some good from a military perspective. This restriction could be defended by appeal to prudence. Parties to a war should not waste their resources on destructive acts that have no military value. Seen in this way, this is not a moral principle. At the same time, accepting this rule might reflect some recognition of the humanity of an enemy and an acceptance of minimal duties toward members of the enemy group.[2] It could be accepted by someone who thought that it was morally wrong to harm enemies unless these harms produced some good result for one's own side. At the same time, because it permits any act that has military value, accepting this rule is cost-free from a military perspective.

Any militarily necessary attack is permissible. This rule is more restrictive than the prior one because it requires that attacks be necessary rather than merely valuable. Suppose, for example, that victory is near and that a large-scale attack that would inflict great casualties on the enemy might attain victory quickly. An alternative option is smaller-scale attacks that would cause few enemy casualties but would bring victory less quickly. In this case, the large-scale attack would satisfy the military value criterion but would not pass the necessity test. While the necessity rule forbids tactics that the military value criterion would allow, it is nonetheless extremely permissive since it allows any type of attack that is required for victory.

Any attack that is militarily valuable and whose negative effects are proportional to the positive value of the military goal is permissible. The proportionality requirement focuses on the relationship between the positive value of a military goal and the negative value of the harms inflicted to achieve it. It requires that the damage be proportionate to the gains. An attack that might be necessary for achieving a particular objective might still be wrong because it causes disproportionate damage. Utilitarianism is often identified with the proportionality requirement because it too calls for considering both the positive and negative effects of actions and requires that we reject actions whose positive effects are outweighed by their negative effects.

Because the proportionality requirement takes account of the losses incurred by the enemy, it reflects some regard for the well-being of the enemy and possibly a recognition of rights that they retain, even in war. It forbids "overkill," excessive damage in relation to the value of the military goal. This differs from the necessity criterion, which allows as much force as is necessary to achieve the goal but does not consider the relation of the goal's value to the damage done.

Combatants may be attacked, but noncombatants may not be intentionally killed or injured unless doing so has significant military value. This rule

---

[2] Larry May stresses the fundamental role of a principle of humane treatment in *War Crimes and Just War* (New York: Cambridge University Press, 2007).

imposes a more specific restraint than the proportionality rule. It is the first rule on the list that provides special protection for noncombatants. It does this by setting up a presumption against attacking them at all. This presumptive immunity does not absolutely bar attacks on civilians. It can be overridden if direct attacks on civilians would achieve significant military results.

Combatants may be attacked, but noncombatants may not be intentionally killed or injured except in supreme emergencies. This view, which plays a central role in Michael Walzer's theory, has the same structure as the previous rule. Both rules pick out civilians for special protection and thereby place a specific restriction on the targets of military attacks. In addition, both rules allow noncombatant immunity to be overridden. This rule, however, sets more stringent conditions on the circumstances under which attacks on civilians are permissible. Achieving a significant military objective is not enough. Instead, intentionally attacking civilians is permissible only in extreme emergencies, when countries face imminent defeat at the hands of an especially dangerous enemy and have no alternative means of defense.

Combatants may be attacked, but noncombatants may not be intentionally killed or injured. This view, which I call strong noncombatant immunity, is a strict, absolute prohibition. Noncombatants may not be the targets of attacks – period. Such attacks are prohibited by this rule even if they are militarily necessary, would achieve significant military gains, satisfy a proportionality test, or ward off a supreme emergency threat. Of the rules so far described, only this one prohibits all terrorist acts.

Neither combatants nor noncombatants may be intentionally killed or injured. Even the strongest noncombatant immunity principle permits attacks on enemy soldiers. Pacifists extend the restriction so that neither combatants nor noncombatants are permissible targets. As a result, none of the killing and injuring that occurs in war is morally permissible.

CONCLUSION

Each of these rules provides a distinct answer to the question "who may be the intended target of a military attack?" The first four say nothing explicit about the nature or status of an attack's victims. The second four impose some limits on attacks against civilians, but the constraints vary in strength. Only the "strong noncombatant immunity" and the pacifist view absolutely forbid attacks on civilians. Because pacifism imposes similar constraints on attacking combatants, it does not recognize a special status for noncombatants. Instead it simply bans any attacks on human beings, whether they be civilians or soldiers.

For people who are not pacifists but want to condemn all terrorist attacks, the "strong noncombatant immunity" view is the only option that accomplishes this purpose. In the following chapters, I will try to show why the "strong noncombatant immunity" rule should be accepted. Since this view is rejected by the theories I have discussed, I will begin my defense by returning to these theories. For each view, I will try to show that we should reject its case against strong noncombatant immunity. We should do so either because the theory as a whole is mistaken or because the specific arguments it offers against noncombatant immunity are flawed. In the case of utilitarianism, I will argue that rule utilitarianism actually supports strong noncombatant immunity.

CHAPTER 8

The realist challenge to the ethics of war

Realism is generally understood as the view that morality does not apply to the conduct of states, especially states at war. Some realists reject this interpretation, but even if (contrary to fact) no serious thinker ever held this version of realism, the idea expressed is powerful and strikes many people as plausible.[1]

The realist, "morality does not apply" view challenges the whole idea of an ethic of war. If it is correct, there can be no moral duty for countries and their leaders to accept noncombatant immunity. Or, if the only moral duty that nations and their leaders have is to pursue their own national interest, then there can be no duty to refrain from attacks on enemy civilians. From the realist perspective, terrorism and other attacks on civilians might be legitimate because anything goes so long as it is in the national interest.

Because of realism's influence, any serious attempt to defend noncombatant immunity or other restrictions on the conduct of war must begin by showing why the realistic perspective is defective. My aim is to show that, while realists have some insights, their inferences about the inapplicability of morality to war and international relations are mistaken.

WHY REALISM SEEMS ATTRACTIVE

Realism is generally seen as a tough-minded, no-nonsense perspective. By contrast, people who think that morality is relevant to war and international relations are often portrayed as naive idealists. Since no one wants to

[1] For the "morality does not apply" interpretation of realism, see Marshall Cohen, "Moral Skepticism and International Relations," in Charles Beitz *et al.*, eds., *International Ethics* (Princeton: Princeton University Press, 1985), 3–4; Holmes, *On War and Morality*, 56; Nigel Dower, *World Ethics* (Edinburgh: Edinburgh University Press, 1998), 18;. B. Coppieters and N. Fotion, eds., *Moral Constraints on War* (Lanham, Md.: Lexington Books, 2002), 1–2. David Hendrickson criticizes this interpretation in "In Defense of Realism," *Ethics and International Affairs* 11 (1997), 19–54; as does Robert Myers in "Hans Morgenthau's Realism and American Foreign Policy," *Ethics and International Affairs* 11 (1997), 253–70.

be seen as naive or unrealistic, there is a certain appeal to accepting the realist view. Realism gains added appeal because it cuts through the hypocritical moralizing that is so common in politics. Political leaders often invoke high moral values even while they ruthlessly pursue their own nation's interests or, perhaps, their own personal interests. Realists dispel the moralistic fog and expose what is actually happening. They may not offer an uplifting vision, but at least it seems free of hypocrisy.

Realism seems especially appealing in thinking about war, a violent struggle in which both the lives of individuals and the most vital interests of a nation may be at stake. In this context, it does not seem foolish to say "it's a nasty world, and we have to do whatever is necessary to take care of ourselves." If we accept this, then the prospect of people accepting noncombatant immunity will look like a pipe dream.

Although realism is identified with classic writers like Thucydides and Machiavelli as well as more recent thinkers in international relations, it is not merely an academic theory. Most people are familiar with the idea that morality takes a back seat when wars occur, and many people accept this idea, even if they wish it were not so. Realism extends this view more generally to international relations.

TERRORISM AND THE IMPLICATIONS OF REALISM

To see why realism is deeply flawed and provides no grounds for rejecting noncombatant immunity, it is worth recalling the power and plausibility of many moral denunciations of terrorist acts. The shock and moral outrage provoked by the September 11 attacks were deep, genuine, and expressed by people throughout the world. Had someone denied that the attacks were grievous wrongs, the denial would have reflected badly on whoever expressed it rather than casting doubt on the wrongness of the attacks. Moreover, if asked why the attacks were wrong, the most natural answer is that they killed innocent people.

I know of no realist thinker who spoke out after the September 11 attacks to say that moral condemnations of terrorism are misguided or naive. Yet, realists could not honestly join in these moral condemnations. Honest realists must say either that morality does not apply to terrorist attacks or that such attacks are only wrong if they harm the national interest.[2]

---

[2] Jack Donnelly describes how discomfort with these types of implications leads some realists to amend their views in "Twentieth-Century Realism," 96–7.

Because amoral realists evaluate such acts only from the perspective of interests, they could say that the September 11 attacks harmed the interests of the United States and benefited the interests of Al Qaeda, but they could not say that they were morally wrong. People who hold the moralized version of realism would, in fact, have to go farther and say that there is a moral duty to engage in terrorist acts if they would promote the national interest. They are committed to this conclusion because the moralized realist view evaluates all actions from the point of view of their own national self-interest.

Taking this point of view, however, leads to odd results. It implies that what made the September 11 attacks wrong was the fact that they damaged the national interests of the United States. This perspective allows US citizens to condemn the September 11 attacks, but the basis on which it does this is entirely self-centered. It is not a basis for moral judgment that we could expect other people to use. It would be absurd for Norwegians, Bolivians, Australians, Tanzanians, or Malaysians to use the interests of the United States as their sole standard for evaluating these actions.

An apparently more reasonable approach might recognize that every nation or group would use its own interests as the moral basis for evaluation, but this also yields an unappealing outcome. The problem with this interest-based moral criterion is that it implies that the moral status of terrorist acts depends on the interests of whoever is judging them. If we assume that groups that use terrorism generally do so because they believe it will benefit them, then this view requires us to say that terrorist acts are right for those people whose interests they promote and wrong for those whose interests are harmed.

This paradoxical evaluation of acts as both right and wrong may be the reason why some people move from moralized realism to amoral realism. When we use the national interest as a moral standard, we are led to the view that the same action can be both morally right and morally wrong. Since this seems absurd, some people may think it more reasonable to believe that these acts are neither right nor wrong and that moral judgments of them simply don't make sense.

The lesson is that realists have a hard time making sense of moral condemnations of terrorism. As a result, they are unable to judge any terrorist acts morally and must reject widely held, plausible moral judgments about terrible acts of violence. The more confident we are that terrorist acts (as well as acts of genocide, torture, enslavement, and other abuses) can be genuinely wrong, the more confident we will be that realism is false.

THE ILLUSORY PLAUSIBILITY OF REALISM

If it seems absurd to deny that certain horrible acts are genuinely immoral, why does realism seem so plausible? One reason is that it is easy to confuse certain reasonable views about morality and the national interest with realism's unreasonable views about them. Realism sounds reasonable because it is easy to confuse it with certain commonsense moral beliefs that differ substantially from realism. Commonsense morality contains the view that *political leaders have a duty to consider the national interest when making judgments about national policy.* Realism contains the similar-sounding but radically different view that *political leaders have a duty to consider NOTHING BUT the national interest when making judgments about national policy.*

Similarly, commonsense morality says that *national leaders have a moral duty to promote the interests of their own countries and its citizens.* Moralized realism transforms this into the view that *national leaders have an EXCLUSIVE moral duty to promote the interests of their own countries and its citizens.* While almost no one denies that rulers have a duty to promote the national interest, that commonsense view differs from the idea that the sole moral duty of leaders is to promote the national interest.[3]

Commonsense morality	Political realism
In making judgments about national policy, leaders have a duty to consider the national interest.	In making judgments about national policy, leaders have a duty to consider *nothing but* the national interest.
National leaders have a moral duty to promote the interests of their own countries.	National leaders have *an exclusive* moral duty to promote the interests of their own countries.

These pairs of statements look and sound similar but are radically different. Most people would reasonably accept the statements in the left column, but if they fail to see that they differ from the statements in the right column, they will mistakenly take realism to be a reasonable view.

By asserting that the national interest is the only thing that matters, realism instructs leaders and citizens to evaluate actions and policies by their effects on the national interest and on nothing else. This is the stuff out of

---

[3] For the contrast between exclusive and non-exclusive forms of national concern, see my *Patriotism, Morality, and Peace.*

which fanatical nationalism is made. It is the same attitude found in groups that engage in terrorist actions. They, too, think that the only thing that matters is the interests of their group or political cause.[4]

By contrast, commonsense morality denies that the national interest is the only thing that matters morally. Even if there is a primary duty to one's own nation and its interests, there are still secondary duties to citizens of other countries. In a similar way, while parents no doubt have primary duties to their own children, that does not mean that they have no moral duties to other children. All of us recognize that it would be wrong for parents to kill or injure other children simply to benefit their own.

The difference between these two views is extremely important from the perspective of the ethics of war. If there are moral constraints on the means by which wars are fought, these constraints consist in duties to members of the enemy nation. For example, the duty not to kill prisoners of war is the recognition of a limit on the permission to kill in warfare; it is a duty to members of the enemy force in spite of the fact that they are the enemy. If the realist claim is true, however, then there can be no moral duty to refrain from killing prisoners of war. Likewise, noncombatant immunity is a moral duty to civilian members of an enemy nation, and the basis for this duty is that these are human beings whose rights and interests must be considered in our deliberations about how we should act.

Once we distinguish exclusive, fanatical promotion of one's nation's interests from reasonable dedication to the national interest, we can allow that in international relations, and certainly in war, it is permissible for people to give a reasonable degree of priority to their own country's interests. This degree of partiality toward our own nation, however, is compatible with giving other people a proper level of human consideration.

WHY REALISTS GO ASTRAY

Realism, as I have described it, is a prescriptive view. It tells us that nations should base their policies on their own interests alone. This prescription about how nations ought to act is rooted in a descriptive view about how nations actually do act. According to this descriptive view, nations act solely in their own collective interests. The prescription is supposed to follow from this. In a "dog eat dog" world, no individual dog has moral obligations to consider the interests of the others.

---

[4] Aleksandr Pavkovic discusses this in "Towards Liberation," 58–71.

In its extreme form, the realist's description says that no nation ever acts to promote the interests of others. This is implausible.[5] Surely nations and other groups sometimes respond to the needs and interests of others, even when doing so does not advance their own interests. Helpful responses to natural disasters, for example, are instances where the motivation often appears to be humanitarian. The same seems to be true of some cases in which diplomatic efforts or even wars of intervention are motivated by a desire to protect people from being harmed by their own government or by warring groups within their country.

Nonetheless, the realist description, though not true in every instance, makes an important point. On the whole, nations – like individuals – are strongly motivated by what they perceive to be their own interests, and their behavior is often aimed at promoting their interests. Moreover, realists are surely right that public officials have a strong duty to act in the interests of the people they represent. There would be something wrong with national leaders who felt no special duty to promote the interests of their own countries and used political office primarily to advance the interests of others.

Unfortunately, realists draw mistaken conclusions from these plausible points. They believe that we face an either/or choice between interest-based policies and morality-based policies. Leaders, on this view, must choose between acting for their own country or acting for others.

WHEN INTERESTS AND MORALITY CONVERGE

The most important error in this view is that it overlooks the fact that morality and self-interest often converge. It is generally in the interests of people of all nations, for example, that aggressive war be seen as immoral. A world without aggressive war would almost always be better for everyone than a world in which aggressive wars are permitted. No one has an interest in being attacked, and for this reason, every nation has an interest in other nations accepting the rule "do not engage in non-defensive, unprovoked attacks on others."

This argument is based on Hobbes's insight that individuals have a strong interest in forsaking the "state of nature," a situation of total liberty in which there is no government, no morality, and in which individuals have unconstrained rights to promote their interests. The result is so bad for

[5] For a more complex account of moral motivations in international affairs by a realist, see Hans Morgenthau, *Politics Among Nations: The Struggle for Power and Peace*, 2nd edn (New York: Alfred A. Knopf, 1954), chapter 16, "International Morality." For criticisms of both the prescriptive and descriptive versions of realism, see Brian Orend, *The Morality of War* (Peterborough, Ontario: Broadview Press, 2006), chapter 8.

all that Hobbes thought it rational for people to give up some freedom for the sake of security and to accept a system of laws that limits everyone's freedom. Each of us agrees not to kill or steal in exchange for everyone else accepting the same constraints on their behavior. Beginning with our own interests, we come to see that moral and legal limits on what we can do to others are rational to accept.[6]

This is not to deny that morality and self-interest can and do conflict with one another. Since the time of Plato, philosophers have recognized the difference between the desirability of everyone else behaving morally and the desirability of acting morally oneself.[7] Nonetheless, for most people most of the time, their interests are supported by the existence of a moral code that requires some respect for the interests of others. To the extent that the realist view suggests otherwise, it is mistaken.

Realists also exaggerate the contrast between morality and self-interest in another way. Morality does not generally require extreme altruism or a lack of concern about oneself or one's own group. It does not require either individuals, nations, or other groups to forsake the pursuit of their own interests. At the international level, morality does not prevent nations from acting self-interestedly, but it does impose constraints on how this is done. Realists are certainly right that there are sometimes painful conflicts between morality and the national self-interest, but they fail to recognize that morality can enhance the national interest as well.

MORALITY VS. MORALISM

Although realists are wrong to reject morality, they are right that an excessive focus on moral ideals can have damaging effects. Their criticisms of morality, however, often fail to distinguish morality from moralism.[8] Moralism is the tendency to focus excessively on moral values as causes of conflict and to appeal to simplistic moral arguments as justifications for policy.

Morality degenerates into moralism when interests and pragmatic concerns are ignored in understanding the actions of other nations and groups. When the interests of adversaries are ignored, the idea emerges that our conflicts with them exist solely because they are evil or committed to an evil ideology. By ignoring interests and automatically attributing evil motives to adversaries, a moralistic perspective keeps people from seeing the legitimate

---

[6] Hobbes's central arguments are in *Leviathan*, part 1, chapters 13, 14, and 17.
[7] This is the point of the story of Gyges in Plato's *Republic*, book 1.
[8] Marshall Cohen uses these terms to make a different anti-realist argument in "Moral Skepticism and International Relations," 6–9.

interests of others and suggests that force alone can resolve conflicts. As a result, moralists may miss the chance to use peaceful means of dealing with conflicting but legitimate interests.

Moralism also blinds people to the role played by one's own interests in motivating national policy. *We* are seen as motivated by the highest values while *they* are seen as purely evil. Just as moralistic explanations ignore the interests that others may be defending, so they may ignore the ways in which one's own motivations may be less lofty than the moral ideals that are invoked to justify actions and policies.[9]

When moralism eclipses attention to interests, people often lose sight of vitally relevant practical factors of exactly the sort that realists emphasize. Advocates of the 2003 United States attack on Iraq, for example, cited the lofty goals of overthrowing a ruthless dictator and spreading democracy. Realists might remind us, however, that occupying and running a country is no easy task, that it might be costly in both lives and money, and that high ideals are not enough to assure success.

Even when realists raise important points, however, their understanding of morality is flawed. In contrasting morality and interests, they suggest that caring about whether goals are achievable and whether the costs of achieving them are excessive does not matter morally. But these factors are as important from the perspective of morality as they are from the perspective of self-interest. When we know that people will kill and die, injure and be injured in a war, it is morally essential to know both what the prospects of success are and what are the likely costs of such an effort. Morality forbids frittering away things of great value in pursuit of ends that may not be achievable. While realists and others often assume that practical considerations play no role in moral deliberation, a sensible moral perspective will never overlook them.

Realists, then, are wise to criticize moralism but wrong to think that this critique undermines the view that morality applies to nations as well as individuals. In fact, by rejecting morality, realism rejects valuable moral constraints and may encourage leaders to engage in the unconstrained, reckless pursuit of national goals.

LEGITIMATE AUTHORITY: A REALIST OBJECTION

While I have argued that realism makes the moral criticism of terrorism impossible, realists might respond to this criticism by appealing to the view of Bruce Hoffman and others that violent acts are instances of terrorism only when

---

[9] David Hendrickson notes the dangers of a moralistic approach in "In Defense of Realism," 35–7.

they are carried out by non-governmental groups. With this definitional claim in mind, realists might argue that their theory applies only to the behavior of nations and governments and that they can condemn terrorism because terrorism is carried out by non-governmental groups. Thus, when realists say that international relations are governed by interests alone and not by morality, they are describing interactions *between nations*. They are not talking about non-governmental groups like Al Qaeda, the Tamil Tigers, the IRA, and others.

These groups (and the individuals who compose them), realists could argue, are bound by morality because they are not states. Unlike governments, they lack the authority to engage in political violence. Members of these groups are simply criminals and have neither a legal right nor a moral right to use violence in the way that governments are authorized to do. According to this argument, realism does not stand in the way of criticizing terrorism. Realists can condemn terrorist acts like the September 11 attacks or the Madrid railway bombings because they were carried out by non-governmental groups rather than governments.

This response is weak because it misidentifies the reasons for the widespread condemnation of terrorist acts. This condemnation has very little to do with whether these acts are carried out by states or non-state groups. If we discovered that the September 11 attacks were actually carried out by governmental covert forces, we would not suddenly change our view and think that our condemnation of the attacks had been mistaken.

Even if we agree to apply the word "terrorism" only to attacks carried out by non-governmental groups and call similar attacks by governments by another name (such as "civilian victimization"), this should have no impact on our moral evaluations of these acts. If we found out that the September 11 attacks were carried out by governmental forces and agreed to classify them as "civilian victimization," we would still condemn them as morally wrong. Realists, faced with a change of view about the perpetrators of these attacks, would have to alter their moral evaluation of them. They would have to say that they had mistakenly condemned these acts as immoral, thinking that they were carried out by "non-state actors." Having learned that they were carried out by a government, realists would have to say that the attacks were neither morally right nor morally wrong. I find it hard to believe that this response could enhance the credibility of the realist view.

THE LEGITIMATE AUTHORITY TO WAGE WAR

There are additional problems with this defense of realism. Central to the defense is a recognition of the authority of states to use violence for political purposes and a denial of that authority to non-state groups.[10] This recognition of state authority as legitimate, however, implicitly makes a moral claim and is thus inconsistent with realism's rejection of morality. Moreover, there is no reason to think that all states have legitimate authority or that all non-state groups lack it.

Anyone who believes that there can be morally legitimate political revolutions must reject the idea that governments alone have legitimate authority and that non-state groups never have this authority. The common view that the American Revolution was morally justified presupposes that the colonists had a legitimate right to use violence to end British rule. The story, as told in the Declaration of Independence, is that the British government had possessed legitimate authority to rule the American colonies but gradually lost its legitimacy through persistently unfair, unreasonable policies. The Declaration's list of a long "train of abuses and usurpations" by the British government is meant to provide the evidence to establish that Britain had lost the legitimate authority to rule the colonies. As a result of this loss, the colonists claimed that they themselves now possessed the legitimate authority to rebel, to rule themselves, and to fight to enforce their claims. When they made these claims, the signers were "non-state" actors.

Anyone who agrees with the Declaration's assertions must accept two points: first, that established governments can lack legitimate authority and second, that non-governmental groups can acquire legitimate authority when they can reasonably claim to speak for the members of their society.[11] Yet the realist objection assumes that legitimacy always belongs to governments in power. As a result, realists implicitly grant a kind of moral authority to governments that they deny to non-state groups. When realists make judgments about the possession of legitimate authority, these are either moral judgments or functionally equivalent to them.

LIMITS ON LEGITIMATE AUTHORITY

Even if governments or other groups have legitimate authority to use violence against enemies, this does not mean that they have unlimited authority to do whatever is in their power. The moral authority to use

---

[10] One need not be a realist to see legitimate authority as relevant to the justification of terrorism. For a discussion of this by a non-realist, see McPherson, "Is Terrorism Distinctively Wrong?," 524–46.

[11] For defenses of the view that non-governmental groups may possess legitimate authority, see Bruno Coppieters, "Legitimate Authority," in Coppieters and Fotion, eds., *Moral Constraints on War*; Steinhoff, *On the Ethics of War and Terrorism*, chapter 1.

power is always limited. A police officer has the authority to carry and use a weapon to enforce the law but not to use the weapon against a personal enemy. A teacher has the authority to assign grades to students but not to base grades on a student's religion, race, or willingness to pay for them. These types of moral and legal limits apply to all officials, including those in the military and those at the highest levels of government.

Advocates of noncombatant immunity grant to legitimate governments the right to engage in wars of defense, but they deny that "anything goes" in the government's pursuit of victory in war. The principle of noncombatant immunity is a "side constraint" that limits the ways in which countries at war may pursue victory. Even if people are pursuing victory in a just war and have a clear right to fight, they may not attack civilians as a means to achieving victory.[12]

A full ethic of war would make clear what may be done in fighting and what is prohibited. Whatever constraints it contains will apply to governments and will also apply to non-governmental groups. In certain circumstances, non-state groups may have a right to use force on behalf of those they represent, but they too are morally limited in the tactics they may use. Even if insurgent or revolutionary groups have a just cause and legitimately represent others, that authority does not include a right to use terrorist tactics that kill and injure innocent people.

The bottom line is that realists are wrong to think that actions of government should be viewed completely differently from the actions of non-governmental groups. Both are bound by principles of morality that limit what they may do to achieve their goals.

CONCLUSION

Although realism is an influential view whose power often undermines confidence in moral judgments about the conduct of war, its radical challenge to an ethic of war rests on confusions. Refuting realism is not sufficient for establishing noncombatant immunity, but it is an important step in that direction because it shows that there are legitimate questions about what actions are morally permissible in war.

---

[12] The term "side constraints" comes from Robert Nozick, *Anarchy, State, and Utopia* (New York: Basic Books, 1973).

CHAPTER 9

An ethic of war for reasonable realists

Having tried to show that there are good reasons to reject the realist's rejection of morality, I want to look at the question of what rules a realist should accept for evaluating conduct in war. I raise this question for a few reasons. First, addressing it is in part a fall-back strategy that is aimed at unrepentant realists who are not swayed by arguments for rejecting realism altogether. Second, addressing this question is a helpful way to begin the transition from an "anything goes" view that focuses exclusively on the national interest to a more restrictive ethic of war that recognizes broader moral duties.

In the chart below, I identify two forms of realism and associate them with the principles "anything goes" and "any attack that has military value is permissible." The necessity view is also associated with realism. I will try to show that reasonable realists will reject these three views and accept the constraints that are supported by the principle of proportionality.

Degree of Permissiveness/ Restrictiveness	Type of Theory	Possible *Jus in Bello* Rules
Most Permissive	Extreme realism	Anything goes.
	Realism	Any attack that has military value is permissible.
	Necessity	Any militarily necessary attack is permissible
	Proportionality	Any attack that is militarily valuable and whose negative effects are proportional to the value of the aim is permissible.

If "anything goes" seems too extreme a view to attribute to realists, it is worth recalling that realists often describe the international realm as a Hobbesian state of nature, and Hobbes characterized this state by saying that "The notions of Right and Wrong, Justice and Injustice have there no place."[1] "Anything goes" is clearly the message of amoral realism because it recognizes no moral constraints on national behavior, while moralized realists are committed to the rule that "anything goes that is in the national interest."[2]

Given these realist views, it might seem that there is no more to be said about where realists should stand on an ethic for the conduct of war. I believe, however, that if we begin with a moral perspective that is not unduly demanding, we can show that reasonable realists should reject the first three views on the chart and accept the proportionality rule, which permits attacks that are *militarily valuable and whose negative effects are proportional to the value of the aim.*

Obviously, accepting the proportionality principle means giving up beliefs that are often seen to be at the heart of realism. Why should realists revise their views about morality, war, and international relations? First, as I have tried to show, because their views rest on confusions that lead them to adopt much more extreme views than they have to. Second, because realists can acknowledge moral limits on the means of fighting wars while still endorsing a primary concern with a nation's interest. In "In Defense of Realism," David Hendrickson describes realism in just this way and approvingly quotes Montesquieu's statement that "nations should do to one another in times of peace the most good possible, and in times of war the least ill possible, without harming their true interests."[3]

Once we distinguish between exclusive, fanatical dedication to the national interest and a reasonable dedication to the national interest, we can allow that in international relations and certainly in war, it is permissible for people to give a reasonable degree of priority to their own country's interests while still giving people in other nations their proper due. The challenge, of course, is to identify what "proper due" means. Here I will interpret it as minimally as possible so that my arguments will stand a chance of persuading people who feel a very strong priority for their own country but are open to reason and to recognizing the humanity of other people. The argument will not take realists all the way to noncombatant

---

[1] Thomas Hobbes, *Leviathan*, I, XIII.
[2] For a self described realist who rejects this characterization, see Hendrickson, "In Defense of Realism."
[3] Ibid., 22.

immunity, but it will further weaken the view that morality should play no role in the conduct of war and international relations.

"Anything goes" is obviously the most permissive rule possible since it places no constraints on what leaders or nations may do. To see why it is unreasonable, the first thing to notice is that it has no linkage with the national interest. While "anything goes" permits countries to kill and injure people even on a whim, appeals to national interest justify such actions only when they have a beneficial effect on the nation. In an "anything goes" world, there is no distinction between gratuitously inflicting harm and inflicting harm to achieve a positive goal. If "anything goes," then people in other countries have no moral standing and count for nothing in our deliberations. We may harm them even if it does us no good. In the context of war, "anything goes" allows the infliction of suffering that has no military value and makes no contribution to victory. It is hard to see how one could claim this to be a reasonable principle.

A more reasonable rule of war that realists can accept is that it is permissible to engage in attacks that have military value. Although this rule is considerably more restrictive than "anything goes," it imposes no limits on actions that might be useful in warfare. It does, however, make the permissibility of actions conditional. It is only if harmful actions have military value that they may be done. If actions that harm others fail to satisfy this condition, they are not justified and ought not to be done. Accepting this requirement, however, does nothing to impede a country's ability to fight effectively or achieve victory. There is, therefore, no reason why people who are concerned about their own country's interests should reject it.

Unlike "anything goes," the "military value" rule recognizes a presumption against harming members of the enemy group. If reasonable realists reject useless violence against the enemy, it must be because they see that these people are human beings like themselves and have some moral standing. For this reason, they may not be harmed gratuitously. Although the "military value" requirement is a very weak constraint on war-fighting, it is significant because it acknowledges the possession by the enemy of rights and claims on us, in spite of the fact that they are outsiders with whom we are at war. At the same time, because the "military value" rule permits any action that is useful in war, there is no reason for a realist to reject it.

FROM MILITARY VALUE TO MILITARY NECESSITY

The term "military necessity" has different meanings. I use it to highlight the fact that not every action with military value is necessary. Thus, if realists want to defend the legitimacy of doing whatever is necessary to defend the national interest, they should agree that, if some actions have military value but are not necessary for victory, they ought not to be taken.

The kind of case I have in mind is this. Imagine that an army can reach a military objective by going through a small city. Perhaps this is the shortest route to their destination. If they go through the city, however, they are likely to provoke resistance, and the chances are high that civilians will be killed and parts of the city destroyed. Still, something of military value will be achieved because the attacking army will reach its objective as quickly as possible.

Suppose, however, that there is an alternate route that avoids populated areas. While the alternate route is longer, taking it will neither diminish the army's chances of achieving its military goal nor increase the risk to its own troops. It will, however, diminish the likely harms to enemy civilians. Because an alternative exists, the first strategy is not militarily necessary even though it has military value. While the military value rule permits either attack, the military necessity rule does not. Choosing the first strategy would not be justified because the additional harm to the city and its inhabitants would not be necessary.

Although the necessity rule is more restrictive than the military value rule, it permits anything that is necessary for victory and thus would not interfere with the attempt to win the war. There is, therefore, no reason for people concerned about the national interest to reject it. Even the most minimal consideration for potential victims would require that unnecessary damage be avoided, and this can be done at no sacrifice of the interests of the attacking nation.

FROM NECESSITY TO PROPORTIONALITY

If reasonable realists accept the limits imposed by the necessity rule, then there is an equally good reason for them to accept a proportionality rule. Suppose there is a military objective that has some value and that the necessary means of achieving the objective involve many enemy casualties and large-scale destruction of resources that have no military value. The necessity rule would permit this attack because it is necessary to achieve the objective.

Suppose, however, that the military value of the objective is small. If so, one might think that the attack is wrong because the benefits do not outweigh the damage caused by the attack. This judgment appeals to a proportionality rule that says that *any attack that is militarily valuable and whose negative effects are proportional to the value of the aim is permissible.* This principle would forbid this attack because the harms inflicted are disproportionately large by comparison with the military value of the goal.

To see why a reasonable realist would accept the proportionality requirement, consider the following case. Suppose there is a sniper in a village. It would be valuable to kill the sniper, but the sniper is clever and hard to find. It would be possible to kill the sniper by bombing the whole village, but this would result in many deaths and great destruction. If this is the only feasible strategy for achieving this goal, the bombing of the village could be described as both valuable and necessary. Nonetheless, the damage required appears to be disproportionate to the value of the objective.

One reason why a reasonable realist might accept the proportionality rule emerges if we consider both what it means for something to be necessary and what it means for an objective to have only a small value. In attributing small value to the objective, we are saying that it makes a small contribution to victory. In saying this, we mean that its contribution to victory is very small and that achieving the objective is not necessary for victory. In my first description, "necessity" meant necessary to achieve the objective. This claim appeals to a second type of necessity. In the last section, the focus was on whether a particular attack was a necessary *means* to achieve a particular military objective. "Necessity," then, is ambiguous. It can refer to something's being necessary to achieve an objective (such as killing the sniper), or it can refer to a specific objective being necessary for victory.

In the case of the sniper, we can ask how important it is to kill the sniper and gain control of the village. If gaining control of the village is not important, then the objective of killing the sniper has small value. One can forsake it without loss to one's prospects for victory. In this case, a reasonable realist could accept the verdict of the proportionality rule. This would reflect a willingness to make some small sacrifices to the national interest in order to avoid a large negative impact on the people in the enemy village.

Suppose, however, that control of the village is important and that not killing the sniper will impose large costs to one's own war effort. Or, to put the point more abstractly, suppose that the military objective has very high value and that the only way to achieve it is with very high casualties among the enemy population. In this situation, the proportionality rule does not forbid the bombing. The greater the value of the objective, the greater the destruction and harm that is permitted by the proportionality principle. When there is a pressing need to achieve a military objective, the proportionality rule does not forbid even very destructive attacks.

If this is the case, then the reasonable realist can accept the proportionality rule because it forbids very destructive attacks only when their aim is to achieve low-value objectives. When the value of the objectives is great, proportionality permits high levels of destruction.

There is reason to think, then, that people with strong concerns for the national interest can accept the proportionality rule because it does not require their armies to forgo important gains. It tells them only that it should apportion the destructiveness of its attacks to the importance of its military objectives. Thus, even though the proportionality rule is more restrictive than the previous rules, it still imposes no absolute bans on the types of tactics used or the destruction that they cause.

FURTHER REASONS FOR ACCEPTING CONSTRAINTS ON THE WAGING OF WAR

Although realists often argue against any moral constraints on the conduct of war, I have argued that they can support some constraints without sacrificing any significant freedom of action. There are additional reasons why reasonable realists should accept limits on the use of destructive power in war. The first is that agreed-upon limits on war-fighting can be beneficial to their own national interest. In some cases, nations accept constraints in order to get other nations to accept them. If particular constraints are mutually beneficial, accepting them on condition that the others do so is clearly worthwhile. It diminishes the costs of war to all involved.

A second reason why realists should accept constraints on the conduct of war arises from the problems of knowing what is actually in the national interest and the often poor track record of leaders in determining this. While people often defend actions related to war by invoking the national interest, these appeals to national interest can actually refer to three distinct things:

1. what *actually* promotes the national interest;
2. what national leaders *believe* promotes the national interest; and
3. what national leaders *say* promotes the national interest.

Realists often speak as if leaders know what is in the national interest. What drives actual policies, however, is what leaders believe is in the national interest and what they tell citizens is in the national interest.

Once we distinguish the national interest itself from leaders' beliefs about it, we can see that there is a problem of *fallibility*. Even if we agree on which goals are in the national interest, knowing which actions or policies promote those goals is often difficult. Wars are frequently entered into because of predictions that they will enhance the national interest, and tactics in war are employed because of predictions that they will make victory more probable. Often, these judgments are based on unfounded views. Wars that are started with expectations of quick victory bog down into stalemate, and destructive tactics that are used to achieve victory fail to do so and only escalate the level of violence for all.

Beyond this, there are problems of *truthfulness*. Leaders often say that war and the tactics of war are in the national interest in order to gain support for themselves and their policies. In these high-stakes situations, there are often strong incentives for presenting false information and making unfounded predictions. Leaders say that if their policy is not followed, disaster will occur, while if their policy is followed, all will be well. Often they have no evidence to support their claims, and frequently what evidence is available suggests that their claims are false.

While realists often talk as if international affairs are driven by the rational pursuit of national self-interest, this is false. Hans Morgenthau, an influential twentieth-century realist, conceded that

the contingent elements of personality, prejudice, and subjective preference, and of all the weaknesses of intellect and will which flesh is heir to, are bound to deflect foreign policies from their rational course.[4]

Having cited sources of fallibility, Morgenthau also recognizes problems of truthfulness:

Especially where foreign policy is conducted under conditions of democratic control, the need to marshal public emotions to the support of foreign policy cannot fail to impair the rationality of foreign policy itself.[5]

If a public cannot be counted on to support rational policies, then national leaders will give them false information or use emotive, inflammatory messages, whichever is required for gaining or sustaining support for a policy.

These difficulties in knowing the genuine interests of a nation or group raise serious problems, not just for realists but for anyone concerned about acting well, whether it be in the pursuit of the national interest or the

---

[4] Morgenthau, *Politics Among Nations*, 7. [5] Ibid.

interests of a global human community. But these issues pose special problems for realists because they claim to know how to manage international affairs in a rational way and do not want to be deflected by morality and other factors that they regard as subjective or emotional.

Given the high degree of uncertainty in predicting outcomes, the moral of the story is that we should be very cautious in our approval and use of violent methods. We should be cautious about entering wars, and during a war, when violence is inevitable, we should not easily succumb to the illusion that unconstrained warfare is in our own interest. Escalation in wars often increases casualties to one's own troops as well as a legacy of suffering for families and friends of those who serve in the military. In addition, it often increases suffering among enemy populations without any serious benefit to the country inflicting the suffering. The short-term effects of violence are the ones that are most easily predicted. The long-term political results are the most difficult, and we should factor in these uncertainties whenever we evaluate war-related policies and tactics. As a result, great caution should be exercised in deciding that the infliction of harm and suffering on others is in the national interest.

CONCLUSION

I have tried to show that reasonable realists will accept some moral obligations to other countries and peoples. By thinking that the pursuit of the national interest requires a rejection of morality, realists have failed to see that moral constraints on warfare are worth respecting in their own right and can sometimes be accepted without sacrificing the national interest.

While I have argued that there is no sacrifice entailed in the move from "anything goes" to a proportionality rule on war-fighting, I cannot make that claim about accepting noncombatant immunity. Acceptance of stronger constraints might require sacrifices for a nation or people, and these sacrifices may be both morally right and detrimental to the national interest.

If realists were correct that morality did not apply to warfare, there obviously could be no serious case for noncombatant immunity. That is why it is important to see that the realist challenge to morality in war is much weaker than is often thought.

CHAPTER 10

Walzer on noncombatant immunity as a human right

We generally assume that most people don't have to be convinced that other people – including those who are not citizens of our own country – matter morally. That is why the phrase "human rights" resonates so strongly. The belief that every person has some claim to decent treatment, no matter what society they belong to, is part of the humanitarian strand of commonsense morality, and I appealed to it in my effort to move reasonable realists from "anything goes" to proportionality as a criterion for justified acts of war.

My challenge now is to justify moving beyond proportionality to rules that explicitly recognize noncombatant immunity from deliberate attacks. Even if I succeed, there will still be questions about the strength of noncombatant immunity. Is it merely a weak presumption against attacking civilians that allows attacks when they yield some significant military value? Is it a stronger prohibition that permits attacks on civilians only in very extreme cases? Or, is noncombatant immunity an absolute prohibition that bars attacks on civilians under any circumstances?

WALZER ON NONCOMBATANT IMMUNITY

I will begin my discussion of these questions by considering Michael Walzer's treatment of them in *Just and Unjust Wars*.[1] This is a good starting place because Walzer asks and answers both these questions and others that I discuss. One of Walzer's central goals in *Just and Unjust Wars* is to defend the principle of noncombatant immunity. In addition, Walzer discusses terrorism and appeals to the principle of noncombatant immunity to condemn terrorism in the strongest terms.

Walzer not only affirms noncombatant immunity, he also tries to provide it with a firm philosophical basis. Prior to developing his own view, Walzer considers whether a utilitarian approach to the ethics of war might be useful.

[1] Walzer, *Just and Unjust Wars*.

His verdict is that utilitarianism cannot provide a strong basis for supporting protections for civilians. Walzer's view is that the strongest case for noncombatant immunity must appeal to fundamental human rights that are possessed by all people.

To set Walzer's discussion in the context of the array of possible *jus in bello* rules, I will explain how he first moves from the proportionality principle (which he identifies with utilitarianism) to strong noncombatant immunity and then moves back to a form of noncombatant immunity that allows exceptions in the extreme circumstance that he calls a supreme emergency.

Type of Theory	Possible *Jus in Bello* Rules
Proportionality	Any attack that is militarily valuable and whose negative effects are proportional to the value of the aim is permissible.
Weak noncombatant immunity	Combatants may be attacked. Noncombatants may not be intentionally killed or injured unless doing so has significant military value.
Noncombatant immunity with a supreme emergency exception	Combatants may be attacked. Noncombatants may not be intentionally killed or injured except in supreme emergencies.
Strong noncombatant immunity	Combatants may be attacked, but noncombatants may not be intentionally killed or injured.

WALZER'S REJECTION OF PROPORTIONALITY AND UTILITARIANISM

As we have seen, the proportionality principle requires that whatever harms are caused by a military attack must be proportionate to the military gains. Military tactics that do great damage are only justified if they can be expected to yield substantial military gains. This principle is sometimes interpreted as a version of the utilitarian principle that we should always act to produce the best possible consequences. In the context of war, this translates into the view that the positive value of a military gain must be greater than the amount of harm that it causes.

Walzer prepares the way for his own rights-based view by trying to show why a utilitarian proportionality principle is inadequate. Since utilitarians believe that the purpose of morality is to enhance human life and since one obvious way to do this is to diminish suffering, one might think that the utilitarian principle would help to limit the horrors and destructiveness of war. To show the weaknesses of utilitarianism, Walzer discusses the views of the nineteenth-century utilitarian, Henry Sidgwick. According to Sidgwick, it is wrong for people who are engaged in fighting a war to cause "any mischief [i.e., harm] which does not tend materially to the end [achieving victory], nor any mischief of which the conduciveness to the end is slight in comparison with the amount of mischief."[2] Walzer's interpretation of Sidgwick's view is that:

What is being prohibited here is excessive harm. Two criteria are proposed for the determination of excess. The first is that of victory itself, or what is usually called military necessity. The second depends upon some notion of proportionality: we are to weigh "the mischief done," which presumably means not only the immediate harm to individuals but also any injury to the permanent interests of mankind, against the contribution that mischief makes to the end of victory.[3]

Putting Sidgwick's view into the framework I have described, I see him as combining the ideas of military value and proportionality. In saying that any "mischief" done must "tend materially to the end," he means that actions that do harm must make some positive contribution to victory. Suffering must not be caused if it is useless or gratuitous. And, as Walzer notes, Sidgwick invokes proportionality in requiring that the benefits of an attack must not be "slight" in comparison to the harms inflicted.

If Walzer can show that these criteria are too weak, that will strengthen the case for moving to a stronger, explicit ban on attacking civilians. In addition, if Walzer can make a compelling case for a strong principle of noncombatant immunity and can also show that utilitarians cannot support this principle, then he will have discredited utilitarianism as well.

Walzer raises two serious criticisms of Sidgwick's use of proportionality.[4] The first is that in practice the proportionality rule fails to constrain people's behavior in wartime conditions. Proportionality, he says, "turns out to be a hard criterion to apply." As a result, "Any act that contributes in a significant way to winning the war *is likely to be called* permissible" (emphasis added).[5]

Walzer does not say that the proportionality principle is mistaken. Rather, he says that because it is difficult to apply, it fails to constrain

---

[2] Ibid., 129, quoting Henry Sidgwick's *The Elements of Politics* (London: Macmillan, 1897), chapter 16, section 2.

[3] Walzer, *Just and Unjust Wars*, 129.

[4] Walzer also criticizes utilitarianism for tending to confirm "our customs and conventions, whatever they are" (133). This criticism is doubly strange, given the strong reformist agenda of utilitarian thinkers and the emphasis in Walzer's own writings on the role of "shared understandings" (i.e., customs and traditions) in moral thought. See, for example, his *Interpretation and Social Criticism*, chapter 1.

[5] Walzer, *Just and Unjust Wars*, 129.

how people actually fight. People at war almost always see victory as so important that virtually any action that contributes to victory will be seen as proportionate. As a result, every action with any military value at all will be "called permissible." Rules of war, Walzer says, must be clearer and less discretionary if they are to have any effect on behavior. Proportionality leaves too much room for judgment and interpretation, which are bound to be skewed under conditions of fear and uncertainty. What we need, Walzer writes, are "clearcut rules – moral fortifications ... that can be stormed only at great moral cost." In his view, a rule like "do not attack civilians" will be more effective than "do not attack civilians unless the harms done to them are proportionate to the value of victory."

RIGHTS, UTILITY, AND THE RAPE OF THE ITALIAN WOMEN

Walzer's second criticism of utilitarianism is that, even if proportionality could be properly applied, it would permit actions that ought to be forbidden. To support this point, he describes a World War II case in which Moroccan mercenaries were hired to fight with Free French forces in Italy. Their contract included a "license to rape and plunder in enemy territory." As a result, a "large number of Italian women were raped."[6] Walzer uses this case to discredit utilitarianism. His basic argument has the following form:

1. The rape of the women was wrong.
2. Utilitarianism would judge the rapes to have been right if they had led to victory and if the positive value of victory outweighed the negative value of the women's suffering.
3. Therefore, utilitarianism is false.

The form of argument is a *reductio ad absurdum.* Walzer takes it as obvious that it is wrong to allow mercenaries to rape women. If it is obvious that rape is wrong and if utilitarianism could approve it, then utilitarianism must be false.

Walzer does not actually say that utilitarians would approve of this license to rape. In fact, he concedes that they might condemn it. Their reason, however, would be that the contribution of the rapes to victory was too

---

[6] Ibid., 133–4. Walzer's source for the rape example is Ignazio Silone, "Reflections on the Welfare State," *Dissent* 8:2 (Spring 1961), 189. For discussions of rape and sexual violence in war, see Slim, *Killing Civilians,* 60–70; and Sally Scholz, "War Rape's Challenge to Just War Theory," in Lee, ed., *Intervention, Terrorism, and Torture.*

"slight" to justify the harm to the women. This reason, Walzer says, "hardly gets at the root of our condemnation of rape."[7] Even if utilitarians condemn the rapes, they do so for the wrong reason.

Utilitarians, Walzer says, have to concede that allowing rape could be morally right, and he cites Francisco de Vitoria's view that allowing soldiers to sack a city might be permissible if it acted "as a spur to the courage of the troops."[8] Since Vitoria understands "sacking" a city to include murdering and torturing innocent people and raping women, Walzer sees him as providing a utilitarian defense of giving soldiers a license to rape.

Walzer's key point is not that utilitarianism or the proportionality principle actually approve of rape. It is that they *could* approve of rape as a war tactic if the right circumstances were to occur. Walzer (understandably) wants a solider, less contingent condemnation. "Surely," he writes, "our judgment does not hang on the fact that rape is only a trivial or inefficient 'spur' to masculine courage." Our condemnation of the license to rape has a different basis.

> Rape is a crime, in war as in peace, because it violates the rights of the woman who is attacked. To offer her as bait to a mercenary soldier is to treat her as if she were not a person at all but a mere object, a prize or trophy of war.[9]

Rape, Walzer says, is wrong not because it is disproportionate or fails to maximize utility. It is wrong because it violates the rights of its victims. Even if it were proportionate or if its overall effects were good, it would still be wrong.

WALZER ON THE ETHICS OF HOW TO FIGHT

In building his own ethic of *how* to fight, Walzer appeals to basic rights to defend the two principles embedded in the principle of discrimination: the principle of combatant *non*-immunity, which allows soldiers to be attacked in war, and the principle of noncombatant immunity, which forbids attacks on civilians.[10] Walzer derives both these principles from rights that he

---

[7] Walzer, *Just and Unjust Wars*, 134.

[8] Francisco de Vitoria, *On the Law of War*, quoted in ibid., 134. Walzer cites Vitoria, pp. 184–5, but does not specify the edition. For the relevant passages (question 3, articles 2 and 7), see Francisco de Vitoria, *Political Writings*, ed. A. Pagden and J. Lawrence (Cambridge: Cambridge University Press, 1991), 317–18, 322–4, especially section 52, page 323. It is not clear that these passages support Walzer's utilitarian interpretation of Vitoria.

[9] Walzer, *Just and Unjust Wars*, 134.

[10] Colm McKeogh discusses the theory and history of the principle of discrimination in *Innocent Civilians*.

believes all human beings possess. The following passage contains his most important statement on the distinction between what is permissible in fighting a war and what is forbidden.

A legitimate act of war is one that does not violate the rights of the people against whom it is directed … [N]o one can be threatened with war or warred against, unless through some act of his own he has surrendered or lost his rights. *This fundamental principle* underlies and shapes the judgments we make of wartime conduct.[11] (Emphasis added.)

The basic idea here is that all people have a right to life, and for this reason other people do not have a right to attack them. This immunity to attack, however, can be lost or given up. One way it can be lost is by illegitimately attacking another person. People who are attacked have a right of self-defense, and that means they can respond to illegitimate attackers by trying to kill them if that is what defense requires. Trying to injure or kill an illegitimate attacker does not violate the attacker's rights because these rights are lost by people who launch unjustified attacks on others.

A second way to give up the immunity to attack is by becoming a member of an army or taking part in a war. Immunity to attack, Walzer says, is everyone's natural state and is retained as long as people do nothing to alter it. Soldiers lose their natural immunity when they acquire the status of being soldiers. People who have not changed their status or engaged in attacks remain civilians and retain their immunity to attack.

For Walzer, noncombatant immunity follows directly from a fundamental principle about people's rights. It rests, he says, on the recognition that noncombatants "are men and women with rights … [who] cannot be used for some military purpose, even if it is a legitimate purpose."[12]

TERRORISM

Walzer devotes a whole chapter to terrorism in *Just and Unjust Wars*. Given his strong affirmation of noncombatant immunity, it is no surprise that Walzer strongly condemns terrorism. Since he defines terrorism as "the random murder of innocent people" and since he believes that all attacks on innocent people are wrong, this condemnation flows naturally from the "fundamental principle" that justifies noncombatant immunity. Walzer

---

[11] Walzer, *Just and Unjust Wars*, 135.   [12] Ibid., 137.

restates his condemnation of terrorism in a later essay, saying, "I take the principle for granted: that every act of terrorism is a wrongful act."[13]

We can understand the scope of Walzer's categorical condemnation of terrorism by looking at his comments on the nature of terrorism. Walzer notes that the word "terrorism" is "most often used to describe revolutionary violence" (i.e., violence by anti-governmental forces), but he challenges this usage and points out that the "systematic terrorizing of whole populations is a strategy of both conventional and guerilla war, and of established governments as well as radical movements."[14] The fact that the term is generally associated with insurgent movements is, he says, a victory for established governments. In his view, however, we are misled if we do not see that governments also engage in terrorist acts.

Moreover, he notes, prior to World War II, revolutionaries had mostly targeted government officials and persons with social and economic power. They had not targeted innocent people and often took steps to spare them.

[T]errorism in the strict sense, the random murder of innocent people, emerged as a strategy of revolutionary struggle only in the period after World War II, that is, only after it had become a feature of conventional war.[15]

Since Walzer sees terrorism as a tactic and rejects agent-focused definitions, he often applies the terrorist label to both governments and anti-government groups. He explicitly describes the Allied city bombings in World War II as instances of terrorism. Discussing the objections of a British admiral to "the terror bombing of German cities," Walzer notes that the target of the bombings was the civilian population, and that the purpose of "terror bombing … was the destruction of civilian morale."[16]

Given Walzer's principles and his broad use of the word "terrorism," it certainly comes as a surprise when (as I described in chapter 6) Walzer defends the British "terror bombings" of German cities by claiming that Britain faced a supreme emergency early in the war. Since Walzer powerfully affirms the immunity of civilians, condemns terrorism in the most sweeping terms for attacking civilians, and criticizes utilitarians for permitting violations of the rights of civilians, his introduction of the supreme emergency exception seems to be a shocking reversal. Yet, it is clear that neither Walzer's initial views nor his supreme emergency exception are arrived at in a careless manner. Having given what he regards as strong reasons for noncombatant immunity, he also tries to give strong reasons to

---

[13] Ibid., 197; "Terrorism: A Critique of Excuses," in *Arguing About War*, 52.
[14] Walzer, *Just and Unjust Wars*, 197.   [15] Ibid., 198.   [16] Ibid., 197–8.

show that the ban on attacking can be overridden in certain extreme cases when the stakes are unimaginably high and the options for action are severely limited.

DEFENDING THE SUPREME EMERGENCY EXCEPTION

Walzer's defense of the supreme emergency exception comes in two stages. The first, which I sketched in chapter 6, describes a model case of a supreme emergency, the threat posed by Germany to Great Britain in 1940. Because of its Nazi ideology, Germany represented a special, extraordinary type of threat. It was, Walzer writes, "an ultimate threat to everything decent in our lives," and the consequences of its victory "were literally beyond calculation, immeasurably awful ..." Because this extraordinary threat was also imminent, Britain faced a "supreme emergency."[17]

While Walzer stresses that Britain was in a supreme emergency because of the imminence and the extraordinary nature of the German threat, two additional conditions had to be satisfied in order to justify attacks on civilians. The attacks must have a chance of being effective, and there must be no effective alternatives. Walzer believes that all four conditions were met in 1940 when Britain launched bombing attacks on German cities. That is why he believes that these attacks were justified.[18]

Walzer emphasizes that most of the city bombings in World War II did not pass this test and were not justified. There was no supreme emergency, he says, by late 1942. While the German threat was still extraordinarily evil, it was no longer imminent, and other means of resistance were available. Both the United States and the Soviet Union had joined Britain by this time, and the Soviet army had weakened the Germans on the Eastern front. In these changed circumstances, Walzer believes, the ban on attacking civilians should have been reinstated. Nonetheless, the attacks continued, and most of the Allied city bombings – including the fire-bombings of Dresden and Tokyo and the atomic bombings of Hiroshima and Nagasaki – occurred after 1942. Walzer strongly criticizes these later attacks on civilian targets because they do not pass the supreme emergency test.

[17] Ibid., 253. See, too, 228–32, where Walzer frames the problem and describes the view he will embrace later in the book, and his subsequent essay, "Emergency Ethics," in *Arguing About War*, 33–50. Gerry Wallace develops a similar argument in "Terrorism and the Argument from Analogy," *Journal of Moral and Social Studies* 6 (1991), 149–60.

[18] For an interesting account of this period, see John Lukacs, *Five Days in London: May 1940* (New Haven: Yale University Press, 1999). It is not obvious from Lukacs's account that the German threat was widely seen as "extraordinary" in Walzer's sense.

Walzer's discussion of Britain's situation early in World War II leads him to revise his earlier version of the principle of noncombatant immunity. He now adds what I will call "the supreme emergency exception." This states that the prohibition on attacking civilians is overridden in circumstances where there is a combination of extraordinary threat, imminent threat, no alternative effective means of response, and reason to believe that attacking civilians will succeed in diminishing the threat. This is the criterion that underlies Walzer's defense of the early bombings and his criticism of the later ones.

The second stage of Walzer's argument extends the supreme emergency exception to other types of cases. While Walzer's first argument stresses that Nazi Germany posed a threat to all civilized values, he goes on to consider cases of extreme threats that are limited to specific nations and asks,

Can a supreme emergency be constituted by … a threat of enslavement or extermination directed against a single nation? Can soldiers and statesmen override the rights of innocent people for the sake of their own political community?

His reply is that he is "inclined to answer this question affirmatively, though not without hesitation and worry." Walzer's reason for accepting this extension of the supreme emergency exception rests on his understanding of the role-based duties of soldiers and statesmen.

What choice do they have? They might sacrifice themselves in order to uphold the moral law, but they cannot sacrifice their countrymen. Faced with some ultimate horror, their options exhausted, they will do what they must to save their own people.[19]

For Walzer, leaders may do whatever is necessary to defend their nation and its people from extreme threats. In these circumstances, everything is permitted.

In a third extension of the supreme emergency doctrine, Walzer uses it to defend the strategy of nuclear deterrence.[20] While many argue that the threat of responding to a nuclear attack with a retaliatory nuclear strike maintained the cold peace of the Cold War, carrying out that threat would surely have been a massive violation of civilian life. Of course, making the threat by itself is not fatal or injurious to anyone, and if it works, one can

---

[19] Walzer, *Just and Unjust Wars*, 254.
[20] Ibid., chapter 17. Henry Shue supports much of Walzer's supreme emergency view but criticizes Walzer's use of it to justify nuclear deterrence in "Liberalism: The Impossibility of Justifying Weapons of Mass Destruction," in Sohail Hashimi and Steven Lee, eds., *Ethics and Weapons of Mass Destruction: Religious and Secular Perspectives* (Cambridge: Cambridge University Press, 2004), 155–9. For Walzer's response, see the same volume, 163–7.

only welcome the result. Even if one applauds the success of nuclear deterrence strategies, however, one may wonder about extending the concept of an emergency to a situation that may exist as long as there are rival nuclear powers. Moreover, since a nuclear deterrence policy requires that any leader of a nuclear power must be committed to ordering mass slaughter should deterrence fail, one may wonder whether we can both support nuclear deterrence and claim to have a fundamental commitment to the immunity of civilians.[21]

THE PROBLEM OF DIRTY HANDS

The status and role of leaders play a crucial role in Walzer's defense of the supreme emergency exception. While individual soldiers must honor noncombatant immunity even if it requires risking their lives, leaders are different. As Walzer explains in his later essay "Emergency Ethics,"

> [N]o government can put the life of the community itself and all of its individual members at risk, so long as there are actions available to it, even immoral actions, that would avoid or reduce the risk. It is for the sake of risk avoidance or risk reduction that governments are chosen. That is what political leaders are for; that is their task.[22]

Walzer does not flinch from saying what this task is. In the "rare and terrible moments" that constitute a supreme emergency, political communities require of their leaders that they "take on the guilt of killing the innocent."[23] When they do this, they do a great wrong because "the destruction of the innocent, whatever its purposes, is a kind of blasphemy against our deepest moral commitments."[24] Nonetheless, it seems, they also do a great right.

These claims about the duties of leaders link up with Walzer's well-known essay on the problem of "dirty hands."[25] There are two different questions intertwined in the dirty hands problem. Does the leader do the right thing when violating a deep moral norm? And, is the leader morally blameworthy for this action? The paradox arises because the intuitively plausible response to both questions is "yes." We think both that the political leader has (in some sense) acted rightly and that the leader is morally tainted because of this act. Ordinarily, if we think that someone

---

[21] For a history of the moral tensions between these views as reflected in US public opinion after World War II, see Conway-Lanz, *Collateral Damage.*
[22] Walzer, *Arguing About War*, 42.   [23] Ibid., 45.   [24] Walzer, *Just and Unjust Wars*, 262.
[25] Walzer, "Political Action: The Problem of Dirty Hands," in Marshall Cohen et al., eds., *War and Moral Responsibility* (Princeton: Princeton University Press, 1974).

ought to be blamed or feel guilty for an act, then we think that the person ought not to have done the act. In this case, however, we believe both that the act was the right thing to do and that it is something for which guilt should be felt and attributed. Having dirty hands, on this view, is a moral price that people in political life must pay.

When we apply this to the supreme emergency situation, the result appears to be that the right thing for a political leader to do is to order attacks on innocent people. Nonetheless, even though this is right, it is something that others could not justifiably do and is a violation of a deep moral norm. For this reason, the leader's hands are dirty.

It is worth noting that one of Walzer's main motivations in raising this problem is to criticize utilitarianism. Walzer believes that utilitarians cannot even recognize the dirty hands problem. If the leader has maximized utility, then utilitarians will say that he has acted rightly and that feeling guilty would be inappropriate. Walzer thinks that his own rights-based approach preserves the possibility of feeling guilty about a right action. Even though the action is right in the circumstances, it nonetheless violates people's right to life, and it remains appropriate for leaders to feel guilty and for others to attribute guilt to them.

It is puzzling that Walzer thinks this is a special problem for utilitarians. Just as he and other rights theorists support overriding a right when there are compelling reasons to do so, so utilitarians support actions that severely harm some people in order to achieve the highest level of utility that is possible in the circumstances. Similarly, just as rights theorists explain how one might feel guilty about right actions that violate people's rights, so utilitarians can explain how one might feel guilty about imposing great suffering on some people in order to create greater benefits for others. If there is a paradox of dirty hands, it is no more or less a problem for utilitarians than for anyone else.[26]

From the perspective of the ethics of war, the dirty hands problem is a distraction because it focuses on blameworthiness for actions rather than the rightness or wrongness of actions. My main concern, like Walzer's, is whether attacking civilians can ever be permissible. On this issue, his answer is "yes." The supreme emergency view, he says, provides "an account of when it is permissible (or necessary) to get our hands dirty."[27]

---

[26] For defenses of utilitarianism against this criticism, see Kai Neilsen, "There is No Dilemma of Dirty Hands" and Tom Sorell, "Politics, Power, and Partisanship," both in Paul Rynard and David Shugarman, eds., *Cruelty and Deception: The Controversy Over Dirty Hands in Politics* (Peterborough, Ontario: Broadview Press, 2000).

[27] Walzer, *Arguing About War*, 46.

The clarity of this answer is blurred because Walzer also says that killing the innocent is "a kind of blasphemy against our deepest moral commitments."[28] How can we fit this statement with Walzer's defense of the view that intentionally killing civilians is morally permissible in supreme emergencies? How can an action be right and at the same time be a "blasphemy against our deepest moral commitments"?

Interpreting Walzer on this issue is not easy. I will mention two ways of dealing with these apparent contradictions and the related "dirty hands" problem.

1. We can interpret Walzer to be saying that the British bombings and other justifiable, "dirty hands" actions are morally permissible. If we adopt this view, as I am inclined to do, then Walzer's view contains a contradiction. He refers to noncombatant immunity as one of our "deepest moral commitments." Nonetheless, he believes that noncombatant immunity should be violated in this case. This shows that, however deeply we may be committed to respecting the rights of innocent civilians, this is not our deepest commitment. Our – or at least Walzer's – deepest commitment is to preserving a way of life against an imminent, extraordinary threat.

2. We can interpret Walzer to be saying that "dirty hands" actions are morally prohibited but nonetheless are permissible according to non-moral standards that trump morality in these circumstances. This would be a move from morality to a realist perspective. On this view, morality would condemn the supreme emergency bombings, but morality would give way and cease to apply in these extreme circumstances. The realist standards that would apply are the standards that are appropriate for judging these actions.[29]

Whichever of these interpretations we accept, violating noncombatant immunity turns out to be permissible. Whether this is because morality itself allows violations or because other standards trump morality in these cases does not matter.

CONCLUSION

Walzer's ethic of war is marked by strong affirmations of noncombatant immunity and equally strong defenses of certain violations of

---

[28] Walzer, *Just and Unjust Wars*, 262.
[29] This is David Hendrickson's interpretation of Walzer in "In Defense of Realism." Brian Orend discusses several interpretations of the supreme emergency view in *The Morality of War*, chapter 5.

noncombatant immunity. Each of the following statements plays a central role in his thinking about the ethics of war.

1. Utilitarianism and the proportionality principle cannot provide a strong basis for noncombatant immunity.

2. Only a doctrine of human rights can provide a strong basis for non-combatant immunity, a basis that guarantees the immunity of civilians from attack.

3. Civilians may not be attacked in war because they have a natural right to life and, unlike soldiers, have done nothing to forfeit that right.

4. Because civilians have immunity to attack and because terrorism attacks civilians, all terrorist acts are wrong.

5. The World War II bombings of German cities were terrorist acts, but some of them were justified because they occurred during a supreme emergency.

6. Since intentional attacks on civilians are justified in a supreme emergency, the prohibition on attacking civilians is not absolute.

Obviously, there are tensions between statements 1–4 and statements 5–6. One way to describe them is by seeing them in the context of the spectrum of possible *jus in bello* rules. In the early part of his discussion (1–4), Walzer appears to defend "strong noncombatant immunity," but he later (5–6) shifts back to the weaker idea of "noncombatant immunity with a supreme emergency exception." If Walzer is right, then noncombatant immunity, though stronger than a mere presumption, is not an absolute prohibition. For this reason, any defense of an absolute prohibition against attacking civilians must show why it is a mistake to accept the view that violations of noncombatant immunity are morally justified in a supreme emergency.

CHAPTER 11

The supreme emergency exception

If Walzer's ethic of war-fighting consisted entirely of a strong prohibition on intentional attacks on civilians and a restrictive rule regarding collateral damage killings, it would provide a strong basis for condemning all terrorist acts. But, as we have seen, Walzer does not see noncombatant immunity as an absolute, exceptionless constraint on how war may be fought. Instead, he believes that under "supreme emergency" conditions, noncombatant immunity gives way, and civilians become permissible targets.

PROBLEMS WITH THE SUPREME EMERGENCY VIEW

In spite of the plausibility of the supreme emergency doctrine, it raises serious problems, both in itself and in its relations to other aspects of Walzer's ethic of war. The most obvious problem is the inconsistency between Walzer's supreme emergency doctrine and his categorical condemnation of terrorism. If terrorism is, as Walzer says, the random or indiscriminate killing of civilians for the sake of a political goal, then the pre-1942 British bombings of German cities were terrorist acts. These attacks certainly satisfy the conditions in the definition of terrorism I have defended. They were acts of serious, deliberate violence that were committed as part of a campaign to promote a political agenda, the defense of Britain from German attack. They targeted large but limited numbers of people in order to influence a larger group and the leaders who make decisions for it. In this case, some German civilians were killed and injured in order to lower the morale of the German people generally, and this in turn was expected to convince German leaders to end the war. Finally, the attacks were deliberately intended to kill and injure innocent people.[1]

---

[1] For informative histories of the British and American air wars, see Stephen Garrett, *Ethics and Air Power in World War II*, and "Terror Bombing of German Cities in World War II"; and Ronald Schaffer, *Wings of Judgment*. Alex Bellamy challenges Walzer's historical account and raises other objections to the supreme emergency exception in "Supreme Emergencies and the Protection of Non-combatants in War," *International Affairs* 80 (2004), 829–50.

Walzer acknowledges these facts and describes the attacks as "terror bombing," the aim of which was to destroy civilian morale. If these attacks were permissible because it was a supreme emergency, then terrorism is morally permissible under at least some conditions. Walzer comes close to acknowledging the possibility of justified terrorism in a reprinted version of his essay "Terrorism: A Critique of Excuses." In a brief, parenthetical addition to this essay, Walzer asks whether terrorism could be justified in a supreme emergency and answers that:

It might be, but only if the oppression to which the terrorism claimed to be responding was genocidal in character. Against the imminent threat of political and physical extinction, extreme measures can be defended, assuming that they have some chance of success. But this kind of threat has not been present in any of the recent cases of terrorist activity. Terrorism has not been a means of avoiding disaster but of reaching for political success.[2]

Though this remark is ambiguous, it appears to recognize the possibility of justified terrorism. If it does, that would eliminate one inconsistency in Walzer's view. Acknowledging the possibility of justified terrorism would require Walzer to retract his statement in the very same essay that he "take[s] the principle for granted: that every act of terrorism is a wrongful act."[3]

THE STATUS OF NONCOMBATANT IMMUNITY

While a change of Walzer's evaluation of terrorism would solve one problem, the inconsistency created by the supreme emergency doctrine goes much deeper. It is not only the condemnation of all terrorist acts that is inconsistent with the supreme emergency view. In addition, the supreme emergency exception conflicts with Walzer's assertion that the principle of noncombatant immunity is a fundamental principle in the ethics of war. The depth of Walzer's problem is revealed in the important passage (quoted earlier) in which he introduced and defended noncombatant immunity.

A legitimate act of war is one that does not violate the rights of the people against whom it is directed … [N]o one can be threatened with war or warred against, unless through some act of his own he has surrendered or lost his rights.

---

[2] Walzer, *Arguing About War*, 54.
[3] Walzer, *Just and Unjust Wars*, 197; *Arguing About War*, 52. This categorical condemnation of terrorism remains in the reprinted essay and appears just before Walzer's new remark about terrorism and supreme emergencies.

This fundamental principle underlies and shapes the judgments we make of wartime conduct.[4] (Emphasis added.)

The supreme emergency doctrine shows that the "fundamental principle" Walzer asserts is in fact not fundamental. When enough is at stake, it may be set aside, and it cannot be said to "underlie and shape" *all* the judgments that either "we" or Walzer himself make of wartime conduct. If noncombatant immunity, the right not to be warred against unless one has surrendered that right, can be overridden, then some competing principle or value must be more fundamental than it.

In fact, Walzer appeals to two incompatible absolutes in different parts of his discussion. The first is the individual human right not to be attacked unless one has forfeited one's immunity. The second absolute emerges in Walzer's explanation of why attacks on civilians are permissible in a supreme emergency.

[I]t is possible to live in a world where individuals are sometimes murdered, but a world where entire peoples are enslaved or massacred is literally unbearable. For *the survival and freedom of political communities* – whose members share a way of life, developed by their ancestors, to be passed on to their children – *are the highest values of international society.*[5] (Emphasis added.)

While the first "fundamental principle" that affirms the rights of individuals is absolute, the passage just quoted stresses group rights and affirms the "survival and freedom of political communities" as the "highest values of international society." By embracing the supreme emergency exception, Walzer commits himself to the view that group rights take precedence over the rights of individuals.

This tension between moral individualism and political communitarianism is the deepest theoretical tension in Walzer's view. If communities have priority, then noncombatant immunity is a weaker constraint than Walzer has acknowledged. If individuals have priority, then the well-being of communities cannot justify overriding noncombatant immunity, even in supreme emergencies. Walzer's choice is vividly expressed in a later essay, where he writes "Supreme emergency is a communitarian doctrine."[6]

These tensions in Walzer's view echo features of commonsense morality. In some circumstances, we readily affirm the absolute rights of individuals.

---

[4] Walzer, *Just and Unjust Wars*, 135.   [5] Ibid., 254.

[6] Walzer, "Emergency Ethics," in *Arguing About War*, 45. David Luban criticizes Walzer for prioritizing the rights of states over individual rights in "Just War and Human Rights," in Charles Beitz *et al.*, eds., *International Ethics* (Princeton: Princeton University Press, 1985), 195–216. Walzer's reply, "The Moral Standing of States: A Response to Four Critics," is in the same volume, 217–37.

At other times, with other problems in mind, we affirm the importance of defending political communities, even if it severely damages individuals. Here, as elsewhere, Walzer's problems are our problems because they reflect the serious tensions and inconsistencies in our moral thinking about war.

CAN WALZER'S VIEW BE MADE CONSISTENT?

Can Walzer's claims about individual rights and supreme emergencies be brought together in a consistent whole? As with the problem of terrorism and the supreme emergency doctrine, it is possible to state a logically consistent view. But, there are costs to doing so.

It could be said that Walzer never treated noncombatant immunity as an absolute principle. Although he appears to hold this absolutist view early in his book, by the end, his commitment to noncombatant immunity is qualified in two ways. First, it is qualified by what he says about collateral damage to civilians. In his view, morality permits some actions that cause civilian deaths and injuries when they are unintended and when steps to prevent them have been taken.[7] Second, noncombatant immunity is qualified by the fact that it does not apply in every wartime situation. While it applies in ordinary wars, it does not apply in a supreme emergency. In both ways, noncombatant immunity is not an absolute. The implication for rights is that individual rights take priority in ordinary circumstances, but group rights trump individual rights in supreme emergencies.

Walzer explicitly embraces this view in "World War II: Why Was This War Different?," an essay that preceded *Just and Unjust Wars*. There he writes:

It is tempting, though it would be wrong, to say that Nazism requires us to recognize the limits of the absolute. It is more prosaic, and probably right, to say ... that the rules are not absolute. They establish very strong presumptions against certain sorts of actions, like the deliberate killing of noncombatants. They are not irrebuttable presumptions, however.[8]

There is, then, a plausible case for the view that Walzer's basic position is logically coherent, even though some of his remarks about which principles are fundamental stray from it.

---

[7] See Walzer, *Just and Unjust Wars*, 151–9. I discuss his views and others' on collateral damage in chapters 17 and 18.
[8] Michael Walzer, "World War II: Why Was This War Different?," in Marshall Cohen *et al.*, eds., *War and Moral Responsibility* (Princeton: Princeton University Press, 1974), 103.

There is nothing inherently contradictory about a non-absolute version of noncombatant immunity. Just as there is no inconsistency in the rule "thou shalt not kill except to defend one's own or another's life from attack," so there is no inconsistency in the rule "thou shalt not harm civilians except when harms to them are collateral damage or are inflicted in supreme emergency circumstances."

RIGHTS AND UTILITY REVISITED

Walzer's problem is that the version of noncombatant immunity that allows exceptions is inconsistent with the strong, rights-affirming position that he initially uses to defend noncombatant immunity. While there is no contradiction in affirming that noncombatant immunity can sometimes be overridden, making this shift undermines the argument that Walzer gives to support his rights-based view and to refute utilitarianism.[9]

Recall Walzer's discussion of the rape of the Italian women. Walzer uses this case to undermine the credibility of utilitarianism and to defend the virtues of a rights-based approach. Walzer contrasted his own categorical condemnation of the rapes with the weaker, conditional evaluation required by utilitarianism. Even if utilitarians could judge the rapes to be wrong, he argues, they could only reach that conclusion after asking whether the military gains achieved by the permission to rape were valuable enough to justify the raping of the women. By contrast, Walzer simply condemns the rapes because they violate the rights of the women. Because no other factors are relevant, we can know that the rapes were wrong without knowing anything about whether the harms inflicted were proportionate to the achievement of the military objective.

The supreme emergency doctrine, however, is a proportionality test. It says that when the evils that threaten are great enough and there are no other ways to defend against them, it may be permissible to take actions that would normally be prohibited. Anyone who accepts the supreme emergency doctrine must admit that if all we know is that women are being raped or cities bombed, we cannot know whether the act is right or wrong. Knowing whether the rapes are right or wrong requires knowing that the evil being resisted is ordinary rather than extraordinary, that the threat is not imminent, and that there are other effective ways to combat it. The simple, direct condemnation of the rapes on the grounds that they violate human

---

[9] Walzer describes tensions between rights-based and utilitarian arguments in his 1988 essay "Emergency Ethics," in *Arguing About War*, 35–40.

rights is no longer sufficient. The wrongness of these acts for people who accept the supreme emergency view is conditional in just the way that it is for utilitarians or others who embrace a proportionality rule. Walzer acknowledges this when he describes the supreme emergency doctrine as "the utilitarianism of extremity" and concedes that, in supreme emergency circumstances, "the only restraints upon military action are usefulness and proportionality."[10]

Of course, it is bizarre to think that giving soldiers a license to rape could play a major role in warding off an extraordinary threat, and one might plausibly condemn the rapes for this reason. But that argument expresses the idea from Sidgwick that Walzer ridiculed, the idea that permitting the rapes was wrong because it could only make a "slight" contribution to victory.

Walzer's own view is quite similar to that of Vitoria, whom Walzer cited as the source for a utilitarian-style defense of rape. Vitoria, after asking whether "it is lawful to allow our soldiers to sack a city," replies that sacking a city

is not of itself unlawful if it is necessary to the conduct of the war, whether to strike terror into the enemy or to inflame the passions of the soldiers ... But this sort of argument licenses the barbarians among the soldiery to commit every kind of inhuman savagery and cruelty, murdering and torturing the innocent, deflowering young girls, raping women, and pillaging churches. In these circumstances, *it is undoubtedly unjust* to destroy a Christian city *except in the most pressing necessity and with the gravest of causes* but if necessity decrees, it is not unlawful, even if the probability is that the soldiery will commit crimes of this kind.[11] (Emphasis added.)

Vitoria sees these acts as detestable, barbaric crimes against their victims. Nonetheless, though "undoubtedly unjust," these acts are justified "in the most pressing necessity and with the gravest of causes." Although we don't know what Vitoria has in mind by "the most pressing necessity" or "the gravest of causes," his language suggests something like the urgency and extremity that Walzer invokes in his discussion of supreme emergencies.

Overall, the problem for Walzer is twofold. Because he admits the relevance of contingencies to determining when violations of individual rights are justified, he complicates the judgments that were supposed to flow so readily from a belief in human rights. Once the supreme emergency exception is introduced, Walzer can no longer fault utilitarians simply

[10] Walzer, *Just and Unjust Wars*, 231. Walzer is mistaken in calling his view a type of utilitarianism, as Daniel Statman points out in "Supreme Emergencies Revisited," *Ethics* 117 (2006), 58–61.

[11] Vitoria, *On the Law of War* in *Vitoria: Political Writings*, 323.

because they might approve of violating rights. Nor can he fault them for basing their judgments on contingent facts rather than simple principles. He, too, approves of sometimes violating rights, and he, too, bases his judgments on contingent facts rather than simple principles.

ARE SUPREME EMERGENCIES COMPATIBLE WITH NONCOMBATANT IMMUNITY?

A defender of Walzer's view could insist that, while the problems I have described are embarrassments, the heart of Walzer's view remains consistent and worthy of acceptance. The basic view is that the principle of noncombatant immunity is a very strong presumption against attacking civilians but not an absolute prohibition. The reason that noncombatant immunity retains great force is that supreme emergencies are rare, abnormal events. Walzer makes this point in a later essay. Responding to the criticism that his view weakens noncombatant immunity, he writes,

Supreme emergency is not in fact a permissive doctrine … Properly understood, supreme emergency strengthens rights normality by guaranteeing its possession of the greater part, by far, of the moral world. That is its message to people like us: that it is (almost) the whole of our duty to uphold the rights of the innocent.[12]

This reply to the charge that the supreme emergency view is too permissive might be correct but only if two conditions are met. First, supreme emergencies must be extremely rare, i.e., genuinely extraordinary. Second, the concept of a supreme emergency must be clear enough to provide criteria that enable people to distinguish supreme emergencies from other threats that do not justify violating noncombatant immunity.

Walzer acknowledges these conditions. He writes:

If we are to adopt or defend the adoption of extreme measures, the danger must be of an unusual and horrifying kind … It is necessary to search for some touchstone against which arguments about extremity might be judged. We need to … mark off the regions of desperation and disaster.[13]

The requirements of unusualness and conceptual clarity are related. If the concept of a supreme emergency is unclear, then many cases – including ones that Walzer would exclude – may qualify, and supreme emergencies will not be unusual. If they are not unusual, then invoking the supreme emergency permission to attack civilians would become the rule rather than an exception, and what would be unusual would be compliance with

---

[12] Walzer, "Emergency Ethics," in *Arguing About War*, 50.   [13] Walzer, *Just and Unjust Wars*, 253.

noncombatant immunity. The key question, then, is: does the concept of a supreme emergency meet the demands for clarity?

HOW CAN WE IDENTIFY A SUPREME EMERGENCY?

Walzer describes supreme emergencies in two ways. Sometimes he writes broadly about threats to civilized values and uses the language of psychological horror. Nazism, he says, was "at the outer limits of exigency, at a point where we are likely to find ourselves *united in fear and abhorrence.*" It "was *an ultimate threat to everything decent in our lives.*" If Nazism were victorious, the results would be "literally beyond calculation, *immeasurably awful*" (emphasis added). Sometimes, Walzer uses more specific language, as when he identifies a supreme emergency as "a threat of enslavement or extermination directed at a single nation …"[14] There are, then, two types of criteria for a threat's being extraordinary. One uses moral and psychological standards (a threat to everything decent, immeasurably awful) while the other cites specific forms of treatment (enslavement, extermination) that might be inflicted on human beings.

It is not clear how these criteria are related. One possibility is that the "enslavement or extermination" criterion provides an objective measure of what counts as "an ultimate threat to everything decent in our lives." A second possibility is that these examples are only illustrations of the type of situation that might constitute an "ultimate threat." If they are only illustrations, then other threats might qualify as well. In addition, if they are illustrations, it makes sense to ask whether there could be enslavements and exterminations that do not threaten civilized values. If the answer is "yes," then some threats of enslavement or extermination would not constitute a supreme emergency.

It may sound absurd to suppose that a threat of enslavement or extermination might not be an "ultimate threat to everything decent in our lives" and "immeasurably awful." Yet, people routinely praise Athens for its high level of civilization even though the Athenians had slaves. And the Founding Fathers of the United States are greatly revered even though some owned slaves and others who were not slave-owners nonetheless voted to allow the institution of slavery. Somehow, the broader Athenian culture and the United States prior to 1865 avoid the taint of being called a threat to everything decent in our lives in spite of their incorporation of the institution of slavery. Likewise, regarding exterminations, many societies,

[14] Ibid., 253, 254.

including the United States, have histories that include genocide and ethnic cleansing. Perhaps there were more supreme emergencies than one might think. Or, perhaps, there are instances of extraordinary threats that we do not experience as violations of "everything decent in our lives."

If we are not clear about the criteria for a supreme emergency, we will lack what Walzer acknowledges to be essential: an adequate "touchstone against which arguments about extremity might be judged." This is clearly a momentous judgment since the decision that a supreme emergency exists licenses the violation of the rights of civilians not to be intentionally killed and injured.

DEFECTS OF THE SUPREME EMERGENCY CRITERION

Walzer seems to treat the supreme emergency exception as a familiar principle and suggests that it played a role in the decision to bomb German cities. Apart from one quotation from Churchill, however, he offers no evidence that decision-makers involved in the Allied bombings thought in this way.[15] Had they used Walzer's reasoning, they might have halted city bombings when the "supreme emergency" was over. In fact, the bombings increased as the war went on and more air power became available. Likewise, although Walzer denies that the Japanese threat ever constituted a supreme emergency, American bombings of Japanese cities went ahead simply to achieve victory. Indeed, American decision-makers and the public at large displayed greater animus toward the Japanese than toward the Germans.[16]

If any of the World War II bombings satisfied the supreme emergency condition, it was a coincidence. Walzer's reasoning was not used by those who planned, approved, and carried out bombings that explicitly targeted civilian areas. In fact, many of those who advocated the bombing campaigns had been converted to the strategy of aerial bombardment of cities in the 1920s and 30s. During this period, Giulio Douhet and other air war advocates urged direct attacks on civilian targets as an alternative to the type of slaughter of soldiers that occurred in World War I. Long before

[15] See ibid., 245, for the Churchill quote. For thoughtful discussions of Walzer's view that include attention to Churchill, see Shue, "Liberalism," and Stephen Lammers, "Area Bombing in World War II: The Argument of Michael Walzer," *Journal of Religious Ethics* 11 (1983), 96–114.
[16] On American attitudes toward the Japanese, Germans, and Italians during World War II, see Paul Fussell, *Wartime* (New York: Oxford University Press, 1989), chapter 9.

there was a supreme emergency, many people had embraced this strategy, and, when war came, they simply applied it.[17]

To make matters worse, Walzer's own application of the supreme emergency criterion is neither compelling nor plausible. Walzer believes that the bombings of Japanese cities were never justified because the Japanese never constituted a supreme emergency threat. Unlike the Germans, he says, "Japan's rulers were engaged in a more ordinary sort of military expansion."[18] In a powerful critique of Walzer's view, Tony Coady responds that:

Walzer's relatively benign view of Japanese aggression is hard to take seriously. I feel inclined to say "Tell that to the Chinese." In the Japanese invasion of China in the 1930s it is soberly estimated that more than 300,000 Chinese civilians were massacred in Nanking alone in a racist rampage of raping and beheading and bayoneting that lasted six weeks. Nor was the racist and anti-civilisational behaviour of the Japanese warriors much better in the rest of South-East Asia during the war.[19]

Didn't the Japanese pose an extraordinary threat to the Chinese and other Asian peoples? It is hard to believe that people subjected to the treatment Coady describes would see their situation as anything other than a supreme emergency. Nonetheless, Walzer casually denies this and classifies Japanese war-making as "ordinary."

Coady's criticism reveals the large element of subjectivity in Walzer's own application of the "supreme emergency" criterion. For whatever reason, Walzer did not think that the massive atrocities committed by the Japanese constituted "an ultimate threat to everything decent in our lives." If the test for this is the sense of horror we experience in learning about these events, it is plausible to think that a vivid awareness of the massive rapes and killings carried out by the Japanese will affect many people with the same horror that a vivid awareness of German atrocities produces. And if they do not, this may call into question the use of this psychological criterion.

Judging that a threat constitutes a supreme emergency seems to depend so much on our emotional responses to various kinds of horror that any

[17] For these developments, see Tami Davis Biddle, *Rhetoric and Reality in Air Warfare: The Evolution of British and American Ideas About Strategic Bombing, 1914–1945* (Princeton: Princeton University Press, 2002), and Ronald Schaffer, *Wings of Judgment*, 20–34.

[18] Walzer, *Just and Unjust Wars*, 267–8.

[19] Tony Coady, "Terrorism, Just War and Supreme Emergency," in Coady and O'Keefe, *Terrorism and Justice*, 17. Coady develops these points further in *Morality and Political Violence*, chapter 14.

large-scale wars might easily qualify as supreme emergencies for the people threatened by them and for at least some onlookers. There is no shortage of such cases. Even at lower levels of violence, people who are subjected to brutal rule that makes it impossible to live normal, secure lives are likely to see their own situation as a supreme emergency for them. As a result, they might believe that their situation justifies terrorism and unconstrained violence. It is not clear that Walzer could show that these people are mistaken since any form of extended oppression is a threat to civilized values.[20]

Walzer's application of the "supreme emergency" concept suggests an odd paradox. Since he believes both that city bombings were not justified after 1942 and that noncombatant immunity is a central value of civilized life, it follows that the Allied bombings themselves were a threat both to German civilians and to the fundamental rules of civilized warfare. If the use of "obliteration bombing" made the Allies into an extraordinary threat, then perhaps Germany and Japan also faced a supreme emergency and would have been justified in using any means necessary and available to fight the Allies.[21]

One way to avoid these problems is to reject the broad language Walzer uses in discussing Nazi Germany and to rely on the more specific language he uses in discussing threats to single countries. There he is more precise: a country faces a supreme emergency when it is confronted with "a threat of enslavement or extermination."

This criterion is clearer, but it too has defects. First, it does not support Walzer's view about the British because Britain never faced a threat of enslavement or extermination. While the Nazis explicitly sought to exterminate Jews and Slavs, they took no steps to exterminate the French or the Scandinavians, and their racist ideology provided no reason to think that genocide or enslavement awaited the British. So, if we replace Walzer's vaguer language with these more precise terms, we will conclude that Britain faced a very serious threat but not a supreme emergency. If Britain's bombings were justified, it is because others faced these extraordinary threats. In this case, however, since Jews and Slavs continued to face imminent threats of enslavement and extermination after 1942, it is not clear that Walzer should say the supreme emergency ended when the Americans

---

[20] James Sterba applies the supreme emergency label to the situation faced by Palestinians in "Terrorism and International Justice," in James Sterba, ed., *Terrorism and International Justice* (New York: Oxford University Press, 2003), 214–15.

[21] The term "obliteration bombing" is used by John C. Ford in his 1944 essay "The Morality of Obliteration Bombing," *Theological Studies* 5 (1944), 261–309.

and Soviets entered the war on Britain's side. While the threat to Britain may no longer have been imminent, it remained imminent to millions of other people until the end of the war.

OPENING THE FLOODGATES

It is not obvious that people threatened by grave but lesser threats should accept the "extermination or enslavement" criterion for a supreme emergency. If the Japanese, for example, had planned to massacre half the population of China and to dominate but not enslave the rest, that would not have satisfied this criterion for a supreme emergency. It is hard to believe, however, that any nation would see this outcome as anything other than a huge disaster that ought to count as a "supreme emergency."

These interpretive problems undermine the value of Walzer's theory from the perspective of practical morality. Suppose that Walzer's rule – "Never attack civilians except in cases of supreme emergency" – were incorporated into our ethic of war. The connotations of the expression "supreme emergency" and the lack of clear criteria for its application strongly suggest that most people would see any urgent, threatening situation as a supreme emergency. Consider the reaction of people in the United States to the September 11 attacks. Though serious and frightening, these attacks came nowhere near satisfying Walzer's criteria, and yet many people would find the expression "supreme emergency" quite apt to describe the situation after these attacks. Many Americans felt that their way of life was threatened, that civilized values were threatened, and that any means of combating terrorism would be justified. Responding to the attacks, US officials claimed that the Geneva Conventions and international laws banning torture were no longer applicable. Nor, they claimed, were legal and constitutional requirements to authorize surveillance of US citizens still binding. Rightly or not, US officials believed that the attacks created an extraordinary but enduring emergency in which constraints that might have been reasonable in the past had to be rejected or suspended for the future.

The language of supreme emergency is too vague and its application to particular situations too dependent on people's subjective responses. People who accept it as a criterion will end up forsaking noncombatant immunity in cases that Walzer himself would not regard as extraordinary threats. As Tony Coady writes: "[I]t is hard to resist the suspicion that 'supreme emergency' is too elastic [and that] admission of this exception is likely to generate widespread misuses of it."²² This echoes Walzer's own argument against the proportionality rule. In practice, Walzer argued, proportionality would not constrain military behavior because it is vague, and soldiers and leaders will see the damage caused by virtually any promising tactic as proportionate to the attainment of victory.

In the end, the supreme emergency doctrine may be more likely to provide a language for justifying exceptions than a rule for maintaining noncombatant immunity. Rather than severely restricting the abrogation of noncombatant immunity, it opens the floodgates. Walzer himself suggests that the terror bombings and other attacks on civilians in World War II set the stage for the spread of the terrorization strategy to revolutionary insurgents across the world. The tactics of one war set precedents for the next.²³

CONCLUSION

Walzer tries hard to defend both a strong version of noncombatant immunity and an opening for permissible violations in extraordinary circumstances. His attempt fails, however, and undermines three of his central goals: a categorical condemnation of terrorist acts, the defense of noncombatant immunity as a "fundamental value," and the restriction of the "supreme emergency" concept to a very limited set of circumstances.

Walzer's views reflect the tensions within commonsense moral thinking about war. People want to condemn terrorists who wantonly kill and injure innocent people, and they want to value civilian immunity. At the same time, when the need to defend one's own nation and its values is strong, the constraints that protect enemy civilians are weakened and often fall away. In fact commonsense morality is more permissive than Walzer's theory. Public responses to the World War II city bombings suggest that commonsense morality approves of attacks on enemy civilians when these attacks will hasten victory and save the lives of one's own military. Because it is less restrictive than Walzer's "supreme emergency" exception, commonsense morality provides an even weaker basis for condemning terrorism than Walzer's theory.

Walzer's view is initially appealing because it condemns terrorism and other attacks on civilians in absolute terms while at the same time providing

---

²² Coady, "Terrorism, Just War and Supreme Emergency," 18, 20.
²³ Walzer, *Just and Unjust Wars*, 198. Kenneth Brown stresses the bombings as setting precedents in "'Supreme Emergency': A Critique of Michael Walzer's Moral Justification for Allied Obliteration Bombing in World War II," *Manchester College Bulletin of the Peace Studies Institute*, 13:1–2 (1983), 6–15.

an opening to allow drastic measures in extreme circumstances. The failure of Walzer's attempt to combine these in a consistent way leaves us with a difficult choice between flexibility and absolutism. Which of Walzer's inconsistent views is correct? His initial absolute condemnation of attacks on civilians? Or his later recognition of exceptional cases in which such attacks are permissible?

CHAPTER 12

Rights theories, utilitarianism, and the killing of civilians

It seems so obvious that terrorism is always wrong because it attacks innocent people. But the obviousness dissipates when we take a wider view and consider more general beliefs regarding war and conflict. To be credible, categorical condemnations of terrorism seem to require that we embrace an ethic of war that absolutely prohibits attacks on civilians. But this requirement is rejected by many attractive views. Even a rights-based approach like Walzer's fails to condemn all instances of intentionally killing civilians in war. The fact that many thoughtful people have reached this position should perhaps lead us to wonder whether the strong noncombatant immunity position is correct. Perhaps at a personal level, one can simply treat this as bedrock and say "here I stand; I can do no other." But in a philosophical inquiry, the question needs to be asked: is an absolute prohibition on attacking civilians a reasonable moral demand? If not, then the correct ethic of war will not prohibit all attacks on civilians.

REVIEWING THE OPTIONS

To put this issue in perspective, recall the most commonly discussed ethical principles on the conduct of war. (I leave aside realism and other relatively unconstrained principles.)

Proportionality	Any attack whose negative effects are proportional to its positive value is permissible.
Weak noncombatant immunity	Noncombatants may not be intentionally killed or injured unless doing so has significant military value.
Noncombatant immunity with a supreme emergency exception	Noncombatants may not be intentionally killed or injured except in supreme emergencies.
Strong noncombatant immunity	Noncombatants may not be intentionally killed or injured.

As we have seen, the proportionality view is associated with utilitarianism because it requires that the damages done by attacks in war must be outweighed by their military benefits. While proportionality gives no special status to noncombatants, it leads rather naturally to the second option, weak noncombatant immunity. Generally speaking, one can best achieve military objectives by weakening the military forces of the enemy rather than killing and injuring noncombatants, who have no direct role in the fighting. Attacks on civilians, then, will have less military value to include in a utilitarian analysis, and if they achieve less militarily, the harms done are less likely to be offset by military benefits. Therefore, a utilitarian might adopt the rule "don't attack civilians" as a default position or rule of thumb. This rule would provide a weak form of noncombatant immunity because it would be understood that, if a particular attack on civilians had sufficient military value, it would be permissible.

The next option is the type of view that requires much more than normal military value to justify attacking civilians. Walzer's noncombatant immunity with a supreme emergency exception is a view of this type. While I have strongly criticized Walzer's supreme emergency view, my criticisms do not show that the idea of such an exception is mistaken. A defender of a supreme emergency view could avoid the force of my criticisms by making three amendments to Walzer's view. First, the amended view would acknowledge that noncombatant immunity is not fundamental and can be overridden by other values. Second, it would accept that terrorist acts can be justified under supreme emergency conditions. Third, it would provide criteria for extreme cases that are clear enough to diminish the role of arbitrary, subjective influences and lessen the likelihood of unjustified extensions of the principle.[1] These revisions would make the supreme emergency view immune to the criticisms I have made. The result would be a view many people will sympathize with, seeing it as a reasonable compromise between a too-permissive ethic of war that gives too little protection to civilians and a too-demanding ethic that fails to respond to the circumstances of people who face extraordinary threats.

There seem, then, to be four views that have some degree of plausibility: 1) proportionality, 2) weak noncombatant immunity, 3) noncombatant immunity with an exception for extreme cases, and 4) noncombatant

---

[1] Igor Primoratz defends an amended supreme emergency view in "Civilian Immunity in War," in Primoratz, ed., *Civilian Immunity in War*. Primoratz applies his view to the Palestinians in "Terrorism in the Israeli-Palestinian Conflict," *Iyyun: The Jerusalem Philosophical Quarterly* 55 (January 2006), 27–48. Saul Smilansky uses another version of an extremity principle to evaluate several actual cases of conflict in "Terrorism, Justification, and Illusion."

immunity as an exceptionless, absolute rule. Because option 4 is the only one that allows us to condemn terrorist acts categorically, I want to see whether a convincing case can be made for it.

A PROBLEM OF METHOD

Looking at these options, the question arises: what method can we use to determine which, if any, of these views is the correct one? How can we tell what is the moral truth about noncombatant immunity?

A common philosophical method of dealing with problems in practical ethics is to consult our commonsense "intuitions" and figure out what these beliefs imply about a problem. Although this method is often useful for tackling difficult problems, I do not think that it works in this case. The reason is that our ordinary moral understandings are thrown into confusion by the phenomenon of war. When it comes to war, we cannot solve these problems simply by getting clear about "our" moral beliefs because our commonsense moral beliefs are confused and contradictory.

A second method is to see whether various moral theories can help us find solutions. Two theories that I have mentioned are utilitarianism and the theory of rights. I have also described Walzer's attempt to show that utilitarianism cannot support noncombatant immunity and that only a rights-based theory can successfully do so. Walzer is not alone in believing this. It is a standard view among both utilitarians and anti-utilitarians that utilitarianism cannot justify a strong principle of noncombatant immunity. According to the standard view, the only hope for establishing strong noncombatant immunity is to appeal to a rights theory or some other deontological approach.

I want to challenge the conventional wisdom on this subject, first by showing why rights theories have no special advantage in justifying noncombatant immunity, and second by developing a utilitarian argument in support of strong noncombatant immunity. Before doing this, however, we need to see why it has been so widely believed that any defense of noncombatant immunity must be supported by non-utilitarian approaches to ethics.

THE SIMPLE ARGUMENT AGAINST A UTILITARIAN DEFENSE OF NONCOMBATANT IMMUNITY

Utilitarianism identifies the rightness and wrongness of actions with the value of their results. For this reason, utilitarians say that an action that leads to better results than other available actions is morally right. Although utilitarians differ on exactly what makes results good or bad, the traditional answer is that results are good if they involve pleasure, happiness, or well-being and are bad if they involve pain, unhappiness, or ill-being. Utilitarians are also committed to the view that it is often possible to make at least rough estimates of amounts of good and bad. If it were not, then we could not judge the results of different actions to be better or worse than one another.

For utilitarians, the costs of war – the negative results of deaths, injuries, and destruction – make war presumptively wrong. Nonetheless, going to war can be morally justified if worse results – for example, more deaths, injuries, and destruction – are the likely effects of not going to war. Similarly, when utilitarians consider the ethics of how to fight in a war, they urge us to determine which tactics are morally best by seeing what the results of using or not using them are likely to be.

The utilitarian approach gives rise to a simple and powerful argument against noncombatant immunity. Since utilitarianism bases judgments of the rightness and wrongness of actions on the value of their results, it seems obvious that utilitarians would accept the following view:

If there are circumstances in which intentionally killing civilians creates more well-being than other available actions, then intentionally killing civilians is the right action in these circumstances.

Suppose there are no circumstances in which killing civilians creates more well-being than not killing them. Even so, from the utilitarian point of view, there is nothing wrong in principle with killing civilians. Whether it is right or wrong is entirely contingent on the circumstances. And, it is hard to see how we could know in advance that there can never be circumstances in which attacking civilians would maximize utility. This is why people say that utilitarians see moral rules or principles as "rules of thumb," rough guides that may apply in many circumstances but which should be readily rejected whenever following them would not maximize utility.

Some people find this utilitarian reasoning very plausible. They reject noncombatant immunity because it requires us to avoid killing civilians even when killing civilians would produce better results than not doing so. Douglas Lackey supports this criticism of noncombatant immunity by imagining the case of a military officer faced with a choice between two possible ways to achieve a particular military objective. One possible attack, call it A, will cause 1,000 civilian deaths while the other, B, will kill 10,000 soldiers. A utilitarian analysis would pronounce A to be the right act. After all, it seems obvious that the right thing to do is to minimize overall deaths.

Why should it matter whether those killed are soldiers or civilians? Even if it is generally better to avoid killing civilians, in this case, the results seem to justify a different view.[2]

While this is a plausible argument, it is clear that the resulting view would not support a categorical condemnation of terrorist acts. If there are circumstances in which terrorist acts would lead to better consequences than other tactics, then this utilitarian reasoning would lead to the view that in these cases, terrorist acts are right. Suppose, for example, that terrorist tactics will overthrow a vile and oppressive government. Although civilians will die, a greater number of civilians will die if the government remains in power. Or, suppose that non-terrorist strategies against this government would cause more total casualties than attacks on civilians. In either case, utilitarian reasoning would justify terrorist attacks.

Lackey's brief discussion of terrorism illustrates this approach. Having rejected noncombatant immunity, he uses a proportionality principle as the "crucial moral test" for evaluating terrorism, asking:

> Can terrorism serve a just cause in such a way that its good effects substantially outweigh the bad? The verdict of history is clear: almost never. Most terrorists do not support just causes. As for the few that do, their actions are almost invariably ineffective.[3]

Although Lackey criticizes actual terrorist attacks and says that they are "almost never" justified, his position could be restated more positively. Instead of "almost never" justified, he could have echoed R. M. Hare's judgment that terrorism is "very seldom" justified. While this too has a negative sound, it definitely implies that terrorism is *sometimes* justified.[4] While Lackey criticizes terrorists because they typically lack a just cause and are "almost invariably" ineffective, his overall view commits him to saying that if they did have a just cause and if their attacks on civilians were effective, then these attacks could be justified. In spite of his negative language, Lackey seems to confirm what critics say: utilitarian reasoning undermines noncombatant immunity and opens the door to justifying terrorist acts.[5]

---

[2] Douglas Lackey, *The Ethics of War and Peace* (Englewood Cliffs, N.J.: Prentice Hall, 1988), 64–5.
[3] Ibid., 85.
[4] R. M. Hare, "Terrorism," in *Essays on Political Morality* (Oxford: Oxford University Press, 1989), 42. For a more positive articulation of the "possibly justified in some circumstances" view of terrorism, see McPherson, "Is Terrorism Distinctively Wrong?"
[5] Burleigh T. Wilkins gives a utilitarian defense of terrorism in *Terrorism and Collective Responsibility*, chapter 2. For criticism of Wilkins's argument, see Khatchadourian, *The Morality of Terrorism*, 80–6.

While Lackey and others use utilitarian arguments to defend this conclusion, others see this use as a confirmation of the moral baseness of utilitarianism. They charge that the utilitarian method of calculating benefits and losses undermines the role of conscience and our sense of humanity. In this sharply critical spirit, Stuart Hampshire writes that

The utilitarian habit of mind has brought with it a new abstract cruelty in politics, a dull, destructive political righteousness: mechanical, quantitative thinking, leaden academic minds setting out their moral calculations in leaden abstract prose, and more civilised and more superstitious people destroyed because of enlightened calculations that have proved wrong.[6]

In a similar spirit, Thomas Nagel writes that "it is particularly important not to lose confidence in our absolutist intuitions [including the belief that killing innocent people is wrong] for they are often the only barrier before the abyss of utilitarian apologetics for large-scale murder."[7] Nagel believes that our "absolutist intuitions" that certain kinds of actions are simply wrong in themselves are needed to support central human values. Like Walzer, Nagel rejects utilitarianism because its evaluations are subject to ever-changing contingencies of fact and circumstance. Because Nagel believes that utilitarian reasoning could support large-scale murder in the "right circumstances," he rejects it as a morally depraved view.

THE SIMPLE ARGUMENT FOR A RIGHTS-BASED DEFENSE OF NONCOMBATANT IMMUNITY

Just as it has seemed clear to many people that utilitarianism cannot support noncombatant immunity, it has seemed equally clear that an approach based on individual human rights provides strong support for noncombatant immunity. This is because rights limit what people may do to one another, and noncombatant immunity is a limit placed on what people may do in pursuit of military victory. This makes it plausible to invoke rights to explain why violating noncombatant immunity is wrong. The following argument articulates this approach and illustrates its plausibility.

1. When people have rights, these rights may not be overridden simply because doing so will achieve an important goal or maximize utility.

---

[6] Stuart Hampshire, "Morality and Pessimism," in Stuart Hampshire, ed., *Public and Private Morality* (Cambridge: Cambridge University Press, 1978), 4.

[7] Thomas Nagel, "War and Massacre," in M. Cohen et al., eds., *War and Moral Responsibility* (Princeton: Princeton University Press, 1974), 6; originally published in *Philosophy and Public Affairs* 1 (1972). Richard Norman makes a similar criticism of utilitarianism in *Ethics, Killing, and War* (Cambridge: Cambridge University Press, 1995), 11.

2. People have a right to life, i.e., an immunity to attacks that would kill them.
3. It is wrong to violate people's rights, even when it would achieve an important goal or maximize utility.
4. Killing civilians in war violates their right to life.
5. Therefore, it is wrong to kill civilians in war, even if this could achieve victory in a just war or maximize overall well-being.

This argument must be supplemented with an explanation of why the right to life gives civilians immunity to attack but does not give that same immunity to soldiers. But, as we see in Walzer's discussion, soldiers are generally thought to have partially sacrificed their right to life. When people become soldiers, they gain a right to kill but lose their immunity to being killed. People who are noncombatants have not given up their immunity to attack, and, for this reason, it is wrong to kill them, even for a good cause.[8]

Rights theories are very attractive in this context. They appear to call for a recognition of rights that is not left to contingencies of circumstance. If "large-scale murder" is wrong because it violates people's rights, then it would not be made right by the fact that valuable goals might be achieved in this way. Rights theorists have been strong defenders of protections for individuals that a utilitarian theory seems incapable of supporting.

The attractiveness of the rights approach is enhanced by the stirring pronouncements of prominent rights theorists. John Rawls, for example, strongly affirms individual rights in this well-known statement:

Each person possesses an inviolability founded on justice that even the welfare of society as a whole cannot override. For this reason ... the rights secured by justice are not subject to political bargaining or to the calculus of social interests.[9]

Robert Nozick makes similar claims about rights as bulwarks of moral protection:

Individuals have rights, and there are things no person or group may do to them (without violating their rights) ... [I]ndividuals are ends and not merely means; they may not be sacrificed or used for the achieving of other ends without their consent. Individuals are inviolable.[10]

Likewise, Ronald Dworkin, in *Taking Rights Seriously*, describes rights as "trumps," i.e., moral reasons that override other kinds of reasons:

---

[8] Walzer, *Just and Unjust Wars*, 134–5.
[9] John Rawls, *A Theory of Justice* (Cambridge, Mass.: Harvard University Press, 1971), 3–4.
[10] Nozick, *Anarchy, State, and Utopia*, ix, 31.

Individual rights are political trumps held by individuals. Individuals have rights when, for some reason, a collective goal is not a sufficient justification ... for imposing some loss or injury upon them.[11]

These statements make clear how the language of rights is often used to affirm the importance of constraints on how goals may be achieved.

It is easy to see why it is appealing to think about noncombatant immunity from a rights perspective. If each individual is inviolable and has rights that may not be overridden, then we can make sense of noncombatant immunity as an absolute constraint on the fighting of wars. Belligerent countries in a war are permitted to do many things in pursuit of victory, but killing civilians is not a permissible means to victory because it violates people's rights.

WHY RIGHTS THEORIES ARE LESS PROMISING THAN THEY SEEM

While the language of rights lends itself to strong affirmations of various kinds of immunity, it does not necessarily support strong rights, and it certainly does not automatically justify an absolute right of noncombatant immunity. The reason for this is simple and even uncontroversial. Many rights, perhaps even most rights, are not absolute. For this reason, violations or infringements of them are often permissible. Dworkin, though best known for the idea of rights as trumps, acknowledges that rights do not always take priority over other considerations.

Rights may also be less than absolute; one principle might have to yield to another, or even to an urgent policy ... We may define the weight of a right ... as its power to withstand such competition. It follows from the definition of a right that it cannot be outweighed ... [by] the ordinary routine goals of political administration, but only by a goal of special urgency.[12]

Rights, Dworkin makes clear, are not always absolute. Sometimes, there are legitimate reasons to override them.

In some cases, the feature of overrideability is actually built into the expression of a right. The Fifth Amendment to the United States Constitution, for example, affirms certain rights when it says that no person "shall be deprived of life, liberty, or property, without due process of law." While this amendment affirms several important rights, it also indicates how those rights can be lost or overridden, namely, through "due process of

---

[11] Ronald Dworkin, *Taking Rights Seriously* (Cambridge, Mass.: Harvard University Press, 1978), xi.
[12] Ibid., 92.

law." Clearly, these rights are not absolute since people may be deprived of them through a legal process. Moreover, whether or not these rights are strong and secure will depend on the nature of the legal processes by which people may be deprived of them. If a trial by a "kangaroo court" is deemed to be sufficient for due process of law, one's rights are not worth much. In practice, the words of the amendment are compatible with both very strong and very weak understandings of these rights.

People's rights can also change in different circumstances. As we have seen, our understanding of the right to life is radically altered by war. During wartime, soldiers gain a right to do many things that are forbidden in ordinary circumstances. At the same time, the soldier's right to life no longer makes her immune to attack. The mere fact, then, that someone has a right to something does not guarantee that this right is always operative.

Sometimes rights are understood to be contingent on certain conditions even though we don't always make that explicit. Someone who gets a parking sticker for a beach parking lot has a right to park there, but that right does not guarantee a space if the lot is already full. The right to park is really a right to park on the condition that there are empty spaces. That is much weaker than a right to park that allows its bearer to eject others from spaces when the lot is full. People who own a parking space have the right to eject others, but in the beach sticker case, the right to park is usually much weaker.

As these examples show, rights vary considerably in strength. They can be weak as well as strong, and they do not always trump other considerations. Once we see this, it is evident that merely using rights language – rather than the language of utility – will not guarantee strong rights. In fact, it is possible to use rights language to articulate the whole range of views on noncombatant immunity. Political realism could be stated as the view that civilians have a right not to be attacked except when it is in the interest of a nation at war to do so. Even the idea that "anything goes" in time of war can be translated into the view that people have a right not to be attacked in ordinary life, but in war, that right no longer applies. So there is nothing about rights language that guarantees strong protections.

The fact that rights do not always trump is clear from Walzer's theory. He affirms a relatively strong version of noncombatant immunity, but that right gives way to a right of people faced with a supreme emergency to defend themselves by attacking noncombatants. Although Rawls affirms the "inviolability" of individuals, he explicitly endorses Walzer's supreme emergency exception to noncombatant immunity.[13]

---

[13] John Rawls, *The Law of Peoples* (Cambridge, Mass.: Harvard University Press, 1999), 98–9.

The choice, then, between a weak, easily overrideable form of noncombatant immunity, a stronger version of noncombatant immunity that can only be overridden in a supreme emergency, and an absolute right of noncombatants not to be attacked exists within a rights theory perspective. Merely adopting this perspective will not tell us which, if any, of these views is correct. While the rhetoric of rights theorists suggests that rights are always inviolable and always trump other considerations, it is easy to see both that this is false and that it is not really held by those who use this rhetoric.[14]

For this reason, even if we believe that noncombatant immunity is a right, we must still ask how strong a right it is. Moreover, because rights-based views can differ among themselves about the strength of this right, we need a method to determine which view is correct. How do rights theorists determine the strength of noncombatant immunity? How do they decide whether a particular right is absolute? And, if they decide that it is not absolute, how do they know what it takes to override it?

WHY THIS IS A HARD PROBLEM FOR RIGHTS THEORISTS

One reason why these issues are difficult for rights theorists is that the problem of whether noncombatant immunity is an absolute or whether it includes a supreme emergency exception arises out of a conflict of rights. In fact, it arises out of a conflict within a single, very important right, the right to life. Although the right to life sounds like a simple, familiar right, it is in fact a package of multiple rights, and, unfortunately, the different rights within this package can conflict with one another. As a result, the right to life seems to be at war with itself.[15]

To see why, consider what the right to life is a right to. The most central idea is that this right gives people an immunity to being killed. Because you have a right to life, other people have no right to kill you. Understood this way, the right to life is a negative right (a right *not* to have something done to you) that is connected to a negative duty (the duty of others *not* to kill you). But that is not all. The right to life also includes a right to defend ourselves against fatal attack and other grievous harms. Moreover, with

---

[14] Nozick comes closest to maintaining the absoluteness of certain rights, but even he seems to concede something like an extreme emergency exception in a footnote comment; *Anarchy, State, and Utopia*, 30. Nozick's willingness to respect property rights even at the cost of great suffering reveals a less appealing aspect of absolute rights.

[15] Jeremy Waldron discusses the problem of conflicting rights in "Rights in Conflict," *Ethics* 99 (April 1989), 503–19.

respect to killing in self-defense, there is widespread agreement that severe harms other than death – for example, rape, torture, disablement – can justify self-defensive killing.[16]

The mere fact that people have a duty not to kill others unjustifiably does not guarantee that they will not try to do so, and such attacks unfortunately occur with great frequency. When they occur, the right of self-defense allows the intended victims to prevent the attackers from inflicting death upon them. This aspect of the right to life is a positive right. It confers a permission on victims of attacks to act in their own defense.

These components of the right to life are familiar and uncontroversial, and, when looked at in a certain way, they fit together nicely. Taken together, the negative right not to be killed and the positive right to defend ourselves work together to give each person a certain level of protection. But there is also a latent conflict between these aspects of the right to life. The positive right to defend one's own life allows a person to attack and, if necessary, kill others. But killing other people seems to violate their immunity to attack. Seen in this way, the immunity to attack and the right to self-defensive killing seem to cancel each other out. Other people's immunity to attack seems to block my right to kill them in order to save myself.

This is where the familiar idea that people can lose their immunity enters the picture. If people lose their immunity when they unjustifiably attack others, then when people defend themselves against an attacker, they do not violate the attacker's right to life. This is because the attacker, by threatening the life of another person, forfeits – at least temporarily – the right not to be killed. In this sense, the right not to be killed is not inalienable. It can be lost when people engage in unjustified, life-threatening attacks on others.[17]

Nor is the right to defend oneself an unlimited right; it does not allow people to do whatever will prevent being killed by an attacker. Jan Narveson, in a well-known criticism of pacifism, goes too far when he says that having a right to personal security implies that "one has a right to whatever may be necessary to prevent infringements" of this right.[18] The right to prevent our own death allows some defensive actions but not every

---

[16] Jane English discusses non-lethal threats that justify self-defensive killing in "Abortion and the Concept of a Person," *Canadian Journal of Philosophy* 5 (1975), 233–43.

[17] Judith Thomson criticizes the forfeiture model in "Self-Defense and Rights," in her *Rights, Restitution, and Risk* (Cambridge, Mass.: Harvard University Press, 1986), 33–7. David Rodin defends it against her criticisms in *War and Self-Defense*, 70–9.

[18] Jan Narveson, "Pacifism: A Philosophical Analysis," *Ethics* 75 (1965), 266. Jenny Teichman criticizes Narveson's claim in *Pacifism and the Just War* (Oxford: Basil Blackwell, 1986), 31–6.

possible means of defense. If someone is about to shoot you from a crowded bus and your only weapon is a hand grenade, you do not have a right to blow up the bus in order to save your life. Your right to defensive action allows you to attack only the person responsible for the attack and does not extend to killing other people on the bus.

Of course, if our lives are threatened, we will very much want to do whatever is necessary to defend ourselves, and abstaining from protective measures will not be easy. Nonetheless, our right to defend ourselves has limits. The person trying to shoot you from the bus may have forfeited his right not to be attacked, but other people on the bus have not forfeited their immunity to attack. You violate their rights if you kill them to protect yourself.

The clash between the right not to be attacked and the right to defend oneself against attack is such an important feature of the right to life that it is worth illustrating this clash with other examples. Suppose that you are walking down the street and a person whom you know to be an expert knife thrower tries to kill you by throwing a knife in your direction. Suppose further that you can save yourself by pulling a passerby in front of you so that the knife will plunge into the passerby's body rather than into yours. This is not a permissible way to protect yourself because it violates the immunity rights of the passerby. Your right to defend yourself does not include the right to deflect the danger onto an innocent person.[19]

For a real-world case, consider Paul Fussell's powerful essay "Thank God for the Atomic Bomb."[20] Fussell argues that anyone like himself who experienced combat and actually faced the prospect of invading Japan in World War II would support the use of the atomic bomb to end the war and spare themselves from further fighting. He derides critics of the atomic bombings who did not themselves experience the horrors of combat. To see that Fussell's right to life did not justify the atomic bombings, we simply have to consider whether the atomic bombings would have been right if Fussell's life was the only one saved. No matter how strong his desire to live and to avoid further combat, his rights did not extend as far as atomic attacks on cities as a means of protecting himself. In saying this, I do not mean to trivialize either Fussell's desires or his rights. The key point is that

---

[19] Noam Zohar discusses this and related cases in "Innocence and Complex Threats: Upholding the War Ethic and the Condemnation of Terrorism," *Ethics* 114 (2004), 734–51. See, too, Judith Thomson's discussion in "Self-Defense," *Philosophy and Public Affairs* 20 (1991).

[20] Paul Fussell, "Thank God for the Atomic Bomb," in *Thank God for the Atomic Bomb and Other Essays* (New York: Summit, 1988), 13–37; followed by comments by Michael Walzer and Fussell's reply, 38–44.

others have the same rights, and their rights impose limits on what any individual may do to protect himself.

IMMUNITY RIGHTS VS. PREVENTION RIGHTS

What these cases reveal is the tension between two aspects of the right to life: the immunity-to-attack component and the permission-to-defend-oneself component. This tension underlies a number of controversial issues. One set of these that has been much discussed by philosophers concerns defense against innocent threats and innocent aggressors. An innocent aggressor is a person who attacks you but who, for one or another reason, is not morally culpable for the attack. Perhaps he or she is deranged or has been hypnotized and ordered to kill you. An innocent threat is a person who is endangering you but not through any action that he or she is carrying out. A common example is a person who has fallen from a building and who will crush you. As happens in philosophical examples, you have a ray gun that you can use to disintegrate the falling person's body. In both cases, you can save yourself by killing a morally innocent person. David Rodin summarizes and assesses the philosophical debate about these cases and their implication, noting that:

> Most modern commentators … agree that one would be justified in acting against both an Innocent Aggressor and an Innocent Threat. Furthermore, this view is explicitly endorsed in most legal jurisdictions … But the consensus view is not correct: it is generally not justifiable to save oneself by killing an Innocent Aggressor or Innocent Threat … The reasons for this stem from considerations deep in the theory of rights.[21]

Rodin disagrees with other theorists because he believes that there is an important constraint on killing another to save one's life. This is permissible, he thinks, only when the person who is the threat is morally responsible for that threat. Others, however, think that the right of the person being threatened to take steps to save herself overrides the lack of moral responsibility on the part of the innocent threat. The debate here is about which aspect of the right to life takes priority in these cases, the negative right of immunity to attack or the positive right of defense against threats to one's life.[22]

We don't need philosophers' examples to see these tensions at work. Consider the debate about access to guns. People who support strong rights

---

[21] Rodin, *War and Self-Defense*, 80–81.
[22] For Rodin's full argument and useful references to the opposition, see ibid., 79–99. For an important defense of a similar view, see Jeff McMahan, "Self-Defense and the Problem of the Innocent Attacker," *Ethics* 104 (1994), 252–90.

to own guns believe that owning a weapon enhances their ability to defend themselves and think that the right of self-defense justifies a right to own a gun. Their opponents stress the dangers created by widespread ownership of guns. The gun-owner – or others with access to his gun – is able to inflict harms on others that he could not readily inflict without a gun. This, along with the possibility of accidents, increases the danger to others. One person's increased capacity to defend himself is another person's increased vulnerability to attack and accidental harm. If everyone owned a gun, each person's defensive rights would be strengthened while everyone's immunity rights would be weakened.

The same issue was at the heart of the Bernhard Goetz case. In December 1984, Goetz shot four young men on a New York subway because he feared that they were going to attack him.[23] One of the men was paralyzed for life. Assuming both that Goetz genuinely feared for his life and that the young men had not yet taken any steps toward attacking him, the question emerges whether he had a right to shoot them. Here, too, the right to defend oneself conflicts with the right of immunity to attack. If we understand the right of self-defense as a very strong right that permits people to shoot anyone that they fear, then the immunity rights of potential victims are clearly weakened. They lose their immunity and become permissible targets because they are feared, even if they have not initiated an attack and have no intention of doing so. On the other hand, if we understand the immunity right as a very strong right that protects people from being attacked unless they actually initiate an attack against someone, then the right of self-defense is understood in a weaker way because fear of attack is not a sufficient justification.

We can think about this conflict of rights by imagining a continuum that represents the strength of each aspect of the right to life. Stronger immunity rights place more restrictions on defensive rights while stronger defensive rights limit the scope of immunity. Each right's strength is inversely proportional to the other's.

	Negative right not to be killed			Positive right to defend oneself	
Strength of Right	100	75	50	25	0
	0	25	50	75	100

---

[23] George Fletcher describes the events surrounding the Goetz case and analyzes the issues it raises in *A Crime of Self-Defense: Bernhard Goetz and The Law on Trial* (New York: The Free Press, 1988).

In a world where positive defensive rights were total and no immunity rights existed, Narveson's claim that the right to life permits any necessary defensive action would be true, as would the realist's view that "anything goes" in the name of self-defense. This view of rights matches Hobbes's conception of the right to life in the state of nature. According to Hobbes, people in the state of nature have complete rights both to defend themselves and to advance their interests. They have no immunity rights against attack by others, however, because everyone has the same complete rights to attack anyone else in order to defend themselves and advance their interests.

As the table shows, immunity rights in Hobbes's state of nature would be at the 0 level while defensive rights would be 100.[24] The opposite extreme is occupied by pacifism. Absolute pacifists reject all violent acts because they see immunity rights as absolute. They do not recognize defensive rights at all if those rights are understood to include the right to use violent means of defense.

We could use this continuum to illustrate all the views on the ethics of war-fighting that I have discussed. Noncombatant immunity raises the level of immunity rights while diminishing the power of the right to defend oneself. Similarly, in the debate between absolute noncombatant immunity and the supreme emergency exception, the supreme emergency exception strengthens the right of defense at the cost of weakening the immunity right of noncombatants.

CONCLUSION

My aim in this chapter has been to reveal a problem, not to solve it. The conventional wisdom is that utilitarianism cannot effectively support non-combatant immunity and that rights theories can. I have tried to show that rights theories provide no guarantees of immunity to attack and no magic solutions to problems about the relative strength of noncombatant immunity. Rather, questions about the strength of noncombatant immunity are a problem within rights theory because both immunity rights and defensive rights are central to the right to life. Since these aspects of the right to life conflict with one another, we need to figure out how to do justice to both of them. The language of rights gives us a vocabulary to formulate this problem, but it does nothing to solve it.

---

[24] Hobbes, *Leviathan*, part I, chapter XIV.

CHAPTER 13

Immunity rights vs. the right of self-defense

If we take rights seriously, how do we resolve the tension between different parts of the right to life? How do we tell which takes precedence in conflict situations? Is it the right of people not to be attacked? Or the right of people to defend themselves when their lives are threatened? A common philosophical method for trying to deal with hard questions like these is to begin with easy cases and see if we can extrapolate from them. Perhaps this familiar strategy can help us to determine whether we should accept absolute noncombatant immunity or recognize exceptions in extreme cases when attacking civilians is the only means of resisting an extraordinary threat.

If we decide that defensive rights take precedence, then people who are in dire enough circumstances may have a right to engage in terrorist acts, whether they be bombings of cities by powerful air forces or the use of small bombs in markets and buses. If we decide that immunity rights take precedence, then no matter how dire the circumstances or how severe the threat, no one has a right to protect themselves by killing innocent people.

THE SIMPLE MODEL OF JUSTIFIABLE DEFENSE IN ORDINARY LIFE AND IN WAR

In standard, uncontroversial cases of justified self-defense, there is no clash between immunity rights and defensive rights. This is what makes these cases uncontroversial. If someone unjustifiably tries to kill you, you have a right to defend yourself from attack and to use lethal force if necessary. Your right to injure or kill the person attacking you rests on two factors. First, by injuring or killing this person, you can prevent the loss of your own life. Second, in injuring or killing the attacker, you are harming the person who is responsible for the unjustified attack on your life.

This second requirement of responsibility for an attack is central to our ordinary understandings of self-defense. It is not sufficient that we can protect our own life by attacking another person. The right of self-defense permits us to harm the attacker because the attacker is responsible for the threat against us. By initiating the attack, the assailant loses his immunity, and the victim gains a right to kill the attacker as a means of defense.

Even in this case, however, there are constraints on what you have a right to do. If, for example, you can protect yourself by hiding or escaping, then killing the attacker is not necessary, and you have no right to do so. Or, if you can defend yourself by inflicting a lesser harm than death, then you have a duty to inflict the lesser harm. Even when you defend yourself against a culpable attacker, that person retains elements of immunity. When there are no alternative means of self-defense, however, an intended victim has a right to kill the attacker. This is our model case for justified killing in self-defense.

This model serves as a launching point for our usual understanding of the ethics of war-fighting. In individual self-defense cases, we have a right to defend ourselves, but we may not defend ourselves by harming people other than the attacker, even if doing so is required for our own defense. Recall the case of using a passerby to block a knife that has been thrown by someone who is trying to kill you. If the passerby has no role in the attack, you may not use that person to shield yourself from attack. While this would succeed in protecting you, the person being harmed is not the one who is responsible for intentionally endangering you.

If we extrapolate from these examples to the case of war, we get the idea that it is permissible for soldiers in a war to kill enemy soldiers because the enemy soldiers are a threat and are responsible for their being a threat. Individual soldiers are, of course, not responsible for the war itself, but they are responsible for the threat that they impose on others whom they attack.

If this is the basis for justifying attacks on enemy soldiers, then it appears to follow that soldiers may not attack non-combatants – even when doing so might have protective value – because noncombatants are not imposing a threat on anyone. While civilians can lose their immunity by taking a direct role in military activities, unless they do this, they are no threat and remain immune to attack. This standard view is the one Walzer draws on in his initial defense of noncombatant immunity: we may only attack people who through some act of their own have lost their immunity.[1] By extension, states at war are similarly restricted in the means they may use to win. Even if attacking civilians might have military value, this is prohibited.

---

[1] Walzer, *Just and Unjust Wars*, 135.

When we use the simple model, we treat the ethics of war as an extension of the ethics of individual conflict. Since we are familiar with the moral rules that govern individual behavior, we extrapolate from them to cases involving the actions of nations or other groups. Just as individuals have rights of immunity and rights of self-defense, so nations and other groups have parallel rights. And, their rights have similar limitations. War is individual conduct writ large.

PROBLEMS WITH THE SIMPLE MODEL

Unfortunately, the use of the simple model for understanding both combatant non-immunity and noncombatant immunity faces serious problems. In the most usual cases, the right to defend one's life does not permit acting in ways that kill innocent people, even if such actions might prevent the loss of one's own life. But warfare is a different circumstance, and the generally accepted rules of warfare depart in significant ways from the individual self-defense model. The rules about killing and other acts of violence in war are generally understood to be much more permissive than the rules that govern violent acts in ordinary life.

If we extrapolate from our ordinary morality to circumstances of war, we would say that soldiers have a right of self-defense that allows them to kill enemy soldiers who are attacking them. But the rules of killing in war are much more permissive. Soldiers are permitted to attack enemy soldiers at any time, whether they are attacking or not. They may attack enemy soldiers who are sleeping and present no current threat to anyone.[2] Moreover, soldiers may attack military personnel whose role is not to engage in fighting, such as soldiers who transport equipment, repair vehicles, or prepare food. Although these soldiers play a role in the overall military effort, they pose no direct, immediate threat to anyone. If soldiers attack and kill them, the attacking soldiers are not acting in self-defense because they are not under attack. Yet, we generally take it for granted that attacks on noncombat military personnel are permissible. In saying this, I do not mean either to approve or criticize this practice. My point is simply that the moral rules that govern permissible killing in war are much more permissive than the rules that govern violent acts in ordinary life.

A further difference between the ethics of war and the ethics of everyday life is the much more permissive approach to actions that result in civilian deaths and injuries as side effects of attempts to defend oneself. Recall the example of the attacker on the bus. The right to defend oneself from being

---

[2] Walzer calls this the problem of the naked soldier and argues that such persons are permissible targets in *Just and Unjust Wars*, 138–43. Larry May rejects this idea in *War Crimes and Just War*, chapter 5.

shot by a person on a crowded bus does not include a right to throw a hand grenade into the bus even if this would kill the attacker and save one's own life. Our ordinary understanding of self-defense forbids actions that cause deaths to innocent people as side effects of a defensive action. Even police officers, who have stronger rights to use lethal force than ordinary citizens, are not authorized to fire into crowds of people in order to kill a dangerous criminal.[3] In warfare, however, it is generally accepted that soldiers sometimes have a right to attack military targets even if they know that innocent people will also be killed by their attack.

These differences between everyday ethics and the ethics of war cast some doubt on the method of extrapolating from one to the other. War is a distinctive circumstance in which actions that are among the most strongly forbidden in ordinary life become routine. This radical shift in moral presumptions about what is permissible adds to the confusion about what is permissible or forbidden in war.

The fact that war is a special circumstance is one reason why it is difficult to resolve the problems raised by the supreme emergency doctrine. That doctrine acknowledges that intentionally targeting civilians is not something that people ordinarily have a right to do, even in war. But, in extraordinary cases, the supreme emergency view says that the balance between immunity rights and defensive rights tips in the other direction of defensive rights. When people face a dire enough threat and have no other effective means of defense, their right to defend their nation or group becomes stronger while the immunity rights of noncombatants become weaker. Opponents of supreme emergency argue that the immunity of noncombatants remains unchanged and that dire circumstances do not justify an exception to absolute noncombatant immunity. Why, they ask, should the immunity rights of civilians in an enemy country be diminished by the dire situation of other people? If the civilians of the enemy country are not responsible for this dire situation, how could it be right to attack them?

THE RELATIONS BETWEEN INDIVIDUAL AND COLLECTIVE RIGHTS OF DEFENSE

While the standard method of thinking about these issues uses the kinds of extrapolations I have described, our views about the ethics of individual

---

[3] Douglas Lackey contrasts military action and police activities in "The Good Soldier versus the Good Cop. Counterterrorism as Police Work," *Iyyun: The Jerusalem Philosophical Quarterly* 55 (January 2006), 66–82.

behavior become stretched and altered when we extend them to the collective actions of countries at war. As a result, actions are permitted in war that are not permitted in individual cases. Perhaps the moral of the story is that the rights of nations and other groups are fundamentally different from the rights that individuals possess. If that is true, then it would be a mistake to try to derive the ethics of war from our views of individual rights in non-war situations.

The chart below describes four models for understanding both the morality of killing innocent people as a means of defense and the relationship between individual and collective rights. The views in columns A and C give different answers to questions about whether there is sometimes a right to kill innocent people, but they both support the method of extrapolating from individual rights to the collective case. The views in B and D differ from one another about whether there is a collective right to attack noncombatants, but both reject the method of inferring collective rights from individual rights.

	A (Nagel)	B (Walzer)	C (Sterba)	D
Uses method of inferring collective rights from individual rights.	Yes	No	Yes	No
Is there an individual right to kill innocent people to defend oneself?	No	No	Yes	Yes
Is there a collective right to kill civilians to defend a nation or group?	No	Yes	Yes	No

In approaching the problem of absolute noncombatant immunity vs. the supreme emergency exception, position A begins with standard cases of individual self-defense and claims that the right to individual defense is limited to attacking people who are directly responsible for the attack. For this reason, there is no right to kill innocent people in order to save one's own life. Position A then claims that, because killing innocent people is forbidden at the individual level, it is also forbidden at the collective level. This view recognizes no difference between the individual and collective levels and bases its moral understanding of war on extrapolations from the ethics of individual self-defense.

Thomas Nagel presents this type of view sympathetically when he writes that "hostile treatment of any person must be justified in terms of something *about that person* which makes the treatment appropriate." If we justifiably kill someone, the relevant fact about the person we kill must be that he or she is attacking us and therefore is not innocent. Later, Nagel directly links this individual case to the situation in war. He writes that the "deliberate killing of the innocent is murder, and in warfare the role of the innocent is filled by noncombatants."[4] According to Position A, then, if killing innocent people is murder at the individual level, comparable acts are murder at the collective level.[5]

Position B agrees with A that, at the individual level, there is no right to kill innocent people in order to save one's own life. Unlike A, however, B holds that different rules operate at the collective level. For this reason, a "no" answer at the individual level does not imply a "no" answer at the collective level. Michael Walzer holds this view. Although he often argues in the manner of Position A (using what he calls the "domestic analogy"), he rejects this method and shifts to Position B in his defense of the supreme emergency exception. Thus, discussing the individual right to self-defense, he writes:

> It is not usually said of individuals in domestic society that they … morally can strike out at innocent people, even in the supreme emergency of self-defense. They can only attack their attackers.[6]

When he defends the supreme emergency exception, however, Walzer explicitly invokes the idea that there is a special moral logic that applies at the collective level. "But communities," he writes, "in emergencies, seem to have different and larger prerogatives." In a passage quoted earlier, Walzer tries to explain why communities have a right to attack noncombatants in supreme emergency circumstances.

> [I]t is possible to live in a world where individuals are sometimes murdered, but a world where entire peoples are enslaved or massacred is literally unbearable. For the survival and freedom of political communities – whose members share a way of life, developed by their ancestors, to be passed on to their children – are the highest values of international society.[7]

The point here seems to be that, as terrible as the murder of individuals is, the horror of enslaving or massacring collectives – entire peoples, political communities – is dreadful in a special way. The difference is not only quantitative. It is not simply that a larger number of people is involved

---

[4] Nagel, "War and Massacre," 13, 19.
[5] Jeff McMahan uses the method of Position A to reveal discrepancies between the rules generated by extrapolating from the individual level and the traditional rules of war. He concludes that traditional views of the ethics of war are severely defective. For his criticisms, see his "Innocence, Self-Defense, and Killing in War," and "The Ethics of Killing in War."
[6] Walzer, *Just and Unjust Wars*, 254.   [7] Ibid.

when groups are attacked and killed.[8] Rather, it is different because the group sustains a form of common life, and this common life faces destruction along with the individual human beings. The moral requirements of individual life do not apply when communities and the forms of life they sustain are threatened with destruction.

Walzer's view is that attacks on innocent people that are prohibited at the individual level are sometimes permissible at the collective level. His argument for this discontinuity is weakly developed, however. Obviously, he can't appeal to the individual level to support his claim because he holds that the individual and collective level differ in this case. Instead, he counts on our sharing his horror at the prospect of the destruction of a way of life. This is a weak argument, however. Many things threaten a community's way of life. Some current examples are television, advertising, and immigration, all of which threaten various ways of life and are perceived by many people to be such threats. Although these threats are serious sources of tension in the world, it is doubtful that combating them would justify killing innocent people. This communitarian path is in fact a dangerous one to go down.[9]

Moreover, Walzer clearly overstates the facts when he says that "a world where entire peoples are enslaved or massacred is literally unbearable." Whether life is bearable or unbearable for people seems to depend largely on our immediate circumstances. Even if we are troubled by evils that befall others, most of us find life quite bearable if we and those we care most about are safe and secure. The fact that genocides continue to occur and that it is difficult to gain support for stopping them should make us skeptical of Walzer's claim that "the survival and freedom of political communities ... are the highest values of international society."

While Walzer rejects the method of inferring collective rights from individual rights, there is an alternative strategy for defending the priority of collective rights of defense over immunity rights. According to this argument, even at the individual level, we recognize cases in which it is permissible to kill innocent people. For that reason, we should be able to understand how individual and collective ethics work in parallel ways and

---

[8] For Walzer's rejection of quantitative considerations, see ibid., 262.

[9] For a defense of a strong communitarian form of patriotism and its militaristic implications, see Alasdair MacIntyre, "Is Patriotism a Virtue?," The Lindley Lecture (Lawrence, Kans.: Philosophy Department, University of Kansas, 1984). For criticisms of MacIntyre's view, see my "In Defense of 'Moderate Patriotism,'" *Ethics* 99 (1988–9), 535–52. Both essays are reprinted in Igor Primoratz, ed., *Patriotism* (Buffalo, N.Y.: Humanity Books, 2002).

why killing innocent people is sometimes permissible at both levels. James Sterba uses this strategy, represented in column C, to support both the supreme emergency exception and the view that terrorism can sometimes be morally justified.[10]

STERBA'S DEFENSE OF SUPREME EMERGENCY
ATTACKS AND TERRORISM

Sterba's argument has four parts. First, he argues that there are cases in ordinary life when it is permissible to kill innocent people. Second, he extrapolates from this view of individual ethics to support the supreme emergency exception to noncombatant immunity. Third, he concludes that terrorist acts can sometimes be morally justified even though they target innocent people. Finally, he applies his view to the case of the Palestinians and argues that their dire circumstances justify terrorist tactics against Israeli civilians.

Sterba begins with an example that various philosophers have discussed. A number of people are exploring a cave when a rock slide traps them inside. To make matters worse, the cave is filling with water. They manage to find a small exit hole, but the first person who tries to exit is too large and gets stuck in the opening. He can neither escape nor free himself to let others through. The group has one stick of dynamite, but if it blows open the exit hole, it will kill the person who is stuck there. Is it morally permissible for the other people to save their lives by blowing open the hole and thereby killing the person stuck there?[11]

In one version, a "yes" answer is extremely plausible. Suppose that the person's head is stuck in the hole so that he too will die as the cave fills with water. In that case, since he will die anyway, there seems to be a strong case for at least saving the others. But in the more relevant version, the person's head is above ground so that he will not drown and may eventually be able to get out. Sterba believes that members of the group would be justified in using the dynamite to free themselves even though this will kill the person who is stuck. Because the person stuck in the exit hole is an innocent person, Sterba infers that it is sometimes permissible to kill an innocent person. But, he reasons, if it is permissible to kill an innocent person in this case, then in situations involving war and violent conflict, there can also be

---

[10] Sterba presents this argument in "Terrorism and International Justice."
[11] The example (used for a different purpose) appears in Philippa Foot, "The Problem of Abortion and the Principle of Double Effect," *Virtues and Vices* (Oxford: Oxford University Press, 2002), 21.

instances where killing innocent people is morally permissible.[12] If this is true, Sterba says, then the prohibition on killing innocent people is not an absolute.

Unlike positions A and B on the chart, Sterba's view C gives a "yes" answer to the question about the right of individuals to kill an innocent person as a means of defense. He then uses this answer as the basis for a "yes" answer at the collective level. He believes that, once we recognize that the ban on killing innocent people in ordinary life is not absolute, we will see that the principle of noncombatant immunity is also not absolute. Having seen that, we will accept the view that violations of noncombatant immunity can be justified in supreme emergency circumstances and that terrorist acts committed in supreme emergency conditions can be morally justified.[13]

Defenders of the absolute version of noncombatant immunity have two options in trying to refute Sterba's argument. The first option is to argue that he is simply wrong about the cave example and that the people in the cave have no right to save themselves by dynamiting the opening and killing the person stuck in the exit hole. If that is true, then Sterba does not establish the right to kill innocent people at the individual level. A second option is to argue that, even if Sterba is correct about the cave example, he is wrong to think that we can extrapolate from it to the circumstances of war and wrong to conclude that violations of noncombatant immunity are sometimes permissible. This reply expresses Position D on the chart. It concedes the permissibility of killing innocent people at the individual level but denies its permissibility at the collective level.[14]

I will consider both challenges to Sterba's argument and try to show that, while Sterba may be right about the cave case, he is wrong to think that he can reasonably extrapolate from it to conclusions about collective rights involving war and terrorism.

THE CAVE EXAMPLE RECONSIDERED

Sterba's view is certainly plausible. All of the people in the cave are equally innocent, and none has a greater right to escape than the others. Moreover,

---

[12] Sterba, "Terrorism and International Justice," 212ff.

[13] Tom Sorell defends violations of moral rules in emergency situations in "Morality and Emergency," *Proceedings of the Aristotelian Society* 103 (2002), 1–37; see 28 n4 for a case like Sterba's.

[14] Noam Zohar distinguishes between individual and collective ethics in "Collective War and Individualistic Ethics," *Political Theory* 21 (1993), 606–22. Zohar appeals to an individual ethic (view A) to support noncombatant immunity while using a collectivist ethic (view B) to justify the permissibility of attacking soldiers.

if the exit is dynamited open, many more people will be saved, while a greater number will perish if, out of respect for the immunity right of the person blocking the exit, they do nothing. Most of the appeal of Sterba's argument rests on this second reason, that more people will be saved if the dynamite is used. Sterba stresses this feature when he writes:

> Suppose there were ten, twenty, one hundred, or whatever number you want of spelunkers trapped in the cave. At some point, won't the number be sufficiently great that it would be morally acceptable for those in the cave … to save themselves rather than the large person [who is blocking the exit hole]?[15]

This may sound like a utilitarian argument, but it can also be seen as an argument for resolving a conflict of rights by considering the consequences. If all of the people trapped in the cave have an equal right to live, then perhaps the best we can do in trying to respect the rights of all is to save as many as possible.

Having argued that killing innocent persons is sometimes morally permissible at the individual level, Sterba applies his reasoning to the collective level and argues that terrorism can sometimes be justified in a similar way. While Sterba accepts a presumption against attacking innocent people, he explicitly offers rules for determining when these immunity rights may be overridden.

> Now one might think that … acts of terrorism could never be morally justified. But this would require an absolute prohibition on intentionally harming innocents, and such a prohibition would not seem to be justified … Specifically, it would seem that harm to innocents is justified for the sake of achieving a greater good when the harm is 1. Trivial … 2. Easily reparable … 3. Nonreparable but greatly outweighed by the [beneficial] consequences of the action.[16]

Essentially, Sterba appeals to a proportionality principle to determine when it is permissible to harm innocent people in order to achieve some beneficial result. In his view, if defending someone from serious harm requires violating the rights of an innocent person, that violation is justified if the harm to the innocent person is either trivial or easy to repair. More importantly, even if the harms are neither trivial nor reparable, inflicting them may still be justified if they are greatly outweighed by the benefits. That is why the dynamiting in the cave is justified, and it is the same reason why attacks on civilians in supreme emergency cases are justified. Even though these actions violate rights, the benefit in lives saved is so large that violating these rights is justified.

---

[15] Sterba, "Terrorism and International Justice," 212.   [16] Ibid., 211–12.

In order to test this conclusion and Sterba's rules for justified violations of the right to life, we can compare the cave case with two other, much discussed examples, the organ transplant case and the trolley case.

In the organ transplant case, each of five people is suffering from serious damage to a different bodily organ, and all will die if they cannot receive transplants. It would be possible for a surgeon to save all five by killing one healthy individual, harvesting the five organs from that person's body, and transplanting them into the five dying people. As in the cave case, more people would live if this were done. Nonetheless, there is widespread agreement that this action would be wrong. From this, it seems to follow that saving the greater number of people does not by itself justify an act. If one of the people suffering from a diseased organ tried to justify the act of killing the healthy person by appealing to the right to save his life, we would surely reject his claim. In this case, the right of the healthy person to his own organs and his immunity to being attacked seem clearly to take precedence over the needs and rights of the other five.

In the trolley case, a runaway trolley is speeding down a track toward five people. The driver can divert the trolley to another track on which one person is standing. Diverting the trolley will result in one death while five will die if nothing is done. In this case, diverting the trolley and lessening the number of deaths seems preferable to allowing it to continue on the track toward the five people. Unlike the transplant case, where we would think that the person whose organs were taken was murdered, we would not think that the person who diverted the trolley had murdered the one person killed. While the difference between the trolley case and the transplant case is a matter of debate, the view that diverting the trolley so as to minimize deaths is morally justified is accepted by many people who reject killing the healthy person in the transplant case.[17]

If we think that killing the healthy person is wrong even if it saves five lives but that it would be right to divert the trolley so that it will kill one person rather than five, then we might try to judge the cave case by asking which it resembles. Is blowing up the person blocking the exit hole like killing a person to harvest his organs? Or is it like diverting a runaway trolley from a track with five people on it to a track with one? If we think that the cave case is more like the transplant case, then we are likely to think it wrong

---

[17] For an influential analysis of both the transplant and the trolley case, see Judith Thomson, *The Realm of Rights* (Cambridge, Mass.: Harvard University Press, 1990), chapters 5–7. The trolley example appears in Foot, "The Problem of Abortion and the Principle of Double Effect," 23.

to dynamite the exit open. If, however, we see it as more like diverting the trolley, then we may think it is permissible.

Suppose that we accept Sterba's view that it is morally permissible to blow open the hole in the cave at the cost of killing the person stuck in it. It is important to see that it does not follow from this judgment that violating noncombatant immunity is permissible in war. Nor does it follow that terrorism is permissible. The reason is that the cave case differs significantly from cases involving war and political conflict, and these differences undermine the analogy between them.

The cave example is a highly specific circumstance, a freakish accident that is not likely to be repeated. For this reason, judging that it is permissible to blow open the hole blocked by a person does not have widespread implications for how we behave in other cases. If we try to generalize from the cave case to others like it, we have to know what features make a situation like the cave case. If, however, what distinguishes cases like this is their freakish nature, then the permissibility of killing in this case does not generalize to other, non-freakish kinds of situations.

In order for Sterba to use the cave example as a precedent, he has to read the moral of the story very differently. He believes that the key feature in the cave case is that one can save a much larger number of people by killing some small number of people. He then generalizes this conclusion to all cases of this type to get the conclusion that, whenever it is possible to save many lives by killing a few, it is permissible to do so. The problem with accepting this view is that it would require us to accept the idea that it is morally permissible to kill the healthy person in the transplant case in order to save five lives. Yet, the transplant case seems to involve a clearly wrong act.

One reason we may find the transplant case so clearly wrong is that it is a repeatable situation. There are millions of people in desperate need of organ transplants and millions of healthy people who could be killed so that their healthy organs could be used in life-saving transplants. Permitting a killing in this case is readily generalizable in horrific ways. While few of us expect to find ourselves in the cave circumstance or other comparable situations, the transplant case has implications for everyone. Every healthy person who visits a doctor would have to fear for his or her life, and even ill people who might benefit from this process by receiving healthy organs would have to fear that they might be killed for their other healthy organs.[18]

---

[18] John Harris describes arguments for an organ harvesting system in "The Survival Lottery," *Philosophy* 50 (1975), 81–7.

The circumstances that give rise to war and political conflict are much more like the transplant case than the cave case. War and conflict are relatively common, and the choices about how and whether to limit the means of violent conflict have recurred throughout history and promise to face human beings for the foreseeable future. Walzer tried to describe supreme emergencies as so extraordinary and unusual that they were freakish, thus limiting the extent to which people could generalize from permissible violations in these circumstances to permissible violations in others. But in the world of political conflict, people are very prone to believe that they are in an extraordinary situation. And, whenever people are victims of political violence or are severely abused or oppressed, their suffering and the threats they face will doubtless feel extreme to them.

As these extreme situations seem more and more common, we are probably less willing to relax the constraints on how people behave in them. It is only when they are genuinely freakish, as with the cave case or the trolley case, that we may feel comfortable permitting otherwise forbidden behavior. So, the first error in Sterba's argument is his generalizing from one bizarre case to a whole range of war-related cases that are common rather than freakish. The costs of accepting more permissive rules with respect to warfare are much greater than the costs of making a permissive judgment about a bizarre, idiosyncratic event.

A second disanalogy is that, in the cave instance, we have precise information about the likely effects of blowing open the hole or choosing not to do so. We know what the costs and benefits in terms of lives taken and saved will be. The case of war is quite different. There, we face pervasive uncertainty. When we adopt a more permissive rule about who may be attacked, we may think that allowing violations will lead to many benefits. Often, however, the predicted benefits do not occur. While the odds were high that the large person in the cave would die and that many others would be saved, no one could have known that the Allied bombings of cities would have their desired effect. In fact, later analysts concluded that these bombings did not significantly help to defeat Germany.[19] Likewise, though Sterba uses his argument to defend Palestinian terrorist attacks against Israeli civilians, a plausible argument can be made that these terrorist attacks have worsened the situation of Palestinians and diminished their prospects for achieving a viable state. I need not take sides on that issue here. My point is that Sterba unjustifiably makes inferences from a philosophical example

---

[19] A. C. Grayling discusses the evidence on this issue in *Among the Dead Cities: The History and Moral Legacy of the WWII Bombing of Civilians in Germany and Japan* (New York: Walker, 2006), 91–116.

about which we have perfect information to a real world case in which the results of killing innocent people are extremely hard to predict.[20]

A third difference between the cave example and warfare is that the decision of the people in the cave is not motivated by hatred, the desire for revenge, or other emotions that often make people want to kill or injure their enemies. The people in the cave are out for a pleasant adventure and have no ill will toward one another. They decide to act in a way that kills one member of their group because they are desperate and see this as the only way to save themselves. They have no other reasons for wanting to kill the person who is stuck in the exit hole. Warfare and violent political conflict, however, create circumstances in which people are highly motivated to harm others. If these powerful motivations are to be controlled so as to prevent grave, gratuitous suffering, then strict rules are needed.

Once we see how different these cases are, it becomes clear that the moral rules that apply to them are likely to be very different. Sterba's attempt to infer a collective right to attack civilians from a right of individuals in a freakish situation does not succeed. Even if individuals do have a right to protect themselves in the way that Sterba thinks, it does not follow that there is a group right to attack civilians in war or to use terrorist tactics to advance political goals.

IS THIS A RESOLVABLE PROBLEM?

Although the rights perspective is helpful in supporting a presumption in favor of noncombatant immunity, it does not suggest an obvious way to decide between absolute noncombatant immunity rights and noncombatant immunity with an extreme emergency exception. If others can use the rights perspective to reach a decision, I would be pleased by that, especially if it supports noncombatant immunity as an absolute right. My intention is not to argue against the existence or importance of rights. I just don't see how to resolve this issue from the rights perspective.

Some might urge the use of a Kantian approach or a social contract theory to resolve the issue. Here, too, I encourage others to do this but do not see how to proceed myself. The Kantian principle that we should never use a person "as a means only" but should always treat persons as "ends in themselves" sounds promising. It would certainly appear to rule out terrorist acts, since terrorism uses attacks against civilians as a means of

---

[20] For additional support for Sterba's claim that Palestinian terrorism has been justified, see Ted Honderich, *Humanity, Terrorism, Terrorist War* (London: Continuum, 2006), 94–118.

promoting a political goal. But this Kantian principle also appears to rule out the killing of soldiers. The basic method of war is to kill or disable soldiers as a means to defeating the enemy. This seems equally to use persons as means only and not as ends in themselves.

Kant's theory also requires that justified moral rules or judgments must be universalizable and capable of serving as laws for a "kingdom of ends," a society in which all members recognize the intrinsic value of all others. This approach strongly resembles the social contract theory view that moral rules are justified if they would be accepted as part of a contract to regulate people's interactions. I find these ideas useful in supporting the view that people possess both a right not to be killed, i.e., an immunity to attack, and a right to act in their own defense. But I do not see how these Kantian ideas can help us to resolve the conflict between immunity rights and defensive rights.[21]

Another possibility is that the conflict between different parts of the right to life is insoluble and creates an intractable moral dilemma. If there is a clash between two equally strong rights and no way to resolve it, then the proper response is to lament the tragic fact that some of our deepest moral beliefs conflict with one another. This seems to be Nagel's view. Although Nagel excoriates utilitarianism for allowing such moral horrors as "large-scale murder" and praises moral absolutism for insisting that some actions "are supposed *never* to be done," he nonetheless acknowledges that in "situations of deadly conflict, particularly where a weaker party is threatened with annihilation or enslavement, the argument for resorting to atrocities can be powerful, and the dilemma acute." Nagel's worry is the same one that leads Walzer to posit the supreme emergency exception. Unlike Walzer, who resolves the dilemma in favor of defensive rights and accepts that "resorting to atrocities" can be justified in a supreme emergency, Nagel thinks that we may face a "moral blind alley" in which "there is no honorable or moral course … to take, no course free of guilt and responsibility for evil."[22] Perhaps the only way to act on one's defensive rights is to violate the equally weighty immunity of rights of others.

---

[21] Kant's ideas on using people as means and the kingdom of ends appear in his *Grounding for the Metaphysics of Morals*, trans. James Ellington (Indianapolis: Hackett, 1981), 36–40. Kant discusses warfare in *The Metaphysical Elements of Justice*, trans. John Ladd (New York: Macmillan, 1965), 114–25 (part II, section 2, "The Law of Nations").

[22] Nagel, "War and Massacre," 6, 23. For interesting comments on moral absolutes and clashes between them, see Stuart Hampshire, "Public and Private Morality," in Hampshire, ed., *Public and Private Morality*, 40–5.

Before agreeing that we have reached this impasse, I want to try to resolve these problems by approaching them from a utilitarian perspective. I want to argue that the usual understanding of utilitarianism – among both its friends and its foes – is mistaken and that a utilitarian moral theory can justify an absolute commitment to the principle of noncombatant immunity. If this can be done, one of its implications will be that terrorist acts are always wrong.

CHAPTER 14

A rule-utilitarian defense of noncombatant immunity

If we ask what utilitarianism implies about warfare, two plausible but radically different answers come to mind. The first answer derives from the fact that utilitarianism was devised, promoted, and embraced by humanitarian reformers whose chief aim was to improve the conditions of human life by reforming social and political institutions. For utilitarians, war, even though sometimes justifiable, is always a great evil. Jeremy Bentham called war "mischief upon the largest scale."[1] It involves the extensive use of violence against persons, resulting in death, injury, pain, disability, and the loss of loved ones. War often damages or destroys the physical and social infrastructure that supports and enhances human life – government facilities, sources of economic productivity, institutions like hospitals, schools, and museums, and objects such as roads and houses. For these reasons, utilitarians will seek to limit both recourse to war and the damages caused in the course of war.

According to this "humanitarian" reading of utilitarianism, utilitarians would find the principle of noncombatant immunity very attractive as a means to limit the damaging effects of war on human life. Since noncombatant immunity places most of the population of belligerent nations and warring groups off limits to intentional attack, honoring that principle would greatly diminish the human costs of war. From this perspective, it seems obvious that utilitarians would favor noncombatant immunity.

There is, however, a strong contrary pull in utilitarian thinking. Since utilitarians view the rightness and wrongness of acts as dependent on their consequences, if circumstances arise in which attacking civilians would yield

---

[1] Jeremy Bentham, "Of War, Considered in Respect of Its Causes and Consequences," Essay 3 in "The Principles of International Law," www.laits.utexas.edu/research/poltheory/bentham/pil/index.html. Essay 4 of "The Principles of International Law" is called "A Plan for an Universal and Perpetual Peace." For doubts on the authenticity of these works, see Gunhild Hoogensen, "Bentham's International Manuscripts Versus the Published 'Works,'" http://www.ucl.ac.uk/Bentham-Project/journal/hoogensn.htm.

better consequences than refraining from such attacks, then it appears that utilitarians will allow – perhaps even require – violations of noncombatant immunity. If, for example, attacks on civilians would end a particular war quickly and thereby diminish the war's overall damage to human life, then attacks on civilians would appear to be justified from a utilitarian perspective.

Arguments like these have convinced most people that utilitarianism cannot support a prohibition on attacking civilians. If it supports any rule at all, it would be "minimize casualties." Such a rule would require belligerent groups to do no more harm than necessary to achieve specific military objectives and win the war as a whole. In some cases, that might mean avoiding civilian casualties, but in principle, civilians would be no more immune to attack than soldiers.

Although this second interpretation of utilitarianism is extremely plausible, I will defend the first, "humanitarian" reading of utilitarianism and will try to show how utilitarianism can provide strong support for an absolute version of noncombatant immunity. I am not arguing that utilitarian flexibility is always wrong or that absolute prohibitions are always better than rules that allow for exceptions. Nor is it my view that highly contextualized, discretionary judgments are never justified. What I want to show is that there are special reasons that justify an absolutist approach to noncombatant immunity.

ACT VS. RULE UTILITARIANISM

Like other "isms," utilitarianism comes in various forms. One main distinction is between act utilitarianism and rule utilitarianism. Act utilitarians tell us to apply the principle of utility – do whatever will produce the best overall results – on a case-by-case basis. Faced with a choice between actions that we could perform, we should always perform the action that will produce the best consequences, where being "best" is generally understood to mean what produces the most happiness or well-being. The spirit of act utilitarianism is hostile to rigid rules that prescribe in advance what ought to be done in every case. It urges us to look at the individual case itself. Of course, if one knew that a particular action would have spillover effects, influencing others to act in harmful ways, that would need to be considered by an act utilitarian. If the immediate effects of an action A are better than those of an alternative action B, the act utilitarian might nonetheless do B if the negative effects of A on other people's behavior tip the utility balance. In general, however, act utilitarians think that we should size up whatever situation we are in and opt for whatever action is most likely to yield the best consequences in that situation.

Although this view has a great deal of appeal, it faces serious problems. Among other things, it does not take seriously enough the problems of bias and fallibility. Bernard Gert, criticizing act utilitarianism, describes it as "the right kind of moral system for a society of omniscient persons." Unfortunately, as he reminds us, "there are no omniscient persons."[2] (Or if there are, they are not us.) By telling people simply to do whatever is best in each circumstance and leaving it to each of us to determine what act has the best consequences, we give people too much discretionary power and ignore both our fallibility and our bias in favor of ourselves and others we care about. If morality simply consisted of the rule "do whatever you think is best" and contained no general requirements or prohibitions, it would unleash everyone to act in a completely open-ended way. The prospect is a frightening one, especially in circumstances of war, where people act in fear and generally feel intense hostility toward the enemy.

Of course, act utilitarians do not say "do whatever you think is best." They say "do what will have the best consequences overall." But in practice, this boils down to telling people to do whatever seems to them to produce the best consequences. We know, however, that people (ourselves included) often judge these matters badly – that they are unduly swayed by their own personal desires, that they give unequal weight to different people's interests, and that they are often mistaken about the relevant facts. If we know from experience that certain general rules or practices are likely to promote good effects, then we will want to urge people to follow these rules rather than to exercise their own judgment in every case.

Consider, for example, the choice between an open-ended rule like "drive safely" and more specific rules like "stop at red lights," "do not travel more than 30 miles per hour in residential areas," "do not drive when drunk," etc. The first rule, like the act-utilitarian principle, is very general and leaves it up to individuals to determine what is the best way to drive in each circumstance. Yet, people are notoriously bad about judging what is the best thing to do when they drive. Even with specific rules, drivers constantly endanger themselves and others. If there were no specific rules, even more people would be killed and injured by cars.

In addition to ignoring widely shared cognitive and emotional limitations, act utilitarianism seems to overlook the role of moral rules in structuring and coordinating people's behavior. Gert, though not a

---

[2] Bernard Gert, *Morality: Its Nature and Justification* (New York: Oxford University Press, 1998), 206.

utilitarian himself, points out the positive effects of knowing how most people will act in certain types of situations. He writes:

> If everyone knew that they were allowed to deceive, break a promise, cheat, or break the law whenever they justifiably believed that their particular act ... would cause no harm, then no one would be able to depend on people obeying these rules with the consistency that is needed for social stability.[3]

Act utilitarianism seems to overlook the fact that social stability can make a large contribution to human well-being and that the ability to predict that people will act according to rules plays an important role in maintaining social stability. Act utilitarianism fails to appreciate the significance of recurrent types of actions and over-emphasizes the particularity of individual actions.

It is worth noticing that strict rules are generally assumed to be necessary in war. There is a "chain of command" and duties of obedience to anyone above oneself in this chain. Soldiers are trained to obey orders and not told simply to do whatever they think is best. Although there are circumstances that require tactical flexibility and discretionary judgments and even cases in which orders should be disregarded, the framework of the chain of command provides a structure for coordinating people's actions in chaotic, dangerous circumstances.

These are a few reasons for rejecting act utilitarianism and for believing that an adequate ethic of war will include at least some specific rules.[4] These conclusions strongly suggest that we should consider a rule-utilitarian approach.

The basic idea of rule utilitarianism has two parts:

1. A moral rule is justified if its inclusion into our moral code would create more utility than either some alternative rule or no rule at all.
2. A specific action is morally justified if it conforms to a justified moral rule.

According to rule utilitarians, we should judge the morality of individual actions by reference to general moral rules, and the correct moral rules are those rules whose general acceptance would maximize well-being.

From this perspective, the question I have been investigating would take the following form: Which would create more overall benefits, a rule that

---

[3] Ibid., 206. For similar points by a utilitarian, see Russell Hardin, *Morality Within the Limits of Reason* (Chicago: University of Chicago Press, 1988).

[4] R. G. Frey defends act utilitarianism against common criticisms in "Introduction: Utilitarianism and Persons" and "Act-Utilitarianism, Consequentialism, and Moral Rights," both in Frey, ed., *Utility and Rights* (Minneapolis: University of Minnesota Press, 1984), 3–19, 61–85.

absolutely prohibits attacks on noncombatants? Or a rule that forbids such attacks except in extreme emergency situations? Or, alternatively, would the rule that generates the highest level of utility make no special distinction between combatants and noncombatants and simply aim to minimize suffering overall?

CAN UTILITARIANISM SUPPORT ABSOLUTE RULES?

Because there is such widespread skepticism that a utilitarian theory could support an absolute ban on anything at all, I will begin by showing how an absolute prohibition can be justified on utilitarian grounds. My argument will build on Richard Brandt's discussion in "Utilitarianism and the Rules of War."[5] Although Brandt rejects noncombatant immunity, his account of the rule utilitarian method illuminates many key issues and is useful in countering the automatic assumption that utilitarianism cannot support an absolute prohibition.

Brandt raises the question of absolute prohibitions in response to Thomas Nagel's scathing attack on utilitarianism in "War and Massacre." Nagel, drawing on the "situationist" reading of utilitarianism, makes the plausible claim that utilitarianism would approve of large-scale murder in circumstances in which it would yield better results (i.e., greater utility) than other available options. According to Nagel, utilitarianism cannot support absolute prohibitions of even the most abominable actions. Because nothing is absolutely forbidden from a utilitarian perspective, the employment of its method leads to what Nagel calls "the abyss of utilitarian apologetics for large-scale murder."[6]

Brandt responds to Nagel's criticism by trying to show that utilitarianism can support absolute prohibitions of certain types of actions. He does this by framing what he takes to be the basic moral question about war and then explaining how a utilitarian would attempt to answer it. The question is "What, from a moral point of view, ought to be the rules of war?" In order to make progress, Brandt proposes replacing it with the question: "What rules would rational impartial people, who expected their country at some time to be at war, want to have as the authoritative rules of war …?" His utilitarian perspective enters the picture because Brandt believes that rational,

---

[5] Richard Brandt, "Utilitarianism and the Rules of War," in Cohen *et al.*, eds., *War and Moral Responsibility*, 25–45. Page references refer to this edition. Brandt's essay originally appeared in *Philosophy and Public Affairs* 1 (1972) and is reprinted in his *Morality, Utilitarianism, and Rights* (Cambridge: Cambridge University Press, 1992).

[6] Nagel, "War and Massacre," 6.

impartial people would choose those rules whose acceptance would "maximize long-range expectable utility for nations at war."[7] He then sets out to
discover what rules would pass this utilitarian test.

Brandt claims that this approach to the ethics of war can support the view
that "certain kinds of actions are morally out of bounds absolutely and no
matter what the circumstances."[8] This possibility, he argues, becomes clear
once we separate the two levels of moral deliberation and see that reasons
that are appropriate at the general, rule-making level are not appropriate for
specific situations. At the general level, the key question is "what moral rules
should we accept as part of an ideal moral code?" The rule-utilitarian answer
is that we should include those rules whose "acceptance and enforcement
will make an important contribution to long range utility."[9]

Once these justified moral rules are in place, judgments about how to act
in specific circumstances are to be made by reference to the rules. As Brandt
says, "in making decisions about what to do in concrete circumstances, the
rules are absolutely binding. In the rule-utilitarian view, immediate expe-
diency is not a moral justification for infringing the rules."[10] Here, Brandt
rejects the act utilitarian idea that we should act in concrete circumstances
in whatever way will yield the most benefits. He rejects this because,
although an act might be best in a particular circumstance, giving people
a general permission to do that type of act would lead to overall worse
results. Once a rule is justified because its inclusion in our moral code
maximizes utility, then individuals are morally required to follow that rule
and do wrong if they break the rule and act in accord with their own utility
calculations for a specific case.

This reasoning allows Brandt to respond to Nagel that "a rule-utilitarian
may quite well agree … that certain kinds of actions are morally out of
bounds absolutely and no matter what the consequences." And, he adds, "A
rule-utilitarian is certainly in a position to say that utilitarian considerations
cannot morally justify a departure from these rules."[11]

Of course, not every rule will have this degree of stringency. There is a
range of possibilities between having no rule at all and having an absolute
rule, and rule utilitarians will adopt for each rule the level of stringency that
will yield the best results. Some rules might be "rules of thumb" that can be
disobeyed whenever a person judges that she can act more beneficially by
breaking the rule. Other rules might require very specific reasons to justify
violations. For example, the rule against killing other people includes

---

[7] Brandt, "Utilitarianism and the Rules of War," 30. [8] Ibid., 26. [9] Ibid., 30. [10] Ibid., 27.
[11] Ibid., 27.

specific exceptions such as self-defense or the defense of other people under threat. The fact that there are recognized exceptions in this case does not mean that people can simply exercise their discretionary judgment to determine what is best to do. Rather, there is both a very strong presumption against killing others and a prior understanding of what things count as good reasons for violating the general rule. Finally, the most stringent rule is an absolute prohibition of a type of act. What Brandt makes clear is that, if an absolute rule of noncombatant immunity could be justified by appeal to the beneficial results of its acceptance, the fact that more utility could be gained in a specific instance by violating that rule would not justify its violation.

Brandt himself thinks that rule utilitarians would not accept noncombatant immunity as an absolute principle. He even says that "It is conceivable that ideal rules of war would include one rule to the effect that anything is allowable, if necessary to prevent absolute catastrophe."[12] Thus, although Brandt's key point is that rule utilitarianism is open to the possibility of absolute prohibitions, he seems to concede that Nagel was correct when he charged that even "large-scale murder" could (in principle) be justified by utilitarians in some instances.

Brandt's full reply to Nagel has two parts. First, he says, if absolute prohibitions of types of actions can be justified by the beneficial effects of their acceptance, then utilitarians can support them. Second, if there are no absolute prohibitions that can be justified by this standard, then such prohibitions should not be included in an ideal moral code. If these prohibitions are not justified, the fact that utilitarianism rejects them does nothing to discredit it as a moral theory.

BRANDT ON NONCOMBATANT IMMUNITY

There is no doubt that Brandt rejects noncombatant immunity. He explicitly says that actions like the "obliteration bombing" of cities in World War II could be morally justified. In defending this view, he stresses that such tactics are justified only if they are based on certain sorts of reasons. Bombing cities is not justified if it is carried out for revenge rather than to achieve war-related benefits. It could be morally justified, however, if it is used as a "deterrent reprisal," and there is evidence that it will deter similar attacks. In addition, Brandt "does not exclude the possibility" that

---

[12] Ibid., 27 n3. Brad Hooker discusses "disaster prevention" exceptions from a rule-utilitarian perspective in *Ideal Code, Real World* (New York: Oxford University Press, 2000), esp. 134–6.

"widespread civilian bombing" could be justified if it could undermine civilian morale and thereby bring an end to the war.[13]

These points make clear that Brandt does not accept noncombatant immunity. His comments on obliteration bombing exemplify the usual understanding of what utilitarianism implies about warfare. According to Brandt, no particular type of attack – not even large-scale bombings that intentionally kill huge numbers of civilians – is necessarily wrong. Instead, the rightness or wrongness of such attacks depends on whether there is sufficient evidence to justify the belief that their military value will exceed their large-scale negative effects. The strongest criticism Brandt can make of bombing cities for the purpose of diminishing civilian morale – i.e., bombing cities as a terrorist act – is that it "could be justified only rarely, if at all."[14] The reason that they are rarely (if ever) justified is that they generally don't work, i.e., they do not diminish civilian morale sufficiently to end the war. For this reason, Brandt is comfortable saying that these sorts of bombings are generally wrong. Nonetheless, because he lacks empirical evidence to claim that they never could succeed, he is unwilling to say that they are always wrong.

APPLYING THE RULE-UTILITARIAN METHOD TO NONCOMBATANT IMMUNITY

While I reject Brandt's conclusions about noncombatant immunity, I support the method that he describes for determining whether noncombatant immunity should be accepted as an absolute constraint. Here is how I understand the steps that the method would use to evaluate noncombatant immunity.

Step 1 clarifies the conditions under which a moral rule about war is justified.

1. *The correct moral rules for warfare are those that would be adopted by rational impartial people who expect that their country will at some time be at war and want to have authoritative rules for the conduct of war.*

What justifies particular rules of war is that they would be accepted by "rational impartial people." These people must be rational in the sense that they can think logically, consider the effects of accepting some rules rather than others, and assess evidence about whether various possible rules will (or will not) have better effects than others. They must be impartial because

---

[13] Brandt, "Utilitarianism and the Rules of War," 39.   [14] Ibid., 39.

they must formulate rules that are in the interests of everyone rather than tailoring the rules to the advantage of a particular group.

Once the rules are incorporated into the moral code, people acting on them need not act impartially. Countries at war are permitted to be partial to themselves. Morality allows them to strive to defeat their enemies as long as their actions comply with the rules that have been accepted. In a similar way, laws that regulate business competition should be drawn up impartially, but once the rules are in place, people in business can try to do better than their competitors. What they are forbidden to do is to use means of competition that are prohibited by the impartially chosen rules.

2. *Rational impartial people would adopt those rules of war whose acceptance would maximize overall utility.*

This affirms the utilitarian principle itself as the standard that rational impartial people would use to evaluate potential rules. This is plausible because impartial people would want a rule that promotes overall well-being and that determines this by considering the interests of all people equally. The utilitarian principle does this.[15]

3. *To maximize utility, rules must allow effective war-fighting while minimizing suffering and destruction.*

This step assumes that war can sometimes be a legitimate means of protecting people's interests. In a fully worked-out utilitarian ethic of war, the same method would be used to justify the judgment that war itself can sometimes be justified. Presumably, the argument would be something like the following rough sketch: If we contrast a rule that permits warfare under some conditions with one that forbids it entirely, the rule that permits war would have better effects overall. Why? Because if people were not permitted to defend themselves from violent attack or severe violations of their rights, others who are willing to use violence to attack or oppress people would feel encouraged to do so. By contrast, if morality permits the use of violence for self-defense and resistance to oppression, then some would-be aggressors would be defeated and others would be deterred. Permitting war and violence for defensive purposes promotes utility by raising the cost of aggression and by throwing its success into doubt.

Once we accept that war can be a legitimate means of defending fundamental interests, it seems to follow that morality must permit people to use at least some forms of effective fighting to defend themselves. A morality

---

[15] Will Kymlicka discusses the relations between impartiality, equal consideration, and the utilitarian method in "Rawls on Teleology and Deontology," *Philosophy and Public Affairs* 17 (1988), 173–90.

that forbids all means of effective fighting would undercut the possibility of acting on the permissibility of war.

This point about effective means may appear to be a matter of common sense, but it raises great difficulties. What exactly does it mean to say that people must be allowed to use *effective* means of fighting? "Effective means" cannot mean tactics that are guaranteed to succeed since success cannot be guaranteed no matter what means are used. Nor can it mean that people are permitted to use whatever tactics maximize the odds of victory since that would imply that "anything goes" if it enhances the prospects of victory. As we have seen, this view rejects almost all constraints on fighting.

What we need here is something like the idea of a "fighting chance." The permissible means of fighting have to include tactics that allow a belligerent to put up a good fight, but they cannot be so extensive as to rule out all constraints. Winning a war is not the only relevant factor that rational impartial people will consider in devising the moral rules for warfare. Since war is so damaging, they will want rules that aim to reduce the suffering and damage that are war's inevitable effects.

Rational impartial people who expect their countries to be at war will want to insist that the rules of war satisfy both conditions: they must permit the use of effective means of fighting, and they must diminish the destructive effects of war as much as possible. These people will know, however, that effective means cannot guarantee success and that, even if understood as the means needed for a "fighting chance," this cannot be guaranteed to all groups. Some groups may not have this level of resources available to them.[16]

4. *If absolutely prohibiting attacks on noncombatants would minimize the destructive effects of war while still permitting effective war-fighting, then rational impartial persons will adopt the principle of noncombatant immunity.*

This simply points out that, if absolute noncombatant immunity satisfies condition 3, then it would be adopted by rational impartial people who are devising a code for the conduct of war.

5. *If an absolute prohibition of attacks on civilians is justified on rule-utilitarian grounds, then it ought to be followed even when people believe that they can do more good or less harm in particular circumstances by attacking noncombatants.*

---

[16] Shannon French discusses and rejects the argument that terrorism can be justified because weaker parties to a conflict are less bound by rules of war in "Murderers, Not Warriors," in James Sterba, ed., *Terrorism and International Justice* (New York: Oxford University Press, 2003), 31–46.

This point reaffirms the idea that if an absolute rule is adopted, it would be wrong for people to ignore it. Once the rule is adopted, it ought to be followed, even by people who think they can act more beneficially in particular instances.

This last step reveals an error in Brandt's argument about obliteration bombing. He seemed to think that bombing civilians in cities could be morally justified because it might sometimes maximize utility. In reasoning this way, however, he inadvertently shifts from his rule-utilitarian method to an act-utilitarian approach.[17] In his reply to Nagel, he showed that an act that maximizes utility in a particular circumstance could still be wrong. If it would maximize utility to have a rule that forbids obliteration bombing, then such bombing would be wrong even when it succeeds. Brandt defends obliteration bombing but never tries to show that rules permitting it would maximize utility. His argument can only work if we accept the act-utilitarian method and abandon the rule-utilitarian method that Brandt himself advocates.

The five-step argument I have given does not by itself prove the utility of accepting noncombatant immunity. This is clear from the word "if" in statements 4 and 5. This set of statements sets the stage for the key question: *Would the acceptance of an absolute version of the principle of noncombatant immunity maximize utility?* This question is a factual question. We can answer it only by predicting the results of accepting this rule rather than others, and any such prediction must be based on empirical evidence. Pure reason won't help us. We have to look at the facts and try to understand the effects of various ways of fighting wars. In addition, we have to compare the results of accepting absolute noncombatant immunity with other available options: no special immunity for civilians; a weak, easily overrideable form of immunity; or immunity with an exception for extreme cases. To justify any of these rules requires trying to predict the results of accepting each of them and then choosing the one that promises to yield the best overall effects.

THE BASIC UTILITARIAN ARGUMENT FOR NONCOMBATANT IMMUNITY

Why should we expect that adopting a rule that bars attacks on civilians would maximize utility? The basic empirical evidence for this rule has two parts to it: first, there is the evident fact that there are many more civilians

---

[17] I am indebted to John Troyer for pointing out Brandt's tendency to shift from rule-utilitarian to act-utilitarian reasoning in his essay.

than combatants. For this reason, if civilians were immune from attack, that would significantly diminish the potential destructive impact of war on human life and human well-being. Second, there is the fact that people in the military play a direct role in fighting a war and therefore that killing or disabling combatants is generally more likely to weaken an enemy's war-fighting capacity than killing or disabling people who are not involved in war-fighting. Effective war-fighting generally requires attacking the enemy military. This may not be true in every case, but it is plausible that it is generally true.

In support of the first point, the experience of twentieth-century wars is certainly relevant. Consider the following chart, which contains estimates of both absolute numbers and percentages of military and civilian deaths in several wars:

War	Military	Civilian	Total
World War I	95%	5%	37 million
World War II	52%	48%	60 million
Korean War	16%	84%	700,000
Vietnam War	10%	90%	1.25 million[18]

While the numbers of people killed in these wars are staggering in and of themselves, the increase in civilian casualties is particularly striking. Almost half of the 60 million people killed in World War II and 80–90 percent of the deaths in Korea and Vietnam were civilian victims. But it is not just the numbers that matter. There is also the contribution to effective war-making that these casualties are supposed to make. There is no reason to believe that the civilian deaths significantly diminished the fighting capacity of the belligerents. If they did not, then these civilian casualties did not significantly enhance either side's prospects for victory. As long as combatants could fight on, the civilian deaths did not directly weaken the enemy forces and therefore did little to achieve military success.

Overall, then, it is reasonable to predict that rejecting noncombatant immunity leads to more deaths overall while achieving less military value. Acceptance of, and adherence to, a noncombatant immunity rule would have greatly diminished the damage to human life and human well-being caused by the wars after World War I.

---

[18] "Casualties of War," in Donald Wells, ed., *An Encyclopedia of War and Ethics* (Westport, Conn.: Greenwood, 1996), 55–6.

While the basic argument rests on empirical premises with a great deal of inherent plausibility, these premises can certainly be challenged. For example, World War I was massively destructive, killing millions of soldiers, but generally less destructive of civilian life. A critic could argue that military casualties would have been lower had civilian targets been attacked. While this is possible, the evidence of World War II suggests that it is unlikely. Increased attacks on civilian targets in World War I would simply have broadened the field for destructive activity. Anyone making the argument that World War I would have been less destructive in total lives if attacks on civilians had been permitted would have to establish two counterintuitive claims: first, that vastly increasing the number of people who constitute permissible targets would have decreased overall casualties of the war, and second, that attacking people who were not engaged in fighting would have made a greater contribution to winning the war than attacking people who were actually engaged in combat. Neither of these is plausible.[19]

Still, it is not true that attacking civilians can never have military value. In *Targeting Civilians*, Alexander Downes points out that attacks on civilians are more common in wars that aim to conquer and annex territory than in other wars. As he says,

[W]hen a belligerent seeks to conquer territory but fears that the population will rebel and pose a permanent threat to its control over the area, a strategy of civilian victimization designed to eradicate that group is a likely outcome.[20]

In this type of war, attacking civilians can have military and political value for a particular party to a conflict. It is in these cases that ethnic cleansing and genocide are tempting because the aim is to clear a territory of its population. If the aim is to clear a territory, we cannot say that attacks on civilians will be without value for that side. In many wars, however, their value as targets is much less than the value of fighters on the enemy side. Even in the case Downes describes, the civilians represent at most a potential, not an actual, threat. As long as they do not violently resist the invaders, they remain noncombatants, and from a broader utilitarian perspective, allowing attacks on them will only increase overall casualties. In fact, acceptance of the importance of noncombatant immunity may be one of the few constraints on the temptation of groups to engage in ethnic cleansing and genocide.

---

[19] Civilians were targeted by air attacks and blockades in World War I. The greatest constraints on such attacks were technological rather than moral.

[20] Downes, *Targeting Civilians*, 178–9. For examples of population displacement, confinement, and genocide, see Slim, *Killing Civilians*, 71–85, 128–31.

Finally, to restate a key point: when we evaluate rules of war, we do not evaluate them from the perspective of the interests of a particular people or group. Rather, we evaluate them from the perspective of rational impartial people who know that their countries are likely to engage in war and want rules that will permit warfare while diminishing the suffering that warfare causes.

IS THERE A RULE-UTILITARIAN CASE FOR THE SUPREME EMERGENCY EXCEPTION?

Why should we believe that accepting absolute noncombatant immunity will lead to better results than noncombatant immunity with a supreme emergency exception? Consider defensive rights and immunity rights in ordinary life. In ordinary life, people do not generally have a right to kill other people, but in extreme circumstances, when their own or other people's lives are threatened, people are permitted to kill those who initiate attacks on them. If faced with the choice between an absolute "do not kill" rule and a "do not kill except in extreme circumstances of attack on oneself (or others) and no other options of defense," one could plausibly argue that we maximize good results by permitting the self-defense exception. Allowing defensive violence puts would-be attackers on notice that they may face a violent response to their attack. Thus, including the exception is likely to provide a disincentive for initiating unwarranted attacks. Essentially this is the same type of argument that utilitarians can use to justify defensive war as a legitimate exception to a "do not go to war" rule.

The question here is whether this same reasoning can justify the supreme emergency exception to noncombatant immunity. Why wouldn't a rule-utilitarian analysis support noncombatant immunity with a supreme emergency exception rather than an absolute ban on attacking civilians?

In answering this question, it is important to keep in mind what it means to include the supreme emergency exception in our moral code. If we recognize this exception, we would be constructing an ethic of war that would tell people that, although they are generally forbidden to attack civilians, there are some circumstances in which this is permitted. We would then describe the circumstances along the lines of Walzer's view: an extraordinary threat, the prospect of imminent defeat, no alternative effective strategies of resistance, and some prospect of success by adopting the tactic of attacking enemy noncombatants. In other words, we would publicly announce that deliberately killing civilians is sometimes morally permissible. Should we do this?

Bernard Gert, in an insightful discussion of the circumstances under which violations of established moral rules are justified, says that "the morally decisive question" is "What effects would this kind of violation being publicly allowed have?" Elaborating on this point, Gert explains:

[I]t is not the consequences of [a] particular act that are being considered, but the consequences of … everyone knowing that this kind of violation is allowed … for one is acting impartially in violating a moral rule only if one would be willing for everyone to know that they also are allowed to violate the rule in the same circumstances.[21]

Although Gert is a critic of both utilitarianism and Kant's theory, these remarks echo ideas in both Brandt's rule utilitarianism and Kant's moral theory.

According to Brandt, the test for the morality of specific actions is whether they conform to rules whose acceptance into a moral code would maximize utility. It is the acceptance into the moral code that is tested by the consequences, not the rightness or wrongness of particular acts. If an exception to a rule is accepted into a moral code, that exception will be known by all to whom the code applies. Brandt, like Gert, believes that when we evaluate a rule, we need to focus on the effects of there being public knowledge that a certain type of action is permitted or forbidden.

Similarly, Kant's point in stressing the universalizability of moral rules and judgments is that people may not make moral judgments or invoke moral rules unless they are willing to have those same judgments and rules applied by everyone. Kant, too, in suggesting that moral judgments be seen as legislation in a kingdom of ends, requires that every moral judgment and the principles behind it be capable of inclusion into a a an ideal moral code that would be suitable for people who regarded themselves and others as ends in themselves.

The problem with Kant's view, taken by itself, is that it fails to provide an adequate method for determining what rules can be universalized and what rules would be suitable for members of a kingdom of ends. The problem in this case arises from a conflict between immunity rights and defensive rights. It pits two strong interests against one another. We want to universalize both the strongest possible rights of immunity to attack and the strongest possible rights to defend ourselves, but the strength of each of these rights diminishes the strength of the other. In considering what to universalize or support as legislation for a kingdom of ends, we find

---

[21] Gert, *Morality*, 236–7.

ourselves in a bind. We don't know what we favor because the two things that we want are inconsistent with one another. Kant's tests do not tell us how to determine what has priority.

The rule-utilitarian approach resolves this problem by tying the solution to a goal, the maximization of utility. This is the point behind Mill's criticism of Kant's moral theory. After praising Kant's work, Mill goes on to say that Kant

fails, almost grotesquely to show that there would be any contradiction … in the adoption by all rational beings of the most outrageously immoral rules of conduct. All he shows is that the *consequences* of their universal adoption would be such as no one would choose to incur.[22]

As Mill, Brandt, and Gert emphasize, it is the *consequences* of universal adoption of a rule or an exception that matter. What we want are rules of war whose acceptance would maximize human well-being. With that goal in mind, we now have a test that we can use to evaluate whether non-combatant immunity with a supreme emergency exception is superior to an absolute ban on attacking civilians.

Why might the supreme emergency exception not pass the rule-utilitarian test? One problem, which I raised earlier, is that the supreme emergency principle is both vague and likely to be applied in an arbitrary, subjective manner. Even Walzer's applications seem personal rather than principled. Recall Tony Coady's criticism of Walzer for casually denying that the Japanese threat constituted a supreme emergency. As Coady points out, the Japanese massacred over 300,000 Chinese civilians in just six weeks in the single Chinese city of Nanking. Countless Chinese people were beheaded, bayoneted, and raped.[23] Yet, Walzer excludes the Japanese threat from the supreme emergency category while including the German threat to Britain. His doing so does not instill confidence in his criterion.

Suppose that we decide to classify the Japanese threat to the Chinese and other Asian peoples as a supreme emergency, and suppose that we infer from this that attacks against Japanese civilians might have been justified in these circumstances. Would our acknowledgment of a supreme emergency threat justify the Chinese in massacring, beheading, and raping hundreds of thousands of Japanese civilians? Is a permission to engage in this behavior something that we want to include in a moral code that will be known to all?

---

[22] John Stuart Mill, *Utilitarianism*, chapter 1, paragraph 4.
[23] Coady, "Terrorism, Just War and Supreme Emergency," 17. On the Japanese attacks on China, Coady cites Iris Chang, *The Rape of Nanking: The Forgotten Holocaust of World War II* (New York: Penguin, 1998).

And if this specific behavior sounds too dreadful to permit, it is important to recall that the bombings of German cities that Walzer's exception permits involved the creation of huge firestorms in which thousands of ordinary Germans were asphyxiated or burned to death. No doubt, active Nazis and Nazi supporters were among the victims. But so were those who opposed the Nazi regime.

We know, of course, what the German government did to millions of people, but our moral code condemns those actions just as it condemns the actions of the Japanese military in Nanking. If we recognize supreme emergency exceptions in our ethic of war, we are considering permitting similar behavior in extreme circumstances as opposed to banning it absolutely. From a utilitarian point of view, the worry is that permitting such behavior even under the direst circumstances will lower the bar for justifying such acts, that it will broadcast the message that such behavior may sometimes be justified and will thus lend its weight to increasing the use of such methods.

In order to prohibit an unwanted message of permissiveness about these types of actions, there would have to be extremely clear criteria for determining that a supreme emergency exists. In addition, we would have to have some confidence that people would apply these criteria judiciously to determine whether the threats they face are ordinary or extraordinary. The process of applying these criteria is greatly complicated by the strong partiality that people feel toward their own group. This partiality will cause people to judge that things that happen to "us" – i.e., to our group, whoever "we" happen to be – are extraordinary threats while things that happen to others – including massacres, beheadings, mass rapes, etc. – are "ordinary." Normal tendencies, such as greater fear for oneself and for people one cares about as well as heightened concern about one's own society and its way of life, will lead to skewed judgments. They will also encourage people to set the standards for extraordinary threats lower when considering one's own group and making them more stringent for others.

The same points apply to the criteria that require imminence, the lack of alternative means of defense, and the probable success of the immunity-violating actions. In times of great stress, fear can make threats appear more imminent, while limited imagination and the desire for vengeance can make it appear that there are no alternatives. Finally, in a desperate situation, the prospects for the success of immunity-violating acts may appear to be greater than they are.

The decisive judgments on these issues will be made by the leaders of nations and other groups. These leaders share the normal biases in favor of their own people and are likely to feel a special responsibility for their group. They will be likely to err on the side of over-protecting their own group rather than protecting its enemies, thus further weakening the barrier to use of the exception.

The prospects for judicious judgments on these matters are weakened further by the fact that history shows leaders of nations and other groups to be extremely fallible. The history of warfare is, in many ways, a history of erroneous judgments. If we have to rely on political leaders to judge whether the circumstances are properly considered a supreme emergency, there is little reason to be confident that they will get it right even if they try. The incentives for genuine trying are weaker than the incentives for thinking oneself justified in using all available means against a serious threat to one's own people. Nor should we overlook the huge pressures on leaders to win, whatever the cost.

There are good reasons for thinking, then, that it would not be beneficial to include a supreme emergency exception in a publicly known moral code. In fact, although Walzer's use of the term "supreme emergency" was inspired by remarks by Winston Churchill, Churchill himself applied this term to circumstances (both early and late in the war) that Walzer judges not to have been supreme emergencies at all.[24] The actual history of this concept's use calls into question the idea that it is clear enough to limit its application appropriately. It seems likely to be applied too permissively and thus to contribute to escalated violence and increased damage to human life. For this reason, it will not maximize utility to include this exception in our moral code.

REPLY TO A POWERFUL CRITICISM

Having given my rule-utilitarian defense of an absolute prohibition on attacking civilians, it is tempting to say "I rest my case." That is not possible, however, because there are counterarguments that need to be considered. In the next chapter, I will consider criticisms of noncombatant immunity that are made from a utilitarian point of view. In closing this chapter, I will respond to an extremely powerful objection raised by Igor Primoratz against an argument for absolute noncombatant immunity that is similar to the one I have given.

Primoratz himself supports noncombatant immunity but allows an exception that is similar to the supreme emergency exception. In defending

---

[24] Walzer, *Just and Unjust Wars*, 243–61.

this exception, he responds to an argument by Tony Coady against the supreme emergency exception. Coady argues that adopting the supreme emergency exception to noncombatant immunity "is likely to generate widespread misuse of it" and concludes that "we surely do better to condemn the resort to terrorism outright with no leeway for exemptions ..."[25]

Primoratz grants that Coady's argument might have weight in some circumstances, but he describes one circumstance in which, he says, "its relevance may be much doubted."

Think of a people facing the prospect of genocide, or of being "ethnically cleansed" from its land, and unable to put up a fight against an overwhelmingly stronger enemy. Suppose we said to them: "Granted, what you are facing is an imminent threat of a moral disaster. Granted, the only way you stand a chance of fending off the disaster is by acting in breach of the principle of civilian immunity and attacking enemy civilians. But you must not do that. For if you do, that is likely to generate widespread misuse of the exemption." Could they – indeed, should they – be swayed by that?[26]

Although Primoratz's final question is not directly answered, it is clear that his answer is that these people could not and should not be swayed by this argument. For this reason, Primoratz concludes that noncombatant immunity is "an *almost* absolute principle." Noncombatant immunity, he says, trumps all other moral considerations "with one exception: that of a (narrowly understood) moral disaster."[27]

Primoratz's forceful objection, though originally directed at Coady, raises a powerful challenge to the view I have defended. Why, he asks, should people who are facing such a severe threat be worried about the possibility that others will "misuse" the exception that would be required to justify their own attacks on civilians? Does the "misuse" problem make any sense in this context? This challenge requires careful consideration.

Notice, first, that Primoratz raises two separate questions: *could* these people be convinced not to defend themselves by violating civilian immunity? And, *should* they be convinced not to defend themselves in this way? To ask whether they *should* be convinced is to question the absolute version of civilian immunity, but it does not actually provide an argument against it. Suppose that Gert and Brandt are correct that the test of an action is whether it conforms to rules that are part of a publicly known moral

[25] Coady, "Terrorism, Just War and Supreme Emergency," 20. While Coady defends absolute noncombatant immunity and often uses consequentialist arguments, he rejects utilitarianism. For overlaps and contrasts between my views and Coady's, see chapter 14 of his *Morality and Political Violence*.
[26] Primoratz, "Civilian Immunity in War," 39.   [27] Ibid., 39–40.

code. And suppose that the test for a rule's being accepted is whether its acceptance maximizes utility. Then, if absolute noncombatant immunity passes this test, it is the correct moral principle, and the people described by Primoratz should not violate this principle.

Primoratz's argument simply assumes that the description of these people's situation will lead his readers to see that people in this circumstance have a right to defend themselves by violating noncombatant immunity. But all that the case really shows is that they would have a powerful motivation for doing anything whatsoever to defend themselves. While the description of their plight should elicit our sympathy, it does not prove anything. Instead, it only reraises the question of which takes priority: rights of self-defense or rights of immunity to attack.

To elicit a fair answer to his question, Primoratz should also describe the plight of the innocent members of the enemy group who would be victimized by the defending group's attacks. If we had an equally vivid sense of their suffering, it is not so clear that we would agree that the people Primoratz describes have a right to violate these other people's immunity. My guess is that, if we are impartial and have comparable descriptions of both groups, we might well be torn between their competing claims and unable to say what is right. Do Palestinians, for example, have a right to bomb buses carrying Israeli children if the Palestinians and their children face the "moral disaster" of being ethnically cleansed from their land? Or do Israeli children retain their immunity from attack even if Palestinians face a genuine moral disaster, a situation of prolonged deprivation for themselves and for their children?[28]

The whole point of Brandt's model and Gert's discussion is that we cannot answer these questions without thinking about the consequences of having a rule that permits or forbids the kinds of attacks in question. If we focus on the individual case alone, we cannot know what is right or wrong. Primoratz's argument is rhetorically powerful, but it presents the case in a one-sided way, focusing only on the suffering of one group while ignoring the suffering that would be inflicted if attacks were launched against innocent members of its enemy. The argument presupposes – rather than proves – that in this instance, the attacks would be justified if they were the only way for the group to ward off the threat of a "moral disaster."

---

[28] Primoratz argues that the Palestinians have faced a genuine "moral disaster." Nonetheless, he denies that Palestinian terrorism has been morally justified because it has had no reasonable chance of success. For this view, see his "Terrorism in the Israeli-Palestinian Conflict," 35–8.

Primoratz's second question – whether people *could* be swayed by the argument for noncombatant immunity – raises a different issue. People in extreme and dire circumstances may be unable or unwilling to restrain themselves, even if the means of defense that they use are wrong. If people could not be swayed by moral considerations in this situation, there are several conclusions we could reach. We might decide that the moral requirements are simply too demanding, that they expect more of people than they can do. This claim, in turn, can be understood either as the view that *no* human beings could comply with this moral demand, or as the view that some people cannot comply with it.

I assume that the second answer is more plausible. Suppose that there are people who cannot help themselves and thus engage in wrongful acts when faced with a moral disaster. We might conclude that, although these people were wrong to defend themselves by attacking civilians, their dire circumstances provide a partial excuse that mitigates their blameworthiness. We would certainly want to distinguish such people from others who kill out of hatred or attack civilians though they have other means of effective self-defense.[29] A defender of absolute noncombatant immunity could certainly accept the view that we should have sympathy for people whose desperation drives them to act wrongly toward others. This, however, is quite different from giving up the view that such attacks are wrong. While Primoratz makes vivid the inclination to reject the absolute version of noncombatant immunity, he does not actually show that this is the right thing for people in this circumstance to do.

CONCLUSION

In this chapter, I have used a rule-utilitarian argument to show that an absolute version of noncombatant immunity is superior to weaker versions of this principle. In particular, I have tried to show why one of the most appealing alternatives to an absolute principle – the principle of noncombatant immunity with an exception for supreme emergencies – is defective. In the next chapter, I will reply to utilitarian critics of noncombatant immunity.

---

[29] Hugo Slim describes a variety of motivations and perspectives that lead to attacks on civilians in *Killing Civilians*, chapter 4.

CHAPTER 15

Why utilitarian criticisms of noncombatant immunity are mistaken

Why does utilitarianism seem so unlikely a basis for noncombatant immunity? Two features of utilitarianism account for this. The first is that utilitarian morality has a goal, the promotion of overall well-being. Noncombatant immunity, however, is a constraint on action. It places limits on how people can pursue their goals. The second feature is that utilitarians have vigorously opposed what they saw as rigid, tradition-bound moralities that consist of useless, often harmful taboos. This feature can easily express itself as hostility toward the idea that rules and principles play an important role in morality. Rules, however, play many important roles in human life. Social life as we know it would be impossible if there were not a set of well-known, widely accepted rules. We could not function if we were unable to generally trust people to tell the truth and keep agreements most of the time. Having explicit rules about these and other actions helps to sustain the necessary level of predictable behavior.

Most moral rules are not absolute. We recognize that violations of them are sometimes permissible. There are times when killing, stealing, lying, breaking promises, etc. are the right thing to do. (Strictly, of course, a permissible exception is not a *violation*.) One reason why there are permissible exceptions is that it is hard to fashion general rules that work in all cases because we cannot anticipate all the conditions we will face in the future. That is why utilitarians often urge us to consider the effects of individual actions rather than conforming to existing rules.

There is, therefore, something unexpected about a utilitarian defense of an absolute prohibition on killing civilians in war. Nonetheless, there are good reasons for embracing a rigid rule in this case. Given the pressures of war, less than absolute rules are likely to be bent and stretched, and given the serious harms caused by actions in war, the costs to human life of this bending and stretching can be extremely high. For this reason, if a rule provides important protections for people, it may make sense to express it in the strongest possible form. This is perhaps why the international laws of war developed after World War II are expressed in absolute terms: "The civilian population as such, as well as individual civilians, shall not be the object of attack. Acts or threats of violence the primary purpose of which is to spread terror among the civilian population are prohibited."[1] My aim is to solidify the standing of these firm principles by showing that they can be justified from a rule-utilitarian perspective.

My use of utilitarian theory in this book is positive. I am not trying to refute non-utilitarian moral theories and perspectives and would be happy to see noncombatant immunity justified from these other points of view. If different theories and perspectives converge on the same conclusions about the ethics of war, that convergence would strengthen whatever conclusions they reach and make it more likely that people with different overall beliefs would accept and comply with them. Even within utilitarianism, however, there is probably little support for noncombatant immunity. For this reason, I want to focus on arguments that utilitarians have given against noncombatant immunity and show why they are mistaken.[2]

BRANDT'S REJECTION OF NONCOMBATANT IMMUNITY

One surprising feature of Richard Brandt's "Utilitarianism and the Rules of War" is the ease with which he rejects noncombatant immunity and accepts the idea that rule utilitarianism permits "substantial destruction of lives and property of enemy civilians ... when there is good evidence that it will significantly enhance the prospect of victory."[3] Brandt takes this stand with very little analysis or discussion, and, as I will show, his main arguments against noncombatant immunity are inconsistent with his own theory and thus fail to provide rule-utilitarian reasons for rejecting noncombatant immunity.

One reason why Brandt does not accept noncombatant immunity shows the powerful influence of political realism. Brandt in fact abandons his own rule-utilitarian method because he accepts a powerful, realist constraint on the types of rule that may be included in an ethic of war. This constraint appears at the end of an argument to support Brandt's basic position, the view that: "[R]ational impartial persons would choose rules of war that

---

[1] Protocols to the 1977 additions to the Geneva Conventions, Protocol 1, chapter 11, article 51. 2.

[2] Haig Khatchadourian criticizes utilitarian defenses of terrorism and, in effect, makes a utilitarian case against terrorism in *The Morality of Terrorism*, 63–86.

[3] Richard Brandt, "Utilitarianism and the Rules of War," 36.

would maximize expectable utility."[4] After giving two arguments for this view, Brandt appears to be restating it but in fact asserts a radically altered version of it. He writes,

> The rules of war, then, *subject to the restriction that the rules of war may not prevent a belligerent from using all the power necessary to overcome the enemy*, will be ones whose authorization will serve to maximize welfare.[5] (Emphasis added.)

This statement includes an idea that I will call the National Security Exemption. This newly added idea allows belligerents to use "all the power necessary to overcome the enemy." I call it an "exemption" because it makes nations at war exempt from the requirements of a genuinely utilitarian morality.

There are several things to see about this addition. First is its extreme permissiveness. It essentially allows nations at war to do anything that is required to win. In effect, it is the equivalent of the "anything goes" position associated with realism. The second important point is that Brandt's support of this restriction is not the product of a rule-utilitarian analysis. Rather, it imposes a restriction on the scope of the rule-utilitarian method by saying that a rule that prevents countries from doing whatever is necessary to win will not even be eligible for a utilitarian analysis. Even if it could be shown that a rule forbidding attacks on civilians would maximize utility, Brandt would reject it because it limits what nations may do in pursuit of victory. Finally, Brandt gives no utilitarian reasons to justify the National Security Exemption and thus ignores his own method in making this significant alteration to his view.

This is not to say that he offers no defense of the National Security Exemption. His argument for it begins by citing the very high stakes in some wars. A nation in a high-stakes war, he says, "considers overpowering the enemy to be absolutely vital to its interests." As a result, "the utility of victory is virtually set at infinity."[6] For these reasons, he says,

> In this situation, we must simply take it as a fact that neither side [in a war] will consent to or follow rules of war which seriously impair the possibility of bringing the war to a victorious conclusion.[7]

In making this argument, Brandt seems to be saying that we need to be realistic in our reflections on the rules of war and that being realistic

---

[4] Ibid., 32.   [5] Ibid., 32.   [6] Ibid., 33, 37.   [7] Ibid., 34.

requires us to support only those rules that warring parties will actually accept.[8]

Even if Brandt is right that nations will reject rules of war that make it difficult to achieve victory, it is hard to see why this refusal should determine the contents of our ethic of war. Consider a parallel case. Suppose that we are considering a rule that prohibits killing except in self-defense and that we believe that this rule will be rejected by people who earn their living as contract killers. While members of this group will reject a rule that prohibits murder for hire, we would not take this fact as a decisive reason to reject the rule against murder. Similarly, in our moral reflections on the rules of war, we should not set aside a rule simply because it would be rejected by those to whom it applies, especially when rule utilitarianism has been recommended as the proper method for determining what the rules of war should be. Brandt's reason for embracing the National Security Exemption is inconsistent with his own rule-utilitarian view.[9]

UTILITARIANISM AND THE FACTS OF LIFE

While Brandt goes wrong in accepting the National Security Exemption, his error reflects a deep problem for utilitarians. Rule utilitarians support moral rules based on factual predictions about the effects of accepting these rules. The rules of morality are supposed to be based on facts and not on fantasy. Perhaps the world would be better if "love thy neighbor as thyself" were the basic moral rule, but we live in a world in which people generally love themselves much more than most others. A moral code that required pure altruism would be unfit for use in our world, and we might express this by saying that it is unrealistic to expect people to behave in a totally altruistic manner. We "simply take it as a fact" (as Brandt put it) that people are not totally altruistic and that no moral code will change this.

Similarly, we might be tempted by the idea that we can maximize utility by accepting the pacifist rule never to engage in war. If everyone accepted and complied with that rule, we would have a world without war and without the human suffering caused by war. The problem is that, even if we

---

[8] See ibid., 34, where Brandt claims that his view reflects international law; for support, he cites L. Oppenheim, *International Law*, 7th edn (New York, 1952), 226. For the claim that Oppenheim's view has been "decisively rejected" by international law, see Christopher Greenwood in D. Fleck, ed., *The Handbook of Humanitarian Law in Armed Conflicts* (New York: Oxford University Press, 1995), sections 133–4.
[9] Brandt rejects the view that rules and practices are morally valid simply because they are accepted in "Some Merits of One Form of Rule-Utilitarianism," in his *Morality, Utilitarianism, and Rights*, 119–20.

include the rule "do not go to war" in our moral code, we can predict that some people will continue to use war and violence as means of personal or group aggrandizement. This suggests that it is unrealistic to expect pacifism to lead to a world without war.

These arguments against total altruism and pacifism sound reasonable, but they raise a problem for my criticism of Brandt's argument for the National Security Exemption. If it seems reasonable to reject total altruism and pacifism by saying that we must "simply take it as a fact" that people will not abide by them, how can I criticize Brandt for arguing that we must "simply take it as a fact" that nations will reject rules of war that forbid them from "using all the power necessary to overcome the enemy"?

In fact, it is possible to use these arguments against altruism and pacifism without accepting Brandt's "realistic" concession to what nations will accept as rules of war. One problem with Brandt's argument is that it overlooks the fact that a rule can be justified even if there is less than perfect compliance with it. The fact that some people will violate a rule against murder does not show that we should not include a rule forbidding murder in our moral code. Perfect compliance is not required for a rule to be justified. What is required is that compliance by most people is psychologically possible.[10] We can reject a rule requiring total altruism because we know that perfectly altruistic behavior is impossible for people. In addition, it is unlikely to maximize utility since a certain amount of self-concern is a useful trait.

Regarding pacifism, it is true that it would be unrealistic to expect that no one will initiate violence simply because there is a rule against it. By itself, however, that fact does not show that pacifism is mistaken. What it does show is that if we predict that some people will violate rules against violent aggression, then we need a rule in our moral code that tells us how we may respond to people who use violence. A pacifist rule is one possibility, but so is the commonsense morality view that people should be able to defend themselves against aggressive violence and severe oppression. A rule-utilitarian defender of commonsense morality will argue that a rule that allows victims to resist, even violently, can increase utility by deterring some would-be attackers from starting wars. In a world where some will use violence unjustifiably, the utilitarian value of permitting defensive action against attackers is what justifies a rule that permits violent responses rather than one that forbids all recourse to violence.

Brandt goes wrong because he rejects strong constraints on war-making simply because he expects that nations will do whatever is necessary to

---

[10] For discussion of this issue, see Hooker, *Ideal Code, Real World.*

achieve victory. What he ought to do is to note this tendency and then ask how our moral code should handle this problem. And, after formulating some possible rules, he should use the rule-utilitarian method to decide which rule's acceptance would maximize overall utility.

IS COMPLIANCE WITH NONCOMBATANT IMMUNITY POSSIBLE?

If we include noncombatant immunity in our ethic of war, we can predict that there will still be deliberate attacks against civilians. Nonetheless, there are reasons for predicting that people can and will accept this rule. According to a major study funded by the International Committee of the Red Cross, there is already widespread support for civilian immunity throughout the world.[11] People often react with special horror when civilians are killed and often think that this is worse than the deaths of soldiers. If noncombatant immunity is affirmed as an important humanitarian value, many people will come to see obedience to it as a deeply important moral value. This public support, along with serious, continuing efforts to teach the rule to those in the military and to the general public, can help to produce general compliance with it.[12]

In teaching this value within the military and even within non-governmental insurgencies, the idea of military honor can play an important role. This ideal helps to keep people in the military from acting immorally because it allows them to differentiate themselves from murderers and to see themselves as dedicated to civilized values. If they believe that anything goes, they are rejecting all civilized values. In the past, even revolutionaries and insurgent groups embraced a strong code of honor that led them to attack public officials and to avoid killing innocent civilians.[13]

A rule that calls for absolute noncombatant immunity is not utopian in the way that universal altruism or pacifism are. It does not take away people's right to defend themselves. Nor does it prohibit people from using many methods and tactics of war that have some promise of effectiveness. Moreover, even partial compliance with noncombatant immunity can greatly diminish the suffering caused by war. Because people are capable of restraint

---

[11] For an international study of popular opinion on noncombatant immunity, see the International Committee of the Red Cross, *The People on War* (Geneva: ICRC, 2000; available as a PDF file at www.icrc.org).

[12] Colin Kahl argues that the US military has made progress in taking civilian immunity seriously in "In the Crossfire or the Crosshairs?"

[13] Walzer discusses the revolutionary code of honor in *Just and Unjust Wars*, 198–203.

even under dire circumstances, we do not need to accept the idea that people must be permitted to do whatever might seem conducive to victory in war.

DOES THE NATIONAL SECURITY EXEMPTION MAXIMIZE UTILITY?

Brandt's use of the National Security Exemption is inconsistent with rule utilitarianism because it restricts the scope of the rule-utilitarian method. It says that even if someone proposes a rule whose acceptance would maximize utility, he will not support it if it requires constraints that nations will reject. The National Security Exemption frees nations from the restrictions of morality while placing a restriction on the application of the rule-utilitarian method.

My criticism of Brandt to this point is methodological. I have shown that he fails to use his own utilitarian method. What I have not yet shown is that the permission to do whatever is necessary for victory cannot be morally justified. Suppose that Brandt had introduced the National Security Exemption and then shown that we could maximize utility by allowing countries at war to use "all the power necessary to overcome the enemy."[14] If accepting this rule would yield more utility than accepting a rule that prohibits belligerents from acting in this way, then rule utilitarianism would support the exemption. That is the case Brandt should have tried to make. Had he done so, however, I believe that a utilitarian analysis would show that we should reject a rule that allows countries at war to do whatever is necessary to win.

One might think that the main problem with this rule arises from a clash between the interests of humanity and the interests of a particular country. That is indeed a serious problem. The National Security Exemption might benefit particular nations but only at a high cost to humanity generally. Recall that the rules of war allow partiality toward one's own side but are chosen by "rational impartial people" in order to promote the overall interests of humanity. Brandt's overly permissive rule places no limits on the damage to be done if that is necessary for victory.

I want to emphasize another problem that is easy to overlook. This is the problem of whether the pursuit of victory is actually in the interest of a particular country at war. While it is generally plausible to assume that victory is more in the national interest than defeat, it does not follow that fighting for victory is always in a nation's interest. Presumably many defeated countries have reached the conclusion that they would be better off losing a war than continuing to fight. More tragically, countries often

---

[14] Brandt, "Utilitarianism and the Rules of War," 32.

continue to fight long after it has ceased to be in their interests. Since realists seem to assume that states act in their own interest (rather than morally), they often fail to stress how common it is for governments and political leaders to pursue policies that damage their nation's interests. As Fred Iklé notes in *Every War Must End*, "governments tend to lose sight of the ending of wars and the nation's interests that lie behind it, precisely because fighting a war is an effort of such magnitude."[15] Conducting a war is so consuming a process that, once war has begun, political leaders often fail to assess whether it should be continued. As Iklé notes, after surveying many historical cases,

If a statesman decides to go to war, or to reject opportunities for ending an ongoing war, he must somehow assume that fighting – or fighting on – will improve the outcome. Far too often, this assumption receives no analysis.[16]

Iklé's point is not simply that leaders make mistaken judgments. It is that they may not even consider whether continuing to fight is worthwhile. The issue often "receives no analysis."

In addition, judgments about what actions are required in order to win are often mistaken. Iklé notes the decision by Germany to initiate unconstrained submarine warfare in World War I. Though German leaders were confident that this would defeat Britain within a few months, they failed to see that it would bring the United States into the war and that US entry would shift the balance against Germany. Germany would have been better off, he says, if it had negotiated an armistice in 1916 rather than after its defeat in 1918. Indeed, he says, Britain would also have been better off since it would have been spared two years of costly fighting. While escalating the war through unrestricted submarine attacks would be permitted by the national security rule, it failed to advance Germany's interests and greatly increased the overall costs of the war. There are numerous examples of such failures of judgment and planning by national leaders, and these failures have resulted in severe damages to their own nation's interest and to the well-being of human beings generally.[17]

---

[15] Fred Iklé, *Every War Must End*, revised edn (New York: Columbia University Press, 1991), 2.
[16] Ibid., 20.
[17] Ibid., 42–50. On the incompetence of government leaders as a cause of World War I, see Jonathan Glover, *Humanity: A Moral History of the Twentieth Century* (New Haven: Yale University Press, 2000), chapter 21. Similar points about poor decision-making can be found in Robert Dallek, *The American Style of Foreign Policy: Cultural Politics and Foreign Affairs* (New York: Alfred A. Knopf, 1983). Thomas Ricks describes the incompetence of the Bush administration in *Fiasco: The American Military Adventure in Iraq* (New York: The Penguin Press, 2006).

This fallibility is not simply the result of limited information. National leaders often fail to examine alternative policies and to use available evidence in an objective manner. These cognitive failures have been noted by many scholars. Their work shows the error in simply assuming that national leaders know how to act in the national interest. One especially dangerous factor stressed by Dominic Johnson is the tendency of leaders to be over-optimistic about war and its possible outcomes. Johnson's survey of the scholarly literature shows the pervasiveness of these phenomena.

A RAND study found that even limited wars "often cost more and last longer than anticipated." Richard Ned Lebow found that in brinkmanship crises that led to war, leaders "grossly misjudged the military balance between themselves and their adversaries. In every instance they were confident of victory." John Stoessinger discovered "a remarkable consistency in the self-images of most national leaders on the brink of war. Each confidently expects victory after a brief and triumphant campaign. This recurring optimism ... assumes a powerful momentum of its own and thus becomes one of the causes of war."[18]

Moreover, once these over-optimistic expectations lead to war, it is difficult for leaders to acknowledge their errors and find ways to limit the damage. As Iklé notes, "Government leaders often fail to explore alternatives to the policies to which they became committed, and they may even unconsciously distort what they know so as to leave their past predictions undisturbed."[19] When their over-optimistic expectations collapse, they may escalate the fighting in an effort to win a war that should not have been started and whose continuation is not in the nation's interest.

Because these are recurrent phenomena in official decision-making about war, rule utilitarians would be very wary of consecrating a rule that allows leaders to do *whatever* they believe is necessary for victory. Indeed, the opposite is true. Given the need for strong constraints on national leaders in wartime contexts, there are good utilitarian reasons for rejecting an open-ended, ultra-permissive rule like the National Security Exemption.

NONCOMBATANT IMMUNITY VS. MINIMIZING CASUALTIES

The most common utilitarian argument against noncombatant immunity, not surprisingly, is that it will fail to maximize utility. Earlier, I briefly cited

---

[18] Dominic D. P. Johnson, *Overconfidence and War* (Cambridge, Mass.: Harvard University Press, 2004), 3.
[19] Iklé, *Every War Must End*, 16.

the version of this argument developed by Douglas Lackey. Lackey claims that utilitarian reasoning cannot justify a rule that forbids attacks on non-combatants. He defends his view by comparing two possible strategies for achieving a military objective. Strategy A targets civilians and is expected to cause 1,000 enemy civilian deaths. Strategy B targets combatants and is expected to kill 10,000 enemy soldiers. According to Lackey, because A causes many fewer deaths than B, the principle of utility clearly favors A, even though it attacks civilians. From a utilitarian perspective, what matters is the amount of harm inflicted, not whether the harm is done to soldiers or civilians.[20]

Generalizing from Lackey's example, it is plausible to claim that rule utilitarianism justifies the following two-part rule of war: i) choose the means of attacking the enemy that will cause fewest total deaths and injuries; and ii) count military and civilian casualties equally. Using these criteria, it is plausible to claim that utilitarians should reject the principle of noncombatant immunity and replace it with the rule "minimize casualties."

Earlier I argued that a noncombatant immunity rule can greatly diminish the human costs of war because there are many more civilians than members of the military and because military casualties are generally more likely to weaken one's enemy's capacity to fight than civilian casualties. The upshot of these two points is that excluding noncombatants will tend to limit overall casualties. Although this argument is plausible, it does not show that Lackey is mistaken. In the case he describes, more lives can be saved by attacking civilians and sparing military personnel. If a utilitarian aim in war is to minimize casualties, why not simply accept the rule "minimize casualties"? Why bother with noncombatant immunity at all?

PROBLEMS WITH LACKEY'S ARGUMENT

Lackey's argument relies on a method that is used in many philosophical discussions (including mine). The method uses artificial examples to identify the essential aspects of problems so as to make them easier to resolve. Unfortunately, artificial examples often omit important factors. As a result, their simplicity can be misleading rather than illuminating.

---

[20] Lackey, *The Ethics of War and Peace*, 64–5. Other utilitarians who reject absolute prohibitions in war are Jeffrey Whitman, "Utilitarianism and the Laws of Land Warfare," *Public Affairs Quarterly* 7 (1993), 261–75; and N. Fotion and G. Elfstrom, *Military Ethics* (Boston: Routledge and Kegan Paul, 1986); see especially chapter 9, "Civilians and the Military."

The case Lackey describes has the following features:
1. two strategies of attack are known to be equally effective;
2. the exact number of casualties for each can be predicted;
3. the breakdown of civilian versus military casualties is clear and precise.
Since the example is imaginary, Lackey can confidently describe the results of the two attacks. There are no facts to show that he is mistaken. The accuracy, precision, and certainty of his fictional "predictions" are central to making his criticism of noncombatant immunity look so strong. In fact, it is just these features that make the example unrealistic.

In Lackey's description, killing a smaller number of civilians will lead to victory. But what if it does not? Will more civilians be killed? And how certain is the military commander about these predicted outcomes? In actual cases, commanders can never be as certain as Lackey is. How much uncertainty is tolerable here? How confident would one have to be in order to target civilians rather than soldiers? Even from a purely military perspective, isn't there some concern about leaving the 10,000 enemy soldiers unharmed and ready to fight on another day? Can the decision be made based simply on today's battle without thinking about tomorrow? Perhaps there are situations that match Lackey's example, but if they are atypical, they may provide a weak basis for any general rules for an ethic of war.

While minimizing casualties is surely a worthy aim, it may be harder to act on the "minimize casualties" rule than to act on the principle of non-combatant immunity. Minimizing casualties requires both predictions and probability judgments. This may make it a more difficult rule to follow than the rule "do not attack civilians." It is generally easier to tell when the principle of noncombatant immunity has been violated than it is to tell when the "minimize casualties" rule has been violated. Although it is often difficult to discriminate between combatants and noncombatants, claims about minimizing damage are subject to both predictive uncertainty and difficulties in comparing actual and hypothesized casualties. While both rules will be subject to the pressure to attain victory and the stresses of battle, the noncombatant immunity rule will generally provide clearer guidance than "minimize casualties."

There are other problems with Lackey's argument. Because his example narrows the focus of our thinking so severely, it excludes important issues that go beyond the particular case but are essential to generating a reasonable rule. Brandt conveys a better sense of the complexities when he introduces a complex moral rule to evaluate particular attacks in war. His perhaps convoluted description of factors that need to be considered highlights complexities that Lackey's discussion overlooks. According to Brandt,

A military action (e.g., a bombing raid) is permissible only if the utility (broadly conceived, so that the maintenance of treaty obligations of international law could count as a utility) of victory to all concerned, multiplied by the increase in its probability if the action is executed, on the evidence (when the evidence is reasonably solid, considering the stakes), is greater than the possible disutility of the actions to both sides multiplied by its probability.[21]

This rule and its embedded amplifications identify many factors that are missing from Lackey's example and the reasoning he applies to it.

By citing the impact of an attack on the maintenance of treaty obligations and international law, Brandt both lengthens and widens the frame of reference for relevant effects. Instead of focusing only on an attack's immediate benefits and harms, Brandt considers the post-war future and the impact of a type of attack on the conduct of international affairs. Although these longer-term effects are hard to predict, we know that attacks in wartime often set precedents for the future and thus can have significant effects that go well beyond their immediate impact. Jonathan Glover describes how the British blockade of Germany in World War I, which caused widespread starvation among German civilians, served as a precedent for later use of aerial bombardment against civilian populations. These bombings of cities then set the stage for the atomic bombings of Japan, which in turn helped to create an acceptance of nuclear threats to kill millions in a single blow.[22] Lackey's argument ignores entirely the factor of precedent-setting and the impact on events outside of the particular made-up case.

Even in the near-term future, the commander's choice may reverberate in unintended ways. While the commander may be trying to act humanely by minimizing total casualties, the enemy may see the attack as the intentional slaughter of a thousand civilians. In response, the enemy may launch brutal reprisals. The result may be an escalation of violence as each side increases the intensity of its attacks in response to the other.

Another factor that Brandt's rule highlights is the fact that we are dealing with probabilities, not certainties. Our decisions are always based on evidence that may vary in strength and credibility and that is always to some extent incomplete. These are the kinds of factors often referred to as the "fog of war." In Lackey's example, there is artificial clarity rather than

---

[21] Brandt, "Utilitarianism and the Rules of War," 37.
[22] Glover, *Humanity*, 115. Kenneth Brown also stresses the importance of precedent-setting in "'Supreme Emergency.'"

fog, and the uncertainties of real wars are excluded from his deliberation about the ethics of war.[23]

Interestingly, simplified scenarios that resemble philosophers' examples are often used by military and political thinkers to justify particular strategies. When this happens, their conclusions have the same defects as the conclusions that philosophers draw from unrealistic examples.

Consider a historical case. In the aftermath of World War I, various theorists of air power concluded that the military carnage of World War I could be avoided in future wars if enemy cities were attacked by air. Rather than having armies fight and kill each other in order to protect their homeland, air attacks on the homeland itself could force a quick end to the war. While more civilians might die, wars themselves would end more quickly, and many lives would be spared. As in Lackey's case, the choice was between a smaller number of civilian casualties and a larger number of military casualties, and the claim was made that higher levels of harm to civilians at the start of a war would diminish the overall casualties of the war as a whole.[24]

There are a number of problems with this utilitarian argument for air strikes on cities, however, and these problems emerged clearly in the experience of World War II. First, the air power theorists overestimated the ability of air strikes to attack cities in a militarily effective way.[25] Second, they overestimated the negative impact on civilian morale. Although it had been predicted that attacks on cities would undermine support for war, the effect was to strengthen enemy resolve. Oddly, while people often think that, when enemy civilians are attacked, their support for the war will weaken, they somehow fully expect that, when "our" civilians are attacked, that will only strengthen their determination to see the war through to victory.

The actual result of an unconstrained air war was the decimation of German and Japanese cities and a huge increase in total war casualties, as the

---

[23] On the uncertainties of war, see Iklé, *Every War Must End*, chapter 2, "The Fog of Military Estimates." Also relevant is Errol Morris, "The Fog of War," a film interview with Robert McNamara.

[24] On the development of these air war strategies, see Schaffer, *Wings of Judgment*, and Biddle, *Rhetoric and Reality in Air Warfare*.

[25] For overviews of the bombings and their effectiveness, see Grayling, *Among the Dead Cities*, chapter 7, and Michael Bess, *Choices Under Fire: Moral Dimensions of World War II* (New York: Alfred A. Knopf, 2006), chapter 5.

number of civilians killed and injured skyrocketed. World War II can be seen as an experimental test of the hypothesis that overall casualties can be diminished by ignoring noncombatant immunity and taking the war to the enemies' cities. The result of this experiment counts strongly against the hypothesis.

Moreover, beyond the war itself, a legacy of this "total war" was the entrenchment of attitudes and beliefs that made it possible for people to develop strategies for the use of nuclear weapons. These strategies assumed the willingness of the nuclear powers to kill millions of people. The acceptance of these attitudes and ideas further undermined constraints on attacking civilians and may have contributed to the increased tendency after World War II for civilians to be targeted in all sorts of wars.[26] Defenders of terrorism frequently cite the atomic bombings in order to ward off criticisms of their own terrorist acts.

The key point is that, while it is easy to describe abstract examples in which targeting civilians leads to better outcomes, history shows that widening the scope of permissible targets leads to greater death and destruction. Targeting civilians almost inevitably leads to escalation because the leaders of a country are pressured to attack enemy civilians when their own civilians have been attacked. In both the First and Second World Wars, the German bombing of British cities led to widespread calls for retaliation and revenge. Rather than breaking the will of the English people to fight, it made them angry and vengeful, and leaders of angry, vengeful people will respond by creating more civilian casualties on the opposing side.[27]

We can see the same dynamics in terrorist attacks by non-state insurgents. Discussing the Israeli/Palestinian conflict, David Hirst explains why Palestinian insurgents saw suicide bombing attacks on civilians as an effective strategy in spite of the fact that they tended to provoke Israel into retaliating against Palestinian refugee camps. According to Hirst, the insurgents thought that "[f]or the Israelis … such losses were hard to bear, while their own people, who had little to lose but their camps, could absorb death and destruction with … fatalistic serenity." Palestinian supporters of terrorism also expected Israelis to see suicide attacks as evidence of the "Palestinian determination never to give up the struggle."[28] They predicted that when Israelis saw how determined Palestinians were, they would give in

---

[26] See Michael Walzer, *Just and Unjust Wars*, 198.

[27] Downes, "Desperate Times, Desperate Measures."

[28] David Hirst, *The Gun and the Olive Branch: The Roots of Violence in the Middle East*, 3rd edn (London: Faber and Faber, 2003), 640; quoted in Igor Primoratz, "Terrorism in the Israeli-Palestinian Conflict," 39.

to their demands for independence. The actual result was quite different. As Igor Primoratz describes it,

The waves of suicide bombings ... did generate much insecurity and fear, especially in Israel's cities ... As to the conclusion Israelis tended to draw from such attacks ... it has rather been one of [the] inhuman, or subhuman, nature of the people who could do such things.

This conclusion, Primoratz says, created among Israelis an increased "willingness to tolerate, and indeed call for, the most extreme measures against them [the people responsible for the attacks] and against the entire Palestinian people."[29] Attacks on civilians led not to victory but simply to increased violence and to a situation in which both sides were worse off and farther than ever from a settlement.

When civilians are wantonly attacked, the reaction is that the people who do such things are animals who cannot be dealt with, cannot be negotiated with, cannot be expected to live in a decent, humane way. And, then, in response, the aggrieved country or group commits similar acts, showing the other side that they too are animals who cannot be dealt with, etc. Violating noncombatant immunity produces a psychological escalation spiral, leading both to increased willingness to inflict more damage and decreased willingness to look for ways to resolve whatever led to the war in the first place. Just as honoring noncombatant immunity limits casualties, violating it increases them.

In both inter-state wars and insurgency struggles, attacks on civilians raise the costs of violence while frequently failing to work in the interests of those who use these strategies. But even in cases where these strategies work, that does not show that they are morally permissible. Their permissibility is determined by the overall results of accepting rules that allow or forbid such attacks, and the overall results include the effects on all people, not simply on one group.

LEARNING THE LESSONS OF WORLD WAR II

A. C. Grayling, in his moral assessment of the World War II city bombings, argues that these bombings were war crimes, and he cites the 1977 Protocol I additions to the Fourth Geneva Convention as a retroactive condemnation of the bombings. These additions to the international laws of war include the following provisions:

---

[29] Primoratz, "Terrorism in the Israeli-Palestinian Conflict," 39.

Chapter 1. Article 48 ... the Parties to the conflict shall at all times distinguish between the civilian population and combatants and between civilian objects and military objectives and accordingly shall direct their operations only against military objectives.

Chapter 11. Article 51. 2. The civilian population as such ... shall not be the object of attack ... Acts or threats of violence the primary purpose of which is to spread terror among the civilian population are prohibited.

Article 53. 2. It is prohibited to attack, destroy, remove, or render useless objects indispensable to the survival of the civilian population.

Article 57. 1. In the conduct of military operations, constant care shall be taken to spare the civilian population, civilians, and civilian objects.[30]

These provisions can be seen as the product of the experience of World War II. Though an abstract argument predicted lower casualties if cities were attacked, the experience of the war showed that expanding the range of permissible targets to include civilians tends to increase the costs of war while failing to produce the expected military and political gains.

I see the provisions of the Geneva Conventions and their strong affirmation of the principle of noncombatant immunity as the real implications of the rule-utilitarian method. These are the rules that would be accepted by "rational impartial persons" who expected their countries to be at war and whose aim was to choose rules of war whose acceptance would maximize human well-being.

CONCLUSION

In this and the previous chapter, I have tried to make a utilitarian case for an absolute version of the principle of noncombatant immunity. I believe that one of the highest items on the human agenda should be the attempt to minimize the human costs of war. As technology makes destruction ever easier to carry out, human beings must find ways to strengthen the constraints on the use of means of destruction. This is a common human interest that links people together, no matter what political animosities and conflicts exist between them. We need an ethic of war that is geared toward the protection of human life and not simply toward advancing the interests of particular human sub-groups. Noncombatant immunity is one of the central parts of such an ethic of war, and we need the strongest possible commitment to it.

---

[30] For these provisions and commentary, see Grayling, *Among the Dead Cities*, 235–44.

The utilitarian tradition, with its goal of improving human life, is a valuable source of support for this humane principle. As we think about the ethics of war, it is important to recapture the great humanitarian tradition that gave rise to utilitarian moral theory and to serious efforts to reform social and political practices. It is a loss to us that caricatures of utilitarianism have made it harder to draw on the moral and intellectual resources contained in the utilitarian tradition.

CHAPTER 16

Is noncombatant immunity a "mere" convention?

The principle of noncombatant immunity is often regarded as a central moral truth. Tony Coady speaks of the "depth and centrality of the prohibition on intentionally killing the innocent" and says that it "functions in our moral thinking as a sort of touchstone of moral and intellectual health."[1] I want to preserve its moral centrality, but I have defended it as a derivative principle whose acceptance is connected to the role that it plays in diminishing the suffering caused by war. This particular defense is open to the charge that it reduces noncombatant immunity to a merely useful convention that at best provides weak protection for civilians.

Three aspects of my view invite this charge: my partial reliance on the status conception of innocence; my utilitarian defense of noncombatant immunity; and the resemblance between my defense of noncombatant immunity and a well-known, explicitly conventionalist defense of noncombatant immunity by George Mavrodes.[2] In order to show that I have not reduced noncombatant immunity to a mere convention, I need to show 1) that the distinction between combatants and noncombatants is not purely conventional, 2) that rule utilitarianism is not a conventionalist theory, and 3) that my view differs from Mavrodes's conventionalist view of noncombatant immunity.

IS THE COMBATANT/NONCOMBATANT DISTINCTION MORALLY ARBITRARY?

Defenses of noncombatant immunity often begin by appealing to the idea that it is wrong to kill innocent people. They then infer that killing civilians is wrong. Some critics of noncombatant immunity claim that this defense rests on the error of equating innocent people with noncombatants. Even if intentionally killing innocent people is always wrong, it does not follow that killing civilians is always wrong. The reason it does not follow is that not all

---

[1] Coady, *Morality and Political Violence*, 297.   [2] Mavrodes, "Conventions and the Morality of War."

civilians are innocent. In fact, some critics charge, once we see that we cannot equate civilians with innocent people, this undermines the whole principle of discrimination, which is central to just war theory and the international laws of war. Current international humanitarian law requires that

[T]he Parties to the conflict shall at all times *distinguish between the civilian population and combatants* and between civilian objects and military objectives and accordingly *shall direct their operations only against military objectives.*[3] (Emphasis added.)

Critics argue that the principle of discrimination makes two mistakes: it assumes both that noncombatants are innocent (and thus not permissible targets) and that soldiers are not innocent (and therefore are permissible targets). If some soldiers are innocent and some civilians are not, then the principle of discrimination permits the killing of some innocent people while shielding other non-innocent people from harm.

We can see the assumed equivalence of innocence and noncombatant status at work in an important statement of noncombatant immunity by John C. Ford. He writes:

Catholic teaching has been unanimous for long centuries in declaring that it is never permitted to kill directly noncombatants in warfare. Why? Because they are innocent. That is, they are innocent of the violent and destructive action of war. It is such participation *alone* that would make them legitimate targets of violent repression themselves.[4]

This view has been challenged by a number of recent critics. Robert Goodin argues that we should reject the whole framework of just war theory, including its understanding of why terrorism is wrong. He writes: "For my own part, I doubt that this 'just-war' fixation on the 'killing of innocent civilians' is the best way to analyze what terrorism is and what is (especially) wrong with it."[5] To support his challenge, he imagines

a conscript soldier, who is personally opposed to the war he is being forced to fight, who even voted against the government waging the war and evades orders whenever he possibly can. He is morally innocent – he is fighting under duress.

Goodin contrasts this unwilling soldier with

---

[3] Protocol 1, Additional to the Geneva Conventions, 1977, Article 48; http://deoxy.org/wc/wc-proto. htm.
[4] John C. Ford, S. J., "The Hydrogen Bombing of Cities," in William Nagle, ed., *Morality and Modern Warfare* (Baltimore: Helicon Press, 1960), 98; quoted in Mavrodes, "Conventions and the Morality of War," 79.
[5] Robert Goodin, *What's Wrong With Terrorism?* (Cambridge: Polity Press, 2006), 9.

a civilian who is a ... fervent supporter of the regime and its war effort. She makes speeches, buys war bonds, does all manner of things to lend "aid and comfort" to the perpetrators of the war. She is in some sense "morally guilty", even if her aid and comfort are in no way essential or even remotely helpful to the war effort.[6]

Both international law and the principle of discrimination tell us that the coerced soldier is a legitimate target while the uncoerced, pro-war, civilian activist is immune to attack. Goodin thinks this is absurd.

Jeff McMahan, who has developed this type of criticism most systematically, offers another troubling case. He describes soldiers who are willingly fighting to defend their country against unjust aggression. Although these soldiers pose a threat to enemy soldiers, they are fighting in a just cause, while the enemy soldiers are engaged in an unjust act of aggression. It is odd to think that the just warriors lose their moral innocence by exercising their country's legitimate right of self-defense and equally odd that members of the aggressive army have the same right to attack and kill that is possessed by soldiers who are exercising their right of national self-defense. Why does the principle of discrimination allow soldiers who are involved in aggression to attack anyone at all? According to McMahan, only those soldiers who are fighting in a just cause have a moral right to fight. Contrary to the principle of discrimination, soldiers who are "guilty" of fighting on the wrong side have no right to attack the just defenders.[7]

There are other troubling cases regarding civilians. A standard example is people who work in factories that produce weapons. They are civilians, and yet their role is essential to the war effort. For this reason, most discussions agree that munitions factories and the people at work in them are legitimate targets. The same can be said of so-called "civilian contractors," who work for private companies that carry out tasks that were previously handled by members of the military. Since they carry out essential war-making functions, the fact that they are privately employed, wear no uniforms, and are not part of the military chain of command is not a plausible basis for exempting them from attack.

Likewise, civilian officials who are involved in war-planning, analyzing intelligence data, or making tactical decisions are directly involved in fighting a war even though they never fire a shot. Although they are civilians, their role in the war makes it implausible to claim immunity for them while

---

[6] Goodin, *What's Wrong With Terrorism?*, 18–19.
[7] Jeff McMahan develops his critique of the traditional principle of discrimination in "Innocence, Self-Defense and Killing in War" and "The Ethics of Killing in War."

allowing attacks on uniformed members of the military who repair vehicles or carry food supplies.

Finally, even within international law, the rules depart from the standard principle of discrimination. Some people in the military are immune to attack. These include soldiers who are disabled by wounds, captured, or have surrendered, and certain members of the armed forces with non-combat roles, such as medical personnel and religious chaplains. Conversely, civilians lose their immunity and become legitimate targets if they take up arms against an enemy army.

There are, then, many puzzling departures from the principle of discrimination. These puzzling features, along with the arguments that show a disconnect between moral innocence or guilt and civilian versus military status, seem to show that the contrast between combatants and civilians lacks the ethical significance that has been attributed to it. Certainly, in practice, it is not true that innocence and guilt determine who is or is not a permissible target.

IMMUNITY WITHOUT INNOCENCE

These various objections and problems differ from one another, but their cumulative effect casts doubt on whether the distinctions embodied in the principles of discrimination and noncombatant immunity make logical or moral sense.

A few of these objections are readily answerable. The fact that some people in the military who have noncombatant roles are not permissible targets is not a serious problem. After all, if we can make war more humane by expanding the category of people who are immune to attack, that is a good thing to do. Wounded soldiers who cannot fight represent no threat, and medical personnel tend to the wounded but do not fight. Making them immune to attack is a good thing, even if it creates a rule system that is less neat conceptually.

Likewise, if some civilian officials play a direct role in carrying out a war, then it seems arbitrary to give them immunity from attack. One can expand the category of permissible targets to include them without giving up the claim that the vast majority of ordinary civilians have no such role and should remain off limits to lethal attack.

These points do not address the strongest challenge to noncombatant immunity. The central challenge attacks the claim that we can justify noncombatant immunity by appealing to the principle that killing innocent people is wrong. This basic criticism succeeds, I think, in showing that we cannot derive noncombatant immunity directly from the wrongness of killing people who are morally innocent. Faced with that outcome, there are several possible responses.

The first is to reinterpret innocence, to define it in such a way that virtually all civilians are innocent while virtually all soldiers are not. The status conception of innocence (discussed in chapter 4) is one way to do that. It says that, in the context of war, innocence and non-innocence depend on the status or role that people occupy and not on their moral innocence. Anyone who is in the military and participates in its activities is non-innocent, no matter what their personal feelings about participating in the war are. Because most civilians do not occupy such a role, they count as innocent. (If they play a direct role while not wearing a uniform, that changes their status.) That is what innocence means in this context.

This view may sound somewhat artificial, but we make similar distinctions in other areas of life. In law, for example, people who have committed crimes and are thus factually or morally guilty may nonetheless be legally innocent. In the legal sense of "innocence," people are innocent if they have not been charged with a crime or are acquitted by a jury. They remain legally innocent, even if they in fact committed the crime and are morally guilty of it. The idea that a person is innocent until proven guilty also shows that innocence can be understood in these two senses. Guilt and innocence within the law are status terms.

As this example shows, there is nothing strange about the fact that the meaning of terms like "innocence" can vary in different contexts. Because not every meaning of "innocence" reduces to moral innocence, noncombatants who have no official role in prosecuting a war can be innocent even if they support the war emotionally or politically.

A second possible response is to retain the moral innocence criterion and to reject the principle of discrimination in its traditional form. This approach is defended by Jeff McMahan, who claims that the principle of discrimination should be amended so that it only permits attacks on people who are morally guilty and prohibits attacks on people who are morally innocent. Since those classes do not coincide with the categories of soldiers and civilians, this understanding of discrimination does not justify the view that all soldiers are legitimate targets and that targeting civilians is always wrong.

A problem with the moral innocence interpretation of discrimination is that it is hard to see how it could be used as a rule for governing the conduct of war. An unwilling, anti-war, conscripted soldier cannot in practice be distinguished from those soldiers who enthusiastically occupy their role.

Nor can civilians readily be identified as pro- or anti-war. An ethic of war that is meant to be action-guiding cannot tell soldiers that they may only attack members of the enemy military who are voluntary, enthusiastic participants in the war. Under the circumstances of war, that criterion for being a permissible target cannot possibly be used. Wearing the uniform and bearing arms have to be sufficient.

The same is true of McMahan's view that soldiers are only permissible targets if their country is fighting unjustly. In practice, this will have little or no effect because the issue of whether or not a country is fighting a just war is generally contentious. All countries claim to be fighting justly, and their citizens and soldiers may have a difficult time knowing whether this is true. Since applying the concept of moral innocence is often difficult, defenders of the status conception claim that their interpretation must be accepted if we want to impose some limits on how wars are fought and who may be targeted.[8]

While the status conception and the moral innocence conception lead to radically different theoretical views, they nonetheless provide overlapping answers in many cases. Most ordinary citizens are morally innocent. They either play minimal, inconsequential roles in activities related to war or no role at all. Although the moral innocence criterion cannot do all the work in explaining who counts as a combatant or a civilian, it still applies in many cases. Where it does not, the goal of diminishing the costs of war supports drawing these distinctions as best we can to support restraints on how wars are fought. The fact that they have conventional components does not mean that they are morally arbitrary or unimportant.[9]

In chapter 4, I defended the view that we should combine the moral innocence conception and the status conception of innocence rather than choosing one over the other. In most cases, these views reinforce one another. People who are civilians generally lack causal and moral responsibility for war-fighting and for policies that provoke political violence. When the two conceptions give rise to conflicting answers, as they do in the cases of innocent soldiers and guilty civilians, we can resolve the conflicts by requiring that people satisfy both conceptions of innocence in order to count as innocent in the context of war and political violence.

---

[8] McMahan discusses this objection in "The Ethics of Killing in War," 729–33. For an excellent discussion of theses issues, see Coady, *Morality and Political Violence*, 110–28. Though Coady rejects utilitarianism, his defense of the principle of discrimination draws heavily on consequentialist arguments and his conclusions on this issue overlap with mine.

[9] For discussion of these issues, see Steinhoff, *On the Ethics of War and Terrorism*, chapter 4; Steinhoff criticizes McMahan's view on 92–7.

Goodin's unwilling draftee and McMahan's just warriors satisfy the moral innocence criterion but not the status criterion for innocence. Civilians involved in war efforts or the implementation of allegedly evil policies satisfy the status criterion of innocence but not the moral innocence criterion. Civilians who support a war but play no direct role in it satisfy the status conception because they are civilians and the moral innocence criterion because their role in the war is too small or too indirect to make them morally responsible for the war.[10]

A DEFENSE OF NONCOMBATANT IMMUNITY AS A MORAL CONVENTION

In "Conventions and the Morality of War," George Mavrodes begins by raising these problems about the relationship between moral innocence and noncombatant immunity. He argues that one cannot defend noncombatant immunity by appealing to the idea that it is wrong to kill innocent people. According to Mavrodes, people who use this argument misunderstand the nature of war. As a result, they try to derive the ethics of war from moral beliefs about individual behavior, but, Mavrodes says,

Warfare is not an activity in which individuals engage qua individuals ... They enter into war as members of nations. It is more proper to say that the nation is at war than that its soldiers are at war.[11]

If warfare is fundamentally a form of collective or institutional behavior, then we cannot derive the ethics of war from the ethics of individual conduct.

Mavrodes argues that noncombatant immunity is best understood as a conventional rule that is invented in order to diminish the human costs of war. To clarify this point, he imagines a statesman who sees war as a procedure for settling otherwise irresolvable conflicts but who is disturbed by the high toll of death and suffering created by war. The statesman wonders whether

one could replace warfare with a less costly substitute ... Suppose, for example, that one could introduce a convention ... that replaced warfare with single combat. Under this convention, when two nations arrived at an impasse which would otherwise have resulted in war they would choose ... two men [who] would meet in mortal combat, and whoever won ... would win for his nation.[12]

---

[10] Coady describes degrees of innocence and involvement in *Morality and Political Violence*, 112–13.
[11] Mavrodes, "Conventions and the Morality of War," 81. [12] Ibid., 82.

If adopted, this convention would allow nations to use combat to settle disputes, but by limiting the number of people fighting to two, the casualties caused would be greatly diminished.

As Mavrodes notes, while the single combat model is present in stories like the biblical account of David and Goliath, the idea of replacing war with single combat has failed to gain acceptance. Nonetheless, the statesman's idea suggests a certain kind of project, a search for a less destructive alternative to traditional warfare that might actually be accepted by groups who now resort to war to solve intractable conflicts. Between single combat and all-out war, Mavrodes says, "there lie a vast number of other possible conventions which might be canvassed in the search for a less costly substitute for war."[13]

Mavrodes sees the principle of discrimination as just such a convention.[14] Like the single combat proposal, it is a rule which, if accepted and followed, retains warfare as a means of resolving conflicts while lowering its harmful costs to human life. It does this by designating a part of a belligerent's population as combatants and making all other members of the group immune to attack. According to Mavrodes, if we ask why it is permissible to kill soldiers but not civilians, the answer is that the duty not to attack civilians in war is a "convention-dependent" moral obligation. Although it is introduced for a humane reason, what creates the obligation to avoid killing civilians is the acceptance of the convention. It is like the obligation to drive on the right side of the road, which has a humane purpose but would not exist without the rules of the road. While these obligations are real, their reality depends on the existence of conventions.

While Mavrodes's goal is to defend noncombatant immunity, his view makes the obligations associated with it very fragile. Noncombatant immunity exists only if it is accepted. If acceptance breaks down, the convention ceases to exist, and the "convention-dependent" obligation to avoid attacking civilians ceases as well. This point is made clear by recalling the single combat proposal. No matter how attractive single combat might look as a damage-limiting proposal, it is not embodied in any actual convention. For this reason, no one is morally obligated to comply with it. Likewise, no one would be obligated to obey noncombatant immunity if it was rejected as a convention for governing the conduct of war.[15]

Mavrodes's view would not be surprising if he were talking about international law rather than morality. In international law, rules and principles are legally binding only when they are explicitly accepted by

[13] Ibid., 83.   [14] Ibid., 84.   [15] Ibid., 87.

nations through treaties or implicitly accepted through widely followed customs and practices. Before there were treaties that forbid the killing of soldiers who surrender or are disabled by wounds, such killings were not forbidden by international law and were therefore legal. Nonetheless, from a moral point of view, we might still think that such killings were always wrong, even when they were not adopted as international law.

Similarly, we might think that killing civilians who are not participating in war is morally wrong even if there is no accepted convention that prohibits it. According to Mavrodes, however, noncombatant immunity is only morally binding when there is a convention that supports it. Mavrodes does not believe that the ethics of war is entirely conventional. He sees both the requirement that wars must be fought for a just cause and the proportionality requirement for war-fighting as non-conventional moral principles. But, he claims, noncombatant immunity does not have this status.

IS NONCOMBATANT IMMUNITY MERELY A CONVENTIONAL RULE?

Mavrodes presents his conventionalist argument as a better defense of noncombatant immunity than the argument from innocence. Nonetheless, there is something deeply troubling about it. If the principle of noncombatant immunity is morally binding only if it is accepted, then if we or others reject it, there will be no moral obligation to avoid attacks on civilians. This greatly weakens the status of noncombatant immunity as a moral principle. Douglas Lackey objects to the conventionalist view of the ethics of war for this reason. He writes:

If the laws are merely conventional, it follows that unilateral violations of the law are not the highest form of wickedness, and may be easily justifiable if one is demonstrably fighting for a just cause. If the laws are merely conventional, one is not bound to keep the rules when fighting against opponents who consistently ignore them. If the principle of noncombatant immunity is a mere convention, then should your enemy take *your* civilians as targets, you would be a fool not to take *their* civilians as targets, if it would be a military plus for you to do so.[16]

When we condemn terrorist attacks because they intentionally kill and injure innocent people, we do not think that we are merely invoking a conventional rule that we made up. We think that these acts are wrong, no matter what we or others might think or feel about them. Yet, as Lackey

---

[16] Lackey, *The Ethics of War and Peace*, 61–2.

says, if we see the ethics of war as conventional, that implies that our obligation to obey moral rules of war depends on whether others obey them or not. Conventions only have force as long as people keep to them. When others violate them, our obligation to obey them ceases.

Mavrodes agrees with all these points and even concedes that the convention supporting noncombatant immunity may not exist. It may be, he says, that the principle of noncombatant immunity

is not really operative now in a substantial way. I do not know. Doubtless, it suffered a severe blow in World War II, not least from British and American bombing strategies ... [A] convention of warfare ... has little status except in its actual observance, and depends greatly on the mutual trust of the belligerents; hence it is especially vulnerable to abrogation by a few contrary acts ... [F]or convention-dependent obligations, what one's opponent does, what "everyone is doing," etc., are facts of great moral importance. Such facts help to determine ... what [our] moral duties are.[17]

For Mavrodes, if enough people violate noncombatant immunity, then it ceases to be a convention, and if it ceases to be a convention, there is no longer any obligation to refrain from killing civilians in warfare.

IS RULE UTILITARIANISM A FORM OF CONVENTIONALISM?

These troubling implications of conventionalism challenge my utilitarian defense of noncombatant immunity because it has some important features in common with Mavrodes's view. According to both views, the principle of noncombatant immunity is a device for promoting human well-being by diminishing the destructiveness of war. Noncombatant immunity is conventional in the sense that it is something that human beings create rather than an independent moral fact.

If noncombatant immunity is, from a utilitarian perspective, only a convention, then a utility-based form of noncombatant immunity will be disappointingly weak. Even if the principle says that we ought never to attack civilians intentionally, the absoluteness of the command is undermined by the fact that people may decide for themselves whether to accept this rule or not. If terrorists do not think it applies to them and violate it frequently enough, their actions stop being wrong. This is indeed an odd result. We generally think that if a terrible action is repeated, this makes

---

[17] Mavrodes, "Conventions and the Morality of War," 86.

matters worse. Conventionalism implies the opposite. If a morally terrible action is repeated enough times, it ceases to be morally wrong.

Igor Primoratz criticizes utilitarian defenses of noncombatant immunity for adopting a conventionalist view. Unlike deontologists, who see violations of civilian immunity as intrinsically wrong, Primoratz says, utilitarians see noncombatant immunity as nothing more than a "useful convention." Hence there is nothing intrinsically wrong with violating it. Like Lackey, Primoratz says that if noncombatant immunity is merely a convention, then it only applies if one's enemies follow it. Either everyone obeys it, or it is not morally binding on anyone.[18]

A PARTIAL DEFENSE OF CONVENTIONALISM

These threats to the status of the principles of discrimination and noncombatant immunity might be met either by 1) denying that the conventionalist interpretation of noncombatant immunity weakens it in the way that critics charge; or 2) denying that the rule-utilitarian view is a form of conventionalism. Both of these responses are worth exploring.

Does conventionalism undermine noncombatant immunity? That depends on how we understand what conventions are and what is required for a convention to come into or go out of existence. One point about conventions is uncontroversial: they are not natural and do not exist independently of human beings. Conventions exist because we have created them, either intentionally or through the evolution of norm-generating patterns of behavior.

Lackey, Primoratz, and Mavrodes assume not only that conventions are created but that they are created by reciprocal agreements. As a result, they claim that, if one party violates a convention, then other parties to the convention are free to violate it as well. On this view, conventions depend on everyone complying with them.

There is no reason to accept this view, however, and no reason why utilitarians would encourage it. For example, if bombing cities is prohibited because it greatly increases casualties and if one side in a war bombs cities, utilitarians will not agree that it is now permissible for everyone to bomb cities. Instead, given the purpose of the convention and the harmful effects of violating it, utilitarians will condemn the violations and urge continued restraint by other parties to the convention.

---

[18] Primoratz, "Civilian Immunity in War," 44.

Even if violations become common, that would not by itself destroy the convention. This point is effectively made by Gabor Rona in a defense of international humanitarian law. Rona is responding to critics who say that aspects of international humanitarian law no longer apply in an age of terrorism. This criticism, Rona writes,

implies that existing law has been "overtaken" by facts on the ground and, therefore, must be revoked or ignored. But law does not give way only because it is overwhelmed by the frequency or intractability of violations. Were that the case, everything from illicit drug use to tax evasion to (some might argue) murder would be decriminalized. Rather, it is the shift from opprobrium to acceptance that places prohibitions at risk. Violations may be frequent – even rampant – but the burden remains on those who challenge the wisdom and sufficiency of existing norms to prove their obsolescence.[19]

Rona makes an important point. While laws are conventional in the sense that they are created, it does not follow that universal compliance is necessary for a convention to exist. As Rona makes clear, conventions can exist even when violations are rampant. What matters is how people respond to violations. Although denying that they have any force is one possible reaction, redoubled efforts to increase compliance is another. According to Jean-François Queguiner, this has been the response to terrorism. Increased terrorist attacks on civilians have led to renewed emphasis on civilian immunity as an important value. He writes that although the

expansion of urban warfare [and the] use of asymmetric strategies ... could have entailed a legal erosion of the principle of distinction [i.e., the prohibition on attacking civilians], analysis of state practice reveals, on the contrary, that each violation of this basic rule has sparked solemn reaffirmations of its being the embodiment of one of the fundamental values of international humanitarian law.[20]

Violations, rather than undermining noncombatant immunity, have "sparked solemn reaffirmations" of it.

Although noncombatant immunity has been frequently violated, it continues to be affirmed both in current international law and in public opinion. It is the basis for the especially strong condemnations that terrorism calls forth from many people and is recognized as a central principle of

---

[19] Gabor Rona, "Interesting Times for International Humanitarian Law: Challenges from the 'War on Terror,'" *The Fletcher Forum of World Affairs* 27 (Summer/Fall 2003), 57.

[20] Jean-François Queguiner, "The Principle of Distinction: Beyond an Obligation of Customary International Humanitarian Law," in Howard M. Hensel, ed., *The Legitimate Use of Military Force* (Aldershot: Ashgate, 2008), 175.

civility by many people throughout the world. The "People on War" study commissioned by the International Committee of the Red Cross shows that a very large percentage of people in many countries take noncombatant immunity very seriously.[21] During World War II, when the Allies were bombing German cities, both British and American officials denied that they were intentionally targeting civilians. They recognized that there was a norm condemning this practice. They themselves had invoked this norm early in the war, and although they felt free to violate it, they feared that their actions, if made public, would be condemned.[22]

Contrary to some critics, conventions do not cease to exist simply because they are violated. Critics are right, of course, that violations can lead to erosion of support and to the demise of a convention. But violations by themselves do not destroy a convention or the duties it generates. As long as a critical mass of support for a convention exists, the convention can still generate moral obligations in spite of rejection and violations by some people.

WHY NONCOMBATANT IMMUNITY IS NOT A CONVENTION

Although some of the arguments against a conventionalist interpretation of noncombatant immunity are mistaken, I agree that a non-conventionalist defense of noncombatant immunity will provide a stronger basis for it. What I want to show is that the rule-utilitarian defense of noncombatant immunity is different from Mavrodes's conventionalist defense. As a result, it is not true that utilitarianism reduces noncombatant immunity to a "mere" convention.

To say that a principle is merely conventional suggests that it depends entirely on the fact that people choose to accept it. Any rule that is accepted and acted upon is a convention, and actions become obligatory when a convention makes them into duties. Conventionalism is a purely formalist view. It makes duties depend on a procedure of acceptance and says nothing about their substance or content. Utilitarianism, however, justifies rules by looking at their content and at the consequences of people accepting rules with that content.

The principles in a utilitarian moral code are not conventional in the sense that critics use the word. While rule utilitarians do see people as

---

[21] See the International Committee of the Red Cross, *The People on War*.
[22] Schaffer, *Wings of Judgment*, 69–70.

devising and selecting moral rules, they deny that the status of a rule depends on whether the rule is accepted. Instead, it depends on whether acceptance of the rules will maximize utility. And, whether the rules will or will not maximize utility is an objective fact that is independent of human choice. It is not our choices about whether to accept a rule that create a moral duty to follow them. Rather it is the foreseeable effects of acceptance. These effects are objective facts that are not changeable by our whims or feelings.

This point is true even of rules that have significant conventional components. Consider traffic signals, for example. It is a matter of convention that a red light signifies "stop" and green signifies "go." If people want to change the meanings of these colors or adopt other colors, they may do so. Given these conventions, however, the rule "stop at red lights" is justified by and gains moral importance from the negative effects of going through red lights. Disregarding the "stop at red lights" rule endangers people's lives while obeying it contributes to protecting human life and human well-being. Because "stop at red lights" is justified by its contribution to safety and well-being, it would be wrong to say that it is *merely* a convention. While traffic rules have instrumental rather than intrinsic value and while they do rest on conventional understandings about the meanings of different colors, they still have moral significance. Even if there were no traffic rules, there would be a duty to take precautions while driving. While specific traffic rules are devices for diminishing the harms caused by driving, the duties they generate depend on their effects and not merely on their acceptance.

MAVRODES ON THE RULES OF WAR

Mavrodes sounds like a utilitarian when he introduces his story about the statesman who proposes single combat to diminish the high human costs of war. But we can see that his conventionalist argument differs from utilitarianism by examining his brief discussion of the single combat proposal. Mavrodes dismisses single combat simply because it has never been accepted and thus lacks the status of a convention. Without this status, it is incapable of generating obligations.

Because Mavrodes rejects single combat simply for its lack of acceptance, he never evaluates it in a serious way. Recall that the statesman had wanted to limit the damage caused by war while retaining war as a means for resolving conflicts. Yet these two goals – permitting war and diminishing the suffering it causes – disappear from Mavrodes's discussion. Whether single combat is likely to achieve these goals is irrelevant to his rejection of it.

Suppose we take seriously Mavrodes's idea that there are many possible rules of war and that any of them could generate moral obligations if it were accepted as the governing convention. While Mavrodes describes a spectrum of possible rules, with a proportionality rule at one end and single combat at the other, I find it more illuminating to broaden the range of options. Suppose that the option of an exterminatory war with no restraints during a war and a rule that permits the killing of all members of the losing side is at one end of the spectrum. At the other end is pacifism, which rejects war entirely and claims that no one is a permissible target. Between these, I place a few of the possible "middle" positions in the chart below.

Spectrum of Possible Rules	Permissible Targets	Prohibited Targets
Exterminatory war	Everyone on the enemy side, even after they are defeated	None
Unconstrained war-fighting	Everyone on the enemy side as long as the war continues	No one
Chivalry	All adult men	Women and children
Noncombatant immunity	All soldiers + civilians with direct war role	All civilians except those with direct war role
Single combat	Single designated warrior	All except the single designated warrior
Coin flip with single victim	Designated victim	All except designated victim
Pacifism	No one	Everyone

It is easy to see that utilitarians and conventionalists would respond to these possible rules quite differently. For conventionalists, if people accept a rule that permits exterminating losers, then that convention would generate a convention-dependent right to kill all members of the losing side. In contrast, utilitarians would never accept this rule because it would significantly increase the amount of human suffering caused by war. Even if a critical mass of people on all sides accepted exterminatory war so that it became the governing convention, utilitarians would argue for reform and try to show people that all would be better off by placing limits on the harms inflicted in war.

What about the single combat model? The single combat rule has the same structure as noncombatant immunity. It links being a permissible target with having a combat role and then limits those who have a combat role to the one person who is the designated combatant. As a result, everyone but the designated warrior is a noncombatant, and everyone but the designated warrior is immune from attack. In the standard model articulated by the principle of discrimination, there are many combatants. Nonetheless, the logical division between fighters and non-fighters is the same. Only the numbers differ. The numbers are important, however, because single combat would cause fewer casualties of war than the standard principle of discrimination. For this reason, utilitarians would at least want to evaluate it.

For all of its appeal as a device for limiting the costs of war, single combat is not a reasonable option and is unlikely to promote human well-being. We can see this by considering the idea that we adopt a coin flip procedure rather than single combat. No one would accept this because it trivializes the issues that give rise to the conflict. Like the proposal that intractable disagreements be settled by a coin flip, single combat fails to recognize that matters of great importance may be at stake in a war. If country A will enslave country B and kill half its young, it would not be rational for members of B to accept the results of single combat between designated warriors. They would no more want to entrust their fate to a single warrior than they would want to entrust it to the toss of a coin.[23]

Because people would find these procedures unacceptable, we might predict that the losers would take matters into their own hands to defend themselves. Moreover, from a utilitarian perspective, it would be beneficial to have rules that permit them to do so. Allowing people to struggle against regimes that impose brutal and inhumane treatment on them is likely to have good effects. It is not enough to prohibit the negative effects of war. There must be means of resisting other evils as well. War, for all of its evils, can prevent the cruel and unscrupulous from using violence against others with impunity. The right to resist creates disincentives that sometimes discourage groups from trying to impose their will on others, and if they nonetheless try, the right to resist will sometimes lead to successful prevention of oppressive practices. In his zeal to prevent the harms generated by war, Mavrodes's statesman lost sight of the positive purposes of war and proposed a rule that is unworthy of acceptance.[24]

By contrast the principle of discrimination and the rule of noncombatant immunity allow groups that face serious threats to devote substantial

---

[23] Uwe Steinhoff makes this criticism of Mavrodes's single combat proposal and discusses the issue of conventionalism in *On the Ethics of War and Terrorism*, 64ff.

[24] Here I ignore the challenges to war by the tradition of nonviolent resistance. For a sample of views in this tradition, see Mulford Sibley, ed., *The Quiet Battle* (New York: Doubleday Anchor, 1963); Gene Sharp, *The Politics of Nonviolent Action* (Boston: Porter Sargent, 1973); M. K. Gandhi, *Non-Violent Resistance* (New York: Schocken Books, 1961).

resources to defending themselves. If they are defeated and must face dire consequences, then their surrender will result from their lack of ability to fight on effectively. Utilitarians will favor their right of resistance. At the same time, the utilitarian concern with human well-being will lead to efforts to limit the suffering created by war. Utilitarians will be attentive both to the costs of war and the costs of non-resistance to threats, and they will support rules and practices that allow resistance while containing war's costs in suffering and death. Noncombatant immunity does this more effectively than either single combat or unconstrained warfare.

CONCLUSION

There may be no harm in thinking of noncombatant immunity as a convention that people create, as long as we do not think that what justifies this "convention" is its acceptance. The purpose of the rule is to maximize well-being in a world in which groups pose serious threats to one another and sometimes engage in war. It is the efficacy of the rule in achieving that goal that is the basis for the duties it generates. What justifies it is its contribution to human well-being.

As with the system of traffic rules, the ethical rules of warfare contain purely conventional elements that enable us to implement and act on them. Among these are designations of permissible and impermissible targets that may appear to be morally arbitrary, but these various devices gain their moral importance from their role in protecting human beings from grievous harm. For this reason, it is a mistake to dismiss them as mere conventions that lose their moral force whenever people do not wish to abide by them.

PART IV

*How much immunity should
noncombatants have?*

Introduction: the problem of collateral damage

Since intentionally targeting civilians is a defining feature of terrorist attacks, I have focused so far on whether it can ever be morally right to launch intentional attacks on civilians. But what about attacks that cause *unintended* deaths and injuries to civilians? Many – perhaps most – of the civilian victims of war and political violence are not intentionally attacked. Their deaths and injuries are "collateral damage," side effects of attacks on military targets.

What ethical judgment should we make of attacks that cause civilian deaths and injuries as collateral damage? Are they always permissible? Never permissible? Or sometimes permissible and sometimes not?

The standard view is that collateral damage attacks are often permissible. This view can be found in commonsense morality, traditional just war theory, and international law. All of these perspectives are more permissive with respect to collateral damage killings of civilians than they are of intentional attacks on civilians. But if attacks that kill civilians as collateral damage are permitted and if many civilians are killed in this way, we might wonder about the value of noncombatant immunity. What good is noncombatant immunity if it fails to protect civilians from being harmed by wartime attacks? How can we speak of the *immunity* of civilians if the ethics of war permits attacks that kill and injure large numbers of them?

In confronting these questions, I face two challenges. The first is to state a reasonable view about the rightness or wrongness of collateral damage attacks that harm civilians; the second is to make sure that this view preserves the credibility of my condemnation of all terrorist attacks. The second challenge arises in part because I have criticized traditional just war theory for failing to meet it successfully. I have claimed that just war theory's too permissive treatment of collateral damage harms to civilians undermines it as a credible basis for rejecting all terrorism. The basic credibility problem is this: if an ethic of war permits many killings of civilians, how can it justify the claim that terrorism can never be right because it kills civilians? If we are

truly interested in noncombatant immunity, won't we condemn both intentional attacks on civilians and attacks that unintentionally kill civilians as
collateral damage?

In my discussions of the problem of collateral damage in part IV, I will
continue to refer to the "ethics of war," but I intend this term to be
understood to include the ethics of political violence more generally.
I have argued throughout that moral judgments about these matters should
not be fully determined by the status of those who carry out acts of violence.
For that reason, when I speak of an ethic of war, I see its principles as
applying both to governmental officials and forces and to the various
non-governmental groups (often labeled as terrorists) that engage in
violence for political reasons.

CHAPTER 17

The problem of collateral damage killings

The problem of collateral damage killings and injuries reveals deep tensions in standard approaches to the ethics of war and commonsense morality. We can see the problem by considering the tensions between three commonly accepted beliefs.

1. Warfare is sometimes a morally permissible activity.
2. It is wrong to kill and injure civilians in war.
3. The killing and injuring of civilians in war is inevitable.

Steven Lee describes this set of statements as an "inconsistent trilemma," by which he means that if any two of the statements are true, the third must be false.[1] If harming civilians is both morally wrong and an inevitable result of war (as 2 and 3 say), then it cannot be true (as statement 1 asserts) that engaging in war is sometimes morally permissible. Alternatively, if war inevitably kills civilians but is nonetheless sometimes morally permissible (as 1 and 3 say), then statement 2, which says that killing civilians is never morally right, cannot be true. Once we accept that civilian deaths are inevitable in war, we are forced to conclude either that war is always wrong or that the killing of civilians is sometimes morally right.

DOUBLE EFFECT AND THE TRADITIONAL JUST WAR THEORY SOLUTION

Just war theory tries to solve this problem by interpreting the ban on killing civilians in the light of the principle of double effect, which stresses the moral importance of the distinction between intentionally causing harm and unintentionally doing so. Using this distinction, just war theory avoids the inconsistency by replacing statement 2, the view that killing civilians is always wrong, with 2A.

---

[1] Steven Lee identifies this inconsistent "trilemma" in "Double Effect, Double Intention, and Asymmetric Warfare," *Journal of Military Ethics* 3 (2004), 233–4.

2A. While the *intentional* killing of civilians is always wrong, the *unintended* killing of civilians is sometimes morally permissible.

In making this revision, traditional just war theory implicitly criticizes statement 2 for failing to recognize that intention (or the lack of intention) makes a big difference to the morality of an action. Actions that kill and injure civilians need not be wrong if these harms are not intended.

This principle appears to plays a large role in commonsense morality. We seem to appeal to it, for example, when we explain why we don't think of highway designers as murderers, even though the designers know that their work will lead to highway deaths and injuries. Similarly, if people engaged in war and political violence intend their attacks to kill enemy soldiers, then attacks that unintentionally cause civilian deaths need not be wrong.

As I noted in chapter 8, there are complex versions of double effect that incorporate other requirements. For example, they require that the civilian deaths not be disproportionately large in relation to the expected military value of the attack. I focus on the simpler version of double effect because intentionality and proportionality are distinct requirements that need to be considered separately.[2] In addition, the simple version is widely cited and seems to play an important role in commonsense moral thinking and in philosophical discussions.

A BBC report, for example, describes the principle of double effect as the view that "if doing something morally good has a morally bad side-effect it's ethically OK to do it providing the bad side-effect wasn't intended." Likewise, a report on National Public Radio describes double effect as the doctrine "that an effect that would be morally wrong if it were caused intentionally *is* permissible if unintended, even if foreseen." In his study of attitudes on noncombatant immunity in the United States after World War II, the historian Sahr Conway-Lanz claims that "the importance of right intention became central to the understanding of noncombatant immunity."[3] According to Conway-Lanz, the distinction between intended and unintended harms – which is central to the principle of double effect – helped Americans to resolve the conflict between their belief in protecting civilians

[2] Alison McIntyre criticizes proponents of double effect for building multiple additional ideas into the principle and documents the wide array of differing ideas that are called "the" principle of double effect. For her very thorough analysis, see "Doing Away with Double-Effect," *Ethics* III (January 2001), 219–55.

[3] BBC Team, "The Doctrine of Double Effect," www.bbc.co.uk/religion/ethics/euthanasia/overview/doubleeffect.shtml; National Public Radio, "Critique of the Double Effect," www.npr.org/programs/death/971211.death.html; and Conway-Lanz, *Collateral Damage*, 222.

and their acceptance of both nuclear weapons and the Korean War. Americans felt that their commitment to noncombatant immunity was compatible with their support for nuclear weapons and the Korean War because, whatever civilians might be killed, it was never our intent to kill them.

In chapter 8, I argued that this intention-focused view is mistaken. To show this, I claimed that it could permit an imaginary variation of the September 11 attacks. In my imaginary version, the goal of the September 11 attackers was to damage the World Trade Center and the Pentagon buildings. Although they knew that many innocent people would be killed, killing civilians was not their intention. My claim is that, while this imaginary version could pass the double effect intentionality test, it would in fact be as wrong as the actual attacks. I very much doubt that many people would accept the argument that the imaginary version of the attacks was justified or excusable because the 3,000 deaths were not intended but were simply collateral damage caused by the attacks on the buildings. Lack of intent in such a case would carry no moral weight at all. My example confirms Robert Holmes's criticism that "double effect allows virtually identical acts ... to be judged differently."[4] In actual practice, we would and should judge the real and the imagined versions of the September 11 attacks in the same way.

COLLATERAL DAMAGE HARMS AS VIOLATIONS OF NONCOMBATANT IMMUNITY

While my imaginary example shows that the principle of double effect is defective, it does not explain its defects. We need a clearer understanding of why double effect is morally unhelpful if we are to find the proper basis for evaluating collateral damage attacks.[5]

We can start to see double effect's defects by considering an argument by Howard Zinn. Zinn's argument is part of his criticism of the US decision to go to war in Afghanistan after the September 11 attacks. Writing in December 2001, Zinn cites reports of many Afghan civilians being killed and injured by US military attacks. He cites the many Afghan civilian

---

[4] Holmes, *On War and Morality*, 197.
[5] There is a huge literature on double effect. For a sample, see Woodward, ed., *The Doctrine of Double Effect*. For insightful criticisms, see McIntyre, "Doing Away with Double-Effect"; and Thomas Scanlon, "Intention and Permissibility," *Proceedings of the Aristotelian Society*, supp. vol. 74 (2000), 301–17.

deaths to show that the United States was wrong to go to war in Afghanistan.

In addition to reporting these deaths, Zinn calls attention to the contrast between the outrage felt by many people toward the killing of civilians in the September 11 attacks and the uncritical acceptance of the killing of civilians in Afghanistan. Zinn criticizes people who condemn terrorism but support the US attacks and charges that the attacks that killed Afghan civilians were the moral equivalent of terrorism. "Terrorism and war have something in common," he writes. "They both involve the killing of innocent people to achieve what the killers believe is a good end."[6]

Zinn knows that most people will reject his equating of war and terrorism, and he anticipates that his critics will invoke the distinction between intended and unintended harms to show that the US attacks were not the same as terrorism. He writes:

I can see an immediate objection to this equation: They (the terrorists) *deliberately* kill innocent people; we (the war makers) aim at "military targets," and civilians are killed *by accident*, as "collateral damage." (Emphasis added.)

Zinn tries to show why this objection is mistaken.

Even if you grant that the intention is not to kill civilians, if they nevertheless become victims, again and again and again, can that be called an accident? If the deaths of civilians are inevitable in bombing, *it may not be deliberate, but it is not an accident*, and the bombers cannot be considered innocent. They are committing murder as surely as are the terrorists … *No killing of innocents, whether deliberate or "accidental," can be justified.*[7] (Emphasis added.)

According to Zinn, if civilian deaths are foreseen, then they are not accidents, and if they are not accidents, then the people who order, plan, and carry out the bombings are not innocent. They know enough about the effects of aerial bombardment to foresee that these attacks will kill civilians. As Zinn says, the killing of civilians by these types of attacks has happened "again and again and again." Even if they are not intended, they are certainly foreseeable, and decisions were made to go ahead with the attacks in spite of these foreseeable consequences.

Although Zinn's main point is critical, his argument suggests that, if these civilian deaths had been genuine accidents, then the bombings might have been permissible or excusable. If the people who planned and carried

---

[6] Howard Zinn, "A Just Cause, Not a Just War," *The Progressive*, December 2001, www.commondreams.org/views01/1109-01.htm.
[7] Ibid.

them out could not have known that they would kill civilians, their actions would not be murder. Colm McKeogh defends this same idea in his interpretation of noncombatant immunity. According to McKeogh, non-combatant immunity "prohibits not only the intentional killing of civilians, but also the negligent or non-accidental killing of them …"[8] He writes:

> To be excusable, the deaths of civilians in war must be accidental. The deaths must be, not only unintended but also unforeseen and reasonably unforeseeable … For an attack on a military objective to be just, there must be, not only an intention, but also a likelihood of no civilian deaths occurring as a result.[9]

I will call this view the "foreseeable harm" principle. It says that an action that kills or injures civilians may be permissible if it is both unintended and unforeseeable. If it is intended or foreseeable, however, it is wrong. Unlike double effect, this principle would condemn the imaginary version of the September 11 attacks that I described. The fact that the imaginary attackers went ahead with the attack in spite of the foreseeable harms shows why their action was wrong.

THE FORESEEABLE HARM PRINCIPLE

The foreseeable harm principle can be used to provide an alternative solution to the "inconsistent trilemma" of beliefs about war. Recall that the problem arises out of the tensions between the following three beliefs.
1. Warfare is sometimes a morally permissible activity.
2. Killing and injuring innocent civilians in war is morally forbidden.
3. The killing and injuring of civilians in war is inevitable.
Proponents of double effect replace 2 with 2A.
2A. While the *intentional* killing of civilians is always wrong, the *unintended* killing of civilians is sometimes morally permissible.
Zinn and McKeogh reject double effect and replace 2A with the foreseeable harm principle:
2B. While actions that cause *foreseeable* civilian death are always wrong, actions that cause *accidental, unforeseeable* civilian deaths are sometimes morally permissible.

---

[8] Colm McKeogh, "Civilian Immunity: Augustine to Vattel," in Primoratz, ed., *Civilian Immunity in War*, 83. See also McKeogh's *Innocent Civilians*, 165–73.
[9] Ibid., 170. See too 190 n51, where McKeogh comments on the much-discussed trolley example, stating that it is wrong to divert a runaway trolley from a track on which it will kill five people to a track on which it will kill only one.

2B broadens the set of wrongful actions by forbidding many collateral damage killings that the principle of double effect permits. With 2B substituted for both 2 and 2A, it looks like we can consistently recognize war as legitimate, know that some civilians will die accidentally in war, and forbid actions that foreseeably kill civilians.

CULPABILITY AND THE MODEL PENAL CODE

The foreseeable harm principle downgrades the importance of the distinction between intended and unintended harms and stresses the moral importance of foreseeability. These ideas receive some support from understandings of wrongful action and culpability in legal contexts. The law recognizes that people can be culpable for harms that they do not directly intend. This can be seen in the American Law Institute's Model Penal Code description of types of culpability. The Code's account is directly relevant to the problem of collateral damage killings.[10]

The Model Penal Code describes four types of culpability, based on whether people have performed criminal acts *purposely*, *knowingly*, *recklessly*, or *negligently*. I will quote from and comment on the Code's definitions of these concepts.

Purposely. A person acts purposely … when … it is his conscious object … to cause such a [harmful] result.

Acting *purposely* is the clearest case of acting intentionally. When terrorists target civilians, they are purposely killing and injuring civilians because the harms caused by their actions are the immediate goal of these actions. They are the results that the terrorists consciously seek to produce. Of course, this goal is linked to broader aims, but achieving these broader aims depends, so they think, on their success in killing and injuring civilians.

The fact that terrorists purposely aim for these harmful effects is one reason why we think that these types of actions are so obviously wrong. This point is stressed by defenders of collateral damage killings, who point out that collateral damage deaths are not caused purposely. They assume that because these harms are not purposely brought about, the actions that cause them are not wrong. The next three categories show why this assumption is mistaken.

---

[10] American Law Institute, Model Penal Code. Although I discuss the criminal law, similar points are found in civil law. See, for example, Marc A. Franklin and Robert L. Radin, *Tort Law and Alternatives*, 7th edn (New York: Foundation Press, 2001), chapter 8, "Liability for Defective Products," especially 559, 567, 576.

Knowingly. A person acts knowingly … when … he is aware that it is practically certain that his conduct will cause such a result.

A person who *knowingly* injures another does not aim to cause the injury but nonetheless sees that it is "practically certain" that his action will cause it. While causing harm is not the purpose of the action, it is certainly not accidental. A person who knowingly causes harm is not surprised by the result, and it would not be a stretch to say that he had acted deliberately. This is Zinn's point about aerial bombardments: people who carry them out know from past experience that it is "practically certain" that their actions will cause civilian deaths and injuries. For this reason, they act knowingly and are responsible for the harmful results, even though producing these harms was not their aim.[11]

Recklessly. A person acts recklessly … when he *consciously disregards a substantial and unjustifiable risk* … The risk must be of such a nature and degree that, considering the nature and purpose of the actor's conduct and the circumstances known to him, its disregard involves a gross deviation from the standard of conduct that a law-abiding person would observe in the actor's situation. (Emphasis added.)

In cases of reckless behavior, people know that there is a large risk of harm, but they disregard the risk and act in spite of it. The fact that the word "reckless" is a pejorative term in ordinary language shows that we commonly recognize that acts that cause unintended harms can be wrong. This is not an esoteric idea or legal technicality. Although Zinn does not use the word "reckless" in criticizing US bombings, he implicitly appeals to this concept when he says that people in the military know that aerial bombardments create substantial risks to civilians but continue to use bombing as a tactic in spite of their knowledge of its harmful effects.

Negligently. A person acts negligently … when he *should be aware* of a substantial and unjustifiable risk that … will result from his conduct. The risk must be of such a nature and degree that *the actor's failure to perceive it … involves a gross deviation from the standard of care that a reasonable person would observe in the actor's situation.* (Emphasis added.)

Here too, we have an action that is done without any intention to cause harm. The lack of intention to cause harm is obvious because the person carrying out the action does not even know that the harmful effects will occur. In this case, however, the person's lack of knowledge is itself culpable. Although the negligent person does not foresee the harms he

---

[11] The distinction between acting purposely and acting knowingly parallels Thomas Scanlon's distinction between two senses of "intention" in "Intention and Permissibility," 306.

will cause, they are foreseeable, and he *should know* that they will occur as a result of his behavior. People engaged in dangerous activities have a duty to make themselves aware of the possible harmful results of their actions so that they can take steps to avoid them. Because launching attacks in war is a dangerous activity, anyone engaged in warfare has a duty to consider the unintended effects that their attack may cause. When people act negligently, the fact that they neither foresee nor intend the harms they cause does not absolve them from responsibility.

These definitions from the Model Penal Code give us a richer way to think about the problem of collateral damage. Whether a collateral damage killing is done knowingly, recklessly, or negligently, the presumption is that it is wrong. The only case in which there clearly is no culpability for a collateral damage killing is one in which the attackers could not know that harms to civilians would result. This is McKeogh's view: "To be excusable, the deaths of civilians in war must be accidental. The deaths must be, not only unintended but also unforeseen and reasonably unforeseeable."[12]

A PROBLEM FOR THE FORESEEABLE HARM PRINCIPLE

Although the foreseeable harm principle appears to be superior to the principle of double effect, it gives rise to a problem that threatens to undermine its usefulness in resolving the difficulty of the inconsistent trilemma. To see what the problem is, recall that Zinn uses the foreseeable harm principle in two ways. First, he uses it to criticize aerial bombardment as a tactic because it is known to kill civilians. Second, he uses the principle to condemn a war as a whole. This broader use is evident in his claim that the United States was wrong to go to war in Afghanistan because it was foreseeable that civilians would die as a result. This argument, however, is applicable to almost every war.

If we apply the foreseeable harm principle in this broader way to war itself – rather than more narrowly to specific tactics of war, then it does not solve the inconsistent trilemma problem. In fact, it makes the problem worse by emphasizing the inevitability of civilian harms in virtually all wars. If actions that kill civilians are permissible only when they are unforeseeable and if civilian deaths in war are inevitable and thus always foreseeable, then engaging in war is never morally permissible.

---

[12] McKeogh, *Innocent Civilians*, 170. For related points, see Rodin, "Terrorism without Intention," 762ff.

The conclusion that war is always morally wrong is apparent in Zinn's claim that war and terrorism are morally equivalent. Just as terrorists know that their actions will kill innocent people, people who enter into war know this as well. In neither case are the resulting civilian deaths unforeseeable. That is why the foreseeable harm principle appears to condemn all wars.[13]

LIMITING THE SCOPE OF THE FORESEEABLE HARM PRINCIPLE

The implication that entering into war is always wrong is, of course, not a problem for pacifists. That is what they believe. For people who believe that war can be legitimate, however, this implication of the foreseeable harm principle is a problem. A possible way out of this problem is to claim that the foreseeable harm principle is applicable only to specific acts and tactics of war but is not applicable to war as a whole. As long as we don't apply it to war as a whole, we will not have the problem of ruling out all wars because of their foreseeable harms to civilians.

While restricting the use of the foreseeable harm principle in this way solves the immediate problem, making this restriction appears to be arbitrary and *ad hoc*. After all, if we can simply decide not to apply the principle to war as a whole because we don't like the result, why not decide not to apply it to types of tactics or to specific actions within wars as well? Why not shield anything that we want to defend from criticism simply by saying that the foreseeable harm principle should not be applied to it?

The challenge for people who accept the foreseeable harm principle but believe that war can be legitimate is to find a way to show that this restriction is not arbitrary. In fact, this challenge can be met. There is a non-arbitrary basis for limiting the foreseeable harm principle to tactics and actions within war and not applying it to war itself. We can see this by returning to the highway example. Although highway deaths are foreseeable consequences of highway design and construction, it would be a mistake to conclude that designing highways is always wrong and that no highways should be built.

It makes more sense to apply the foreseeable harm principle to specific techniques of building and using highways. As Richard Wasserstrom points

---

[13] Robert Holmes uses the foreseeability of civilian deaths in modern wars as a basis for defending anti-war pacifism in *On War and Morality*. Richard Wasserstrom examines this argument in "On the Morality of War: A Preliminary Inquiry," in Richard Wasserstrom, ed., *War and Morality* (Belmont, Calif.: Wadsworth Publishing, 1970), 94–101.

out, "in a quite straightforward sense, the highway does not, typically, cause the death of the innocent passenger; the careless driver or the defective tire does."[14] What we need to do, then, is criticize and reject specific design features and methods of highway construction that are dangerous. Similarly we can use the foreseeable harm principle to criticize features of vehicles and of driver behavior that are likely to cause accidents. Even though we know that these dangerous conditions will exist and therefore that highway deaths are inevitable, we apply the foreseeable harm principle to these specific factors and not to highway construction as a whole.

The same point can be made about vaccination programs. We can predict that vaccinations will cause illness and deaths for some people, but we do not condemn all use of vaccines. Because vaccinations achieve important goals in promoting health, we take their use to be legitimate. Instead of condemning all vaccinations, we look at the track record of particular vaccines, the methods of producing and distributing them, and the susceptibility of patients to risks from vaccination. If particular vaccines or methods of producing or using them pose special dangers, we single these out for special attention and either prohibit them or regulate their use. We do not condemn the entire process.[15]

These seem like reasonable responses in the cases of highways and vaccines. With those cases in mind, it is possible to claim that it is not arbitrary to restrict the foreseeable harm principle to evaluating tactics and actions within wars and not to apply it to war itself.

Accepting this restriction does not deprive the foreseeable harm principle of critical force. It can be used to show that types of weapons or tactics that especially endanger civilians are immoral. This argument has been used, for example, as the basis for campaigns to prohibit land mines and cluster bombs because their past use shows that they pose special dangers to civilians. In this case, the foreseeable harm principle generates a morally plausible condemnation of these weapons. The principle can also be applied to specific uses of weapons or specific instances of tactics. In these cases, the target of evaluation is not a general type but a specific action.[16]

If we accept the foreseeable harm principle, we will understand it to apply in these narrower ways and not broadly to war itself. Applied to cases of

---

[14] Richard Wasserstrom, "On the Morality of War: A Preliminary Inquiry," 97. Wasserstrom's point is sensible, but we may wonder how it differs from the slogan: "Guns don't kill people, people do."

[15] Russell Hardin discusses ethical problems raised by the use of vaccines in order to defend consequentialism in "Ethics and Stochastic Processes," *Social Philosophy and Policy* 7:1 (Autumn 1989), 69–80.

[16] Human Rights Watch, "Cluster Bombs in Afghanistan."

collateral damage to civilians, it tells us that actions can be legitimate if the harms caused are genuinely accidental, i.e., neither foreseen nor foreseeable. If they meet these conditions, they are neither reckless nor negligent.

THE PRECAUTIONARY PRINCIPLE

The foreseeable harm principle is one response to the weakness of the principle of double effect. A second alternative to double effect avoids its weaknesses by requiring that people fighting a war take serious precautions to prevent harm to civilians. I will call this idea, which plays an important part in international law, the *precautionary principle*. By requiring people fighting wars to take serious precautions in order to prevent harms to civilians, the Geneva Conventions appear to demand more than both the principle of double effect and the foreseeable harm principle.[17]

Article 57 of the Geneva Protocols, "Precautions in attack," begins by asserting the necessity for precautionary efforts.

1. In the conduct of military operations, constant care shall be taken to spare the civilian population, civilians and civilian objects.[18]

This statement asserts the basic principle and makes clear that active steps must be taken to prevent harm to civilians. The phrase "constant care" emphasizes that these steps must be taken throughout the process of planning and carrying out attacks.

The precautionary principle provides another possible solution to the inconsistent trilemma. It substitutes 2C as a criterion for distinguishing permissible acts that cause civilian injuries from those that are wrong.

1. Warfare is sometimes a morally permissible activity.

2C. While actions that cause civilian deaths are morally wrong if they result from insufficient precautions to spare civilians from harm, actions that cause civilian deaths are permissible if precautionary measures have been taken to avoid or minimize civilian harms.

3. The killing and injuring of civilians in war is inevitable.

---

[17] The key documents in international humanitarian law are in the *Protocol Additional to the Geneva Conventions of 12 August 1949, and Relating to the Protection of Victims of International Armed Conflicts (Protocol 1)*; accessible at www2.ohchr.org/english/law/protocol1.htm. For a description of these provisions, see Kalshoven, *Constraints on the Waging of War*. For a concise, informative overview, see Kretzmer, "Civilian Immunity in War."

[18] See *Protocol Additional to the Geneva Conventions of 12 August 1949*. The precautionary requirements are discussed in A. P. V. Rogers, *Law on the Battlefield*, 2nd edn (Manchester: Manchester University Press, 2004), chapters 4 and 5; and Yoram Dinstein, *The Conduct of Hostilities under the Law of International Armed Conflict* (Cambridge: Cambridge University Press, 2004), 113–40.

2C solves the problem by affirming that war can be a morally legitimate activity as long as serious precautions have been taken to avoid or minimize civilian harms. Even if civilians are harmed (in spite of the precautions taken), that does not undermine the legitimacy of the war.

Michael Walzer defends a version of the precautionary principle in his discussion of the problem of collateral damage. Walzer develops a precautionary requirement that he calls the principle of "double intention." He does this because he, too, sees the traditional double effect principle as insufficiently demanding. "Simply not to intend the death of civilians is too easy," he writes. "What we look for … is some sign of a positive commitment to save civilian lives … And if saving civilian lives means risking soldiers' lives, the risk must be accepted."[19] Walzer stresses both that precautions are necessary and that they must be serious. He is certainly right that, if soldiers increase risks to their own well-being in order to save civilian lives, that would be a powerful sign that their "commitment to save civilian lives" is genuine.

Article 57 of the Geneva Protocols contains several provisions to make clear that efforts to spare civilians must be serious and not perfunctory.

2. (a) Those who plan or decide upon an attack shall: (i) Do everything feasible to verify that the objectives to be attacked are neither civilians nor civilian objects … but are military objectives.

This provision states a duty to confirm the nature of the target prior to an attack. We can see this as a warning against negligence. People acting negligently fail to foresee the harmful results of their actions even though these results are foreseeable. If, however, attackers do "everything feasible to verify" that their target is legitimate but nonetheless mistakenly kill civilians, they would have fulfilled the duty to verify and would not be acting negligently.

After verifying that a planned attack is directed at a military target and not at civilians, combatants must:

(ii) Take all feasible precautions in the choice of means and methods of attack with a view to *avoiding*, and in any event to *minimizing*, incidental loss of civilian life, injury to civilians and damage to civilian objects. (Emphasis added.)

While the ideal aim is to find "means and methods" that will completely avoid harm to civilians, this provision recognizes that this may not always be

---

[19] Walzer, *Just and Unjust Wars*, 155–6. While Walzer sees "double intention" as an amendment to double effect, I think it is better to see it as a separate requirement.

possible. When avoiding civilian harms is not possible, those who plan and carry out an attack must strive to minimize them.

3. When a choice is possible between several military objectives for obtaining a similar military advantage, the objective to be selected shall be that [objective] the attack on which may be expected to cause the least danger to civilian lives and to civilian objects.

This principle applies to the choice of targets. If several targets have roughly equal military value, planners must choose the target with the least expected harm to civilians.

Even though the precautionary principle imposes demands on fighting that neither the double effect principle nor the foreseeable harm principle imposes, there is an important sense in which it is more permissive than the foreseeable harm principle.[20] According to the precautionary principle, if proper precautions have been taken, an attack can be legitimate even if civilian deaths are foreseen. We can see this in the explicit distinction between two goals: avoiding civilian deaths and injuries and minimizing them. If completely avoiding civilian harms is impossible, the precautionary principle allows attacks to go forward if efforts are made to minimize civilian harms. The precautionary principle allows the attack to be made in this circumstance even though harms to civilians are foreseen. The foreseeable consequence principle would forbid an attack in this situation.

THE PRECAUTIONARY PRINCIPLE VS. THE FORESEEABLE HARM PRINCIPLE

Both of these principles should be appealing to people who are serious about the issue of collateral damage to civilians. The clash between these two principles raises difficult questions. Does the precautionary principle permit too much, allowing acts of war that should be prohibited because they cause foreseeable harm to civilians? Or is the foreseeable harm principle too demanding, imposing constraints that are unreasonably stringent and thus not morally required of people fighting wars?

A critic of the precautionary principle might support the claim that it is too permissive by appealing to the Model Penal Code's definitions of acting

---

[20] In *Morality and Political Violence*, 143–4, Tony Coady recognizes the precautionary principle but calls it a "precondition" of the principle of double effect. I find this effort to build precautionary requirements into double effect unconvincing and confusing. Nonetheless, Coady's chapter 7 discussion of collateral damage contains many valuable points.

knowingly and recklessly. Consider a case involving the following sequence of events:

1. An attack on a military target is planned.
2. Civilian casualties are foreseen.
3. There is no way to completely avoid civilian casualties.
4. Precautionary steps are taken to minimize foreseeable civilian casualties.
5. The attack takes place, killing or injuring civilians as predicted.

Using the Model Penal Code terminology, we would not say that the attackers acted *purposely* in killing the civilians, since it was not their "conscious object" to kill them. Nonetheless, the attackers appear to satisfy the Code's criterion for acting *knowingly*, since they were "aware" that it was "practically certain" that their conduct would cause civilian deaths and injuries. The requirements for acting recklessly appear to be met as well. The attackers know that their actions pose "substantial" risks of harm to civilians but "consciously disregard" this fact and act anyway.

Using the Code's analysis, critics could argue that the precautionary principle is too weak because it permits reckless actions. The more restrictive foreseeable harm principle is not open to this criticism. It says that, if people see that they cannot fully avoid foreseeable harm to civilians, then it would be wrong for them to go ahead with the attack.

WALZER'S DEFENSE OF THE PRECAUTIONARY PRINCIPLE

Defenders of the precautionary principle might seek support from Walzer's discussion of these issues. Walzer argues that morality requires a "positive commitment to save civilian lives," even if this means risking soldiers' lives.[21] To illustrate this, Walzer describes a model case of a soldier whose actions exemplify what Walzer thinks is required. The exemplary soldier, Frank Richards, fought in World War I. In his memoir about the war, Richards describes using grenades to attack cellars and bunkers in which German soldiers might be hiding. Prior to throwing a grenade into a cellar, Richards always took the precaution of calling out a warning so as to give civilians who might be inside a chance to exit safely. He gave this warning even though it increased his risk of being fired on by German troops.

---

[21] Walzer, *Just and Unjust Wars*, 155–6. Paul Christopher defends the view that soldiers have a duty to accept risks to themselves in order to spare civilians in *The Ethics of War and Peace* (Englewood Cliffs, N.J.: Prentice-Hall, 1994), 173–7. Eyal Benvenisti criticizes this view in "Human Dignity in Combat: The Duty to Spare Enemy Civilians," *Tel Aviv Law School Working Paper Series*, http://law.bepress. com/taulwps/fp/art11/.

Richards recounts an incident in which he and another soldier had called out twice and were about to throw a grenade into a cellar when a young woman called in reply and revealed that she and several others were in the cellar. Richards writes, "If the young lady had not cried out when she did, we would have innocently murdered them all."[22] Richards's expression "innocently murdered" is somewhat paradoxical, but his meaning is clear. He calls his almost killing these innocent people "murder" because their deaths would have resulted from his deliberately throwing the grenade into a cellar without knowing who was in it. He calls the action "innocent" because he had tried to avoid harming civilians who might be in the cellar. Without a precautionary warning, the killing would simply have been a murder. With the warning, the killing would have been done "innocently."

Walzer uses the example to show that collateral damage killings of civilians may be permissible (or excusable) when precautions have been taken. Because Richards's behavior exhibits a kind of soldierly virtue, it is plausible to think that he acted well. Moreover, as Walzer sees it, Richards would have been acting well even if the woman had not responded to his call and she and the others had been killed by Richards's attack. As Walzer emphasizes,

These are, after all, unintended deaths and legitimate military operations, and the absolute rule against attacking civilians does not apply. War necessarily places civilians in danger … We can only ask soldiers to minimize the dangers they impose.[23]

Walzer's conclusion mirrors the Geneva Protocols, which require soldiers to avoid civilian deaths if possible but allow them to cause civilian deaths if they are unavoidable and precautions have been taken to minimize them. More than that is too much to ask.

IS THE PRECAUTIONARY PRINCIPLE TOO PERMISSIVE?

While friends of the precautionary principle will see this as a case in which soldiers take risks to minimize civilian deaths, supporters of the foreseeable harm principle may see it as a case of soldiers disregarding risks to civilians and launching attacks that they know will sometimes kill and injure innocent people. Which view is right?

---

[22] Frank Richards, *Old Soldiers Never Die* (1933), quoted in Walzer, *Just and Unjust Wars*, 152.
[23] Walzer, *Just and Unjust Wars*, 156.

Given the description of Richards's actions, it seems unfair to accuse him of acting recklessly. After all, he risked his life to provide a warning that might avert the deaths of civilians. Nonetheless, in order to judge his action, we need to know more about his past experiences in this type of situation and his expectations regarding the particular attack.

We know from Richards's account that the situation he describes was not unique. Suppose that, in past cases, Richards had shouted warnings but nonetheless frequently found that his grenade attack had killed civilians rather than soldiers. If so, Richards would come to subsequent situations knowing that there was a substantial probability that his attack would kill or injure civilians. In order for Richards's warnings to be a meaningful precaution, they would have to have some record of success. If they were generally unsuccessful and if Richards still continued his attacks, we might come to see the warning as a meaningless ritual that might have made Richards feel better but failed to save civilian lives.

This scenario raises several questions. Is it enough to do all that you can to minimize civilian casualties if what you do is ineffective? Is taking precautions sufficient if civilian casualties are still foreseeable or if there is still a substantial risk that they will occur? Was Frank Richards an exemplary soldier? Or was he acting recklessly because he was aware of the dangers to civilians and consciously disregarded them?

SOME PROVISIONAL LESSONS

The revised Frank Richards case is instructive for several reasons. First, it sheds some light on the three principles I have discussed, but it also shows how we may face quandaries about individual cases even when we have decided which principles are correct.

Viewed from the perspective of the principle of double effect, Richards acted rightly because he never intentionally killed civilians. Assuming that the deaths that occurred were not disproportionate to the military value of clearing areas of German soldiers, double effect implies that Richards's actions are permissible, both in Walzer's description and in the case I have described.

One might think that the precautionary principle would approve of Richards's actions, but this is not obvious. It will depend on whether shouting the warning counts as a serious precaution or an empty ritual. While precautions need not work in every case, they must have some success to be called a "precaution." Had Richards prayed before each attack, this might reflect well on him as a caring human being, but we would not call it a genuine precaution. So, proponents of the precautionary principle could judge either way, depending on their assessment of the efficacy of the precaution.

The foreseeable harm principle faces a similar issue. If grenades are thrown into cellars after warnings and, to use Zinn's phrase, "again and again and again" the result is dead civilians, then these deaths are foreseeable and the grenade attacks would be wrong. If civilian deaths are infrequent enough, however, then they would cease to be foreseeable, and the foreseeable harm principle would approve of Richards's attacks.

In this type of case, there may be little difference between the precautionary principle and the foreseeable harm principle. If the warning reduces civilian deaths significantly enough, then the precaution is clearly effective, and the civilian deaths might no longer be foreseeable. In other cases, precautions might reduce or minimize civilian deaths but not so much that they would be unforeseeable. In this situation, the two principles would give different answers.

Some of the questions about what counts as a serious precautionary effort to avoid harming civilians are illustrated in a discussion of the 2009 Israeli attack on Gaza, which resulted in 1,300 civilian deaths. Walzer, in an article co-authored by Avishai Margalit, criticizes Israeli troops for endangering Palestinian civilians. In a response to this criticism, two defenders of the Israel Defense Force claim that it made "unprecedented efforts" to "minimize collateral damage," including the distribution of warning leaflets and 150,000 automated phone calls, telling people to leave an area prior to an attack. Responding to their critics, Walzer and Margalit reassert their view that Israel did not do enough to spare civilians and question the efficacy of these warnings. They cite the history of American efforts to create "free fire" zones in the Vietnam War. In that case, US troops told civilians to leave an area and warned that after a certain period of time, the troops would assume that any remaining people were legitimate targets. Walzer and Margalit argue that these types of precautions are ineffective:

In such cases some civilians never leave, despite repeated warnings – because they are old and sick, or because they are caring for relatives who are old and sick, or because they are afraid that their homes will be looted, or because they have no place to go. If an army is committed to taking positive measures to minimize civilian casualties, and to accept "costs" to its own soldiers, then it can't be enough to make phone calls, even a lot of phone calls.[24]

---

[24] The exchange occurs in the *New York Review of Books* 56 (June 11, 2009), 77. The critics, Asa Kasher and Major General Amos Yadlin, are responding to Walzer's and Margalit's "Israel: Civilians and Combatants," in the May 14, 2009 issue.

We can see this exchange as a debate on the question "when is an action a genuine precaution?" Although Walzer uses Frank Richards's warnings as a model precaution in his book, his comments about the Gaza attacks make clear that one cannot tell whether something is a precaution in isolation. While the efficacy of warnings might be a reasonable presumption, as soon as there is an historical track record, that history becomes relevant. Included within the demands of the precautionary principle is a duty to assess the efficacy of precautionary measures. Taking precautions that are known (or should be known) to be ineffective is not a way of meeting the precautionary principle's requirements.

CONCLUSION

What is the correct moral appraisal of acts that kill and injure civilians as collateral damage? At least some such acts must be morally permissible if war is to be a morally legitimate means of defending important interests and values. At the same time, we must be able to say why some acts that kill innocent civilians are morally different from terrorist acts that kill innocent civilians, and the standard, double effect view that they are not intended is too weak an answer.

The foreseeable harm principle has a good explanation for the difference. Terrorist acts are wrong because harm to civilians is foreseen. We know that it is foreseen because it is the intended goal of terrorist acts. Some collateral damage killings of civilians are wrong for the same reason: the deaths of civilians are foreseeable. Other actions that kill civilians as collateral damage are not wrong because the harms were unforeseeable; those carrying out the attack had no reason to think that their attack would cause civilian deaths and injuries.

The precautionary principle gives a different answer. Terrorist acts necessarily fail to take precautions against harming civilians. Since they aim to kill and injure civilians, taking precautions would be self-defeating. Justified collateral damage killings, however, are preceded by serious precautionary measures. In some cases, these precautions avoid civilian deaths entirely. In others, they diminish foreseeable harms to civilians as much as possible but do not completely prevent them. In both cases, the precautionary principle says that the attacks are morally justified.

The precautionary principle and the foreseeable harm principle both attempt to do justice to the seriousness of the question. Their differences leave us still with difficult questions. Is it enough for people fighting a war to reduce foreseeable civilian harms to a minimum? Or must they avoid them entirely? Does morality permit people fighting a war to proceed with actions that they know will kill innocent people?

CHAPTER 18

The ethics of collateral damage killings

The strongest criticism of the precautionary principle is that it allows actions that are morally on a par with reckless behavior. From the perspective of the foreseeable harm principle, the precautionary principle permits attackers to consciously disregard foreseeable harms to civilians and thus approves actions that display a callous indifference to civilian lives. In this chapter I will defend the precautionary principle against these powerful and troubling charges. I will also discuss the principle of proportionality and will argue that, while it plays a role in evaluating collateral damage killings, it must be used as a supplement to the precautionary principle rather than a sufficient principle in itself.

DOES THE PRECAUTIONARY PRINCIPLE APPROVE OF RECKLESS BEHAVIOR?

Contrary to the criticism that the precautionary principle permits reckless killings of civilians, a good case can be made for the view that, if wartime attacks are preceded by serious precautions, they are not reckless, even if they foreseeably kill or injure civilians. This possibility is clearly suggested by the Model Penal Code. It says that a person acts recklessly when he

consciously disregards a substantial *and unjustifiable risk* that … will result from his conduct. The risk must be of such a nature and degree that … its disregard involves a gross deviation from the standard of conduct that a law-abiding person *would observe in the actor's situation*. (Emphasis added.)

The charge that the precautionary principle permits reckless acts focuses on the fact that it allows attackers to act in spite of the prospect of civilian deaths and injuries. However, the criticism ignores two additional features that the Code requires for actions to be reckless. The risk of harm must be "unjustifiable," and the disregard of the risk must involve a "gross deviation" from standards that people would generally observe "in the actor's situation."

Using the Model Penal Code conception of recklessness, then, we need to answer two questions about people who a) are fighting at war, b) take serious precautions to avoid or minimize civilian harms, and c) launch the attack, anticipating that there will be collateral damage harms to civilians. First, are people in these circumstances running an unjustifiable risk? And, second, do their actions grossly deviate from standards that ordinary people would observe if they themselves were in this situation?

A plausible answer to the second question is that if the "actor's situation" is participation in a war, a typical, law-abiding person would probably not see the launching of such an attack as a "gross deviation" from standards of appropriate conduct. While the attacker acts in spite of foreseeable civilian harms, he does so in a violent situation in which he is part of an effort to achieve victory, his own life may be in danger, and he has taken meaningful precautionary measures to minimize civilian damage. This scarcely sounds like someone who is acting recklessly. That is why we respond sympathetically to Walzer's description of Frank Richards's behavior. In these circumstances, it is impressive that he risks his own life by trying to warn civilians prior to a grenade attack.

Indeed, when we consider the precautions taken, we may question whether it is true that the attacker "consciously disregards" the foreseeable harms his action will cause. The phrase "consciously disregards" is ambiguous. If it means to go ahead with an action in spite of the harms it will cause, then it does apply to the attacker in this case. But if "consciously disregards" means to ignore or pay no attention to foreseeable harms, then it is misleading to describe someone who has taken serious precautions to minimize damage as consciously disregarding these risks. By striving to diminish the risk of harm to civilians before proceeding, these soldiers are in fact consciously regarding these harms, not disregarding them at all. And if they are not disregarding them, they are not acting recklessly.

The second feature that is required for an act to be reckless is that the risk it creates must be both substantial and unjustified. If there is some special reason that justifies taking a substantial risk, then the act is not reckless even if it endangers others and even if the agent proceeds, knowing that it is likely to cause serious harm. This raises a problem for the critic of the precautionary principle. The critic argues that the action is wrong (i.e., not morally justified) because it is reckless. But the definition of recklessness requires us to know that an act is unjustified before we can describe it as reckless. For this reason, the charge of recklessness cannot be used by critics to show that the precautionary principle approves of unjustified actions. We know that the precautionary principle approves actions that will cause foreseeable harms, but that is not sufficient for making them reckless and wrong.[1]

While this point undermines the criticism that the precautionary principle justifies reckless action, it also suggests that advocates of the principle have to say more about what justifies the attacks that it approves. In doing so, they may want to draw on the principle of proportionality, a key principle that I have not yet discussed in connection with the problem of collateral damage.

THE VALUE OF AN ATTACK AND THE PRINCIPLE OF PROPORTIONALITY

In explaining how acts that foreseeably harm civilians can be justified, we need to recall the purpose of the act, which is to achieve a military objective that has positive value in the quest for victory. A serious concern about the negative impact of attacks on civilians should not make us lose sight of the positive value of these attacks. Once we attend to both the positive and negative effects of attacks, it is quite natural to justify and defend attacks by appealing to the principle of proportionality. As we have seen earlier, this principle says that attacks that kill civilians may be justified when there is a proportionate relationship between the positive value of the attack and the negative value of the harms to civilians.

The proportionality principle incorporates three different elements: the amount of positive good done by the attack, the amount of negative harm created by the attack, and the relationship between them. Strictly, proportionality deals only with the third. We might think of the first two factors as providing conflicting reasons about an act's justification. The benefits make the action presumptively right while the harms make it presumptively wrong. The relationship between the positive and negative effects – i.e., whether the harms are proportionate or disproportionate to the benefits – provides the verdict. From this perspective, the justification of an attack that harms civilians has two parts: there must be a positive value to the success of the attack; and the negative effects of achieving that positive value must not be disproportionately large.

Earlier, I argued that proportionality is too weak a principle and wrongly permits intentional attacks on civilians. In reintroducing the principle here,

---

[1] David Rodin discusses recklessness in connection with collateral damage attacks in "Terrorism Without Intention."

I am considering a more restricted role for it. I am assuming both that proportionality is applied only to cases of collateral damage harms, not to intentional attacks on civilians, and that it is applied only in conjunction with the precautionary principle. It is used to evaluate the relationship between benefits and harms that is predicted after precautions have been taken to avoid or minimize civilian casualties. It is used to evaluate the remaining, unavoidable harms of the attack.

Proportionality plays this restricted role in international humanitarian law. After requiring that combatants take precautions to avoid or minimize civilian casualties, the Geneva Protocols state that combatants must

refrain from deciding to launch any attack which may be expected to cause … [damage to civilians] which *would be excessive in relation to the concrete and direct military advantage anticipated.*[2] (Emphasis added.)

While this statement stresses the negative value of excessive harm, it implicitly suggests that if the positive value of achieving a military objective is sufficiently great and the foreseeable harms are not excessive, then the action is justified.

By combining the proportionality principle and the precautionary principle, it seems possible to defend the precautionary principle against McKeogh's powerful statement of the foreseeable harm principle. According to McKeogh, "the deaths of civilians in war must be … not only unintended but also unforeseen and reasonably unforeseeable … For an attack on a military objective to be just, there must be … a likelihood of no civilian deaths occurring as a result."[3]

The combination of the precautionary principle and the proportionality principle provides the basis for rejecting this extremely demanding view. According to this reply, attacks that foreseeably will kill civilians are morally justified if:

1. precautions have been taken (both in the choice of a target and the methods of attack) to avoid civilian harms entirely or, when that is not possible, to minimize them, i.e., reduce them to the lowest level that is compatible with achieving the military objective;
2. the foreseeable harms to civilians that cannot be avoided are not disproportionately large in relation to the foreseeable military gains of the attack.

---

[2] Article 57, 2 a (iii). For a brief history of proportionality in international law, see Rogers, *Law on the Battlefield*, 17–23.
[3] McKeogh, *Innocent Civilians*, 170.

If constant care is taken to protect civilians and foreseeable harms are proportionate, then the attacks can be morally justified.

That such attacks may be justified does not mean that anyone should be happy about the outcome. In the circumstances we are considering, however, some allowance has to be made for the difficult context in which these actions occur. As Tony Coady, who supports strong constraints on the use of violence, notes about the ethics of collateral damage killings:

[T]he conduct of war ... is morally impossible unless warriors are allowed knowingly to put noncombatants at risk in certain circumstances. Some modification of the immunity principle to allow indirect harming seems to be in line with commonsense morality in other areas of life and to be necessitated by the circumstances of war.[4]

Coady's reference to areas of life other than war recalls the examples of highway construction and vaccinations that I discussed earlier. In these cases and many others, we think it legitimate to engage in actions that, even after precautions are taken, are likely to have some important harmful effects. The problem of collateral damage is not unique to war.

CAN ATTACKS IN UNJUST WARS BE PROPORTIONATE?

Thomas Hurka has argued that soldiers fighting on the unjust side in a war can never satisfy the proportionality criterion. If the war is being fought for an unjust cause, then victory for the unjust side has no positive value, and actions that contribute to victory have no positive value either. Soldiers fighting an unjust war may try to meet the proportionality standard by avoiding "excessive harm," but this is impossible to do. All the harms they cause are excessive because the positive value of their successes is zero. There is no positive value to outweigh the harms inflicted.[5]

According to Hurka, the morality of actions within a war cannot be evaluated without evaluating the war as a whole. He, like Jeff McMahan and others, believes that *jus in bello*, the ethics of fighting a war, cannot be separated from *jus ad bellum*, the ethics of going to war. If a nation wrongly goes to war, then none of the acts of war its armies carry out can be morally right.

This is a powerful argument, but I believe it is mistaken. One problem with the argument is that it fails to take seriously the effects of rules of war.

[4] Coady, *Morality and Political Violence*, 136.
[5] Thomas Hurka, "Proportionality in the Morality of War," 45.

According to the rule-utilitarian method that I have used, rational impartial people will want military planners and soldiers to take seriously the task of limiting the damage that their attacks cause. Adopting the proportionality rule is one means by which this damage-limiting goal can be carried out. Of course, rational, impartial people will also want countries and groups not to resort to war and violence for inadequate reasons, but even when wrongful wars are launched, it is in the interests of people generally that there be recognized moral and legal restraints on the use of force. Given the sharp disagreements among people about whether a particular side has a just cause or not, it is better to put that issue aside and emphasize to all concerned that they not inflict disproportionate harms in their efforts to achieve victory.

Hurka also overstates the extent to which the overall value of an endeavor completely determines the morality of individual acts performed as part of that endeavor. Consider again the highway designer. Suppose that she is working on a road that has little to no value. It is a "road to nowhere," promoted by corrupt politicians and highway companies. Hurka's view suggests that we should evaluate all the actions done in creating the highway as wrong. Yet, surely we should distinguish the actions of a conscientious highway designer who strives to make this useless road as safe as possible from the actions of a designer who takes no such steps. And just as the actions of careful and careless designers differ morally, so would the actions of soldiers who – though they fight on the wrong side of a war – either take steps to ensure that their attacks are proportionate or fail to do so. There seem to be strong reasons for encouraging these unjust warriors to observe all the justified constraints, including proportionality, on their use of force.

THE ROLE OF PROPORTIONALITY JUDGMENTS IN WAR

While Hurka takes a broad view of the factors to be considered in proportionality judgments, the traditional understanding of the *jus in bello* proportionality principle is that it does not consider the overall justice or value of a particular side's involvement in war. In applying proportionality, it is assumed that victory has a certain positive value for each side. But even if this is not true, it may not matter. When proportionality judgments are made in war, the positive value that is considered is the value of achieving a specific military objective, not the value of victory. Since victory is always very highly valued, using it as the positive value in proportionality judgments would undermine the restraining power of the proportionality principle. Even if a war is launched for trivial reasons, once it has begun, countries and their leaders are very averse to defeat. For this reason, if the question is asked whether some number of civilian deaths is proportionate to the value of victory, the answer will always be *yes*. Because the perceived value of victory is so high, applying proportionality in this way is virtually useless and imposes no real constraint on collateral damage killings.

For this reason, the proportionality principle is applied in a narrower, more focused way. We can see this in the Geneva Protocols, which require that unintended civilian deaths and injuries not be disproportionate or excessive "in relation to the concrete and direct military advantage anticipated" from a particular attack or strategy.[6] Collateral damage to civilians must be weighed not in relation to the value of overall victory but rather in relation to the value of the objective that a specific attack is meant to achieve.

PRECAUTIONS, PROPORTIONALITY, AND JUSTIFICATION

The combination of the precautionary and proportionality principles generates extremely plausible answers to questions about the justifiability of attacks. This is especially true if we describe types of cases somewhat abstractly and contrast those cases in which there seems to be a strong basis for approving an action with those in which approval seems inappropriate.

An attack seems clearly justified if it has four features: 1) The military objective has a very high value because it is *essential* to victory. 2) The attack is *discriminate*, i.e., aimed at a military target and designed to reduce harm to civilians. 3) The predicted civilian casualties are *low*, both in number and severity of harm. 4) There is no way to achieve the military objective that would cause less harm to civilians.

Contrast this with a situation in which the justification is weak because: 1) The military objective is *low* in value. 2) The attack is *indiscriminate*, i.e., not narrowly aimed at the target. 3) Predicted civilian harms are *high* in number and severity. 4) There are other ways to achieve the military objective that would cause less harm to civilians. The table below makes these contrasts clear.

---

[6] Geneva Protocols, article 57, 2 a (iii).

Relevant features	A Strongest case for justified collateral damage harms to civilians	B Weakest case for justified collateral damage harms to civilians
1. Value of military objective	Essential	Low value
2. Degree of discrimination	Discriminate, aimed at military target, designed to minimize harm to civilians	Indiscriminate with respect to military and civilian damage
3. Amount of expected harms to civilians	Very low: small numbers, less serious harms	Very high: large numbers, serious harms
4. Possibility of effective, less harmful alternatives	No	Yes

It is hard to resist the conclusion that an attack with the features in column A would be justified while an attack with features in column B would be wrong.

PROPORTIONALITY VS. THE PRECAUTIONARY PRINCIPLE

I originally introduced proportionality into the discussion to support the precautionary principle by showing that attacks that cause foreseeable civilian deaths can be justified and thus are not necessarily reckless. Once proportionality has been introduced, however, we may wonder whether proportionality is by itself sufficient and thus whether we can drop the precautionary principle as a separate factor. One reason for this thought is that the precautionary principle has not played a major role in philosophical discussions. Even writers who mention precautions do so as additions to other principles. Recall that Walzer sees the precautionary requirement as a gloss on the principle of double effect. More recently, Larry May describes the effort to minimize civilian casualties as somehow implied by proportionality itself.[7] These approaches may suggest that the precautionary principle, in spite of its important role in international law, is not morally or philosophically important.

---

[7] Walzer, *Just and Unjust Wars*, 155–6; May, *War Crimes and Just War*, 220 and 222. See, too, Coady, *Morality and Political Violence*, 143.

If we pare down the criterion in this way, we would view any attack with collateral damage that meets the proportionality criterion as justified. While it would be humane to diminish civilian damage even more, that is not strictly required. If we accept the pared-down proportionality view on collateral damage, we end up with a single ethical principle to govern collateral damage attacks.

Proportionality: unintended but foreseeable civilian casualties must not be disproportionate to the value of the military objective.

Like the other principles discussed, proportionality provides a possible solution to the inconsistent trilemma problem. It takes the places of the other versions of statement 2 that I have discussed.

2D. While actions that cause disproportionate civilian deaths are morally wrong, those which cause civilian deaths that are proportionate to the military value of an attack are morally permissible.

Like the other principles, it aims to make the inevitability of civilian deaths compatible with the legitimacy of war by distinguishing different types of actions that cause these deaths.

If we reject the idea of a one-principle rule for collateral damage and favor keeping the precautionary principle, we will retain proportionality but add others to it. We will favor something like the following more specific and less elegant set of requirements as our ethic of collateral damage harms:

1. Unintended but foreseeable civilian casualties must not be disproportionate to the value of the military objective.
2. Attacks must not be indiscriminate, i.e., they must be directed at military targets, and the damage they cause must – as much as possible – be limited to the target.
3. Steps must be taken to predict civilian casualties, i.e., to actually foresee those harms to civilians that are foreseeable.
4. Precautionary measures must be taken to avoid or minimize foreseeable harms to civilians so as to ensure that civilian casualties are no greater than necessary to achieve the military objective.
5. If foreseeable civilian deaths cannot be further reduced and remain disproportionate, the attack should not be launched.

There are a few points worth noting about the items on this list.

Proportionality appears twice, both in the first and the last item. The first instance in rule 1 highlights the avoidance of disproportionate civilian casualties as a guiding principle. The second appearance in rule 5 calls for a specific judgment about proportionality after precautions have been taken, and it has proven to be impossible to avoid collateral damage to civilians.

Rule 2 prohibits indiscriminate attacks and interprets this to mean both that military targets alone must be attacked and that efforts must be made to limit damage to them. The traditional principle of discrimination emphasizes the first of these by saying that only soldiers may be attacked and that civilians are not permissible targets. What this omits, however, is the precautionary requirement that the damage caused by an attack on soldiers or military objects must, as much as possible, be limited to them. This omission gives the impression that, as long as civilians are not the intended targets, the attack is permissible.

Rule 4 can be thought of as a caution against negligence. The precautionary rule requires steps to avoid or minimize foreseeable harms. The negligent person is not aware of harms that are foreseeable but is still responsible for them. Rule 4 makes explicit the idea that efforts must be made to foresee whatever civilian harms are capable of being foreseen.

How can we decide which set of rules is superior? The rule-utilitarian perspective is useful in this context. If we could tell which set of rules would do a better job of protecting civilians while also permitting effective forms of fighting, we would know which rules ought to be accepted. In making this judgment, we can use historical experience to predict the efficacy of particular rules in promoting well-being in circumstances of war. For this reason, it will be helpful to look at how rules of war are applied in practice.

THE HUMAN RIGHTS WATCH REPORT ON THE 2003 US/IRAQ WAR

In order to examine the efficacy of rules of war for evaluating attacks, I will describe some of the findings in *Off Target*, a 2003 Human Rights Watch report on the first stage of the War in Iraq.[8] This report examines the degree of compliance with international laws of war from the March 20 US invasion to the fall of Baghdad on April 9.

The report is instructive for several reasons. First, it discusses actual types of attacks in a particular war. Second, it shows us how people who are careful in their thinking and strongly concerned about protecting civilians in war justify their evaluations of war-fighting tactics. Third, although the report is retrospective, it indicates the factors that should be considered by people making decisions about how to fight. Finally, although the report evaluates compliance with international law and does not make moral

---

[8] Human Rights Watch, *Off Target: The Conduct of the War and Civilian Casualties in Iraq* (New York: Human Rights Watch, 2003). For this and later Human Rights Watch reports, see www.hrw.org.

judgments, the legal standards it draws on are relevant to any serious reflection on the ethics of war.[9]

I believe that the report shows that it is a mistake to rely too heavily on proportionality and ignore other factors. I will be using the report, then, as evidence for the view that the longer list of rules that emphasizes precautionary requirements is superior to the single proportionality rule. What makes it superior is the fact that it is easier to apply and promises to be more effective in reducing harms to civilians without prohibiting effective fighting.

Off Target evaluates the actions of both the US military and the Iraqi army. (By the Iraqi army, I mean the army of Saddam Hussein's government, not the non-governmental insurgency that developed after the first stage of the war.) I will begin by discussing the report's evaluation of the Iraqi army's tactics. This will both introduce the kinds of criticisms that Human Rights Watch makes and will reveal some of the reasons why proportionality is a difficult standard to apply.

Human Rights Watch criticizes the Iraqi army for numerous violations of international law, including using civilians as human shields, using Red Cross and Red Crescent medical symbols to camouflage military equipment and personnel, engaging in indiscriminate placement of land mines, locating military personnel and equipment in civilian areas such as hospitals and mosques, failing to take precautions to protect civilians in conditions of urban warfare, and disguising military personnel in civilian clothes. These activities endangered civilians by undermining the conditions that make it possible to discriminate between military and civilian targets.[10]

While these criticisms seem quite reasonable, it is important to see that, if we use proportionality as our criterion, it will be hard to tell whether the Iraqi army acted wrongly by engaging in these activities. In order to know, for example, that the Iraqi military's use of a mosque or hospital for military purposes was wrong, we would have to know both the amount of risk to civilians that these actions created and the positive value of the military objective that motivated this tactic. If we do not know both of these, then we cannot judge that the danger posed to civilians was disproportionate to the value of the military objective. The same point is true of all the other practices that Human Rights Watch criticized.

---

[9] Virginia Held rightly stresses international law as a source of "measured normative recommendations for a dangerous world," in *How Terrorism Is Wrong*, 45.

[10] Human Rights Watch, *Off Target*, 66–79.

Because proportionality is a relative measure, one cannot measure it in the abstract. Civilian harms that would be disproportionately large for some objectives might not be excessive for others. Presumably, there is some level of military value that is so high that the risks to civilians created by these Iraqi tactics would be proportionate and thus justifiable by this standard. Since the authors of the report do not consider the expected military value of these tactics, they are in no position to claim that these risks to civilians were disproportionate.

The report relies on the standards of international law to evaluate actions, and these standards include a proportionality requirement that condemns attacks that are "excessive in relation to the concrete and direct military advantage anticipated."[11] Human Rights Watch does not appeal to this standard, however, in its criticism of the Iraqi army. Apparently they did not think they could substantiate that criticism. If proportionality had been their only standard, they would have been unable to criticize these Iraqi army tactics. If it is our only standard, we cannot know whether the report's criticisms are justified or not.

EVALUATING US TACTICS

Human Rights Watch describes both positive steps taken by US forces to protect civilians and tactics that it criticizes for illegally killing and injuring civilians.[12] As evidence of US efforts to protect civilians, the report describes procedures developed by the Air Force to minimize collateral damage to civilians.

U.S. air forces carry out a collateral damage estimate using a computer model designed to determine the weapon, fuze, attack angle, and time of day that will ensure maximum effect on a target with minimum civilian casualties. Defense Secretary Donald Rumsfeld reportedly had to authorize personally all targets that had a collateral damage estimate of more than thirty civilian casualties.[13]

Reviewing the US air war during this stage of the war, Human Rights Watch concluded:

---

[11] Article 57, 2 a (iii).

[12] For sympathetic but sometimes critical discussions of US efforts to protect civilians, see Kahl, "How We Fight" and "In the Crossfire or the Crosshairs?"

[13] Human Rights Watch, *Off Target*, 19. See also Kahl, "In the Crossfire or the Crosshairs?," 16–23; and Mark Benjamin, "When Is an Accidental Civilian Death Not an Accident?," in salon.com, July 30, 2007, www.salon.com/news/feature/2007/07/30/collateral_damage.

For the most part, the collateral damage assessment process for the air war in Iraq worked well, especially with respect to preplanned targets … [I]n most cases, aerial bombardment resulted in minimal adverse effects to the civilian population.[14]

While the procedures for evaluating attacks on pre-planned targets worked well, there was less success with other kinds of attacks. In cases of unplanned attacks on "emerging targets," evaluation procedures were scaled back so that opportunities to strike valuable targets would not be lost. Other unplanned attacks were launched to support US soldiers under fire. In these cases, there was no time for careful review, the need to protect soldiers was urgent, and constraints on how to fight were loosened.[15]

CRITICISMS OF US WAR TACTICS

Human Rights Watch directs some of its strongest criticisms at the program of US bombings whose goal was to kill high-level Iraqi military and government officials. Killing these "high-value targets" was part of a "decapitation" strategy to end the war quickly by killing or disabling the Iraqi leadership.

The US launched fifty air strikes in this decapitation effort. Many were directed at civilian areas and thus placed civilians in danger. None of these attacks succeeded in killing the targeted Iraqi leadership, but they did kill and injure many civilians. Human Rights Watch was not able to determine the total number because they could not investigate all the cases. In the four attacks that they could investigate, forty-two civilians were killed and dozens more were injured. These civilian casualties resulted from less than ten percent of the decapitation air strikes.[16]

The fact that civilians died in these attacks does not by itself show that the attacks were illegal or immoral. Nor does the fact that the attacks failed to achieve their goal. The basis of the Human Rights Watch criticisms is that the attacks relied on flawed information and that US military planners should have seen that, without better information, the attacks were essentially indiscriminate.

Human Rights Watch stresses two features of the weak informational basis of these attacks. In many cases, targeted Iraqi officials were located by intercepts of satellite phones. While these intercepts indicated the presence

---

[14] Human Rights Watch, *Off Target*, 20.
[15] Sarah Sewall describes how too much focus on protecting one's own troops and insufficient concern for protecting civilians can undermine a counter-insurgency war in "Modernizing U.S. Counterinsurgency Practice: Rethinking Risk and Developing a National Strategy," *Military Review* (September–October 2006), 104–5.
[16] Human Rights Watch, *Off Target*, 22–3, 27–41.

of a phone, they did not show that the targeted Iraqi leader was actually present. Even if the targeted official was present, the phone intercept could only locate the phone within a 100-meter radius. The targeted official could have been anywhere within a 31,400 square meter area. As a result, Human Rights Watch notes, "imprecise target coordinates were used to program precision-guided munitions."[17]

The report also criticizes US forces for failing to carry out effective "battle damage assessments" of these attacks. Had US forces evaluated the decapitation campaign, it would have learned that the bombings were ineffective and that they were causing substantial harms to civilians. Lacking such assessments, the air force had no basis for believing that these attacks were effective and no justification for continuing them when they knew that they were likely to produce significant civilian casualties.

If we compare the Human Rights Watch criticisms of the US bombing campaign to disable the Iraqi leadership with the list of principles given above, the violations alleged by Human Rights Watch seem best classified as failures of discrimination and failures to take adequate precautions. The failure of discrimination is a violation of rule 2 on my list:

Attacks must not be indiscriminate, i.e., they must be directed at military targets, and the damage they cause must – as much as possible – be limited to the target.

The decapitation attacks were often launched when it was uncertain that the intended target was present and in spite of the fact that the cell phone intercepts did not accurately identify the intended target's location. As a result, the attacks could not be aimed in a discriminating way.

There was also a failure to take adequate precautions to avoid harm to civilians. This violates rules 3 and 4, which require precautionary measures both to determine the extent of risk to civilians and to minimize civilian harms. Because of time pressures and imprecise information about the targeted officials' locations, these steps were not carried out.

For these reasons, the decapitation attacks failed to meet the standards set by the discrimination and precautionary requirements. Though they used high-tech methods, they were, in a sense, shots in the dark. Given the locations attacked, the probability of hitting civilians appears to have been higher than the probability of hitting the intended targets.

A second focus of Human Rights Watch criticisms is the US military's use of cluster bombs in urban areas. According to the report, in the first

[17] Ibid., 24–5.

stage of the war, US air forces dropped 1,206 cluster bombs containing over 200,000 sub-munitions. US ground forces used almost 11,000 cluster bombs, which Human Rights Watch estimates contained between 1.7 and 2 million sub-munitions.[18] Cluster bombs are both geographically and temporally indiscriminate. The large numbers of bomblets that they release disperse over a wide area and thus pose an immediate danger to civilians. They also pose a danger over time because many fail to detonate immediately. These unexploded "sub-munitions" continue to pose a threat to civilians after their initial use. The history of their use in other wars reveals a long track record of many civilian deaths and injuries.

Here, too, the key criticism is that these cluster bombs are indiscriminate, not in the sense that they intentionally target civilians but rather in the sense that they fail to accurately target military personnel. In this case, the indiscriminateness is inherent in the weapon, though the degree of danger that cluster bombs create varies with the location of the attack. According to Human Rights Watch, while US air forces did not rely heavily on cluster munitions, US ground forces used them extensively in civilian areas where the dangers of harm to civilians were clearly foreseeable.

SOME CONCLUSIONS ABOUT PROPORTIONALITY AND THE ETHICS OF WAR

There are important lessons we can learn from the Human Rights Watch report. One is that the proportionality principle does not supersede the precautionary principle or show it to be redundant. The various aspects of the principle of discrimination and the precautionary principle do real work in assessing particular attacks and providing a basis for plausible moral evaluations of attacks, weapons, and types of tactics. Even if some of the Human Rights Watch evaluations turned out to be flawed because of inaccurate information, the methods of assessment support the value of principles other than proportionality and provide grounds for retaining these other principles in our ethic of war.

The second lesson is how difficult it is to apply proportionality in practice. As Walzer rightly warned, proportionality "turns out to be a hard criterion to apply."[19] Relying too heavily on it can undermine attempts to set meaningful moral standards for evaluating acts of war. Because the US military clearly attached a very high value to killing members of the Iraqi leadership, it is not surprising that they felt that these attacks met the

---

[18] Ibid., 56, 80.   [19] Walzer, *Just and Unjust Wars*, 129.

proportionality standard. Although high-level approval was required for "high collateral damage" attacks that were expected to kill thirty or more civilians, all of the decapitation attacks were approved by the Secretary of Defense. In every case, he thought the risk to civilians was justified.

There are reasons for thinking that the value of killing Iraqi military officials was overestimated. The US defeated the organized forces of the Iraqi government without killing any of these officials. In addition, even if killing these leaders had high military value, determining the expected value of the attacks required factoring in the probability of success. To do this, planners would have to multiply the value of killing the Iraqi leaders by the probability of success. Using such a formula, if we set the military value of an Iraqi leader's death at +100 and assume a 20 percent chance of success, then the expected value would only be +20, which lowers the foreseeable military benefit of each attack.

Psychologically, however, the full value of success probably weighed more strongly than the expected value in the minds of planners. And just as they might be prone to inflate the value of a successful outcome, there are probably psychological tendencies to minimize both the probability of civilian damage and the negative value of civilian deaths and injuries. In any case, US planners certainly thought that the goal of decapitating the Iraqi leadership was so valuable that the dangers posed to civilians did not seem excessive.

Although the language of proportionality is mathematical, what counts as disproportionate or excessive is imprecise and often subjective.[20] Many authors writing about proportionality have noted the sharp contrast between the abstract clarity of proportionality and the many difficulties of applying it in actual circumstances. These problems are worsened by the fact that proportionality judgments are made by people who have different perspectives, values, sympathies, and priorities. As A. P. V. Rogers points out:

The principle of proportionality operates … as a factor for decision makers to enable them to take humanity [i.e., civilian harms] into consideration when doing their military planning. However, commanders are, by the nature of the task they are called upon to perform, likely to put more emphasis on military necessity. Representatives of aid organizations, or indeed journalists, are more likely to put emphasis on humanity. Members of the public of states not involved in the conflict

---

[20] Although Thomas Hurka defends proportionality in "Proportionality in the Morality of War," his discussion makes clear the imprecision of proportionality judgments.

will tend to focus on the human story in the aftermath of an attack, like pictures of children killed in an air raid.[21]

More generally, we can say that there are powerful tendencies both for people responsible for fighting a war and for their supporters to view their own attacks in a positive light and to see the civilian casualties they cause as proportionate. But there are equally strong tendencies for enemies, critics, and bystanders whose primary commitment is to the protection of civilians to view such attacks negatively and to see them as disproportionate. For them, the deaths of civilians weigh very heavily while for others, the positive value of the military objective will seem much more important. There is no objective method for determining who is right.

Overall, then, the principle of proportionality provides at best a very rough guide for making moral assessments and ought not to be our only standard. This is not to say that it should be rejected entirely. In spite of these problems, attackers should certainly try to assess the military value of an attack's objective in relation to the expected harm to civilians. Even though other people will probably disagree with their assessment, attackers should be able to honestly declare that the value of the target is great enough to warrant military actions that they expect will kill or injure some number of civilians.

Moreover, if the attackers can credibly describe the precautionary measures they have taken and if they comply with the more specific requirements of both law and morality, their estimates of proportionality will stand a better chance of being taken as genuine and not merely self-serving. A. P. V. Rogers describes some of the factors required for serious, credible assessments of attacks that kill civilians. He writes:

The mere fact that civilians have been killed and injured ... does not necessarily mean that a state has failed to comply with the requirements of international law. It is necessary to inquire into all the surrounding circumstances to ascertain what was attacked and why, what weapons or tactics were used, what was known about likely collateral casualties and damage, what precautions were taken to reduce these, how the collateral loss or damage was caused and what this amounted to.[22]

Rogers's description helps us to see what is required for morally credible defenses of collateral damage killings. The standard responses to collateral damage deaths – ritualized, mechanical claims that such deaths are

---

[21] A. P. V. Rogers, "The Principle of Proportionality," in Howard Hensel, ed., *The Legitimate Use of Military Force* (Aldershot: Ashgate, 2008), 209. See, too, Henry Shue, "War," in *The Oxford Handbook of Practical Ethics* (Oxford: Oxford University Press, 2003), 747–52.
[22] Rogers, "The Principle of Proportionality," 209.

regrettable and were unintended – only serve to undermine moral credibility and encourage cynicism. If people who are responsible for the deaths of innocent civilians want their justifications to be taken seriously, they must do a better job both of preventing them and of explaining why the actions that cause these harms were morally justified.

CONCLUSION

While collateral damage killings are not a form of terrorism, how our ethic of war deals with them has an impact on the credibility of our condemnations of terrorism. Since both terrorist attacks and collateral damage attacks result in dead and injured civilians, people who condemn one but not the other need to have a good account of their differential responses to these acts. As I have tried to show, some of the standard justifications in the ethics of war – lack of intention and proportionality – are insufficient. Support for a principle that requires strong precautionary measures to avoid or minimize harm to civilians must be part of any credible view.

The moral credibility problem is at the core of the inconsistent trilemma problem. The tensions between these commonly held beliefs are an aspect of the credibility problem. As long as inconsistencies remain in our beliefs, we will appear to be (and may sometimes actually be) hypocritical in our moral stances.

I have tried to show that the inconsistent trilemma can be solved by substituting statement 2E below for the original statement 2, "It is wrong to kill and injure civilians in war."

1. Warfare is sometimes a morally permissible activity.
2E. Attacks that kill and injure civilians are wrong when the attacks that cause these harms are intended to harm civilians, fail to be discriminating in the choice or method of targeting, are negligent, or cause civilian harms that are disproportionate to the value of the military objective. Attacks that kill and injure civilians are permissible when the harms to civilians are unintended, caused by a discriminate attack on a military target, take place in spite of serious precautionary efforts to avoid or minimize civilian harms, and are proportionate to the value of the target of the attack.
3. The killing and injuring of civilians in war is inevitable.

War can be legitimate even if civilian deaths and injuries are inevitable because the civilian deaths are caused by acts that meet the requirements cited in 2E.

In particular, this principle highlights the precautions that must be taken to avoid or minimize civilian deaths. While the need for efforts to spare civilians or minimize civilian casualties is often noted in discussions of the ethics of war, the importance of this as a key principle is seldom stressed. This precautionary principle, I have argued, is the most important one with respect to collateral damage to civilians. When it is adhered to, the resulting actions, even though they cause foreseeable harms to civilians, are not the result of callous indifference to human life. For this reason, it cannot be said that these actions are morally similar to terrorist acts.

Conclusion: terrorism and
the ethics of war

In writing this book, I have focused on a centrally important but relatively narrow issue: the status of civilians in circumstances of war and political violence. Examining this issue, however, has led in many directions and raised many broader issues. In this concluding chapter, I want to return to the five questions I began with and then discuss how they generated new questions that changed the focus of the book. In addition, since utilitarian arguments have played a central role in my defense of noncombatant immunity and since this use of utilitarian ideas conflicts with many widely held views, I want to return to the question of whether utilitarian reasoning can support noncombatant immunity.

FIVE QUESTIONS, FIVE ANSWERS

What exactly is terrorism? Terrorism is a form of political violence, a tactic that can be used both by non-governmental groups and by governments. Terrorist attacks intentionally kill and injure innocent people (or credibly threaten to do so) in order to promote a political agenda. By attacking some limited number of innocent people, they try to influence a broader population or the decision-makers for that group.

If terrorism is in some way especially wrong, what features of terrorism make it especially wrong? Terrorism is especially wrong because it intentionally injures and kills civilians and thus violates the norm of noncombatant immunity. Terrorism rejects this fundamental constraint on political violence.

If terrorism is obviously wrong, as many people think, why do moral condemnations of terrorism often lack credibility? Why do they evoke cynical responses rather than affirmations of respect for human life? Moral condemnations of terrorism often lack credibility because the labeling of acts as terrorism and the negative moral judgments of terrorist acts are often biased. While people who condemn terrorism may think that they do so because innocent people have been killed, their condemnations are undermined by the obvious influence of partisan political perspectives and subjective personal attitudes. They tend to use the word "terrorism" and to condemn attacks on innocent people only in those cases where they have some special sympathy with the victims. When innocent people are attacked by their own country or its allies or when the victims are people for whom they have less sympathy, people generally do not call these attacks "terrorism" and do not condemn them with the same fervor. Though people claim to condemn all terrorism, they often condemn only a subset of terrorist acts. Other terrorist acts are not even called "terrorism" and are approved, condoned, or met with indifference.

What conditions must be met in order for condemnations of terrorism to be morally credible? In order for condemnations of terrorism to be morally credible, the labeling of acts as terrorism must be neutral and nonpartisan, and moral condemnations of terrorist acts must derive from the impartial application of general moral principles. If critics want to say that terrorist acts are always wrong, the most plausible principle that they can appeal to is that it is always wrong to attack civilians. If people believe that some attacks on civilians are morally permissible, their condemnation of all terrorist acts will not be credible.

To be credible, people who condemn terrorism must also take a certain stance on non-terrorist acts that kill and injure civilians. Because it is the killing of innocent people that makes terrorism wrong, people who condemn terrorism must be equally concerned about non-terrorist acts that kill civilians, including acts that kill civilians as collateral damage. While critics of terrorism need not condemn all collateral damage killings of civilians, they must set a high bar for moral approval. Collateral damage killings and injurings of civilians are only permissible if they are carried out after serious precautions have been taken to avoid or minimize civilian harms. People who condemn terrorism lose all credibility when they automatically accept collateral damage killings simply because these killings are not intended or are seen as inevitable effects of war.

Is terrorism always wrong, or can terrorism be morally justified under some circumstances? Yes, terrorism is always wrong. It does not follow, however, that terrorism is necessarily the worst form of political violence. Efforts to exterminate groups of people are not terrorism but are generally much worse than most terrorism. Likewise, collateral damage killings of civilians can be as bad as terrorism if these deaths are foreseeable and no efforts are made to avoid or minimize them. Counter-terrorism campaigns that kill or injure innocent people can be as wrong as the terrorism they are meant to oppose, and conventional wars can be much worse in terms of the total harms that they cause to civilians.[1]

When I began trying to answer these questions, I assumed that deliberately killing innocent people was always wrong and thought that this belief needed no defense. My aim was to work out the implications of an ethic of war that takes seriously the avoidance of killing civilians. In particular, I wanted to show that collateral damage killings had to be taken much more seriously than they are. Like Howard Zinn, whom I quoted earlier, I was deeply troubled both by the number of Afghan civilians killed by US forces in the response to the September 11 attacks and by the apparent indifference of most people to these deaths. I thought that moral consistency required a different response from people who were outraged by terrorism.

In the aftermath of the September 11 attacks, it seemed that no respectable person would approve of terrorism. It took me a while to see that this apparent consensus was an illusion and that many respectable people (and theories) reject the strong principle of noncombatant immunity and thus cannot categorically condemn terrorism. At first, I took this as clear evidence that these views – realism, Walzer's theory, commonsense morality, and act utilitarianism – were false, and I assumed that people would reject these views once they saw that they could not condemn all terrorist acts. At a certain point, however, I began to appreciate more fully how demanding it is to prohibit all intentional attacks on civilians, and this made it more understandable that people would reject an absolute commitment to noncombatant immunity. Proponents of the views that I thought were discredited by their inability to condemn all terrorist acts might actually hold on to their views and admit that attacking civilians could sometimes be morally justified.

Another powerful source of opposition to absolute noncombatant immunity is the strong emotional partiality that most people feel toward their own country or group. People who care most about their own group are not likely to place a high value on protecting members of other groups, especially when they are enemies at war. From this partialist perspective, it may seem absurd to condemn all attacks on civilians, no matter what the

---

[1] This point about conventional wars is stressed by Lionel McPherson in "Is Terrorism Distinctively Wrong?"

circumstances. Because our most intense concerns are partial rather than impartial, it may seem absurd to hold a principle that requires putting the interests of enemies above the interests of people we care deeply about and groups that we strongly identify with.

My original goal was to challenge people's beliefs about terrorism by showing that they actually approved of terrorism when it was done by "our side" against terrible enemies. My point in doing this was not to justify terrorist acts. Rather, it was to urge greater moral consistency and a certain degree of moral humility. By recognizing that we ourselves might approve of terrible acts under some circumstances, we might take a step away from self-righteous, simplistic condemnations of others.[2]

I have not forsaken these goals, but I was forced to expand them when I took seriously the existence of good reasons in support of terrorism and against noncombatant immunity under some circumstances. At that point, I came to see that noncombatant immunity needed to be defended and not merely invoked. Constructing a strong defense of noncombatant immunity became a central aspect of my efforts in writing the book. The attempt to do this led me into many issues in moral theory that I had not expected to deal with – in particular, issues about the right of self-defense and the debates between rights theorists and utilitarians. While my primary motivations and concerns remain practical, I found that having a theory is necessary (at least for me) to have confidence in the correctness of moral claims regarding the conduct of war.

RIGHTS, UTILITY, AND NONCOMBATANT IMMUNITY

The principle of noncombatant immunity is generally expressed in the language of rights. This may suggest that noncombatant immunity should be defended in rights language as well. Such a defense would have to provide us with reasons to believe both that there is a right of noncombatant immunity and that this right takes precedence over the right of people to protect their own or others' lives against attack.

The ethic of war that I have defended gives individuals who are civilians an absolute right against being intentionally attacked as well as a right not to be killed or injured recklessly or negligently. These rights generate duties for people who are fighting. Combatants have a duty to take serious precautions to avoid or minimize civilian harms. There is nothing about utilitarianism

---

[2] Though her views differ from mine in many ways, this is one of Virginia Held's aims in *How Terrorism Is Wrong*.

that stands in the way of asserting that noncombatants have these rights. The clash between utilitarianism and rights theories occurs at the level of justification, not at the level of rules or concrete moral claims. While utilitarianism justifies rights and duties by appeal to considerations of overall well-being, rights theorists justify them in other ways. Although utilitarians and rights theorists (or other deontologists) defend their views differently, they need not disagree about which rights and duties exist.[3]

We can see that there need not be any conflict between these theories on the existence of rights by using George Rainbolt's helpful characterization of the nature of rights. Rainbolt's thesis about the nature of rights is that "X has a right against Y if and only if *a feature of X is a reason* [why] Y has an obligation" to act in a certain way (emphasis added).[4] According to Rainbolt, the key point about rights is that whenever someone has a right to be treated in a certain way, some feature of that person provides the reason or explanation for why others have an obligation to treat her in this way. It is clear that utilitarians can recognize a right of noncombatant immunity in this sense. When they say that X, a noncombatant, has a right not to be attacked by soldiers, they are affirming that X's possession of the feature "being a civilian" provides the reason why others have an obligation not to attack X.

Rainbolt partly supports my claim about the compatibility of rule utilitarianism and rights. He claims that, while act utilitarianism "does not leave conceptual space for rights," there is no reason why rule utilitarians cannot accept rights. His reasons for this view are plausible. When act utilitarians believe that someone has an obligation to act in a certain way, their belief is based on facts about the likely positive effects of this act on overall well-being, not on facts about the features of a particular person. Rule utilitarianism, however, generates rules that can contain rights.[5] If we can maximize utility by accepting the principle of noncombatant immunity, then after we adopt this principle, rule utilitarians will say that certain people should not be attacked because they possess the feature of being a civilian.

Since I have appealed to rule utilitarianism rather than act utilitarianism, I welcome Rainbolt's support for the view that rule utilitarianism can recognize rights. I believe, however, that act utilitarians can recognize rights,

---

[3] Bentham famously rejected rights as "nonsense on stilts" in his "Critical Examination of the Declaration of Rights," reprinted in B. Parekh, ed., *Bentham's Political Thought* (New York: Barnes and Noble, 1973). Mill provides the classic utilitarian defense of rights in *Utilitarianism*, chapter 5, "On the Connection Between Justice and Utility."
[4] George Rainbolt, *The Concept of Rights* (Dordrecht: Springer, 2006), 118.   [5] Ibid., 133–40.

too, as long as the rights are regarded as overrideable. Act utilitarians can recognize a weak form of noncombatant immunity. If attacking civilians generally constitutes gratuitous violence that achieves little of military value, then the fact that someone is a civilian will be a reason for not attacking that person. Hence it would be a right in Rainbolt's sense. While act utilitarians will favor overriding this right, they need not deny that it exists.

These points should make it clear that, at a conceptual and theoretical level, there is no obstacle to utilitarians and rights theorists agreeing on the existence of certain rights while disagreeing about how these rights are best justified.[6]

It is worth noting that historically utilitarians and their philosophical opponents have often seen eye to eye on issues about the ethics of war. Geoffrey Best, in his history of efforts to make war more humane, cites the nineteenth-century debates between Kantians and utilitarians and comments that

One would expect to find arguments about human rights [in war] ... embittered by such contrasting [philosophical] ideas ... Yet I cannot see that it made much difference in practice ... [A]t no stage of my story can I find good cause to judge that one or the other school of thought was more conducive to practical humanity.[7]

Earlier, I cited the bitter attacks on utilitarianism by Thomas Nagel and Stuart Hampshire. Unlike Best, Nagel sees utilitarianism as much less "conducive to practical humanity" because it can justify "large scale murder," and Hampshire faults utilitarian thinking for creating "a new abstract cruelty in politics."[8] Best, however, claims that utilitarians and Kantians were equally involved in efforts to "humanize" warfare.

Nor did utilitarians invent "abstract cruelty in politics." In fact, other thinkers have faulted different philosophies for encouraging such cruelty. Best cites a comment by L. T. Hobhouse that sheds an interesting light on Hampshire's anti-utilitarian remarks. Hobhouse, who was in London and reading Hegel in 1918 when the Germans bombed the city, wrote that he "had just witnessed the visible and tangible outcome of a false and wicked doctrine, the foundation of which lay ... in the book before me." For Hobhouse, it was Hegel's doctrines that provided the impetus for abstract cruelty in politics. After quoting Hobhouse's denunciation of Hegel's

---

[6] For excellent discussions of the relationship between rights and utilitarianism, see L. W. Sumner, *The Moral Foundations of Rights* (Oxford: Oxford University Press, 1987), and David Lyons, *Rights, Welfare and Mill's Moral Theory* (Oxford: Oxford University Press, 1994).

[7] Geoffrey Best, *Humanity at War* (New York: Columbia University Press, 1980), 40.

[8] Nagel, "War and Massacre," 6; Hampshire, "Morality and Pessimism," 4.

philosophy, Best leaves the reader with his own question: "But what doctrine lay beneath the bombings of Dresden or Hiroshima?"[9]

While anti-utilitarians fault consequentialist theories for making moral rights and principles contingent on circumstances, John Dewey saw just the opposite problem in Kantian ethics. In his analysis of German militarism during World War I, Dewey defended utilitarianism and other consequentialist ethical theories against the Kantian view.

Morals which are based upon consideration of good and evil consequences not only allow, but imperiously demand the exercise of a discriminating intelligence. A [Kantian] gospel of duty separated from empirical purposes and results tends to gag intelligence. It substitutes for the work of reason displayed in a wide and distributed survey of consequences … an inner consciousness, empty of content, which clothes with the form of rationality the demands of existing social authorities … [and] which is not based upon and checked by consideration of actual results upon human welfare …[10]

For Dewey, a perspective that ignores the "actual results upon human welfare" is simply socially irresponsible, even if it is labeled with the high-sounding name "Reason."

My point here is not to attack Kant, Hegel, deontology, or rights theory. Other reformers have found inspiration in these views. My aim is to defend utilitarianism against attacks that suggest that it is essentially threatening to core human values. The historical record suggests that a single philosophy can support both positive developments like the humanitarian laws of war as well as inhumane, destructive practices like conquest and genocide. It is easy to see how this happens. Philosophical theories, especially when presented at their most abstract levels, do not dictate practical conclusions. Many other beliefs are required to provide the links between abstract ideas and specific moral rules and judgments, not only about war but about other matters as well. Whatever features of utilitarianism might lead some people to think that it justifies atrocities, there are features of rights theories and other perspectives that can be used for evil purposes as well.

Where utilitarianism is strong is in its emphasis on just the thing that Dewey stressed, attention to the "actual results upon human welfare" of different moral rules, principles, practices, and institutions. Very much in this spirit, William Talbott has argued that we can justify certain universal

[9] Best, *Humanity at War*, 40. The quote from Hobhouse comes from *The Metaphysical Theory of the State* (London: George Allen and Unwin Ltd., 1918), 6.
[10] John Dewey, *German Philosophy and Politics*, revised edn (New York: G. P. Putnam's Sons, 1942), 88. Originally published in 1915, the 1942 edition reprints the original and adds a substantial discussion of the roots of Nazi doctrine in German philosophy.

human rights using what he calls "the historical-social process of moral discovery paradigm."[11] By this he means that in determining what rights should be recognized, we should look at the history of human societies in order to learn what are the consequences for human well-being when certain rights are recognized or not recognized. I have used a similar argument that appeals to the history of warfare. While there may be abstract arguments against noncombatant immunity, the historical record strongly suggests that failure to recognize noncombatant immunity leads to increasing the brutality and destructiveness of war. If our goal is to permit war while also containing its level of destructiveness, a strong effort must be made to entrench the idea of the inviolability of innocent civilians.

RULES OF WAR VS. THE "DEEP MORALITY OF WAR"

Some philosophers attack utilitarianism because they equate it with conventionalism and have a low opinion of any view that reduces ethical principles to "mere conventions." Noam Zohar, commenting on utilitarian defenses of the war ethic, makes both a positive and a negative point about them:

It is hard to contest the assertion that adherence to the rules that constitute the war convention will vastly increase overall utility … [But] if noncombatant immunity is only a convention, it seems difficult to sustain the moral fervor of the condemnation of terrorists. Whatever good effects the convention has, it must first of all be grounded in our moral sense and convictions.[12]

I have argued that rule utilitarianism is not a conventionalist theory because it does not hold that rules are morally binding because they are accepted. Rather, it holds that rules are binding because their acceptance will generate good consequences.

Zohar might acknowledge this but still claim that the rules are a device that we create in order to achieve good ends rather than principles that are "grounded in our moral sense and convictions." This is a very strange remark because it requires us to believe that measures that "vastly increase overall utility" by preventing many deaths and injuries have little or no moral significance from the perspective of "our moral sense and convictions." It is hard to see how any set of reasonable, humane moral convictions could be indifferent to diminishing the destructiveness of war.

---

[11] William Talbott, *Which Rights Should be Universal?* (New York: Oxford University Press, 2005), 35.
[12] Zohar, "Innocence and Complex Threats," 736.

Jeff McMahan develops a point like Zohar's more fully and powerfully. He contrasts the "conventions established to mitigate the savagery of war" with what he calls "the deep morality of war."[13] Like Zohar, McMahan thinks that these conventions can be valuable, but he does not believe that they are the real morality of war, and he uses a version of the moral innocence view to criticize many traditional views of the ethics of war, including the principle of noncombatant immunity.[14]

The moral value that underlies McMahan's view is that people should be treated justly, and this requires treating them as they deserve. From this perspective, the distinction between combatants and noncombatants is much too crude. For McMahan, this distinction is itself a convention and has no intrinsic moral weight. According to McMahan's conception of the "deep morality of war," a "person becomes a legitimate target in war by being to some degree morally responsible for an unjust threat, or for a grievance that provides a just cause for war."[15] Some degree of responsibility is required for a person to be a permissible target, and the stringency of constraints on attacking people varies with their degree of responsibility.

McMahan acknowledges that someone might object to this view, arguing that even if it is "true in principle, it is irrelevant in practice since it is normally impossible to know, of any particular unjust combatant, the degree to which he is morally responsible for the unjust threat he poses ..." And, he replies, "This is largely true."[16] In effect, then, people fighting a war cannot use McMahan's principle to determine their actions because they do not know enough about individual combatants and non-combatants that they face. Not knowing their degree of innocence or responsibility, they cannot actually follow McMahan's rule.

After conceding that it is "largely true" that this knowledge is out of reach, McMahan makes a concession to practicalities, saying that people will have to act "on the basis of presumptions" about the justice of each side in war. And, if they believe that side A is fighting an unjust war, then they should assume that fighters for side A are responsible enough to be attacked. Similarly, while some civilians may be responsible for the injustice of their side in the war, "just combatants should in general err on the side of caution by acting on the presumption that noncombatants are innocent ... "[17]

---

[13] McMahan, "The Ethics of Killing in War."

[14] For simplicity, I ignore a shift in McMahan's view. In "Innocence, Self-Defense, and Killing in War," he uses the language of moral innocence; in his 2004 paper, "The Ethics of Killing in War," 723, he rejects that for the language of responsibility.

[15] McMahan, "The Ethics of Killing in War," 724.   [16] Ibid., 724.   [17] Ibid., 728.

There are two problems with McMahan's view, one concerning the "deep morality of war" and the other concerning the rules that must be accepted for practical purposes. The first problem concerns McMahan's elevation of the status of the allegedly deep morality or war. If the central function of morality is to guide our actions by making clear what actions are permissible and forbidden, McMahan's "deep morality" seems unable to play this central role. If it cannot play the role of guiding behavior, however, it seems very odd to consider it as, in some sense, the real thing while dismissing actual, useable moral principles as shallow substitutes.

This somewhat dismissive contrast between deep and shallow morality is the second problem for McMahan. It is clear that the practical rules that McMahan describes have some moral importance in his eyes. These are the rules that actually tell people what to do in war. McMahan is not happy with them because they are crude approximations of the moral innocence criterion, and they sanction departures from this criterion out of a recognition of the imperfect knowledge that soldiers possess about the enemy. He calls them conventions because they are made-up rules that fail to do perfect justice. Nonetheless, as he himself acknowledges, they seem to be the best we can do in the circumstances.

The problem for McMahan is that he has to take these crude, pragmatically determined rules to be morally important because he really wants people to follow them. And yet, they do not line up exactly with the deep morality he is committed to. One might compare his situation with that of an act utilitarian who reluctantly embraces rule utilitarianism for pragmatic reasons. For the act utilitarian, the deep morality is the act-utilitarian principle itself: in every action, do the most good. Yet, one cannot simply act on this principle because we know that our knowledge is imperfect and our desires and attachments distort our predictions and utilitarian calculations. And, knowing what we do about people generally, we think we often do better by devising and embracing various rules. That is why we have red lights and stop signs rather than leaving it up to individual drivers to determine the expected utility of stopping or going through an intersection. It is why, in the political realm, we have constitutions, procedures, and separation of powers – all of which prohibit individuals from simply acting on their own estimation of what is the best thing to do. Frustrated act utilitarians will see all of these rules and processes as mere conventions that are obstacles to making utilitarian calculations in all individual cases. They will view these conventions as departures from the "deep morality" expressed in utilitarianism's fundamental principle, "maximize utility."

Mill wisely pointed out that "Whatever we adopt as the fundamental principle of morality, we require subordinate principles to apply it by."[18] For utilitarians, these "secondary principles" should be based on what experience teaches about the effects of types of actions and the effects of adopting certain rules. Moreover, the secondary principles that we devise are revisable in the light of experience. As Mill says, "The corollaries from the principle of utility, like the precepts of every practical art, admit of indefinite improvement ..."[19] These corollaries and secondary principles are important and worth supporting, even though they may fail to conform with the "deep morality" of utilitarianism as act utilitarians understand it.

Both Zohar and McMahan concede that the rules of war, including noncombatant immunity, make a serious contribution to human well-being. As deontologists, they face a choice between acknowledging the moral importance of rules that help to save people's lives and denying that these life-saving rules have genuine moral importance. It is hard to believe that they would choose the second of these options. McMahan, in fact, makes it clear that he supports rules that are imperfect yet capable of being acted on, even if he views them as shallow and conventional.

Note that if Mill is right that all moral theories require secondary principles to guide the application of fundamental principles, then it is certainly possible that different theories may converge on similar sets of secondary principles even though they begin with differing fundamental principles. In setting out such principles, we need to avoid thinking that a "secondary" principle is a principle of lesser importance. What is meant here is only that it is not the fundamental principle in a moral view. Rather, it is a principle that we derive from a fundamental principle when we try to discover how best to implement its central values.

DOES UTILITARIANISM GIVE THE WRONG REASONS NOT TO KILL CIVILIANS?

The utilitarian approach to noncombatant immunity has been attacked thoughtfully and forcefully by Igor Primoratz in his essay "Civilian Immunity in War." Primoratz writes that

the consequentialist misses what anyone else, and in particular any civilian in wartime, would consider the crux of the matter. Faced with the prospect of being killed or maimed by enemy fire, a civilian would not make her case in terms of the disutility of killing or maiming civilians in war in general, or of killing or maiming

---

[18] John Stuart Mill, *Utilitarianism* (Indianapolis: Hackett Publishing, 1979), 24.   [19] Ibid., 24.

her then and there. She would, rather, point out that she is a civilian, not a soldier; a bystander, not a participant; an innocent, not a guilty party. She would point out that she has done nothing to deserve, or become liable to, such a fate. She would present these personal facts as considerations whose moral significance is intrinsic and decisive … And her argument, couched in personal terms, would seem to be more to the point than the impersonal calculation of good and bad consequences.[20]

Primoratz is surely right that a person in this situation would be unlikely to offer a crash course in rule-utilitarian reasoning. She would be more likely to make a more personal plea, and any humane person would hope that those who threaten her would be moved by her plea.

Nonetheless, Primoratz's argument does not undermine either the rule-utilitarian argument or any other philosophical defense of noncombatant immunity. Primoratz's use of this example fails to prove his point. It only seems persuasive because of what it leaves out. The example does not acknowledge the existence of the other side. It tells us nothing about the situation of the attackers, who may face circumstances as dire as the woman they threaten. The example says nothing about why the attackers might think it necessary or desirable to kill this woman and others like her.

Suppose that the attackers face a Walzer-type supreme emergency or a Primoratz-type moral disaster. Suppose that they believe that they can only defend their group by resorting to the tactic of killing enemy civilians. Just as the woman in Primoratz's example can point to her innocence, so can they point to the innocence of people in their group and to the severe threats (perhaps including extermination or enslavement) that they and members of their group face. When we understand what is motivating the attackers, it becomes clear that the woman's plea may be insufficient because it is counter-balanced by the similar pleas of the attackers.

Once we are faced with equally desperate pleas from both sides, it is clear that we cannot tell whether to heed the woman's pleas unless we have a way to adjudicate these competing claims. The rule-utilitarian perspective provides a way to adjudicate them. It notes that wars and other threats to people's lives, rights, and well-being exist. It recognizes a right of people to defend themselves against these kinds of attacks and other forms of severe oppression. But it sees, too, that the interests of the threatened group are not the only relevant interests. There is a global human interest in minimizing the destructiveness of war. If groups at war think only of their own interests, they will escalate war to whatever level is necessary to win, and the human interest will suffer as all move toward an "anything goes" approach to

---

[20] Primoratz, "Civilian Immunity in War," 26–7.

warfare. What we need are rules of war that permit people to fight and defend themselves and their group and that impose the constraints on tactics of fighting that are necessary to protect the overall human interest. Since war is likely to be with us for a long time and since the weapons of war have become increasingly destructive, this constraint is extremely important.

The rule utilitarian, looking at the history of warfare and knowing facts about how people are inclined to act in war, seeks to impose a set of rules that protects both the interests of particular groups and the general human interest. I have argued that taking this perspective will generate a rule of noncombatant immunity that will support the plea of the woman in Primoratz's example. If the argument is correct, then that is why her plea takes precedence over whatever reasons the attackers have for being inclined to kill her.

Primoratz's example is appealing because we would like to think that once soldiers or potential terrorists are reminded that their intended victims are innocent people who are not engaged in warfare against them, then these fighters themselves would feel compassion for these people, would be horrified by the thought of killing them, and would spare their lives. They would feel the kind of revulsion that people often think of as the correct reaction to terrorism. The only difference is that the revulsion would not be limited, narrow, and biased. It would be the felt reaction toward any killings of innocent people for the sake of a political goal.

UTILITARIANISM AND THE EMOTIONS

Many people have thought that utilitarianism is incompatible with the idea that it is good for people to be motivated by emotions like compassion, horror, and revulsion. The criticism that utilitarianism makes people "too calculating" is an old one. Mill writes of the charge "that utilitarianism renders men cold and unsympathizing; that it chills their moral feelings toward individuals; that it makes them regard only the dry and hard consideration of the consequences of actions."[21]

This criticism rests on exaggerated contrasts between reason and the passions. These contrasts are drawn too sharply. There is no incompatibility in being concerned both about overall well-being (a kind of abstraction) and about the well-being of concrete individuals. In fact, it is because of an appreciation of the value of individual lives that we care about the effects of

---

[21] Mill, *Utilitarianism*, 19.

actions and rules on people generally. Similarly, it is because we care about people that we want to make reasonable predictions about the effects of our actions and sometimes try to quantify the costs and benefits of different possible actions prior to deciding what to do. Reason is in these cases the partner of the passions.

The integration of emotional responses to individuals and broad concerns about large-scale effects on people is apparent in Hugo Slim's defense of the ideal of civilian immunity. An interesting feature of Slim's language is that it includes appeals both to the individual and the collective levels, to qualitative and emotional responses to people and to quantitative and rational forms of response. In a section on "The preciousness of human life," for example, he writes:

> The main idea behind limited war and its civilian ethic is, of course, that of limited killing. This argument reasons that, even in war, one should kill as little as possible. This is because every human being's life is precious to themselves, to those who love them and, if one is religious, to God as well.[22]

The language of the opening sentences is quantitative, emphasizing that the goal of the limited war idea is to diminish the number of killings of people. In justifying this quantitative goal, however, Slim appeals to the preciousness of each potential and actual victim's life to themselves and to others.

The same integrated appeal to quantitative and qualitative features appears in Slim's concluding argument on the preciousness of life. Slim notes that advocates of civilian immunity may sometimes exaggerate the sanctity of the lives of certain individuals, even those who have done terrible things. They exaggerate in order to make the strongest case for "demarcat[ing] the category of protected persons whom we call civilians." A strong sense of the sanctity of individual lives is necessary, he writes,

> because without it, everyone would be fair game in war ... with the result that massive killing and suffering become the norm, as has often happened. This is a norm which the compassionate view of limited war cannot accept because compassion is essentially positive about every human life.[23]

Closing a book that describes and analyzes the many horrors inflicted on civilians, Slim makes a powerful and passionate case for setting civilians aside as a protected group. In doing so, he invokes compassion as a motivating force. Compassion is important because it motivates people to refrain from violence against others, and compassionate responses to people are incompatible with a norm of war that allows "massive killing and suffering." Like the

---

[22] Slim, *Killing Civilians*, 260–1.   [23] Ibid., 262–3.

rule utilitarian, Slim is concerned about what norms are seen as acceptable for guiding our actions. He is also concerned with quantities of suffering. If the norm allows, encourages, or requires killing civilians, there will be massive amounts of death and suffering. To limit the scope of these harms, we need strong, restrictive norms. These humanitarian norms will be responsive to and resonate with feelings of compassion. At the same time, they will encourage and give support to compassion as the appropriate emotional response to civilians who are vulnerable to attack.

While Slim stresses the positive emotions of compassion and appreciation for the sanctity of life, negative emotions also play an essential role in motivating compliance with humanitarian norms of war. While it is paradoxical for a utilitarian to refer to moral prohibitions as taboos, there is no contradiction in saying that the utilitarian argument for noncombatant immunity supports the idea of making the killing of civilians a powerful prohibition whose violation should be seen as uncivilized and barbaric. The taboo should be strong enough to constrain people's behavior in difficult circumstances. It should make those who attack and kill civilians feel ashamed and guilty. It should also make members of the group on whose behalf these deeds are done feel ashamed and guilty. Though they want their cause to win, they should also want people fighting on their behalf to do so within the limits of a morality that recognizes the humanity of both friends and foes. They should want everyone to respond with horror to the prospect of killing civilians who are not engaged in warfare.

Does seeing this prohibition as a taboo mean that people must be ignorant of or deceived about the real basis of noncombatant immunity? Not at all. The central goal of maximizing well-being and the ideal of acting in accord with rules whose acceptance would promote the interests of all can certainly be known to people. They would feel revulsion against violating the "taboo," but they would also know that it was morally and rationally justified, that its presence in the moral code serves the interests of humanity in a world in which war and violent conflict are likely to continue.

Bibliography

American Law Institute. *Model Penal Code.* Philadelphia: American Law Institute, 1962.

BBC Team. "The Doctrine of Double Effect." www.bbc.co.uk/religion/ethics/ euthanasia/overview/doubleeffect.shtml.

Bellamy, Alex. "Supreme Emergencies and the Protection of Non-combatants in War." *International Affairs* 80 (2004), 829–50.

Benjamin, Mark. "When Is an Accidental Civilian Death Not an Accident?" www.salon.com/news/feature/2007/07/30/collateral_damage.

Bennett, William J. *Why We Fight.* New York: Doubleday, 2002.

Bentham, Jeremy. "Critical Examination of the Declaration of Rights." Reprinted in B. Parekh, ed., *Bentham's Political Thought.* New York: Barnes and Noble, 1973.

"The Principles of International Law." www.laits.utexas.edu/poltheory/ bentham/pil/index.html.

Benvenisti, Eyal. "Human Dignity in Combat: The Duty to Spare Enemy Civilians." *Tel Aviv Law School Working Paper Series.* http://law.bepress. com/taulwps/fp/art11/.

Bess, Michael. *Choices Under Fire: Moral Dimensions of World War II.* New York: Alfred A. Knopf, 2006.

Best, Geoffrey. *Humanity in Warfare.* New York: Columbia University Press, 1980.

Biddle, Tami Davis. *Rhetoric and Reality in Air Warfare: The Evolution of British and American Ideas About Strategic Bombing, 1914–1945.* Princeton: Princeton University Press, 2002.

Bin Ladin, Osama, *et al.* "Jihad Against Jews and Crusaders: World Islamic Front Statement." February 1998. www.fas.org/irp/world/para/docs/980223-fatwa.htm.

Bird, Kai. *The Color of Truth.* New York: Simon and Schuster, 1998.

Brandt, Richard. *A Theory of the Good and the Right.* New York: Oxford University Press, 1979.

Morality, Utilitarianism, and Rights. New York: Cambridge University Press, 1992.

"Utilitarianism and the Rules of War." In M. Cohen *et al.*, eds., *War and Moral Responsibility.* Princeton: Princeton University Press, 1974.

Brown, Kenneth. "'Supreme Emergency': A Critique of Michael Walzer's Moral Justification for Allied Obliteration Bombing in World War II." *Manchester College Bulletin of the Peace Studies Institute*, 13:1–2 (1983), 6–15.

Carr, Caleb. *The Lessons of Terror*. New York: Random House, 2002.

Christopher, Paul. *The Ethics of War and Peace*. Englewood Cliffs, N.J.: Prentice-Hall, 1994.

Clausewitz, Carl von. *On War*. Edited and abridged by A. Rappaport, translated by J. J. Graham. New York: Penguin Books, 1968.

Coady, C. A. J. "Defining Terrorism." In Igor Primoratz, ed., *Terrorism: The Philosophical Issues*. Houndsmills: Palgrave Macmillan, 2004.

Morality and Political Violence. Cambridge: Cambridge University Press, 2008.

"Terrorism, Just War and Supreme Emergency." In T. Coady and M. O'Keefe, *Terrorism and Justice*. Melbourne: Melbourne University Press, 2002.

Coady, Tony, and Michael O'Keefe, eds., *Terrorism and Justice*. Melbourne: Melbourne University Press, 2002.

Coates, A. J. *The Ethics of War*. Manchester: Manchester University Press, 1997.

Cohen, Marshall. "Moral Skepticism and International Relations." In Charles Beitz *et al.*, eds., *International Ethics*. Princeton: Princeton University Press, 1985.

Connell, F. J. "Double Effect, Principle of." In *New Catholic Encyclopedia*, 2nd edn, volume IV. Detroit: Thomson Gale, 2003.

Conway-Lanz, Sahr. *Collateral Damage: Americans, Noncombatant Immunity, and Atrocity after World War II*. New York: Routledge, 2006.

Coppieters, Bruno, and Nick Fotion, eds. *Moral Constraints on War*. Lanham, Md.: Lexington Books, 2002.

Corlett, J. Angelo. *Terrorism: A Philosophical Analysis*. Dordrecht: Kluwer, 2003.

Dallek, Robert. *The American Style of Foreign Policy: Cultural Politics and Foreign Affairs*. New York: Alfred A. Knopf, 1983.

Dardis, Tony. "Primoratz on Terrorism." *Journal of Applied Philosophy* 9 (1992), 93–7.

Dewey, John. *German Philosophy and Politics*. Revised edn. New York: G. P. Putnam's Sons, 1942. Original edition, 1915.

Dinstein, Yoram. *The Conduct of Hostilities under the Law of International Armed Conflict*. Cambridge: Cambridge University Press, 2004.

Donnelly, Jack. "Twentieth-Century Realism." In T. Nardin and D. Mapel, eds., *Traditions of International Ethics*. New York: Cambridge University Press, 1992.

Doran, Michael Scott. "Somebody Else's Civil War: Ideology, Rage, and the Assault on America." In J. Hoge, Jr. and G. Rose, eds., *How Did This Happen? Terrorism and the New War*. New York: Public Affairs, 2001.

Dower, Nigel. *World Ethics*. Edinburgh: Edinburgh University Press, 1998.

Downes, Alexander. "Desperate Times, Desperate Measures: The Causes of Civilian Victimization in War." *International Security* 30 (Spring 2006), 152–95.

Targeting Civilians in War. Ithaca, N.Y.: Cornell University Press, 2008.

Doyle, Michael. *Ways of War and Peace*. New York: W. W. Norton, 1997.

Dressler, Joshua. *Understanding Criminal Law*. 3rd edn. New York: Lexis Publishing, 2001.

Dworkin, Ronald. *Taking Rights Seriously*. Cambridge, Mass.: Harvard University Press, 1978.

Ellsburg, Daniel. *Secrets: A Memoir of Vietnam and the Pentagon Papers*. New York: Penguin, 2003.

Elshtain, Jean B. *Just War Against Terror*. New York: Basic Books, 2003.

English, Jane. "Abortion and the Concept of a Person." *Canadian Journal of Philosophy* 5 (1975), 233–43.

Finnis, John. *Moral Absolutes*. Washington, D.C.: Catholic University of America Press, 1991.

Fleck, D., ed. *The Handbook of Humanitarian Law in Armed Conflicts*. New York: Oxford University Press, 1995.

Fletcher, George. *A Crime of Self-Defense: Bernhard Goetz and the Law on Trial*. New York: The Free Press, 1988.

Foot, Philippa. "The Problem of Abortion and the Doctrine of the Double Effect." In *Virtues and Vices*. Oxford: Oxford University Press, 2002.

Ford, John C., S. J. "The Hydrogen Bombing of Cities." In William Nagle, ed., *Morality and Modern Warfare*. Baltimore: Helicon Press, 1960.

Ford, John C., S. J. "The Morality of Obliteration Bombing." *Theological Studies* 5 (1944), 261–309.

Forde, Steven. "Classical Realism." In T. Nardin and D. Mapel, eds., *Traditions of International Ethics*. New York: Cambridge University Press, 1992.

Fotion, N., and G. Elfstrom. *Military Ethics*. Boston: Routledge and Kegan Paul, 1986.

Franklin, Marc A., and Robert L. Radin. *Tort Law and Alternatives*. 7th edn. New York: Foundation Press, 2001.

French, Shannon. "Murderers, Not Warriors." In James Sterba, ed., *Terrorism and International Justice*. New York: Oxford University Press, 2003.

Frey, R. G. "Act-Utilitarianism, Consequentialism, and Moral Rights." In Frey, ed., *Utility and Rights*. Minneapolis: University of Minnesota Press, 1984.

"Introduction: Utilitarianism and Persons." In Frey, ed., *Utility and Rights*. Minneapolis: University of Minnesota Press, 1984.

Frey, R. G., and Christopher Morris, eds. *Violence, Terrorism, and Justice*. Cambridge: Cambridge University Press, 1991.

Fussell, Paul. "Thank God for the Atom Bomb." In *Thank God for the Atomic Bomb and Other Essays*. New York: Summit Books, 1988.

Wartime. New York: Oxford University Press, 1989.

Gandhi, M. K. *Non-Violent Resistance*. New York: Schocken Books, 1961.

Ganor, Boaz. "Defining Terrorism." www.ict.org.il/ResearchPublications/tabid/64/Articlsid/432/Default.aspx.

Garrett, Stephen. *Ethics and Airpower in World War II: The British Bombing of German Cities*. New York: St. Martin's Press, 1993.

"Terror Bombing of German Cities in World War II." In Igor Primoratz, ed., *Terrorism: The Philosophical Issues*. Houndsmills: Palgrave Macmillan, 2004.

Gert, Bernard. *Common Morality*. New York: Oxford University Press, 2004.

Morality: Its Nature and Justification. New York: Oxford University Press, 1998.

Glaser, Daryl. "Partiality to Conationals or Solidarity with the Oppressed? Or, What Liberal Zionism Can Tell Us about the Limitations of Liberal Nationalism." *Ethnicities* 5 (2005), 489–509.

Glover, Jonathan. *Humanity: A Moral History of the Twentieth Century.* New Haven: Yale University Press, 2000.

"State terrorism." In R. G. Frey and C. W. Morris, eds., *Violence, Terrorism, and Justice.* Cambridge: Cambridge University Press, 1991.

Goodin, Robert. *Utilitarianism as a Public Philosophy.* Cambridge: Cambridge University Press, 1995.

What's Wrong With Terrorism? Cambridge: Polity Press, 2006.

Grayling, A. C. *Among the Dead Cities: The History and Moral Legacy of the WWII Bombing of Civilians in Germany and Japan.* New York: Walker, 2006.

Gross, Michael. "Killing Civilians Intentionally: Double Effect, Reprisal and Necessity in the Middle East." *Political Science Quarterly* 120 (2005–6), 555–79.

Hampshire, Stuart. "Morality and Pessimism." In S. Hampshire, ed., *Public and Private Morality.* Cambridge: Cambridge University Press, 1978.

"Public and Private Morality." In S. Hampshire, ed., *Public and Private Morality.* Cambridge: Cambridge University Press, 1978, 40–5.

Hardin, Russell. "Ethics and Stochastic Processes." *Social Philosophy and Policy* 7:1 (Autumn 1989), 69–80.

Morality Within the Limits of Reason. Chicago: University of Chicago Press, 1988.

Hare, R. M. "Terrorism." In *Essays on Political Morality.* Oxford: Oxford University Press, 1989.

Harris, John. "The Survival Lottery." *Philosophy* 50 (1975), 81–7.

Held, Virginia. *How Terrorism Is Wrong: Morality and Political Violence.* New York: Oxford University Press, 2008.

"Terrorism, Rights, and Political Goals." In R. G. Frey and C. W. Morris, eds., *Violence, Terrorism, and Justice.* Cambridge: Cambridge University Press, 1991.

Hendrickson, David. "In Defense of Realism." *Ethics and International Affairs* 11 (1997), 19–54.

Hensel, Howard M. *The Legitimate Use of Military Force.* Aldershot: Ashgate, 2008.

Herman, Edward. *The Real Terror Network: Terrorism in Fact and Propaganda.* Boston: South End Press, 1982.

Hirschbein, Ron. "Just Terrorism Theory." *Concerned Philosophers for Peace Newsletter* 21 (Spring and Fall 2001), 13–17.

Hirst, David. *The Gun and the Olive Branch: The Roots of Violence in the Middle East.* 3rd edn. London: Faber and Faber, 2003.

Hobhouse, L. T. *The Metaphysical Theory of the State.* London: George Allen and Unwin, 1918.

Hoffman, Bruce. *Inside Terrorism.* New York: Columbia University Press, 1998.

Hoge, J. Jr., and G. Rose, eds. *How Did This Happen? Terrorism and the New War.* New York: Public Affairs, 2001.

Holmes, Robert. *On War and Morality.* Princeton: Princeton University Press, 1989.

Honderich, Ted. *Humanity, Terrorism, Terrorist War*. London: Continuum, 2006.

Hoogensen, Gunhild. "Bentham's International Manuscripts Versus the Published 'Works.'" www.ucl.ac.uk/Bentham-Project/journal/hoogensn.htm.

Hooker, Brad. *Ideal Code, Real World*. Oxford: Oxford University Press, 2000.

Hooker, Brad, Elinor Mason, and Dale E. Miller, eds. *Morality, Rules, and Consequences*. Lanham, Md.: Rowman and Littlefield, 2000.

Hopkins, George E. "Bombing and the American Conscience During World War II." *Historian* 28 (May 1966), 451–73.

Human Rights Watch. "Cluster Bombs in Afghanistan." www.hrw.org/backgrounder/arms/cluster-bck1031.htm.

　Off Target: The Conduct of the War and Civilian Casualties in Iraq. New York: Human Rights Watch, 2003.

Hurka, Thomas. "Proportionality in the Morality of War." *Philosophy and Public Affairs* 33 (2005), 34–66.

Iklé, Fred. *Every War Must End*, revised edn. New York: Columbia University Press, 1991.

International Committee of the Red Cross. *The People on War*. Geneva: ICRC, 2000. http://www.icrc.org.

Johnson, Dominic D. P. *Overconfidence and War*. Cambridge, Mass.: Harvard University Press, 2004.

Johnson, James Turner. *Just War Tradition and the Restraint of War*. Princeton: Princeton University Press, 1981.

　Morality and Contemporary Warfare. New Haven: Yale University Press, 1999.

Kahl, Colin H. "How We Fight." *Foreign Affairs* 85:6 (November–December 2006), 83–101.

　"In the Crossfire or the Crosshairs? Norms, Civilian Casualties, and U.S. Conduct in Iraq." *International Security* 32 (Summer 2007), 7–46.

Kalshoven, Frits. *Constraints on the Waging of War*. 2nd edn. Geneva: International Committee of the Red Cross, 1991.

Kant, Immanuel. *Grounding for the Metaphysics of Morals*. Trans. James Ellington. Indianapolis: Hackett, 1981.

　The Metaphysical Elements of Justice. Trans. John Ladd. New York: Macmillan, 1965.

Kapitan, Tomis. "The Terrorism of 'Terrorism.'" In James Sterba, ed., *Terrorism and International Justice*. Oxford University Press, 2003.

Kavka, Gregory. *Moral Paradoxes of Nuclear Deterrence*. New York: Cambridge University Press, 1987.

Kegley, Charles, ed. *International Terrorism*. New York: St. Martin's, 1990.

Keller, Simon. "On What Is the War on Terror?" In Timothy Shannon, ed., *Philosophy 9/11: Thinking About the War on Terrorism*. Chicago: Open Court, 2005.

Kennan, George. "Morality and Foreign Policy." *Foreign Affairs* 64 (Winter 1985–6). Reprinted in *Morality and Foreign Policy*. Washington, D.C.: US Institute of Peace, 1991.

Khatchadourian, Haig. *The Morality of Terrorism*. New York: Peter Lang, 1998.

"Terrorism and Morality." *Journal of Applied Philosophy*, 5 (1988), 131–45.

Kretzmer, David. "Civilian Immunity in War: Legal Aspects." In Igor Primoratz, ed., *Civilian Immunity in War*. Oxford: Oxford University Press, 2007.

Kymlicka, Will. "Rawls on Teleology and Deontology." *Philosophy and Public Affairs* 17 (1988), 173–90.

Lackey, Douglas. *The Ethics of War and Peace*. Englewood Cliffs, N.J.: Prentice-Hall, 1988.

"The Evolution of the Modern Terrorist State." In Igor Primoratz, ed., *Terrorism: The Philosophical Issues*. Houndsmills: Palgrave, 2004.

"The Good Soldier versus the Good Cop: Counterterrorism as Police Work." *Iyyun, The Jerusalem Philosophical Quarterly* 55 (January 2006), 66–82.

Lammers, Stephen. "Area Bombing in World War II: The Argument of Michael Walzer." *Journal of Religious Ethics* 11 (1983), 96–114.

Lee, Steven. "Double Effect, Double Intention, and Asymmetric Warfare." *Journal of Military Ethics* 3 (2004), 233–4.

ed. *Intervention, Terrorism, and Torture*. Dordrecht: Springer, 2007.

ed. *Morality, Prudence, and Nuclear Weapons*. Cambridge: Cambridge University Press, 1993.

Lifton, Robert Jay, and Greg Mitchell. *Hiroshima in America: A Half Century of Denial*. New York: Avon Books, 1995.

Lopez, George. "The Gulf War: Not So Clean." *Bulletin of Atomic Scientists* 47:6 (September 1991), 30–5.

Luban, David. "Just War and Human Rights." In Charles Beitz *et al.*, eds., *International Ethics*. Princeton: Princeton University Press, 1985.

"Liberalism, Torture, and the Ticking Bomb." In Steven Lee, ed., *Intervention, Terrorism, and Torture*. Dordrecht: Springer, 2007.

"The War on Terrorism and the End of Human Rights." In Verna Gehring, ed., *War After September 11*. Lanham, Md.: Rowman and Littlefield, 2003.

Lukacs, John. *Five Days in London: May 1940*. New Haven: Yale University Press, 1999.

Lyons, David. *Rights, Welfare and Mill's Moral Theory*. Oxford: Oxford University Press, 1994.

MacIntyre, Alasdair. "Is Patriotism a Virtue?" Lawrence, Kans.: Philosophy Department, University of Kansas, 1984. Reprinted in Igor Primoratz, ed., *Patriotism*. Amherst, N.Y.: Humanity Books, 2002.

Mavrodes, George. "Conventions and the Morality of War." In Charles Beitz *et al.*, eds., *International Ethics*. Princeton: Princeton University Press, 1985. Originally published in *Philosophy and Public Affairs* 2 (1975).

May, Larry. *War Crimes and Just War*. New York: Cambridge University Press, 2007.

McIntyre, Alison. "Doing Away with Double Effect." *Ethics* 111 (January 2001), 219–55.

McKeogh, Colm. "Civilian Immunity: Augustine to Vattel." In Igor Primoratz, ed., *Civilian Immunity in War*. Oxford: Oxford University Press, 2007.

Innocent Civilians: The Morality of Killing in War. New York: Palgrave, 2002.

McMahan, Jeff. "The Ethics of Killing in War." *Ethics* 114 (2004), 693–733.
"Innocence, Self-Defense, and Killing in War." *The Journal of Political Philosophy* 2 (1994), 193–221.
"Self Defense and the Problem of the Innocent Attacker." *Ethics* 104 (January 1994), 250–90.
McPherson, Lionel. "Is Terrorism Distinctively Wrong?" *Ethics* 117 (2007), 524–46.
Mill, John Stuart. *Utilitarianism.* Indianapolis: Hackett Publishing, 1979.
Miller, Seumas. *Terrorism and Counter-Terrorism: Ethics and Liberal Democracy.* Oxford: Blackwell Publishing, 2009.
Morgenthau, Hans J. *Politics Among Nations: The Struggle for Power and Peace.* 2nd edn. New York: Alfred Knopf, 1954.
Murphy, Jeffrie. "The Killing of the Innocent." *The Monist* 57 (1973), 527–50.
Myers, Robert. "Hans Morgenthau's Realism and American Foreign Policy." *Ethics and International Affairs* 11 (1997), 253–70.
Nagel, Thomas. *Equality and Partiality.* New York: Oxford University Press, 1991.
"War and Massacre." In M. Cohen *et al.*, eds., *War and Moral Responsibility.* Princeton: Princeton University Press, 1974.
Narveson, Jan. "Pacifism: A Philosophical Analysis." *Ethics* 75 (1965), 259–71.
Nathanson, Stephen. "In Defense of 'Moderate Patriotism'." *Ethics* 99 (1988–9), 535–52. Reprinted in Igor Primoratz, ed., *Patriotism.* Amherst, N.Y.: Humanity Books, 2002.
"Is the War on Terrorism a Defense of Civilization?" *Concerned Philosophers for Peace Newsletter* 22 (Spring/Fall 2002), 19–27.
Patriotism, Morality, and Peace. Lanham, Md.: Rowman and Littlefield, 1993.
"Prerequisites for Morally Credible Condemnations of Terrorism." In William Crotty, ed., *The Politics of Terror: The U.S. Response to 9/11.* Boston: Northeastern University Press, 2004.
"War, Patriotism, and the Limits of Permissible Partiality." *Journal of Ethics* 13 (2009), 401–22.
National Conference of Catholic Bishops. *The Challenge of Peace.* Washington, D.C.: United States Catholic Conference, 1983.
National Public Radio. "Critique of the Double Effect." www.npr.org/programs/death/971211.death.html.
Neilsen, Kai. "There Is No Dilemma of Dirty Hands." In Paul Rynard and David Shugarman, eds., *Cruelty and Deception: The Controversy Over Dirty Hands in Politics.* Peterborough, Ontario: Broadview Press, 2000.
Norman, Richard. *Ethics, Killing, and War.* Cambridge: Cambridge University Press, 1995.
Nozick, Robert. *Anarchy, State, and Utopia.* New York: Basic Books, 1973.
O'Brien, William V. *The Conduct of Just and Limited War.* New York: Praeger, 1981.
Orend, Brian. *The Morality of War.* Peterborough, Ontario: Broadview Press, 2006.
Pape, Robert. *Dying to Win.* New York: Random House, 2005.

Pavkovic, Aleksandar. "Towards Liberation: Terrorism from a Liberation Ideology Perspective." In Tony Coady and Michael O'Keefe, eds., *Terrorism and Justice*. Melbourne: Melbourne University Press, 2002.

Pillsbury, Samuel H. *Judging Evil: Rethinking the Law of Murder and Manslaughter*. New York: New York University Press, 1998.

Primoratz, Igor. "Civilian Immunity in War." *Philosophical Forum* 37 (2005), 41–58. Reprinted in I. Primoratz, ed., *Civilian Immunity in War*. Oxford: Oxford University Press, 2007.

  ed. *Civilian Immunity in War*. Oxford: Oxford University Press, 2007.

  "State Terrorism." In Primoratz, ed., *Terrorism: The Philosophical Issues*. Houndsmills: Palgrave Macmillan, 2004.

  "Terrorism in the Israeli-Palestinian Conflict." *Iyyun: The Jerusalem Philosophical Quarterly* 55 (January 2006), 27–48.

  ed. *Terrorism: The Philosophical Issues*. Houndsmills: Palgrave Macmillan, 2004.

  "What Is Terrorism?" In Primoratz, ed., *Terrorism: The Philosophical Issues*. Houndsmills: Palgrave Macmillan, 2004.

Protocol Additional to the Geneva Conventions of 12 August 1949, and relating to the Protection of Victims of International Armed Conflicts. www.ohchr.org/english/law/protocol1.htm.

Queguiner, Jean-François. "The Principle of Distinction: Beyond an Obligation of Customary International Humanitarian Law." In Howard M. Hensel, ed., *The Legitimate Use of Military Force*. Aldershot: Ashgate, 2008.

Rainbolt, George. *The Concept of Rights*. Dordrecht: Springer, 2006.

Rawls, John. *Law of Peoples*. Cambridge, Mass.: Harvard University Press, 1999.

  A Theory of Justice. Cambridge, Mass.: Harvard University Press, 1971.

Richardson, Louise. *What Terrorists Want: Understanding the Enemy, Containing the Threat*. New York: Random House, 2006.

Ricks, Thomas. *Fiasco: The American Military Adventure in Iraq*. New York: The Penguin Press, 2006.

Rodin, David. "Terrorism Without Intention." *Ethics* 114 (2004), 752–71.

  War and Self-Defense. New York: Oxford University Press, 2002.

Rogers, A. P. V. *Law on the Battlefield*. 2nd edn. Manchester: Manchester University Press, 2004.

  "The Principle of Proportionality." In Howard M. Hensel, ed., *The Legitimate Use of Military Force*. Aldershot: Ashgate, 2008.

Rona, Gabor. "Interesting Times for International Humanitarian Law: Challenges from the 'War on Terror.'" *The Fletcher Forum of World Affairs* 27 (Summer/Fall 2003), 55–74.

Saeed, Abdullah. "Jihad and Violence: Changing Understandings of Jihad Among Muslims." In T. Coady and M. O'Keefe, eds., *Terrorism and Justice*. Melbourne: Melbourne University Press, 2002.

Scanlon, Thomas. "Intention and Permissibility." *Proceedings of the Aristotelian Society*, supp. vol. 74 (2000), 301–17.

Schaffer, Ronald. *Wings of Judgment: American Bombing in World War II*. New York: Oxford University Press, 1985.

Scheffler, Samuel. "Is Terrorism Morally Distinctive?" *Journal of Political Philosophy* 14 (2006), 1–17.

Schmid, Alex P., and Albert J. Jongman. *Political Terrorism*. New Brunswick, N.J.: Transaction Publishers, 1988.

Scholz, Sally. "War Rape's Challenge to Just War Theory." In Steven Lee, ed., *Intervention, Terrorism, and Torture*. Dordrecht: Springer, 2007.

Sewall, Sarah. "Modernizing U.S. Counterinsurgency Practice: Rethinking Risk and Developing a National Strategy." *Military Review* (September–October 2006), 104–5.

Sharp, Gene. *The Politics of Nonviolent Action*. Boston: Porter Sargent, 1973.

Shue, Henry. "Liberalism: The Impossibility of Justifying Weapons of Mass Destruction." In Sohail Hashimi and Steven Lee, eds., *Ethics and Weapons of Mass Destruction: Religious and Secular Perspectives*. Cambridge: Cambridge University Press, 2004.

"War." *The Oxford Handbook of Practical Ethics*. Oxford: Oxford University Press, 2003.

Sibley, Mulford, ed. *The Quiet Battle*. New York: Doubleday Anchor, 1963.

Sidgwick, Henry. *The Elements of Politics*. London: Macmillan, 1897.

Silone, Ignazio. "Reflections on the Welfare State." *Dissent* 8:2 (Spring 1961), 185–90.

Sinnott-Armstrong, Walter. "On Primoratz's Definition of Terrorism." *Journal of Applied Philosophy* 8 (1991), 115–20.

Slim, Hugo. *Killing Civilians: Method, Madness, and Morality in War*. New York: Columbia University Press, 2008.

Smilansky, Saul. "Terrorism, Justification, and Illusion." *Ethics* 114 (July 2004), 790–805.

Solomon, William David. "Double Effect." In Lawrence and Charlotte Becker, eds., *The Encyclopedia of Ethics*, 2nd edn, vol. I. New York: Routledge, 2001.

Sorell, Tom. "Morality and Emergency." *Proceedings of the Aristotelian Society* 103 (2002), 1–37.

"Politics, Power, and Partisanship." In Paul Rynard and David Shugarman, eds., *Cruelty and Deception: The Controversy Over Dirty Hands in Politics*. Peterborough, Ontario: Broadview Press, 2000.

Sparrow, Robert. "Hands Up Who Wants to Die?: Primoratz on Responsibility and Civilian Immunity in Wartime." *Ethical Theory and Moral Practice* 8:3 (2005), 299–319.

Statman, Daniel. "Supreme Emergencies Revisited." *Ethics* 117 (2006), 58–79.

Steinhoff, Uwe. *On the Ethics of War and Terrorism*. Oxford and New York: Oxford University Press, 2007.

Sterba, James, ed. *Terrorism and International Justice*. New York: Oxford University Press, 2003.

"Terrorism and International Justice." In Sterba, ed., *Terrorism and International Justice*. New York: Oxford University Press, 2003.

Stimson, Henry. "The Decision to Use the Atomic Bomb." *Harper's Magazine* 194 (February 1947), 97–107.

Sumner, L. W. *The Moral Foundations of Rights*. Oxford: Oxford University Press, 1987.

Talbott, William. *Which Rights Should Be Universal?* New York: Oxford University Press, 2005.

Teichman, Jenny. "How to Define Terrorism." *Philosophy* 64 (1989), 505–17.
Pacifism and the Just War. Oxford: Basil Blackwell, 1986.

Thayer, H. S., ed. *Pragmatism: The Classic Writings*. Indianapolis: Hackett Publishing, 1982.

Thompson, Janna. "Terrorism and the Right to Wage War." In Tony Coady and Michael O'Keefe, eds., *Terrorism and Justice*. Melbourne: Melbourne University Press, 2002.

Thomson, Judith. *The Realm of Rights*. Cambridge, Mass.: Harvard University Press, 1990.
Rights, Restitution, and Risk. Cambridge, Mass.: Harvard University Press, 1986.
"Self-Defense," *Philosophy and Public Affairs* 20 (1991), 87–96.

Uniacke, Suzanne. *Permissible Killing*. Cambridge: Cambridge University Press, 1994.

United States Catholic Conference. *The Harvest of Justice Is Sown in Peace*, 1993. www.usccb.org/sdwp/harvest.shtml.

Vitoria, Francisco de. *On the Law of War*. In A. Pagden and J. Lawrence, eds., *Vitoria: Political Writings*. Cambridge: Cambridge University Press, 1991.

Waldron, Jeremy. "Rights in Conflict." *Ethics* 99 (April 1989), 503–19.
"Terrorism and the Uses of Terror." *The Journal of Ethics* 8 (2004), 5–35.

Wallace, G. "Area Bombing, Terrorism and the Death of Innocents." *Journal of Applied Philosophy* 6 (March 1989), 3–16.
"The Language of Terrorism." *International Journal of Moral and Social Studies* 8 (Summer 1993), 123–34.
"Terrorism and the Argument from Analogy." *International Journal of Moral and Social Studies* 6 (1991), 149–60.

Walzer, Michael. *Arguing About War*. New Haven: Yale University Press, 2004.
Interpretation and Social Criticism. Cambridge, Mass.: Harvard University Press, 1987.
Just and Unjust Wars. New York: Basic Books, 1977.
"The Moral Standing of States: A Response to Four Critics." In Charles Beitz et al., eds., *International Ethics*. Princeton: Princeton University Press, 1985.
"Political Action: The Problem of Dirty Hands." In Marshall Cohen et al., eds., *War and Moral Responsibility*. Princeton: Princeton University Press, 1974.
Spheres of Justice. New York: Basic Books, 1983.
"World War II: Why Was This War Different?" In Marshall Cohen et al., eds., *War and Moral Responsibility*. Princeton: Princeton University Press, 1974.

Wasserstrom, Richard. "On the Morality of War: A Preliminary Inquiry." In Richard Wasserstrom, ed., *War and Morality*. Belmont, Calif.: Wadsworth Publishing, 1970.

Wells, Donald, ed. *An Encyclopedia of War and Ethics*. Westport, Conn.: Greenwood, 1996.

Whitman, Jeffrey. "Utilitarianism and the Laws of Land Warfare." *Public Affairs Quarterly* 7 (1993), 261–75.

Wilkins, Burleigh T. *Terrorism and Collective Responsibility*. London: Routledge, 1992.

Woodward, P. A., ed. *The Doctrine of Double Effect*. Notre Dame: University of Notre Dame Press, 2001.

Zinn, Howard. "A Just Cause, Not a Just War." *The Progressive*, December 2001. www.commondreams.org/views01/1109-01.htm.

Zohar, Noam. "Collective War and Individualistic Ethics." *Political Theory* 21 (1993), 606–22.

"Innocence and Complex Threats: Upholding the War Ethic and the Condemnation of Terrorism." *Ethics* 114 (2004), 734–51.

Index